A.R. GURNEY

Collected Plays Volume II

1974–1983

A.R. GURNEY

Collected Plays Volume II
1974–1983

CONTEMPORARY PLAYWRIGHTS SERIES

SK
A Smith and Kraus Book

A Smith and Kraus Book
Published by Smith and Kraus, Inc.
PO Box 127, Lyme, NH 03768

First Edition: June 1997
10 9 8 7 6 5 4 3 2 1

The Library of Congress Cataloging-In-Publication Data
Gurney, A.R. (Albert Ramsdell), 1930–
    A.R. Gurney Collected Plays Volume II: 1974–1983. —1st ed.
    p. cm. — (Contemporary playwrights series)
    ISBN 1-57525-027-6
    I Title. II. Series.
    PS3557.U82A6   1995
    812'.54—dc20   95-19638
               CIP

CONTENTS

TO GILBERT PARKER
a good friend and fine agent,
who placed and improved
all these plays and many more.

INTRODUCTION

Ronald Reagan had been President for about a year when *The Dining Room* opened in New York. The cultural conjunction was propitious. Pete Gurney's first broad popular success came at a time when people were in a nostalgic mood. Reagan looked backward to a hazy idealized America that may never have existed in the first place, and tried to persuade people that time had come again. Pete Gurney, shrewdly, looked back over half a century of white Anglo-Saxon protestant ascendancy, and had the wisdom, not to mention the sense of humor, to kiss it good-bye.

The six plays in this collection all link personal and cultural change. Two are set in summer places, where families go for awhile every year as a release from where they live the rest of the time. One is set in an early twentieth century city in transition, while another takes place in a motel—by definition a place of passage. Two are set in particular rooms: a dining room, and the trophy room of a private club. The nostalgic appeal of these plays arises from their delightfully comprehensive anthropological accuracy. Not only are they an encyclopedia of droll, even arcane cultural ritual, but they are written in the perfectly pitched, dry, and very funny voice of the participants themselves. yet even as Pete Gurney is fondly evoking this world, he shows it to be under siege, not from without, but from within.

Pokey in *Children,* Barney in *The Middle Ages,* Charlie in *What I Did Last Summer*—all are aggressively or subversively trying to disrupt the life they grew up in. The architect in *The Dining Room* is actually prepared to demolish the place in the name of progress, although unlike some of the others, he's reluctant to acknowledge why. For Pete Gurney, the germ of this assault lies in the elemental relationship between fathers and sons, husbands and wives.

Early in *The Dining Room,* the archetypal strong father instructs his young son, "Long after you've forgotten that hymn, long after you've forgotten how to factor, long after you've forgotten Miss Kelly, you will remember these pleasant breakfasts around this dining room table…and here is your mother to prove it." This lovely non sequitur perfectly captures the dynamic at the heart of these plays. The men create their world for the women, and justify it by the women.

It is an unself-conscious world, that emphasizes responsibility—what one *will* do—over individual feeling. Yet when responsibility falters, and the will is challenged, it is the women who struggle to adapt and carry on in changing circumstances.

Pete Gurney works by omission to create the cracks and spaces that admit emotion into the lives of his characters. There are a number of important men who never even appear in these plays—Pokey in *Children,* Billy in *The Middle Ages.* The father in *Children* is deceased, away at war in *What I Did Last Summer,* and destroys himself in *Richard Cory.* Even the most amiable and loquacious dad on display, Charles Rusher in *The Middle Ages,* is technically absent because the play is framed as a series of flashbacks at his funeral. The strong, self-assured men in the first act of *The Dining Room* are last seen before intermission scurrying out of an interrupted Thanksgiving dinner after their ancient mother, who has forgotten where she lives. By the second act, their wives and daughters have pretty much taken over the place.

The fathers establish impossible standards which the sons cannot or will not sustain and the women pick up the pieces. When the pieces don't quite fit, the women fill in the gaps. Both mother and daughter in *Children* have more or less longstanding extramarital affairs. Eleanor in *The Middle Ages* struggles to balance her marriage to proper Billy with her enduring love for his improper brother Barney—one of the most outspoken, self-aware, and self-challenging men in this collection. But even Barney's most amusing confession of promiscuity occurs in a scene in which he first appears dressed as a woman. Contrast that revelation to the breathtaking understatement of one father in *The Dining Room,* bewildered by the complexity of his daughter's emotional life: "One time I became romantically involved with Mrs. Shoemaker. We took a little trip together. To Sea Island. Your mother got wind of it, and came right down, and told Betty Shoemaker to get on the next train. That's all there was to it." For the women in these plays, there is inevitably more to it than that, as they engage those feelings the men who made their lives have conveniently left out, or chosen to deny.

The cover of this book is an Edward Hopper painting of a couple at the theatre—an apt choice, because Hopper is a plain, spare American painter with a strong emotional undertow. But there's another artist whose work is interesting to think of in relation to Gurney, and that is Joseph Cornell, who made boxes in which he places objects or even bits of objects—a feather, a photograph, a shard of mirror—the odd juxtaposition of which creates a powerful fascination. The set of *The Dining Room* is a box containing just a table, some chairs, a carpet, and a mirror, which, like the mirrors in Cornell's work, puts a glimpse of the viewer in the box as well. But the emotional objects on display are the exquisitely distilled scenes Pete Gurney juxtaposes to suggest the life and ultimate passing of life in that room. He finds a way, in this play, not to spin the story into the form, but to make the form itself the dramatic event.

At the end of the play, three women set the table for an elegant dinner party. This is the first and only complete table setting in the piece. As in a separate, simultaneous scene one last strong archetypal father says to his son, "Now I want to go over my funeral with you," a great white linen tablecloth billows out over the table behind him, like a shroud. It is, like the small masterpiece that caps this collection, a death, and a celebration, in one image.

David Trainer
June 25, 1997

Children
(1974)
Suggested by a story by John Cheever

AUTHOR'S NOTE

Children is my first attempt to write a full-length, traditionally "well-made" play. It tries to follow the Aristotelian unities of time, place, and action. It was partly prompted by my admiration for John Cheever, but more by my growing awareness that I belonged to an ethnic group as idiosyncratic as any other in America. I had a difficult time getting the play produced in the U.S., however, possibly because a central character refuses to come on stage, and possibly because the play seemed too elitist for the politicized early seventies. In any case, it had fine productions in London and Germany before the Manhattan Theatre Club got wind of it and gave it a try.

ORIGINAL PRODUCTION

Children was first presented in New York City by the Manhattan Theatre Club, Lynne Meadow, Artistic Director, on October 20, 1976. It was directed by Melvin Bernhardt; the set designer was Marjorie Kellogg; costumes were by Patricia McGourty; the lighting designer was Arden Fingerhut; the sound designers were George Hanson and Chuck London; and the production stage manager was Mark Paquette. The cast, in order of appearance, was as follows:

Barbara	Holland Taylor
Randy	Dennis Howard
Mother	Nancy Marchand
Jane	Swoosie Kurtz
Pokey	Gary Smith

Children received its American premiere on January 30, 1976, by the Repertory Company of the Virginia Museum Theatre. It was directed by Keith Fowler.

The play was first produced at the Mermaid Theatre in London, opening on April 8, 1974. It starred Constance Cummings and was directed by Alan Strachan.

CAST OF CHARACTERS

Barbara
Randy
Mother
Jane
Pokey

SETTING

The action of the play takes place during the morning, afternoon, and evening of a Saturday on a July 4th weekend, on the terrace of a large, old summer house, overlooking the sea, on an island off the coast of Massachusetts. The year is 1970.

The terrace occupies most of the stage. It is surrounded by a low sitting wall, and contains primarily old terrace furniture, wicker, metal, and wood, thick with many coats of white paint. There is only an occasional concession to aluminum and vinyl. Behind, there is the side of the house, composed of weathered shingles. Ground-floor windows, framed by shutters, graced with window boxes containing geraniums and petunias, open onto the terrace, and of course a large screen door, which slams closed by means of a rusty, sagging spring.

To the right, screened by shrubs, a path leads off and down to the driveway and the tennis court. To the left, around the corner of the house, another path leads to wooden steps down the bluff to the beach.

NOTES

Everyone in this play should look thoroughly tanned. The clothes they wear—and they are the kind of people who change their clothes a lot—should be bright, summery, expensive-looking, and conservatively stylish.

The songs should not be considered isolated interludes, but rather should contribute to the flow of the play. They should begin as a scene is ending, and fade out only after the next scene has begun. Similarly the light changes should be carefully modulated.

Finally, the house should be used almost as a character in the play. The upstairs shades should be closed for the first scene. The leafy shadows change over its surface during the day. Before the final scene, the lights come on inside, and for the first time we can see something of the interior.

SYNOPSIS OF SCENES

Children

ACT I

*The sound of a group of amateur voices singing, in good, close, genial har-
mony, as if at a beach party. They might be singing a song about morning,
or the sun, or even "Show Me the Way to Go Home." The lights come up on
the terrace. It is very early in the morning. Bright sunlight has begun to slant
across the stage, which will become brighter as the scene continues. No one is
in view. We hear various sounds: birds chirping off right; the slow pound of
the sea off left. Then, off right, the motor of a car getting closer, and the
crunch of its wheels on a gravel driveway. The crunch stops, the motor stops.
Car doors are heard slamming. Then, closer at hand, but still off right, a
woman giggles. Finally, we can make out some of her words.*

WOMAN'S VOICE: Sssshhhh. You'll wake Mother…All right, this is far enough…
Mmmmmm…You'd better go. People will see you…Good night—
ooops, I mean, good morning…

*(Barbara comes on from upstage right. She is tan, lean, and attractive, in her
late thirties. She wears a stylish summer outfit which looks slightly
disheveled, as is her hair. She tiptoes on, carrying her shoes in one hand.
Then she turns back, and waves down and off right. When the car door
slams again, she cringes and puts her finger to her lips. She waves as the car
is heard driving off. She sighs and turns toward the house. Stealthily, she
makes her way on tiptoe toward the screen door. She opens it very carefully,
trying not to make its spring squeak. She is about to enter the house when
suddenly the strident sound of a telephone is heard ringing within. She starts,
jumps back, catches the screen door before it slams shut, and looks around,
frightened, at a loss for what to do. The telephone rings two or three times,
then stops in the middle of a ring, indicating that someone within has picked
up the receiver. Barbara stands in the center of the terrace. Sounds begin
within the house. First children's voices murmuring sleepily and petulantly.
Then a man's voice.)*

MAN'S VOICE: *(Offstage.)* What the hell was that?

WOMAN'S VOICE: *(Offstage. Sleepily.)* I think it was the telephone. I think your
mother answered it.

MAN'S VOICE: *(Offstage. Sleepily.)* At seven o'clock? Jesus Christ.

(Barbara, now unable to enter the house with all the noise, sits down resignedly. Voices continue ad-libbing within. Then after a moment the screen door bursts open and Randy comes out, wrapping a towel around his waist. He is in his early thirties, trim, very tan, and athletically built. He calls back into the house as he comes out.)

RANDY: I'm going for a swim. *(He comes onto the terrace, stops short when he sees Barbara.)* Hey.

BARBARA: Good morning.

RANDY: You look like you just got home.

BARBARA: I did. *(Lying.)* Betsy's car broke down after the movie, so I stayed over at her house.

RANDY: *(Believing her.)* Oh. *(Gesturing toward the house.)* Goddamn phone woke everybody up.

BARBARA: I heard. Who was it?

RANDY: I dunno. Mother got it in her bedroom.

BARBARA: Probably a wrong number.

RANDY: *(Stretching, yawning.)* No. She's still talking. *(Starts right.)* I'm going for a swim.

BARBARA: No kidding.

RANDY: Hey, do you know where the oil is?

BARBARA: The suntan oil?

RANDY: *(Irritably.)* No, not the suntan oil. The oil for the tennis court roller. I was looking all over for it last night.

BARBARA: Did you look in the shed?

RANDY: It's not in the shed.

BARBARA: It used to be in the shed.

RANDY: It's not there, Barbara.

BARBARA: Then I don't know where the oil is, Randy.

RANDY: *(Starting off again.)* Christ, you can't find a thing around here. No one puts things back. I don't mind people using things if they put them back.

BARBARA: Oh stop trying to be like Daddy.

RANDY: *(Turning again.)* You mean, because I'm taking a dip?

BARBARA: No, I mean the lecture about putting things back.

RANDY: You never do, and you never did. I have a game this morning, and the court's a mess.

BARBARA: *(Yawning.)* I didn't take the oil, Randy.

RANDY: You didn't even put the roller back after Labor Day last year. It was out all winter. That's why it's rusty. That's why I have to oil the damn thing.

BARBARA: Did you ever think that the children might have taken it?

RANDY: *(Stopping and turning again.)* Not my children.

BARBARA: Here we go.

RANDY: My children put things back. We've trained them.

BARBARA: So now you're blaming my children.

RANDY: Who lost the pump for the boat?

BARBARA: Oh Randy, that's mean.

RANDY: Who lost the pump?

BARBARA: That's just plain mean. My children are naturally upset, and you start nit-picking about oil and pumps and rollers and—

RANDY: You can't run a house unless people put things back. You can't—

(Both are talking at once. The screen door opens, and Mother comes out of the house. She is in her early sixties, and looks neat and well-groomed, in her good-looking bathrobe, even at this hour of the morning. Randy and Barbara begin to appeal to her immediately and simultaneously.)

BARBARA: Mother, now he's blaming my children because he can't find the oil for the tennis court roller…

RANDY: Mother, I've got a game at ten-thirty and I can't play on that court unless I…

(Mother closes her eyes and puts both hands over her ears.)

MOTHER: Ssshhhh.

(Randy and Barbara stop.)

MOTHER: Just…sshhhh. Let me pull myself together. *(Mother opens her eyes.)* Guess who just telephoned from the mainland?

BARBARA: Who?

MOTHER: Guess who will be on the ten o'clock ferry?

RANDY: Who, Mother?

MOTHER: Guess who decided to join us for the Fourth of July weekend after all? *(Pause.)*

BARBARA: Pokey.

MOTHER: *(Nodding.)* Your brother.

RANDY: Pokey?

MOTHER: Your little brother. With Miriam. And both children. We meet them at eleven-fifteen.

BARBARA: Well, well.

MOTHER: They made up their minds *yes*terday. Drove all night. All the way from Washington.

BARBARA: Typical.

MOTHER: He called from Providence. At seven o'clock in the morning. He said he figured we'd all be up.

BARBARA: Typical.

(Mother nods, looks at her, suddenly notices her clothes.)

MOTHER: Barbara, where have you been?

BARBARA: *(Mechanically.)* Car broke down. Stayed at Betsy's. Just got in.

MOTHER: You must be exhausted.

BARBARA: *(Stretching; yawning.)* I am.

MOTHER: Well, you'll have to stay awake long enough to come to the ferry with me.

RANDY: I can't, Mother. I've got a game.

MOTHER: Oh Randy, you always have a game when I need you.

BARBARA: Why is he coming, Mother?

MOTHER: I suppose because I invited him. Just as I invite both of you. Every year.

RANDY: But he refused, Mother. Remember when we called him last Christmas? He showed no interest.

BARBARA: He hasn't been near this place in—what?—four years?

MOTHER: Five.

BARBARA: That's right. Ever since Daddy died.

RANDY: And now, suddenly, on the spur of the moment...

MOTHER: Well he's changed his mind, that's all. And of course, I'm delighted. I'm thrilled. We'll all be together for the Fourth. What fun. *(Pause.)* It just requires some additional planning, that's all. *(She paces around the terrace, counting on her fingers.)* Let's see. There's Barbara, and Randy, and Jane, and me, and now Pokey and Miriam. That's six grown-ups. And Barbara's two children, and Randy's four, and Pokey's two. That's eight children. Which means a total of fourteen people in this house. We'll have to get more food on the way to the ferry.

BARBARA: And liquor, Mother.

MOTHER: Oh they won't drink much.

BARBARA: No, but we will.

(Barbara and Randy laugh.)

MOTHER: *(Firmly.)* There is plenty of liquor, Barbara.

(Laughter subsides. Mother continues to plan, nervously.)

MOTHER: Now please. Let me think. He'll want his old room, so we'll move all the children out onto the screen porch. Which means changing sheets. Which means stopping at the laundry. And I'll have to get the little MacKenzie girl from down the road to feed the children and help with the dishes. And of course, I've got to come up with his favorite meal tonight. Which means leg of lamb, *and* mint jelly, *and* red raspberries, if I can *find* them, and then there's the Yacht Club Dance, and I suppose I should call and make two more reservations, and—

RANDY: Did he *say* why he decided to come, Mother?

(Pause, Mother looks at him.)

MOTHER: No. He didn't say…

BARBARA: He avoids us like the plague for five years, and then suddenly…

RANDY: Oh he's always doing this. Remember the time he ran away from summer camp? And just arrived, on the doorstep, in the middle of a party?

BARBARA: I remember the time he *left*. Remember that, Mother? You were having some people over for him, and right before they arrived, he walked in with his knapsack packed and said he was hitchhiking out west?

RANDY: I thought he'd settle down, now he's married. Do you think he's quit his job again, Mother?

MOTHER: He didn't say… *(Pause.)* But I know. I know why he's coming. He's coming because of my letter.

RANDY: Your—letter?

MOTHER: My letter. People still write letters, Randy. Occasionally. When they want to say things that can't be said on the telephone. When they want to have things sink in. That's when they write letters. *(Pause.)* And knowing the United States mail, your brother just got that letter yesterday. And apparently it *didn't* sink in. It didn't sink in at all. Because he throws his poor wife and children into the car, and drives all night, and doesn't call until he's practically *here,* so that we can't say no, we can't say relax, we can't say please, before you come, at least let it sink *in. (Pause.)* That's why he's coming.

(Pause.)

BARBARA: What did the letter say, Mother?

(Pause.)

MOTHER: Well first, I said we'd all miss him, and I wished them all a very happy Fourth of July.

BARBARA: And?

MOTHER: And then I asked him to do some serious thinking about the fall.

RANDY: The fall?

MOTHER: The fall. Because in the fall—as I wrote your brother—you three children will get this house.

BARBARA: But—why, Mother?

MOTHER: *(Taking a deep breath.)* Because in the fall, in September, to be exact—now this is a secret. Nobody knows about this— *(Pause.)* In the fall, in September, your Uncle Bill and I are going to be married.

(She turns and strides into the house. Pause. Barbara and Randy look at each other.)

BARBARA: Wow.

RANDY: *(Looking toward the house.)* She told him first. Why does she always tell him things first?

(Pause. They look at each other again, and then of one accord rush into the house after their Mother, calling, "That's great, Mother!"; "That's terrific," "Why didn't you tell us?" etc. The lights dim as we hear congratulations within. The group of voices sings a song like "I Want a Girl" or "Personal Friend of Mine." The song fades as the lights have come up again. The brightness of the overhead sun indicates that it is about eleven-thirty in the morning. After a moment, Jane comes out of the house, a pretty woman in her mid-thirties. She wears a white tennis dress, white hair band, and white sneakers. She carries a tray with two glasses of coke on it, which she puts on a table. Then she calls toward off right.)

JANE: I'm out here, Randy.

(Pause. Then Randy comes on from around the house, now also in whites. He carries a tennis racquet. He glances at Jane, then walks to the edge of the sitting wall. He hauls off, about to hurl the racquet away.)

JANE: Oh don't, Randy! That's a new racquet.

(He looks at the racquet, shakes his head, and tosses it aside. He slumps angrily into a chair.)

JANE: We should have gone to the ferry with everyone else.

RANDY: We had a game.

JANE: Some game.

RANDY: All right. I stank.

JANE: You got so mad.

RANDY: They never knew. We shook hands, and all that.

JANE: They didn't even stay for a coke.

RANDY: They couldn't, Jane. They had to get back to their children.

JANE: They *said* they had to get back to their children. Who are in camp.

(Randy looks at her. Pause.)

JANE: I love the ferry. All that kissing and hugging.

RANDY: Pokey and I don't hug.

(Pause. They sip their cokes.)

RANDY: You know why we lost?

JANE: You got mad.

RANDY: You know why I got mad?

JANE: You're upset about your mother.

RANDY: Not at all.

JANE: It makes sense, psychologically.

RANDY: I said, not at *all,* Jane.

JANE: I mean, you're very close to her. You don't want to see her go.

RANDY: She's not *going* anywhere. She'll be right here, every summer. With all
of us. And Uncle Bill. Who's a great old friend of the family. Who was
one of Daddy's ushers in their wedding, for God's sake. It's perfect. It's
ideal.

JANE: I think so, too.

RANDY: So that's not why I got mad.

JANE: All right.

RANDY: That's not why we lost.

JANE: All right, dear.

(*Long pause; they both look out to sea.*)

RANDY: You want to know why we lost?

JANE: Because of Pokey.

RANDY: No.

JANE: Well you say he always makes you nervous.

RANDY: He's not the reason.

JANE: Well you're always saying that. Everybody says it. Isn't that why you all
call him Pokey? Because he's always poking around, making everybody
nervous?

RANDY: We call him Pokey because he has a poker face.

JANE: Oh.

RANDY: And because he was a slowpoke. He was always holding us up.

JANE: Your mother said it was because he liked to poke around. I remember,
because she said he now has the perfect job. In Washington. Working for
the Department of Justice. She said now he can poke around the entire
country, stirring things up.

RANDY: Oh maybe…

JANE: I'm sure she said that. She said that both her sons had perfect jobs. You
teaching at a boys' boarding school because you love sports and games,
and Pokey poking around for the Department of Justice.

RANDY: O.K., O.K.

JANE: So probably you were nervous about Pokey on the tennis court.

RANDY: Wrong.

JANE: O.K.

RANDY: Just plain wrong, Jane.

JANE: O.K. Skip it.

(Pause. They look out to sea again.)

RANDY: You want to know why we lost? Really?

JANE: I still think—

RANDY: Do you want to know why?

JANE: It's your mother. Or Pokey. Or both. I'll bet you.

RANDY: *(Shouting.)* DO YOU WANT TO KNOW WHY WE LOST THAT GODDAMN GAME OF TENNIS, JANE?

(Pause.)

JANE: Why?

RANDY: Because of the court.

JANE: The court? What's wrong with the court?

RANDY: What's wrong with the *court?* What's wrong with that tennis court, out there? I'll tell you what's wrong with the court. Everything's wrong with the court. You can't see the lines, the net is riddled with holes, the surface is like a battlefield. How can a man play under those conditions? How can a man who is used to a decent court play on a court like that? Daddy wouldn't have played. Daddy would have walked right off that court. I tell the kids, I tell the boys at school, there's no point in playing a game unless you have good equipment. A man's got to be able to count on certain fundamental *things.* It's like Latin. That's why I like Latin. When I'm teaching Latin, I say look for the verb. You can always count on the verb. Find the verb, and everything will fall into place. Now maybe those clods we played tennis with today don't care about these things. Maybe they're used to bad bounces, and foot faults, and wrong scores.

JANE: The score wasn't wrong.

RANDY: He called it wrong. Twice. I had to correct him. Because I care about the score. And I care about lines and nets and smooth surfaces and bounces that I can at least pre*dict.* And that's why we lost, if you really want to know.

(Pause.)

JANE: All right.

(Pause.)

RANDY: And I'll tell you something else. We're going to resurface that court. That's the first thing. That's first on the list, when the house is ours.

JANE: I think Barbara wants to winterize the house. She's always talking about it.

RANDY: Well the court comes first.

(*Pause.*)

JANE: Would you explain something to me, please?

RANDY: What?

JANE: Why do you get the house when your mother gets married?

RANDY: It was in Daddy's will.

JANE: Oh.

RANDY: It's in most wills.

JANE: Oh.

RANDY: The house is in the wife's name until she dies or remarries. Then it goes to the children. It's standard practice.

JANE: Oh. And Pokey understands all that?

RANDY: Of course he does. He's the executor of the will.

JANE: Oh then that explains it.

RANDY: Explains what?

JANE: Why he's suddenly coming up. To handle these legal things.

RANDY: I suppose.

JANE: Oh that's a relief. You know what I thought?

RANDY: What?

JANE: I thought he was upset about your mother.

RANDY: (*Exploding.*) JESUS, JANE—

(*A car horn is heard off right. Car doors slamming, the sound of children's voices.*)

JANE: Well. There they are. (*She gets up.*)

RANDY: (*Getting up.*) So let's get Pokey to chip in on the court, O.K.?

JANE: Does he still play?

RANDY: Of course he does. He's quite good. But I can beat him. I can beat him easily. Even on that crummy court, with those lousy lines, and that stringy net between us, I can still beat him. Ask Mother. Mother will tell you. I can slaughter him.

(*He is off right by now, Jane following him, as the lights change. The group of voices might sing Stephen Foster's "Old Folks at Home." The lights are up by now. It is high noon. The sound of children's voices can be heard occasionally offstage. Mother comes out of the house, now dressed in colorful slacks and blouse. Then Barbara comes out in a change of clothes, carrying a gin-and-tonic. She looks at her mother.*)

BARBARA: Well. He's changing.

MOTHER: (*With a sigh.*) Do you think so?

BARBARA: His clothes, Mother. He's changing his clothes.

MOTHER: Oh.

BARBARA: Thank God he's getting out of that dark suit. He looked like a visiting minister.

MOTHER: *(Glancing toward the house.)* Sssshhhh.

(Pause.)

BARBARA: *(Lower voice.)* What did you think of *her* outfit?

MOTHER: Miriam? She's sweet.

BARBARA: Her *out*fit, Mother. What did you think of that little number?

MOTHER: I thought it was very pretty.

BARBARA: Oh Mother…

MOTHER: Very snappy.

BARBARA: Snappy? That halter job? And no *bra,* Mother?

MOTHER: That's the style these days. *(Pause.)* Apparently.

(Pause.)

BARBARA: What about the children? How did you like them getting off the ferry in their grubby little blue jeans?

MOTHER: Styles change, Barbara.

BARBARA: Oh do they? I don't see you giving my children blue jeans for Christmas. It seems to me I remember nice little boxes from Saks Fifth Avenue.

MOTHER: People live different lives, Barbara.

BARBARA: They certainly do. He looks like a relic from the Eisenhower age escorting a bunch of hippies around.

MOTHER: That's enough, please.

BARBARA: And pale. Don't they allow the sun down in Washington? Is that one of their new laws?

MOTHER: They'll get the sun here.

BARBARA: Let's hope so. Can you imagine us all cooped up here together on a rainy day?

(Pause. Mother shakes her head.)

MOTHER: The first thing he did when he got here, the first thing, he walked right out on this terrace, and looked at the view, and said, "Where's the rose garden? Where's the old croquet court?" So I said, "Erosion, dear. Natural erosion. You just haven't been here."

BARBARA: If there's erosion, Pokey would notice it.

MOTHER: He says we need a seawall.

BARBARA: Oh my God, that costs a fortune.

MOTHER: That's what he says. Otherwise, he says some night we're going to be sitting here drinking, and the whole house will slide slowly into the sea.

BARBARA: Pokey, Pokey, Pokey...

MOTHER: *(With a sigh.)* Well, we've just got to loosen him up, that's all.

BARBARA: How? How do we loosen up Pokey?

MOTHER: By being very affectionate and warm-hearted.

(Barbara laughs; Mother looks at her.)

MOTHER: What's so funny?

BARBARA: The way we were at the ferry?

MOTHER: What was wrong at the ferry?

BARBARA: Nothing. We were all on our best behavior.

MOTHER: We welcomed him with open arms.

BARBARA: A peck for a kiss.

MOTHER: I didn't peck.

BARBARA: We both pecked, Mother. And the children shook hands.

MOTHER: Well what should we have done? Are we supposed to fall all over each other, like that Italian family?

BARBARA: Not at all. We're not the type. *(Pause.)* Except maybe Pokey. Remember how he cried at Daddy's funeral?

MOTHER: We all cried.

BARBARA: But not so *much*. God, tears were streaming down his face. The rest of us were good old undemonstrative Wasps.

MOTHER: I hate that expression, Wasp. Everyone uses it these days, and I loathe it.

BARBARA: It's what we are, Mother.

MOTHER: We are not. We are people, like Italians or anybody else. We love our family, and we're very affectionate when we're not in public. Honestly. *(Pause.)* We all cried. *(Pause.)* I don't like all this smart talk, Barbara. I know you're upset about your divorce, but I don't want to see you turning into a bitter, disagreeable woman. Now you'd better learn to be nice to both your brothers, because you're going to take over in the fall. *(Pause. She looks out to sea.)*

BARBARA: What's the matter, Mother?

MOTHER: Nothing's the matter. *(Pause.)* Except that he never even mentioned my getting married.

BARBARA: No kidding.

MOTHER: Not a word. Not at the ferry, not in the car, not out here, not at all.

BARBARA: No kidding.

(Pause.)

MOTHER: *(Carefully.)* I suppose he mentioned it to you.

BARBARA: No.

MOTHER: You must have brought it up.

BARBARA: I tried. At one point.

MOTHER: What did you say?

BARBARA: Oh I said, "What do you think of the good news, Pokey?" Something like that.

MOTHER: What did he say?

BARBARA: Nothing. He walked away.

(Mother sighs.)

BARBARA: He was fussing with his children.

(Pause.)

MOTHER: The only way it came up with me was when I told him we were having his favorite meal tonight. Do you know what he said? He said, "I hope it's just the family." That's all he said. *(Pause.)* Well. Just the family it will be.

BARBARA: Not Uncle Bill?

(Mother shakes her head.)

BARBARA: Oh Mother, we were going to have toasts. And sing songs. I got some wine.

(Mother shakes her head.)

BARBARA: Uncle Bill's part of the family.

MOTHER: Not to Pokey. Pokey won't even call him Uncle Bill.

BARBARA: We've always called him Uncle Bill.

MOTHER: Pokey hasn't. He calls him Mister. He used to say that Uncle Bill's not his uncle, so why should he call him that. *(Pause.)* Pokey doesn't like him.

BARBARA: Oh Mother.

MOTHER: He doesn't like him. He can be very rude to him. I've seen it. *(Pause.)* That's why I wrote him that letter. So he could get used to the idea. *(Pause.)* I told Pokey first. Before I told any of you. Uncle Bill hasn't even told *his* children yet. But I thought I should tell Pokey. *(Pause.)* So. No Uncle Bill for dinner. No celebration. Just the family. *(She gets up, smiles, squares her shoulders.)* And maybe it's just as well. Aunt Peggy just died in March. We shouldn't be jumping the gun, should we? To be fair to her. So maybe it's just as well if we all just avoided the issue for the weekend, and had a nice family dinner, and then we'll see Uncle Bill at the Yacht Club dance. *(She starts for the house.)* And now I think I'll take a bath before lunch.

(Barbara laughs. Mother turns.)

MOTHER: *Now* what's so funny?

BARBARA: Oh Mother…

MOTHER: What's wrong with taking a bath?

BARBARA: Nothing's *wrong* with it. But have you noticed that since Pokey arrived, everyone makes a dash for the water.

MOTHER: Phooey.

BARBARA: It's true. I went in, Jane went in, the children went in, Randy's still in, and now you're making a beeline for the bathtub.

MOTHER: It's a hot day.

BARBARA: Oh sure.

MOTHER: What's wrong with people keeping clean?

BARBARA: Nothing's *wrong,* Mother. It's just who we are. I think that's why we have to be near the ocean. We have to go through these ritual cleansings.

MOTHER: People feel hot, people feel dirty…

BARBARA: And people feel guilty.

(Pause.)

MOTHER: Guilty? Guilty about what?

BARBARA: Oh lots of things. Money. Having this place when poor people are sweltering in the city. Living off the stock market. All that.

MOTHER: That's ridiculous.

BARBARA: I feel guilty.

MOTHER: I don't, at all.

BARBARA: I do. I feel guilty about my divorce. I feel guilty about— *(She glances toward off right. Pause.)* And Pokey always makes me feel more guilty.

MOTHER: I have nothing to feel guilty about, thank you very much. *(She starts toward the house again.)*

BARBARA: Maybe you do, and don't even know it.

(Mother turns.)

BARBARA: Face it, Mother. That's who we are. We're very repressive people. That's what my psychiatrist said. We survive on repression. That's how we made our money, and that's how we've held onto it. We hold onto things. We hold on. That's our whole bag. And it's time we realized it.

(Mother snorts, strides to the door opens it, then turns.)

MOTHER: I'll tell *you* what it's time we realized. It's time we realized when to drink and when not to drink. I've noticed that glass in your hand, Barbara, and I haven't mentioned it, but now I think it's time I did. I don't like drinking at this hour, and I don't like drinking alone. We have rules about drinking in this house. If your father were alive, he'd make you pour that out. You children are much too casual about alcohol. It's not a toy. *That's* what it's time you realized, frankly, if you want my opinion. *(She goes into the house. The screen door slams behind her. Barbara looks after her, looks at the drink in her hand, shakes her head, settles into her chair, takes a long sip.)*

BARBARA: Oh Pokey, Pokey, Pokey. Welcome home…

(The lights dim. The group of voices might sing "Aura Lee" or "Tell Me Why." The lights are up again. It is about an hour later. Barbara is sound asleep in her chair, her feet up on the wall, her empty glass beside her. Jane comes out of the house, now also dressed in a fresh blouse and slacks.)

JANE: *(Not seeing that Barbara is asleep.)* There's a slight problem with the children.

BARBARA: *(Starting; sitting up.)* What?

JANE: Oh I'm sorry.

BARBARA: That's all right. I had a late night. What's the matter?

JANE: The children. They're using four-letter words.

BARBARA: How did that start?

JANE: I'm afraid with Pokey's children.

BARBARA: Wouldn't you know…

JANE: They just started in saying them. Every word in the book. And the other children took them up. And now four-letter words are being tossed around the infield, over the peanut butter sandwiches, amid gales of laughter.

BARBARA: Did you stop it?

JANE: Oh I tried to. But then I started to laugh. That didn't help much.

BARBARA: Oh Jane…

JANE: It was so funny. At one point, it was like a chant. All the most repulsive words. Even the sitter was doing it. I found myself roaring with laughter. *(She laughs, then checks herself.)* I hope your mother didn't hear.

BARBARA: She's taking a bath.

JANE: Whew. *(She sits down.)* Another problem. Pokey's children call me by my first name.

BARBARA: Did you ask them to?

JANE: Nope.

BARBARA: I think that might be a little fresh, don't you?

JANE: I sort of like it.

BARBARA: Then what's the problem?

JANE: Well now your children want to do it.

BARBARA: Out of the question.

JANE: Otherwise they say it's not fair.

BARBARA: They weren't brought up that way.

JANE: I told them they could.

BARBARA: I'll tell them later they can't. *(Pause.)* Next thing you know, your own children will be calling you Randy and Jane.

JANE: That's what they want to do.

BARBARA: You said no, I hope.

JANE: Oh it wouldn't kill me.

BARBARA: Randy would kill *them*.

JANE: *(Nodding.)* I said that. *(Pause.)* So they'll continue to call me Mummy. *(She shakes her head.)* I hate being called Mummy. I wish I were called Ma. Or Mama Mia. Or just plain old Mom. *(Pause.)* Not Mummy. It reminds me of all those types I went to boarding school with. They called their mothers Mummy, and when they wrote, everything slanted backwards, and they dotted their *i*'s with great, big, empty circles.

BARBARA: I slant backwards.

JANE: *(Sadly.)* So do I. *(Pause.)* It's hard to change. *(Pause.)* Oh. Remind me to pick up some more coke this afternoon.

BARBARA: There's plenty of coke.

JANE: There was.

BARBARA: Mother just got coke. This morning.

JANE: They've been through two big bottles.

BARBARA: Who?

JANE: The children. Just now.

BARBARA: Coke with meals? Mother planned milk.

JANE: Pokey's kids wanted *Coca-Cola*. So the sitter gave it to them.

BARBARA: Are mine having coke? Are yours?

JANE: We had to be fair.

BARBARA: Coke is for people who play tennis. That's the rule.

JANE: Maybe it's a Jewish thing.

BARBARA: Coke? Coke is Jewish?

JANE: No, the idea of no milk with meals. Maybe it comes from Miriam. Maybe it's a Jewish rule.

BARBARA: We have our own rules around here. And one of them is Coke is for people who exercise. Think of their *teeth*. I'll tell the sitter.

(Randy comes in from left. He wears a white monogrammed terry cloth bathrobe which is a little too big for him. His hair is wet from swimming. Barbara sees him, gasps.)

BARBARA: Oh my God!

RANDY: What?

BARBARA: That bathrobe! I thought you were Daddy.

RANDY: Pokey gave it to me this morning.

BARBARA: You'd better get it off before Mother sees it.

JANE: Why?

BARBARA: Daddy wore it the day he drowned. She found it on the beach.

RANDY: I think she'd want me to wear it.

BARBARA: When she's getting married again?

RANDY: Pokey said that doesn't mean she wants to forget Daddy.

BARBARA: *(Shaking her head.)* I want to forget Fred. I can tell you that.

RANDY: That's a little different.

BARBARA: I'll say.

RANDY: Oh. Pokey brought a present for you.

BARBARA: Something of Daddy's?

RANDY: Yep. He held onto a lot of his stuff.

BARBARA: *(Getting up.)* I'll go see. *(She goes into the house.)*

RANDY: *(To Jane.)* Do you think she'd mind?

JANE: Your mother? I don't know.

RANDY: Why should she? She gave me lots of his sport coats.

JANE: That might be a little big for you.

RANDY: It's supposed to be. You're supposed to feel free in it. Daddy would wear all these tight, stuffy clothes, but when he went swimming, this was it. Mother would try to get him to wear a bathing suit when you were around, but he wouldn't do it. He said that swimming was the one time he wanted to feel absolutely free. Remember? He'd roll around in the water like an old walrus. *(He shakes his head.)* I'm the same way. *(He looks at Jane.)* You look great. New outfit?

JANE: Your mother got it for me in the village.

RANDY: I like it.

JANE: You do?

RANDY: Don't you?

JANE: I don't know. I thought I did. But now…

RANDY: What?

JANE: I don't know. After seeing Miriam, I feel so…square.

RANDY: You look great to me.

JANE: It makes me feel like your mother.

RANDY: What's wrong with that?

JANE: I don't know. Here I am in your mother's outfit, and you're in your father's bathrobe, and we're living in your family's house... *(She shakes her head.)* I don't know.

(She walks to the edge of the wall and looks out. Randy watches her, then smiles, and comes to her. He begins fiddling with the back of her blouse.)

RANDY: Then let's take it off.

JANE: *(Giggling.)* Oh Randy, stop it.

RANDY: *(Nuzzling her.)* How about it? A quickie? A little nooner, before lunch? Mmmm? Mmmm?

JANE: *(Laughing.)* What's come over you?

RANDY: *(Opening his bathrobe.)* This. Look. No hands.

JANE: *(Walking away; laughing.)* You're repulsive!

(Randy follows her around. Barbara comes out of the house, carrying a wristwatch.)

BARBARA: *(Holding it out.)* Look what Pokey gave me. Daddy's watch.

RANDY: Hey!

BARBARA: Daddy left this on the beach, too. *(She shakes it.)* Oh, Darn! It doesn't work. *(She looks at it fondly.)* Oh boy. I can remember this. *(Imitating her father.)* Barbara, I want you in this house by ten-thirty. No and's, if's, or but's. I intend to be looking at my watch. *(Pause.)* Pokey kept it. *(Pause.)* I said, "Pokey, don't you want any of these things? What are you keeping for yourself?"

RANDY: What did he say?

BARBARA: Nothing. *(Pause. She sighs, settles back into her chair.)* Well. Anyway, while I was in there, I laid down the law. Milk for everyone. No exceptions. And I told our little teenage townie to take them all out to the meadow for softball as soon as they've finished their ice cream. No children on this terrace. This is absolutely sancta sanctorum for grown-ups. *(Randy has begun to nuzzle Jane again.)*

BARBARA: Oh God, Randy, stop *paw*ing the woman. It's embarrassing. Mother says you do it even in restaurants in New York. Cut it out. What are other people supposed to do when you're doing that?

RANDY: Masturbate.

BARBARA: Oh Jesus.

(She looks at the watch fondly, tries to shake it into running. Randy continues to nuzzle Jane. Then Barbara seems to make up her mind and puts the watch down on the table where it stays, in full view, till the end of the play.)

BARBARA: Randy, do you think you could possibly control yourself long enough for us to have a small, serious conversation before Mother and Pokey come down for lunch?

RANDY: Sure.

BARBARA: Good.

(She smiles icily, he smiles back.)

BARBARA: Do you know, for example, that when Mother gets married, the house goes to us?

RANDY: I know that.

BARBARA: Good. *(Another smile.)* Do you know, also, that I am seriously considering giving up my apartment in Boston, and living down here over the winter?

RANDY: Mother doesn't think—

BARBARA: Mother will be *out* of it, Randy! Now I want to do it, and all I need is a small gas furnace to take care of the bottom floor of the house.

RANDY: We need lots of things.

BARBARA: We need that first, Randy. Now I've looked around, and I know I can get one put in for a song.

RANDY: We need a new tennis court.

BARBARA: Will you let me *fin*ish, Randy? Please. I can get one put in for about two thousand dollars.

RANDY: Two thousand!

BARBARA: That's a bargain, Randy. I've found a builder who will do it almost at cost.

RANDY: We could resurface the court for—

BARBARA: You'll *get* your court, Randy. Next year. Chip in with me for the furnace now, and next year I'll chip in with you on the court! O.K.?

(Pause.)

RANDY: A thousand? Now? I don't have that kind of money.

BARBARA: Oh yes you do.

RANDY: Do you know what they pay me at Saint Luke's School?

BARBARA: Do you know what I pay for rent in Boston? Do you know what Fred gives me for alimony? We've got to get together on this, Randy.

RANDY: I can't afford a thousand.

BARBARA: You can, Randy. You know damn well you can. You have your stocks, and Jane is privately endowed…

JANE: Oh…

BARBARA: You are, Jane, and both of you manage to keep four children in private school, and get them on skis every winter. You can damn well pay for a dinky little furnace, if you wanted to. And you could use it, Randy. You could all come down here. Thanksgiving. And Christmas. We'd all get together. You'd use it more than I'd ever use that court. I mean, what's more important? A home, warmth, shelter—or a goddamn game?

RANDY: You've got a home.

BARBARA: I don't, Randy. I hate Boston. Everyone there is either a professor or a politician. Or both. It's all very moral and earnest, and I hate it, and I want to be here.

RANDY: Mother says you'd last about a week.

BARBARA: I won't, I swear. I'll send the kids to the local schools, and I'll do some writing…

RANDY: Writing?

BARBARA: Children's books. I want to write children's books. I've always wanted to do that. Always.

RANDY: You'd go stir-crazy, sitting around, writing about bunnies, with nobody to see.

BARBARA: I'd see people.

RANDY: Who? Old ladies? Townies?

BARBARA: There are people.

RANDY: Who? You'd never go out, Barb.

BARBARA: I went out last night.

RANDY: With Betsy. To the movies.

BARBARA: *(Blurting it out.)* Says who?

RANDY: Says you. You said so.
(Pause.)

BARBARA: Well maybe I had a date last night. What do you think of that?
(Pause.)

RANDY: Who with?

BARBARA: Never you mind.
(Pause.)

RANDY: Someone who's going to be around all winter?

BARBARA: Maybe.
(Pause.)

RANDY: Who?

BARBARA: That's for me to know.

RANDY: Come on. Who?

BARBARA: None of your beeswax.

RANDY: And you want me to kick in a thousand bucks for some demon lover?
(Pause.)

BARBARA: Promise you won't tell Mother?

RANDY: O.K.

BARBARA: Will you chip in on the furnace?

RANDY: Maybe. It depends.

(Pause. Barbara thinks it over. Finally:)

BARBARA: Artie.

(Pause.)

RANDY: Artie? Artie who? Artie…GRIEBER?

BARBARA: *(Quietly.)* Artie Grieber.

(Pause; Randy whistles.)

JANE: Who's Artie Grieber?

RANDY: Oh my God.

JANE: Who's Artie Grieber.

RANDY: He used to cut the *grass* around here.

BARBARA: He's a builder now.

RANDY: He cut the grass.

BARBARA: He's done very well on the island.

RANDY: I thought he was married. I thought he had kids.

BARBARA: He's getting separated.

RANDY: Artie Grieber… *(To Jane.)* She had a crush on him twenty years ago. *(To Barbara.)* Didn't Pokey catch you with him in the maid's room?

BARBARA: Pokey caught you doing a few things too, kid.

RANDY: *(Shaking his head.)* Artie Grieber. All night, with Artie Grieber.

BARBARA: If you tell Mother, Randy, I swear I'll strangle you.

RANDY: Oh my God, I wouldn't dare tell Mother. *(He sits down.)* Artie Grieber.

JANE: Is it serious, Barbara?

BARBARA: It's beginning to be.

JANE: Do you think you might marry him?

BARBARA: Maybe. I…see a lot of him. I'm seeing him this afternoon.

RANDY: *(Still shaking his head.)* Artie Grieber…Old Artie the grass-cutter… *(He laughs.)* So you want to be here in the winter, and have Artie come in and turn on your furnace, eh?

BARBARA: *(Angrily.)* CUT IT OUT!

(Controlling herself, as he continues to chuckle.)

BARBARA: He does tennis courts, Randy. He could put in a whole new tennis court for you, next year, at half the cost. You get your court, and I get a place to live. Please, Randy. I want this. This is very important to me. Can we get together on this, please?

(Randy looks at her, stops laughing, stands up, wraps his bathrobe tightly around him.)

RANDY: Who do you think I am? Do you think I'd go along with the idea of my sister shacking up all winter in this house with Artie Grieber? Jesus, Barbara. Grow up.

(Pause.)

BARBARA: *(Grimly, quietly.)* Do you know what a Wasp is, Randy?

RANDY: Yes I know what a Wasp is.

BARBARA: I don't think you do. So I'll tell you. Because you are one. A Wasp is a white Anglo-Saxon prick.

RANDY: Big joke.

BARBARA: And I'll tell you something else, brother. I'm going to be here this winter. I'm going to be right here. You wait, buster. You just wait.

JANE: *(Looking toward the house.)* Ssshhh. Your mother.

(A noise within. Then Mother comes out of the house, in different clothes again. She stands at the door, and notices Randy's bathrobe immediately.)

MOTHER: Pokey gave you that.

RANDY: Yes, Mother.

MOTHER: *(Nodding; turning to Barbara.)* And what did he give you ?

BARBARA: *(Indicating the watch on the table.)* Daddy's old wrist watch.

(Mother nods and sits down.)

MOTHER: I wonder what he brought for me.

(Pause.)

RANDY: Do you mind, Mother? My wearing this?

MOTHER: *(Brightly.)* Mind? Mind? Why should I mind? *(She looks him up and down.)* It doesn't fit at all, but why should I mind? *(To Barbara.)* And the watch, of course, doesn't work. *(Pause.)* Pokey asked, he specifically asked for both those things when we were going over your father's possessions.

BARBARA: Why did he give them to us, then, Mother?

MOTHER: *(Grimly.)* I think I can answer that. *(Pause.)* I've just had a long talk with your brother. *(Pause.)* Through the bathroom door. While I was taking my bath. *(Pause.)* In fact… *(Pause.)* I think we should all have a drink before lunch. *(A glance at Barbara.)* Or another drink, in some cases. *(To Randy.)* Randy, go make Bloody Marys. Barbara, there's some Brie left. Get that, and some of those Bremner wafers.

BARBARA: What did he *say*, Mother?

MOTHER: I will tell you when we all have a drink in our hands. Go on, Randy…And get into some clothes while you're doing it, please.

(Randy and Barbara look at her and then go quickly into the house. Jane remains. Pause. Mother looks out to sea then turns to her with a sigh.)

MOTHER: You and I are going to have to work very hard this weekend, Jane. Very hard indeed. We've got a big job on our hands... *(She shakes her head.)* Just keeping things going.

JANE: What do you mean?

MOTHER: *(Shaking her head again.)* Wait till the others get back. *(Pause.)* One thing we talked about, Pokey and I, was that outfit you're wearing.

JANE: This?

MOTHER: That. We talked about that for a while.

JANE: I don't—

MOTHER: He said it was unfair.

JANE: Unfair?

MOTHER: Unfair for me to buy you that, and unfair for me to buy Barbara her yellow sweater, when I didn't buy Miriam anything.

JANE: Oh.

(Pause.)

MOTHER: You didn't tell him I bought it, did you?

JANE: No.

MOTHER: Of course you didn't. He just knows these things. By instinct. Always has. He can sniff out an issue like this a mile away. At Christmas, he could tell if he was one present short without even counting. *(Sighs; shakes her head.)* Pokey, Pokey, Pokey. *(Pause.)* So. I said I bought you that outfit because you needed one. Because you and Randy don't have much money. Because Randy just teaches school. And I said I bought Barbara that yellow sweater because Fred just gives her a pittance for alimony. And I said of course I would have bought Miriam something, but she wasn't here, and I don't dare buy her things when she's not here because I never know what she likes.

JANE: That seems fair.

MOTHER: And I said, all right. This afternoon, I'll take Miriam into the village, and she can buy whatever she wants. On me.

JANE: Did that do it?

MOTHER: No, I don't think so. All I got from that was silence, on the other side of the bathroom door. *(Pause.)* There's always one. In every family. Always one child who behaves like this. Does one of yours always stir things up, Jane?

JANE: Yes.

MOTHER: Who? Which one?

(Pause.)

JANE: I won't tell.

MOTHER: *(Smiling.)* Good. Good for you. *(Pause.)* But in some ways, don't you love that one most of all?

JANE: Yes.

(Pause.)

MOTHER: Even though it's so exhausting, even though it wears you down, even though you spend more time thinking about that one than any of the others…there's a special feeling, isn't there?

JANE: Yes.

(Pause. They both look out to sea.)

MOTHER: Aaaanyway, that was the first thing we talked about, Pokey and I, while I was trying to take a bath, after a very long morning, when he hasn't been here in five years. That was just the first thing.

JANE: Didn't he talk about your getting married again?

MOTHER: *(Laughing ironically.)* He didn't. So I did. Finally, I said, "Pokey, sweetheart, I'm getting *married* in the fall. I wrote you a letter, and you haven't even mentioned it. Don't you at least want to congratulate your mother? Isn't that just a little bit more important than who bought what for whom? Kind of? Maybe? Sort of? Hmmm?"

JANE: And what did he say?

MOTHER: Nothing.

JANE: Nothing.

MOTHER: Nothing. There was more silence. Endless silence. An eternity of silence.

JANE: Maybe he didn't hear.

MOTHER: Oh he heard all right. Because then suddenly he launched into the *big* topic of discussion, and—

(Noise from the house; clinking of glasses and ice.)

MOTHER: And here, thank heavens, comes something to drink.

(Randy enters, now in a polo shirt and khakis, carrying a tray of glasses and a pitcher of Bloody Marys. Barbara follows him with a platter of crackers and cheese. As the scene continues, Randy hands around the drinks, with the appropriate ad-libs. Barbara puts the crackers and cheese in front of her Mother, who cuts it, puts the cheese on the crackers, and hands them out during the conversation.)

MOTHER: Where is Pokey now?

RANDY: With his children.

MOTHER: That's so we can talk it over.

BARBARA: Talk *what* over?

(Randy hands his mother a drink.)

MOTHER: Thank you, dear. *(She takes a long sip.)* Pokey wants you two to buy him out.

(Startled pause.)

RANDY: Buy him *out?*

MOTHER: That's what he said. Buy out his third of the house. In the fall. When it goes to you. When I get married…Have some cheese, Jane? *(She hands Jane a cracker and cheese.)*

BARBARA: He doesn't want it?

MOTHER: He wants his equity. That's what he says…Here, Barbara. Cheese. *(Pause.)*

RANDY: Well…O.K.…

MOTHER: O.K.? O.K.? Randy, my dear love, *think* before you speak. Pokey wants one third of a fair market value. He says that this house, with beach frontage, and a tennis court, and a barn, and five acres of valuable land, is worth at least two hundred thousand dollars. Minimum…Take some cheese, dear.

BARBARA: That means…mmm…over sixty thousand each.

MOTHER: At least.

RANDY: That means we each have to pay Pokey at least thirty thousand.

MOTHER: At least and we can't sell off the land because the will won't allow it, and we can't get another mortgage, because Daddy already did that after he got sick and couldn't work full time.

(Pause.)

RANDY: Then we can't pay Pokey.

MOTHER: Of course you can't. Nor can I. Nor can Uncle Bill.

BARBARA: Did you tell him we can't?

MOTHER: Of course I did.

RANDY: What did he say?

MOTHER: He said we can. If we sell.

(General consternation.)

MOTHER: Oh, yes. That's what he said. Sell this beautiful place, pay a huge capital gains tax, divide up the furniture, and get out of here, lock, stock, and barrel, so that Pokey can have his money.

BARBARA: He doesn't need the money.

MOTHER: He says he does.

RANDY: He's got a good job. He earns more than any of us.

MOTHER: He wants to leave that job.

BARBARA: With the Department of *Justice?*

MOTHER: He doesn't like it. He says it's unfair.

RANDY: Unfair?

MOTHER: He's upset about Civil Rights. He says the Department of Justice is unfair to Negroes. I don't know. He wants to leave.

RANDY: Golly.

MOTHER: Just the way he left Andover. Just the way he left Yale Law School. Just the way he left two other jobs in the past ten years. Just the way he left *here,* summer after summer... *(Ironically.)* whenever things are unfair...

BARBARA: Oh Lord.

MOTHER: And so he says he needs the money to live on. To support Miriam and the children. While he decides what he wants to do.

(Long pause.)

BARBARA: So what's the solution, Mother?

MOTHER: I'll tell you what the solution is not. The solution is *not* to sell. That is *not* the solution.

RANDY: Of course.

MOTHER: Sell this spot? Which has been in the family for over eighty years? Why there's nothing that can compare to it on the island, in the country, in the world! I mean, look, *just* look at that view!

(They all look out.)

MOTHER: Pokey loves it here. In his heart of hearts, he loves it. I know it. And he knows it...My glass is empty, Randy.

(Randy jumps up, takes her glass, and pours her another Bloody Mary.)

MOTHER: It's the same old thing, with Pokey. He leaves. But he always comes back. I mean, he's here, isn't he? He's right here. And he wants us all to make a big fuss.

(Randy gives her her glass.)

MOTHER: Thank you, dear...Remember when he was little? He'd come storming in, his bag all packed, ready to run away, and we'd all have to coddle him like mad. Remember? All those trips down to the drugstore for special ice cream cones? Well that's what he wants now, at thirty-one years old, and I'm afraid we're all going to have to do it...Have some more cheese, Jane.

BARBARA: Do what, though, Mother?

MOTHER: Baby him, dear. Butter him up.

RANDY: Pokey's kind of a hard guy to butter up, Mother.

MOTHER: Not if we work hard. First, I think he needs sleep. He's exhausted from the trip. So I think we should persuade him to take a nap, and keep the children very quiet while he does.

RANDY: But I asked him to play tennis this afternoon…

BARBARA: Oh Randy, God!

MOTHER: Tennis can wait. Next, I think we can all loosen up. Barbara, the children can have *Coca-Cola* if they want it. He complained about that, and I told the sitter they can.

BARBARA: O.K. Fine. Coke with meals. I'll send you the dentist's bills.

MOTHER: And tonight, after he's had a nap and his favorite meal, I think we should try to get him to come to the Yacht Club dance.

BARBARA: He doesn't want to go, Mother. He says he hates costume parties.

MOTHER: Nonsense. He's just forgotten what fun it can be. We'll all go together. I've decided to go as my favorite person, Eleanor of Aquitaine, mother of kings and queens. And Uncle Bill is going as the Great Gatsby. Pokey and Miriam can go as them*selves,* I don't care, but they've got to go. He'll be able to sing, and dance, and see all his old friends. So we've all got to coax him to go.

RANDY: O.K.

MOTHER: And finally, I think we should ask him to stay on. As long as he wants. All summer, if he wants. And if he wants the house to himself, he should have it.

BARBARA: Mother!

MOTHER: It's only fair, Barbara.

BARBARA: But we've made plans!

MOTHER: Change them, Barbara. Pokey comes first.

RANDY: But maybe he doesn't want to be here any more, Mother.

(Pause; she looks at him.)

MOTHER: One thing I *know.* One thing I know without a shadow of a doubt. No one, and I mean no one, can live without roots. No one can cut himself off completely from his background. People are like plants. If they are cut, they last for a while, but then they wither and die. That I know. And that is Pokey's problem. And that we have got to make him realize, before it's too late for all of us. *(Pause.)* Now. Change the subject. I want a picture of all of us here on this terrace together. Randy, go into the coat closet and get Daddy's old *Kodak.* And please call Pokey and Miriam.

(Randy goes into the house.)

BARBARA: Mother, if Pokey takes August, what'll I do?

MOTHER: Ssshhh.

(Randy's voice is heard calling "Pokey" within.)

BARBARA: But I've sublet my apartment, Mother. Where will I go?

JANE: You could stay with us, back at school.

BARBARA: But I don't want to do that.

MOTHER: Ssshhh.

(Randy comes back on with the camera and a package wrapped in brown paper.)

MOTHER: Are they coming?

RANDY: In a while. They're reading to their kids.

MOTHER: In the middle of the *day?*

RANDY: Apparently it's their custom.

MOTHER: Oh…

RANDY: *(Handing her the package.)* But he told me to give you this. He says it goes with the house.

MOTHER: *(Holding it, a little nervous.)* How nice.

BARBARA: Well open it, Mother.

MOTHER: All right.

(She opens it slowly. Everyone watches.)

BARBARA: Look out. It might explode.

(Everyone laughs. Finally Mother gets it open.)

MOTHER: Why it's…

BARBARA: *(Squealing.)* It's the Family *Bi*-ble!

JANE: Bible?

BARBARA: We called it that. It's Daddy's notebook. Look, Randy! *(She takes it from her mother.)* All the old records. *(To Jane.)* We thought it was lost, after he died. *(To Randy.)* Pokey kept this, too. *(To Mother.)* Oh this is a great house-present, Mother!

MOTHER: *(Shaking her head, quietly to herself.)* Pokey, Pokey, Pokey.

BARBARA: *(Sitting on steps, thumbing through the book, as Randy looks over her shoulder.)* Look. Here's the genealogy. All the old names. Ezra, Abigail, Hepsibah…Oh, and here's the account of that fabulous woman. That great, great, great, great, GREAT grandmother, who was raped by Indians, and had her stomach slit open. Remember, Mother? When Daddy used to read that? And she hid herself in a hollow tree for three days, and stuffed her guts back in, and was found and sewn up by her husband, and went on to have eight children?…Remember, Mother? *(Mother nods.)*

RANDY: *(Flipping pages, looking over Barbara's shoulder.)* Hey. Here are all the Ministers. Look at all the Presbyterian ministers.

BARBARA: And here's one of their sermons.

RANDY: *(Reading; laughing.)* "Man is conceived in sin and born in travail… Seek not for salvation in the vast splendors of our bounteous land…the delights of this world have been set as a bait and a snare..." *(Slyly; to Barbara.)* "Forswear the pleasures of this world..."

BARBARA: *(Quickly.)* Isn't that marvelous? Isn't that marvelous, Mother?
(Mother nods, a little grimly. Barbara continues reading.)

BARBARA: Oh, and here come the businessmen. Look at all these inventories. All this money. Look. Daddy estimated all their incomes...

RANDY: And furniture. And china. And horses. And automobiles....Look, even wash cloths are listed. *(To his mother.)* It's all here, Mother.

MOTHER: *(Impatiently.)* I know it's all there.

BARBARA: *(Flipping the pages.)* Oh, and now here are the games. All the old scores of all the old family tennis games. Look: in 1952, Mother and Daddy beat you and me 6–3.

RANDY: *(Taking the book.)* Let me see that...Well, here's where I beat Pokey 18–16. *(To Jane.)* I told you I could beat him.

BARBARA: *(Reading over his shoulder.)* Oh Mother, look. *(She takes the book, shows it to her mother.)* In 1957, you and Daddy beat Fred and me, six–love. I remember that. Fred and I were engaged, and he was visiting, and he could hardly hold a racquet. God, he was horrible. Six–love. I should have read the writing on the wall.

MOTHER: *(Infinitely patient.)* Do you think we can take pictures, please?

RANDY: *(Looking over their shoulder.)* Look. Here's 1963. Here's where Uncle Bill started to fill in.

BARBARA: Because of Daddy's bad heart.

RANDY: Let's see. In '63, Mother and Uncle Bill lost to you and me 7–5.

BARBARA: I remember. Poor Daddy had to watch.

RANDY: *(Taking book.)* Hey, this isn't right. It says here that in 1961, Pokey beat me by default. That's not right.

BARBARA: Oh yes it is. That was the year you threw your racquet at him. And Daddy made you default.

RANDY: Oh yeah...

BARBARA: *(Taking the book, flipping through it.)* Wow. Here are the sailing races, and the croquet games, and even our report cards from school...

RANDY: Who won between Pokey and me in '65. *(He tries to take the book.)*

BARBARA: *(Holding on to it.)* Wait a minute. Here are my marks from Westover. Look. See? An A in creative writing. I told you I could write.

RANDY: *(Pulling at the book.)* Let me just see the tennis scores. I know I beat Pokey in '65. I'm sure of that.

BARBARA: Randy, don't grab!

RANDY: I just want to see '65!

(Mother gets up, comes between them, takes the book, closes it decisively, and puts it on a table.)

RANDY: I just want to see the record for 1965, Mother.

MOTHER: *(Grimly; wheeling on him.)* You won't *find* any record for 1965, dear boy. Because in the summer of 1965, your father *died.* Remember. Taking a long swim, after a big meal, on a hot day, with a bad heart. That's what happened in 1965. *(She shakes her head, tears in her eyes.)* Oh what does Pokey think he's doing, dragging all this stuff up? The bathrobe, the watch, and now that—that stupid, stupid book! What's he trying to do?

BARBARA: It shows he cares, Mother.

MOTHER: Cares? Cares about what? A lot of old names and dates and statistics.

RANDY: These are our roots, Mother.

MOTHER: Not at all. That's just a long boring list. I used to beg your father, I used to beg him when he was working on that thing, I'd say put in the nice things we all did. Put in some of the things *I* organized. Where is a description of the blueberry picking, or the trip to Cuttyhunk, or the singing by the piano, or the time we all got together and made this terrace, stone by stone? Where are the real things? Where is the *life?* I'd beg him to include those things. But he never would. All he cared about was things you could own, and count, and pin down. *(She sits down.)* Now *Please!* Let's take a picture of us all here together, out here on this terrace, in the sun!

(Long pause.)

RANDY: *(Quietly.)* I want a picture of you, Mother.

MOTHER: You have plenty of me.

RANDY: Not alone.

BARBARA: He wants a picture of the bride.

RANDY: I want a picture of Mother.

MOTHER: *(Touched.)* Oh…All right. *(She dries her eyes, folds her hands in her lap, puts her heels neatly together, and tries to smile.)*

RANDY: *(Kneeling; sighing; then looking up.)* Gee. You're still a beautiful woman, Mother.

BARBARA: Portrait of a lady.

(They all look at her. Pause.)

MOTHER: Oh take the picture. Take it. Before I go to pieces completely.

(Randy sights, focuses, takes the picture, as Barbara and Jane look on.)

MOTHER: Now. Someone. Get Pokey.

JANE: I'll get him.

(She hurries into the house. The sound of a car horn can now be heard honking far off right.)

BARBARA: *(With a start.)* Oh my God. That's for me. *(She starts hurriedly off right.)*

MOTHER: Who is it?

BARBARA: *(Glancing defiantly at Randy.)* I've—got a golf game, Mother.

MOTHER: What about the picture? What about lunch?

BARBARA: Too late, Mother. Good-bye. *(She goes off right.)*

MOTHER: *(To Randy.)* Who is that? Why can't they come up and shake hands? I don't like people sitting in cars and tooting their horns. *(Shakes her head.)* There goes the family picture.

(Jane comes out of the house.)

JANE: Miriam's made lunch. It's all ready.

MOTHER: Then we should go in.

JANE: *(To Randy.)* And Pokey wants to take you on in tennis, after lunch. *(Jane goes in.)*

RANDY: *(Eagerly.)* You mean I'll take *him* on.

(He cuts across his mother as she moves toward the house.)

MOTHER: Randy!

RANDY: Oh! Sorry, Mother.

(He holds the screen-door open for her. She goes in, shaking her head. Randy follows, as the lights dim.)

End of Act I

ACT II

The group of voices might sing "I Had a Dream, Dear" or "Careless Love."
Early afternoon light. Shadows are just beginning to appear on the terrace.
The glasses and cheese have been cleared away, but the watch is still on the
table. From off right comes the occasional sound of a tennis game, and at
intervals the sound of children's voices cheering. After a moment, Barbara
comes in from upstage right. She sees Jane, stops, straightens her hair, adjusts
her clothes, puts on a bright smile, and speaks.

BARBARA: Hi.
    (Jane starts, and turns.)
JANE: We didn't expect you back so soon.
BARBARA: We only played nine holes. *(Laughs; does up a button on her blouse.)*
    No. He had to get back to work. Lots of summer construction. *(Pause.)*
    People *work* on this island, if you can believe it. *(Pause.)* I'm seeing him
    again tonight. I'll have to skip the dance.
    (The sound of children cheering and clapping, off right.)
BARBARA: Hey, how come you're not down there watching the big match? It
    looked very heated as I came by. Pokey and Randy dashing around,
    snorting and puffing away. And all the children were sitting in a row on
    the bench. Like vultures. *(She looks at Jane.)* Shouldn't you be down
    there, rooting for your man?
JANE: *(Quietly; shaking her head.)* I'm tired of games.
    (Pause.)
BARBARA: *(A little uneasily.)* Where's Mother? Taking her nap?
    (Jane nods.)
BARBARA: Was she—peeved at me, for ducking out?
JANE: She never mentioned it again.
BARBARA: Then she was peeved. *(Pause.)* Was lunch awful? Was there a lot of
    bickering about the house?
JANE: Not so much…I don't know…I was talking to Miriam.
BARBARA: Oh dear. You got stuck with her.
JANE: Not *stuck*. Not stuck at all. I like her.
BARBARA: So do we all, so do we all. *(Pause.)* What did you talk about, with
    Miriam?
JANE: Oh, I don't know…
BARBARA: Did you talk about the house?
JANE: No.

BARBARA: No?

JANE: We never got to that.

BARBARA: Well you must at least have broached the subject.

JANE: No. I'm sorry. I didn't.

(Pause.)

BARBARA: What *did* you talk about, then?

JANE: Oh…Life, I guess.

BARBARA: *(Laughing.) Life?* How heady.

JANE: Her life.

BARBARA: *Her* life? Does she have one? Does Pokey let her have one?

(Pause.)

JANE: She's thinking of leaving Pokey.

BARBARA: Oh no…

JANE: Unless he decides who he is. She said she wanted him to come up here this weekend. So he could work things out.

BARBARA: Work things *out?*

JANE: She said it's like being married to an elastic band.

BARBARA: Whatever that means.

JANE: I think it means that he's stretched. Between their life. And this.

BARBARA: And which way does she want him to go?

JANE: Either way. Otherwise, she says he'll snap. Or she will.

(Pause.)

BARBARA: I know the feeling.

JANE: So do I.

(Pause.)

BARBARA: Well what's her way?

JANE: Oh her life sounds wonderful.

BARBARA: According to her.

JANE: No really. I think she has a wonderful life.

(Pause. More noise from the tennis game is heard off right.)

BARBARA: So do you. So do you have a wonderful life.

JANE: Oh I know. *(Pause.)* But she…does more.

BARBARA: Such as what?

JANE: She works, for one thing.

BARBARA: Busy, busy, busy…

JANE: No, she's got a profession. People…need her. People count on her. In her work.

BARBARA: What does she call herself?

JANE: I don't even know the title. But she helps families that are falling apart.

BARBARA: *(Bitterly.)* Oh I know that type. I've been through that mill. You sit there, pouring out your soul to those ladies, and they smile, and give you a lot of lingo, or else yawn in your face.

JANE: She didn't yawn in mine.

(Pause; more sounds from right.)

BARBARA: Well you help people, too. You're on some hospital board, aren't you?

JANE: It's not the same.

BARBARA: Of course it's the same.

JANE: *(Shaking her head.)* I'm just there. *(Pause.)* Miriam's getting her Ph.D. That's what she's doing right now. She's upstairs studying for her Ph.D. So she can teach.

BARBARA: Oh, Jews always do that. They're frantic about education.

JANE: And she plays the viola.

BARBARA: The viola! My, my.

JANE: In a string quartet. Once a week, rain or shine, she gets together with three other people, and they play Mozart, and Bach, and Vivaldi together, all evening long. Oh it sounds like so much fun doing that.

BARBARA: Well you sing, Jane.

JANE: I don't sing.

BARBARA: You do, too. You sang in the Nightowls at Vassar, and I hope you'll sing at the dance tonight. I hope you sing *Mood Indigo.* I love the way you do that.

JANE: *(Singing softly.)* "You...Ain't...Been...Blue."

BARBARA: *(Joining her, in harmony.)* "No...No...No..."

(They stop.)

BARBARA: See? You sing. I'll bet Miriam can't sing that.

(More sounds from the tennis off right.)

JANE: She has such a good relationship with her children.

BARBARA: What does that *mean?* A good relationship.

JANE: She lets them grow.

BARBARA: So do you. You've taught them to ski and play tennis...

JANE: But it isn't such a—struggle, with Miriam. She doesn't make them wear things, or say things, or learn things all the time.

BARBARA: And as a result they are spoiled little brats.

JANE: They're wonderful.

BARBARA: They're fresh, they're grubby, they use foul language...

JANE: But they're so...open. They were there all during lunch with us.

BARBARA: Oh I'm sure. Interrupting Mother, debasing the conversation, while our children were out playing a good healthy game of softball. Where are Pokey's kids now?

JANE: Watching TV, I think.

BARBARA: You see? Our children don't do that.

JANE: I know it.

BARBARA: Because we have rules about TV. I imagine Miriam lets them watch it whenever they want.

JANE: She doesn't like rules.

BARBARA: Well that's just the trouble. I think Pokey and Miriam spend too much time giving in to their children, and kowtowing to them, and being around them. I think that's unhealthy. Mother says if you do that, you'll turn into a child yourself.

JANE: I suppose…

(Pause. A big groan is heard off right.)

JANE: But they fight so.

BARBARA: Who fights?

JANE: Our children. Yours and mine.

BARBARA: All children fight.

JANE: Miriam's don't. They never fight. They traveled all night, and they've been up most of the day, and they haven't fought at all.

(Pause. Then Randy comes in from upstage right, in his tennis whites, looking hot and sweaty. He looks at the two women, shakes his head and slumps into a chair.)

BARBARA: Well. Who won?

RANDY: *(Under his breath.)* We didn't finish.

BARBARA: What do you mean?

RANDY: *(Shouting.)* WE DIDN'T FINISH!

(Pause.)

BARBARA: *(Looking at Jane; with a sigh.)* Well. I'm going to go butter up Pokey, and get back into Mother's good graces. *(Indicating Randy.)* He's all yours. *(She goes out upstage right.)*

(Pause.)

JANE: Where's your racquet? *(No answer from Randy.)* Where's your racquet, Randy? *(No answer.)* Did you throw your racquet at him? *(No answer. She shakes her head.)* Oh Randy…

RANDY: I didn't throw it at *him.* I threw it into the poison ivy.

JANE: Oh honestly.

RANDY: It was a crummy racquet. I hated that goddamn racquet.

JANE: In front of the children.

RANDY: I apologized. I said, Come on. I'll get another racquet. I'll get Mother's racquet. Come on. Let's finish the game. But he just walked off the court.

JANE: I don't blame him.

RANDY: You don't *blame* him? For walking away? In front of all those kids?

JANE: *(Shaking her head.)* Throwing your racquet…

RANDY: He walked away from the game!

JANE: Oh Randy…

RANDY: Listen. You know what I think. I think he came up here just to beat me. I really think that. He's been practicing *up,* you know. Oh sure. He's been playing all winter, at this jazzy club in Washington. I have to coach hockey, but he's had all winter to practice up for me. He still isn't much good, either. He's got all these cuts and lobs and drop shots, but his serve is a laugh…

(Jane sighs and starts toward the house.)

RANDY: And I could have won, too. It was my serve when he quit. Do you want to know what the score in games was? Do you—

JANE: *(Suddenly wheeling on him at the door.)* Oh Randy, I don't care! I don't CARE who beats who! I don't care whether you beat Pokey, or whether Saint Luke's School beats Exeter, or whether the Los Angeles Rams win or lose! I don't care! I don't care about scores or goals or points or batting averages! Really! I don't CARE, Randy! I just don't give a SHIT!

(She storms into the house. Randy stands up, amazed.)

RANDY: Hey…HEY!…Hey, WAIT!…What's gotten *into* you?

(He hurries after her into the house as the lights fade. The group sings a campfire song such as "A Man Without a Woman" or "The Blue Tail Fly" or "When Pa Was a Little Boy." The lights have come up again. It is now late afternoon. Shadows are longer across the terrace. Mother has come out of the house. She carries a small watering can and shears, and begins to water the flowers in the window boxes, deftly snipping off the dead blossoms and leaves. Barbara comes out of the house, and stands by the door, watching her. Mother ignores her, stonily working on the flowers. Finally:)

BARBARA: Mother, I'm sorry I skipped lunch.

MOTHER: *(Blithely.)* Oh that's all right. What's lunch? Just a meal. *(She works on the flowers.)* Your brother is here for the first time in five years, it's his first meal here, the whole house is at stake—but what's lunch? Do you think you can make it for dinner?

BARBARA: *(With a sigh.)* Of course, Mother.

MOTHER: You see I don't know. People come and go around here as if it were

Grand Central Station…Now the boys aren't speaking because of that stupid tennis…I suppose now Pokey won't go to the Yacht Club dance.

BARBARA: He doesn't want to go. I've just been talking to him.

MOTHER: Why not? Because of Randy?

BARBARA: Because Uncle Bill is going.

MOTHER: And did you try to persuade him? Did you defend your Uncle Bill? Did you make even the smallest effort to keep this family together?

(Pause.)

BARBARA: I'm not going either, Mother.

MOTHER: Oh fine. That's just fine.

BARBARA: Please don't be mad.

MOTHER: Mad? Who's mad? What makes you think I'm mad.

BARBARA: You won't even look at me.

MOTHER: *(Puttering rather violently with the flowers.)* Do I have to look at you every minute of the day? Do I have to stare at you in order for you to exist? *(Pause; too casually.)* Why do you care how I feel anyway? It seems to me my opinion counts for very little in your life lately.

(Pause.)

BARBARA: What does that mean?

MOTHER: I happened to look out my bedroom window, Barbara, and see Artie Grieber's truck in our driveway this afternoon.

(Pause.)

BARBARA: *(With a deep sigh.)* Here we go.

MOTHER: I saw you give him that kiss. That was quite a kiss. Quite a kiss. To bestow on a yardman.

BARBARA: Not a yardman.

MOTHER: He was the yardman here.

BARBARA: He's a builder now.

MOTHER: Oh I know what he is now. I've seen every tacky summer cottage he's put up. *(Pause.)* And you said you had a golf game.

BARBARA: I didn't want an argument.

MOTHER: You've got one now.

BARBARA: I know it.

(Pause.)

MOTHER: I suppose that's where you were last night.

BARBARA: Yes.

MOTHER: At least you're discreet about it. I'll say that.

BARBARA: Not now. I told him to drive right up to the door. I'm glad you saw.

MOTHER: Well I don't want to see it again. I never liked him. Neither did your father. I don't want to see him around.

BARBARA: It's my life.

MOTHER: It's my house.

BARBARA: Not any more.

MOTHER: Until September! And I will not have you living here while you engage in a cheap, adulterous relationship with a local married man!

BARBARA: He's separated, Mother.

MOTHER: Because of you?

BARBARA: Yes.

MOTHER: He's leaving his family because of you?

BARBARA: Yes. If he can. They're Catholic.

MOTHER: You hardly know him.

BARBARA: I know him very well.

MOTHER: Years ago.

BARBARA: I've known him all along. Every summer.

MOTHER: While you were married to Fred?

BARBARA: Yes.

MOTHER: Don't tell me this is the reason for your divorce!

BARBARA: Yes. Partly. Yes.

MOTHER: I am appalled!

BARBARA: It's true.

MOTHER: I am simply appalled. To leave Fred for that sly, ambitious, social climbing Artie Grieber. I'm appalled.

BARBARA: I love him, Mother.

MOTHER: You can't love him.

BARBARA: I've loved him since I've known him.

MOTHER: What? When he was cutting our grass?

BARBARA: Even then!

MOTHER: That's impossible.

BARBARA: *(Defiantly.)* He was the first boy I ever slept with, Mother.

MOTHER: I won't hear this.

BARBARA: That's why I moved into the maid's room. So he could come back at night. Up the backstairs. And we'd meet on the beach.

MOTHER: I don't want to hear any of this.

BARBARA: Well it's true, Mother. And I love him. And I want to marry him. *(Started to cry.)* And I should have married him all along. I never should have married Fred.

MOTHER: Oh Barbara...

BARBARA: I never liked Fred. I don't like my children.

MOTHER: Barbara, Barbara...

BARBARA: You and Daddy made me marry Fred.

MOTHER: We did no such thing.

BARBARA: *(Crying.)* You did, you did. You brought him around. You turned on the charm. You kept saying he was Our Kind. You kept saying it. That's what you kept saying, Mother.

MOTHER: Stop it, Barbara.

BARBARA: He wasn't my kind. Artie is my kind. And I'm going to live with him, Mother.

MOTHER: Not here, you're not.

BARBARA: Oh yes. Right here. Because he's going to buy Pokey out. And if Randy doesn't like it, he'll buy Randy out. He's got all the money he wants, and he's going to put in a seawall, and winterize this place, and fix it all up, and we'll live here all year round. And I'll see him summers and winters and days and nights and we're going to screw any time we want!

(Mother slaps her hard across the face. Barbara reels back, then speaks very quietly through her tears.)

BARBARA: Oh Mother, you hypocrite! You hypocrite! Pokey just told me you did the same thing with Uncle Bill! For years! And Daddy knew it! And that's why he finally killed himself!

(She runs into the house. Mother stands aghast as the lights dim; then she strides into the house as the song comes up. The group sings a lively romantic song such as "Ain't She Sweet" or a ra-de-de-da version of "In the Evening by the Moonlight." The lights come up again, as the music fades. It is early evening. There is a rosy glow on the terrace now. Mother's shears and watering can are still on the table where she left them. After a moment, Randy comes out of the house. He wears a white, freshly laundered Yale football uniform, including the helmet. He carries a tray full of gin-and-tonic ingredients. He sets the tray down on the table, takes off his helmet, and calls toward the house.)

RANDY: *(Calling.)* Jane?...Are you coming out? *(No answer from within the house. He looks at the tray, looks back toward the house again.)* I'm having a drink. Won't you join me? I don't want to drink alone. *(No answer.)* Come on. You'll feel better once you've had a drink.

(Still no answer. He shrugs, looks at the tray, then begins to fix himself a drink. As he does, the screen door opens and Jane comes out, in her costume. It is her debutante dress, long, all white, perhaps strapless. She also wears

long white gloves, has her hair done in a fancy way, and looks young and lovely.)

RANDY: You. Look. Spec-*tac*ular!

JANE: I feel like a jerk.

RANDY: You look as great as the night I met you…Better. Even better.

JANE: I feel like a real jerk. *(Pause.)* I just showed it to Miriam. She wanted to know why I was going as Little Bo-Peep. When I told her it was my coming-out dress, from my coming-out party, she said, "Ah. The Wasp Bar-Mitzvah."

RANDY: *(Returning to making the drinks.)* That Miriam. I wish she'd lay off.

JANE: *(Defiantly.)* She's wonderful.

RANDY: She bugs me.

JANE: I like her one heck of a lot.

> *(Pause.)*

RANDY: *(Looking at her.)* I won't argue. You look too great. *(He starts to mix drinks.)*

> *(Pause.)*

JANE: *(Suddenly.)* I don't want to go to the damn dance.

RANDY: *(Bringing her a drink.)* Oh come on.

JANE: I don't. I look like a jerk. And everyone else there will look like a jerk. And act like one, too. Last year there were at least twenty debutantes or brides, and another twenty football players or hockey players or lacrosse players and I don't want to go. I don't want to spend a sappy evening trotting around the dance floor with all those jerks.

> *(Pause. Randy puts down his drink, looks at her carefully.)*

RANDY: So you think all our friends are jerks, huh?

JANE: *(Defiantly.)* Yes I do.

> *(Pause.)*

RANDY: Do you think I'm a jerk?

JANE: I think we're both jerks.

> *(Pause.)*

RANDY: Do you think our children are jerks?

> *(Pause. She turns away from him.)*

JANE: I think they could be. *(She turns back to him.)* I think they could turn into jerks very easily.

> *(Pause.)*

RANDY: Who do you think isn't a jerk?

JANE: Oh…

RANDY: Who? Come on.

(Pause.)

JANE: Miriam. Miriam isn't a jerk.

RANDY: I knew it. Why?

JANE: She has a better life.

RANDY: That kook?

JANE: Sssshhh.

RANDY: *(Loud.)* She's a kook! You want to wander around with your boobs bouncing and your hair in your eyes and B.O.?

JANE: She doesn't have B.O.

RANDY: She smells, my friend. She hasn't even been swimming. Smell her some time.

JANE: Sssshhh.

RANDY: That's not a better life, pal.

JANE: It is, it is. They do things, they feel things, they know what's going on. *(Pause.)* We don't. We're babies. We live on an island, here and at school. What have we done with our lives? All we've done is play games. We've missed things, Randy. We've really missed things.

(Pause.)

RANDY: You don't like your life.

JANE: No. I've wasted it.

RANDY: Do you want to change it?

JANE: Yes.

RANDY: Do you want to change—me?

JANE: I don't know.

(Pause.)

RANDY: Do you still love me?

(Pause.)

JANE: I guess…I don't know…

(Randy looks at her for a long time.)

RANDY: Wait there.

(He goes into the house. Jane waits nervously, eyeing the screen door. She picks up her drink, is about to take a sip, and then shakes her head and defiantly puts it down, untouched. In a moment, music can be heard from within a "society orchestra" recording: Bright, bouncing songs from musical comedies in the 50s. Randy comes back out.)

RANDY: Hear that?

(She nods, reluctantly.)

RANDY: Sound familiar?

(She nods.)

RANDY: Remember your party?

JANE: *(Impatiently.)* Randy—

RANDY: Remember your party?

(Jane nods.)

RANDY: You were standing between your parents...holding a huge bunch of flowers...

(He picks a flower from the window box, holds it out to her. She hesitates, then takes it.)

RANDY: And I was visiting Bill Butler after the hockey play-offs at Princeton.

JANE: *(Ironically.)* What was the score?

RANDY: Seven to six in overtime... *(He catches himself.)* Cut it out...I remember coming through the line... *(He pantomimes bowing and shaking hands.)* How do you do? Good evening. *(He reaches Jane, shakes her hand.)* Good evening. Would you like to dance?

JANE: *(Walking away.)* That's not the way it was, Randy. I had to dance with my father first.

RANDY: Still...Would you like to dance?

(She turns; he bows very formally.)

JANE: *(Reluctantly.)* All right.

(She holds out her arms. They begin to dance in the waning light around the terrace, avoiding the furniture. Jane is stiff and reluctant at first. Randy tries a dip.)

RANDY: Remember this?

JANE: *(Smiling.)* Mmmm-hmmmm.

(More dancing. She dances more enthusiastically now.)

RANDY: *(Trying a fancy break.)* I learned this at dancing school.

JANE: So did I.

(They dance closer after a while, cheek to cheek, occasionally turning.)

RANDY: This isn't so bad, is it?

JANE: Mmmm.

RANDY: Dancing on a terrace, on an island, in the sunset, overlooking the sea...

JANE: Mmmm.

RANDY: *(Turning)* If this is wasting our life, baby, vive le wastefulness.

JANE: *(Eyes closed.)* Sssshhh.

RANDY: *(Trying another fancy turn.)* Do you think Miriam can do this?

JANE: Just...sshhhh.

(It is almost sunset now. And the sky is beginning to turn a deep blue behind the house. Randy and Jane, both with eyes closed, now dance very close

together, very sensuously, even though the music continues its bouncy beat.
Suddenly it groans to a stop, as someone has turned off the machine within.
Randy and Jane stop, still holding each other, in a dance position. Mother
comes out of the house. She wears a summer jacket dress, with high heels, and
carries a small traveling bag. She comes out briskly, and speaks very calmly.)

MOTHER: Randy, I want you to do me a big favor.

(Randy and Jane stand looking at her, amazed.)

MOTHER: I want you to go down to the beach, Randy, and get Pokey, bring
him up here, because I want to say good-bye.

RANDY: Mother...

MOTHER: Just do it, Randy. Right now. Please. Uncle Bill is picking me up in
ten minutes. We're catching the eight o'clock ferry, and we're staying
with the Robinson's in Boston, and we'll be married—by ourselves—as
soon as we possibly can. Go *on*, Randy. Please. Get Pokey. The house is
yours. There's a lamb in the oven and spinach on the stove and you can
all fight and argue over dinner all by yourselves.

RANDY: Mother...

MOTHER: Do it, Randy, before I scream.

(Pause. He looks at her, sees her determination, turns, and angrily goes off
left toward the beach. Pause. Mother puts down her bag, looks at Jane.)

MOTHER: I. AM. THROUGH. Through with this house, through with the
children, through with the grandchildren, through with the WHOLE.
DAMN. THING. I am free and clear, as of right now. Take over, Jane.
It's yours, and anyone else's who wants to pay the taxes, and plant the
flowers, and fix the roof, and order the meals, and make the gravy, and
keep things UP! I've had it! Count me permanently OUT!

(Off right, a large bang.)

JANE: *(Jumping up.)* What's that?

MOTHER: That was a firecracker! I just gave out all the firecrackers! To all your
children! Early! I said, Go ahead. Let 'er rip. Make as much noise as you
want. This is *my* independence day. Celebrate it, kiddoes! Make unto the
Lord a joyful noise!

(A string of bangs is heard.)

MOTHER: The Mother country is cutting loose from the colonies! Long live
the Queen!

(Perhaps a Roman candle shoots across the dark blue sky, she calls off toward
right.)

MOTHER: Go on! Get hurt! I don't care! Point those things right at the house!

Set it on fire! Who cares? We won't be here, Bill and I! We'll be off having fun!

(More firecrackers sound.)

MOTHER: Oh, such spectacular fun! We're going to spend every nickel we've got. We're going to travel to Europe and Japan and South America. We're going to get new clothes and new cars and a new apartment! And I'm going to forget Christmas, and Easter, and everyone's birthday, and everyone's size and shape! If someone gets sick, I don't want to hear! If someone loses a tooth, or wins a prize, or needs a dress, or wants a toy, I don't want to know! I don't want to know, I don't want to hear, I don't want to care! I won't have anyone's telephone number, and no one will have mine. I'm unlisted, as of now. If you find me out, I won't be there. I'm gone, I'm finished, I'm through!

(More firecrackers; a great barrage of Roman candles.)

MOTHER: Come on, Bill! Hurry! Take me away! We've got ten good years to go! Oh boy, oh boy, oh boy! At long last, we are about to be the most attractive older couple in the whole, free world!

(Randy comes on slowly from downstage left. His white Yale football jersey is spotted with blood and water. He looks at his mother.)

RANDY: Mother…

(She turns, sees him. Jane moves toward him.)

RANDY: I hurt Pokey, Mother.

(They stare at him.)

RANDY: He—just walked away from me. I tried to tell him to come up, but he just walked away. So I…I just picked up this rock and threw it at him. I hit him in the face…

(Jane gasps and starts off downstage left; Randy grabs her arm.)

RANDY: He's all right. He's bleeding, but he's all right. He's…kneeling in the water. He won't get up. Miriam's there, and his kids.

(Jane roughly breaks loose of his grasp and runs off left. Mother starts after her.)

RANDY: Mother…MOTHER!

(Mother stops almost at the exit, her back to him.)

RANDY: He said something about you. About you and Uncle Bill. That's why I threw the rock. He told a goddamn lie about you.

(Mother turns and looks at him.)

MOTHER: Oh sweetheart. *(She goes to him and hugs him.)* Oh my little baby boy.

(Then she turns and walks away off downstage left toward the beach. Randy

looks after her. A long string of firecrackers. Then the lights fade on him. Song: sung this time by an individual male voice, preferably Randy's, with the others humming in the background: "O Rose, climb up to her window,/ And into her casement reach…/ And say what I may not utter, / In your beautiful silent speech./ And then—who can tell?—she may whisper / While the city sleeps below:/ "I was dreaming of him when you woke me, / But rose, he must never know…")

(The lights come up again; it is night. The terrace is bathed in moonlight. Light also spills onto it from the windows of the house, and for the first time, one can see the cozy rooms inside. The sound off the sea off left, can be heard. Mother's suitcase is still where she left it. Randy sits on the edge of a chair, still in his bloody football uniform, all huddled into himself. After a moment, Barbara comes out of the house. She sees him.)

BARBARA: Nice going.

RANDY: *(Looking up.)* He's all right, isn't he?

BARBARA: Oh fine. Fifteen stitches on his forehead. Scarred for life. But fine.

RANDY: Can't he have it—fixed?

BARBARA: Oh sure he can. But he won't. Not Pokey. He'll wander around for the rest of his life, pointing out his scar, saying, "This is what my brother did. My Wasp brother. Who lost control."

RANDY: Is he leaving?

BARBARA: I have no idea. He's in his room. With the door closed. With Miriam.

RANDY: Is Mother leaving?

BARBARA: I don't know. Last time I noticed, she was sitting out in the car. Talking to Uncle Bill.

RANDY: Where's Jane?

BARBARA: Putting the kids to bed. Half of them plastered with band-aids. They started throwing firecrackers at each other.

RANDY: Oh God.

BARBARA: It was a pretty explosive evening all around.

(Pause, he holds his head in his hands. She watches him.)

BARBARA: I assume *you're* leaving.

RANDY: I guess so.

BARBARA: Oh you booted the ball, Mr. Yale Football player. You really did. Any way you slice it, you lose but good. I'll bet Mother gives Pokey the house all summer, all by himself, and I'll bet he sells it in the fall.

RANDY: *(Shaking his head.)* Oh gee

BARBARA: Oh you'll have a lot of money, my stone-throwing friend. After a huge tax, why you'll still have enough left to rent a cottage down here for a couple of years. And after that, you can send your kids to a YMCA camp. Or why not buy a tent, big enough for all of you? You can all huddle together out of the rain and the mosquitoes in some trailer park in New Hampshire. I'm sure if you drove for twenty miles, you might find a public tennis court where you can wait in line to play.

RANDY: Quit it, please. Lay off.

BARBARA: At least I don't throw large rocks at people when their back is turned.

(Pause.)

RANDY: You lose, too, Barbara.

BARBARA: Oh I might be right here, after all.

RANDY: What do you mean?

BARBARA: Wait and see, kiddo. Just wait and see.

(Mother comes on from upstage right. Both Randy and Barbara stand up instinctively when they see her.)

MOTHER: Randy. Go upstairs, and knock on Pokey's door, and ask him if he'd please come down here. I want to talk to him alone.

(Randy moves toward the door.)

MOTHER: And don't throw anything at him this time, dear.

(He turns protestingly. She waves him out, smiling.)

MOTHER: Go on. Shoo. I know you won't.

(He exits into the house. Barbara stands defiantly, facing her mother. Pause. Mother speaks very coldly to her.)

MOTHER: Your—truck seems to be parked out in the driveway.

BARBARA: *(Equally coldly.)* Thank you. *(She starts out upstage right.)*

MOTHER: Barbara.

(Barbara stops, her back to her mother.)

MOTHER: Ask your friend out there whether he wants you or this house. Ask him that. Ask him what he'd do if he can't have the house. Just ask him. *(Barbara gives her a grim look and exits quickly right. A moment. Mother sighs, then adjusts the chairs. She sits and waits. Then a sound is heard within the house. She turns toward the door. A man appears, a shadowy figure behind the screen, a shadowed bandage on his head.)*

MOTHER: Pokey?

(The shadow stands silently; she sighs.)

MOTHER: Pokey. *(Pause.)* Pokey, you lied to your brother and sister about me. What you said was not the truth. Do you hear me? I won't ask you to apologize, because I know you won't, but you told a lie, Pokey. *(Pause.)*

And now I'm going to tell *you* something. I'm going to tell you a story. I want you to listen very carefully. I don't want you to squirm and become impatient, as you used to, years ago, when I tried to hold you in my lap. *(Pause.)* Once upon a time there was a very naive young girl who decided to marry a very upright young man. And at their wedding, she danced with one of his ushers, who had just married someone else. And for a moment, she was carried away. For a moment, she thought, oh dear, have I married the wrong person? And for a moment, the usher thought the same thing. *(Pause.)* But that was that. She never mentioned it, and neither did the usher, but they knew it, and her husband knew it, and his wife knew it, and they all lived with it, all four of them, for thirty-five years. All four were very good sports about it. They played by the rules, and life went on. *(Pause.)* Do you believe this story, Pokey? I doubt if you do. You never believed the fairy tales I used to tell you. But this one is true. *(Pause.)* Randy would believe it. And Barbara would too. Oh, she'd say it was very dumb. Very dumb of these people to live this way. And maybe it was dumb. Maybe that's what made your father turn to himself so much, tinkering with his notebook, puttering with the house, swimming all alone. Maybe one day he said to himself, Oh, the heck with it, and kept on swimming out to sea. *(Pause.)* Now this woman had three lovely children. And the first two seemed very happy, at least for a while. But the third, the youngest, was not. He seemed to sense something wrong almost the day he was born. He'd look at his mother with dark, suspicious eyes. And as soon as he was old enough, he'd struggle out of her arms. But he'd always crawl back. He'd come, and go. And it went on that way for a long time. *(Pause.)* Well finally, the woman's husband died, and the usher's wife died, and the two of them thought they might spend their golden years together, sailing into a golden sunset, with a golden nest egg between them. But then, at the last minute, the woman—she was an old woman now—changed her mind. It was difficult to do, but she did it. She saw that her two older children had never grown up. And she blamed herself. She said to herself, "I've made my bed, and I must sleep in it. Alone," she said. "Alone." *(Pause.)* So you win, Pokey. I won't marry Uncle Bill. I'll hold onto this house until the day I die. And the children can come here every summer with their children, and I'll pay for it, gladly. *(Pause.)* But you can't come, dear. I won't invite you again. I don't think our family is good for you any more. I think all these years you've been at least trying to grow up, and now the best thing I can do is send you on your way.

I'll try to be as fair as I can at Christmas, and when I die, but I think we should say good-bye to each other, once and for all. I wish you well, dear. I really do. I think you're an impossible person, but I love you dearly, and I hope this will help you settle on something you want to do. I think the best thing you've done is to marry Miriam and have those sweet children. I don't understand them, they're out of my league, but they seem to make you happy, which is more than I could ever do. So good-bye, Pokey. I'll get Randy to take you to the ferry in the morning, and I hope you make it up with him before you leave. He's a good boy, and he was trying to defend me. Good-bye, dear.

(She turns toward the screen, and rises as if to kiss him good-bye. But he has gone. She whispers to herself.)

MOTHER: Good-bye.

(Barbara comes in hurriedly from right.)

BARBARA: *(Breathlessly.)* Mother, what did you mean about the house? Artie wants to know.

MOTHER: *(Calmly.)* I'm keeping the house.

BARBARA: Explain that, Mother.

(Mother walks away from her.)

BARBARA: Mother, he's *wait*ing.

MOTHER: Why don't you tell him you're just a little tired of talking about real estate?

(Barbara looks at her, looks around, sees her father's watch, picks it up, shakes it futilely, looks at her mother again.)

BARBARA: I'll tell him it's later than I thought.

MOTHER: Good idea, dear. Tell him that.

(Barbara goes off toward the driveway, shaking the watch. Randy comes out, now wearing his father's bathrobe.)

RANDY: Mother, I can't find Jane.

MOTHER: I think she's sitting on the beach, dear.

RANDY: *(Beaming.)* I knew it! I knew that's where she was! *(He whips off his bathrobe, tosses it to mother.)* Here. Hold this. *(He runs off toward left, naked, calling.)* Hey, Jane! Hey, Jane!

MOTHER: *(Calling after him.)* Ssshh. You'll wake the children.

(She stands in the moonlight. Then she picks up the bathrobe, holding it limp in her arms, and stands looking out to sea for a moment. Then she walks into the house as the lights fade on her and the screen door slams behind.)

The End

Richard Cory

(1976)

AUTHOR'S NOTE

Richard Cory opened at the Circle Rep under the title *Who Killed Richard Cory?* It was much too long, but I had the chance to boil it down a few years later at the Williamstown Theatre Festival. The play is an attempt to deconstruct and explore the poem by Edwin Arlington Robinson, using it as a tragic framework of inevitability within which the hero is doomed to die. I'm not sure I ever got it right, but there is something in the relationship between Cory and the townspeople which continues to fascinate me. The play is now done here and there, and has recently been adapted into an opera.

CAST

The size of the cast of this play is dependent on the sort of theatre, the shape of the budget, and the kind of production envisaged for it. It would be difficult to do with less than five: one actor to play Richard Cory, and a chorus of two men and two women to play the other roles. On these terms, it should be presented in a kind of reading or concert version. On the other hand, it may be done with a cast of seven, or more. Whatever doubling occurs, one actor only should constantly play Richard Cory, and be cast as much as possible according to type: "clean-favored and imperially slim."

ORIGINAL PRODUCTION

An earlier version of *Richard Cory* was presented by the Circle Repertory Company, in New York City, on March 10, 1976, under the title *Who Killed Richard Cory?* It was directed by Leonard Peters; the setting was by Joan Ferenchak; costumes were by Gary Jones; the lighting was by Arden Fingerhut; choreography was by Bridget Leicester; the musical director was Charles L. Greenberg; and the production stage manager was Marjorie Horne. The cast was as follows:

Howard, Joe, and Chip . . . . Roger Chapman
The Piano Player . . . . Charles L. Greenburg
Prostitute, Emily, and Librarian . . . . Jane Hallaren
Rose, Charlotte, and Grandmother . . . . Patricia O'Connell
Alice, Louise, and Bessie . . . . Sharon Madden
Elise, Mrs. Baker, and Richard's Mother . . . . Joyce Reehling
Eddie, Richard's Father, and an Anarchist . . . . Larry Rosler
Doctor, William, and Chester . . . . M. Jonathan Steele
Frank, Rev. Davis, and Ted Babcock . . . . Robb Webb
Richard Cory . . . . Bruce Gray

This revised version was first presented in the Extension Theatre of the Williamstown Theatre Festival on July 2, 1984. It was directed by Steven Schachter, designed by John Huttman, and lighted by Christina Gianelli. The production stage manager was Carol Klein. The cast was as follows:

Richard Cory . . . . Christopher Reeve
Ensemble . . . . Frank Hankey
Joe Ponazecki
Judith Ann Roberts
Audrey Matson
Laila Robins
Jon Tenney
Mark Wade

SETTING

The play should begin on a bare stage. Whatever scenery, furniture, and props are used should be introduced as the play develops, so that we have the sense of a play taking shape before our eyes.

COSTUMES

Except for Richard Cory, all the actors should be dressed simply, when the play begins. They are, after all, "people on the pavement." As it continues, they may add hats or other accessories to a particular role. Cory, of course, should be beautifully, carefully, and totally costumed in a pearl-gray suit and appropriate hat according to the style of the early twentieth century.

STAGING

The scenes should melt into one another, so that there is a sense of flow to the play. Actors should participate in setting up or striking what is needed for a scene, and when they are not involved, may remain on stage to watch it. If props are used, they should be used consistently. Otherwise, pantomime might be the best bet. In any case, the effect should be one of constant improvisation, cooperation, and speculation as the play circles around the central question of the poem. The actor playing Richard Cory should not participate in any of this stage work, of course.

Richard Cory

An Actor, or Actress, enters and reads from a small, old, leather volume.

ACTOR: *(Reading.)* "Richard Cory," by Edwin Arlington Robinson.
Whenever Richard Cory went downtown,
We people on the pavement looked at him:
He was a gentleman from sole to crown,
Clean-favored and imperially slim.
And he was always quietly arrayed,
And he was always human when he talked;
But still he fluttered pulses when he said,
"Good morning," and he glittered when he walked.
And he was rich—yes, richer than a king—
And admirably schooled in every grace:
In fine, we thought that he was everything
To make us wish that we were in his place.
So on we worked, and waited for the light
And went without the meat, and cursed the bread,
And Richard Cory, one calm summer night,
Went home, and put a bullet through his head.
(He closes the book. Pause. He starts again, from memory.)
Whenever Richard Cory went downtown…
(Other actors begin to come out, the lines are divided among the cast.)
A STREETCLEANER: *(As if pushing a broom.)*
Whenever Richard Cory went downtown,
We people on the pavement looked at him…
A GENTEEL LADY: He was a gentleman from sole to crown,
Clean-favored and imperially slim.
AN ENVIOUS YOUNG MAN: And he was always quietly arrayed…
A YOUNG GIRL: And he was always human when he talked…
A WORKING WOMAN: *(Teasingly, to another.)*
But still he fluttered pulses when he said, "Good morning"…
OTHER WOMAN: *(Dreamily.)* And he glittered when he walked.
A BUSINESSMAN: *(Pompously.)* And he was rich…
YOUNG MAN: *(Yearningly.)* Yes, richer than a king…
GENTEEL LADY: *(Primly.)* And admirably schooled in every grace…

WORKING WOMAN: *(To her friend.)* In fine, we thought that he was every-thing…

DREAMY WOMAN: To make us wish that we were at his place.

WORKING WOMAN: *(Admonishing her.)* In his place.

BUSINESSMAN: *(Snapping out of it, gruffly.)* So on we worked…

YOUNG GIRL: And waited for the light…

STREETCLEANER: *(Continuing his work.)* And went without the meat, and cursed the bread…

YOUNG MAN: And Richard Cory…

SECOND WOMAN: *(Dreamily.)* One calm summer night…

GENTEEL LADY: *(Shivering.)* Went home and…

STREETCLEANER: Put a bullet through his head.

(Pause.)

FIRST ACTOR: Whenever Richard Cory…

A WOMAN: Whenever Richard Cory…

A MAN: Whenever Richard Cory…

(Richard Cory appears. He is thin, handsome, elegantly dressed.)

CORY: *(Politely.)* Good morning. *(He walks across the stage, speaking to them one by one.)* Good morning…Good morning…

OTHERS: Good morning…Good morning…Morning…Morning, sir…

A MOTHER: Good morning, Mr. Cory. *(She nudges a Little Boy.)* Say good morning to Richard Cory.

LITTLE BOY: *(Mustering up his courage, shouting it out.)* Good morning, Richard Cory!

MOTHER: *(Whispering.)* Mr. Cory!

CORY: *(Stopping, smiling, shaking the Boy's hand.)* Good morning.

(He goes off. The others look after him admiringly.)

A WORKER: *(As if shoveling.)* So on we worked…

MOTHER: *(To Little Boy.)* And learned to be polite…

(A Young Man enters a haberdashery store. A Clerk comes up to him.)

CLERK: *(Officiously.)* May I help you, sir?

YOUNG MAN: I want to buy a necktie.

CLERK: What kind, sir?

YOUNG MAN: Oh. Well. Different from those on the rack. Don't you think those look a little—loud?

CLERK: Depends who you are, sir.

YOUNG MAN: And who you want to be.

CLERK: Exactly.

YOUNG MAN: *(Blurting it out.)* I saw a man today named Richard Cory.

CLERK: Ah.

YOUNG MAN: He was dressed more—quietly.

CLERK: *(Selecting a special tie.)* "Dressed" is not the word for Mr. Cory. Mr. Cory is always quietly…arrayed.

YOUNG MAN: "Arrayed?"

CLERK: Like the lilies of the field. Who toil not. Neither do they spin.

YOUNG MAN: I want to look like Richard Cory.

CLERK: *(Producing the tie.)* Try this quiet regimental, sir.

YOUNG MAN: *(Trying it on; as if to a mirror.)* "Good morning." "Good morning."

CLERK: That's very good, sir.

YOUNG MAN: He sort of glitters when he walks. *(Tries walking in front of the mirror.)* I don't quite glitter.

CLERK: You might try new shoes, sir.

YOUNG MAN: How much is the tie?

CLERK: One dollar, sir.

YOUNG MAN: *One?* That's all I have. Just one. *(Pays him.)* Boy. It costs money to glitter.

CLERK: Money helps, sir.

YOUNG MAN: *(Adjusting his tie.)* Well. Thanks. So long. *(Catching himself; more stuffily.)* I mean, thank you. Good morning. *(Pause.)* I don't quite have it yet. *(Goes out.)*

CLERK: *(Calling after him.)* Rome wasn't built in a day, sir.

(The Young Man practices saying "Good morning" to people bustling by. Mrs. Baker, who is Richard Cory's receptionist, has settled into a chair, and is working a telephone switchboard.)

MRS. BAKER: Cory, Pierce, and Paine…Good morning…I'll connect you.

(Millie, a young secretary, approaches her.)

MILLIE: Mrs. Baker, would you give these contracts to Mr. Cory?

MRS. BAKER: I'm busy, Millie. Take them in yourself.

MILLIE: *(Shrinking back.)* Oh I can't. I just can't. I'm too embarrassed.

MRS. BAKER: Now Millie…

MILLIE: But I've still got this boil on my nose. I look awful. He might not even recognize me.

MRS. BAKER: Oh nonsense. Of course he will. Now go on. I'm busy.

MILLIE: But it looks like I've got an entirely different nose. Oh I'll die in there. What will he say?

MRS. BAKER: He won't say anything. He's too much of a gentleman. Now go on in.

(Millie squares her shoulders and goes off. Mrs. Baker continues typing. The Young Man with the new tie comes in.)

YOUNG MAN: I'm answering the advertisement about a clerk for Mr. Richard Cory.

MRS. BAKER: Just wait right there, please.

(She continues typing. Millie comes out.)

MRS. BAKER: Well?

MILLIE: He noticed it.

MRS. BAKER: Oh Millie.

MILLIE: He did. He looked right at my nose. So I said, this isn't my real nose, Mr. Cory. I've got a boil that makes my nose this way. My regular nose is much different.

MRS. BAKER: And what did he say?

MILLIE: *(Romantically.)* He said I had two of the loveliest noses in town.

MRS. BAKER: You see? *(To Young Man.)* Go on in, sir. See what he says to you. He is a gentleman from sole to crown.

(Young Man goes in, Millie goes off dreamily. Mrs. Baker calls after her.)

MRS. BAKER: Millie, they say boils are a question of diet. Have you been going without meat? *(Mrs. Baker exits.)*

A RELIGIOUS MAN: *(Crossing the stage.)* Wait for the light! Watch and wait. Wait for the light.

(Cory crosses by him.)

RELIGIOUS MAN: Read about the light, mister?

CORY: No thank you.

RELIGIOUS MAN: *(Calling after him.)* It is easier for a camel to go through the eye of a needle than for a rich man to enter the Kingdom of God.

CORY: *(Stops, turns, comes back, takes a pamphlet.)* Thank you. *(He reaches for his wallet.)*

RELIGIOUS MAN: *(Shaking his head.)* The light is free, sir. Store up treasure in heaven.

CORY: *(Bemusedly.)* I'll try. Thank you. *(He goes off.)*

RELIGIOUS MAN: *(Calling after him.)* Watch and pray! Jerusalem will fall to the ground! Wait for the light! *(He goes off the other way.)*

(At a newsstand)

JOE: *(A newsman.)* Paper! Morning paper! Leading citizen dead! Read all about it!

(People buy papers from him.)

JOE: Thank you, sir! Thank you, ma'am…I knew him, you know. I knew Richard Cory… *(He addresses the audience.)* Whenever Richard Cory came downtown, he'd stop by my stand on his way to work. I'd have his *New York Times,* hot off the boat, ready and waiting…

(Folds it with a flourish as Cory comes on.)

JOE: Morning, Mr. Cory… *(Hands him the paper.)*

CORY: Good morning, Joe. *(Takes the paper; hands him the correct change.)*

JOE: Thank you, sir.

(Cory begins to move on, then stops, turns back.)

CORY: Quite a stack of papers there, Joe.

JOE: Yes, sir.

CORY: Quite a pile. The *Times.* And then all the others underneath.

JOE: Yes, sir.

CORY: We're quite a country.

JOE: Yes, sir.

CORY: Papers in different languages; Polish, French, Italian, Hebrew…

JOE: The *Times* keeps 'em from blowing around, sir.

CORY: *(Casually shuffling through the papers.)* I've often wanted to look under the *Times. (He browses through the papers, then stops, looks, looks at Joe.)* Hmmm. What's this, Joe?

JOE: What, sir?

CORY: *(Indicating.)* This particular journal.

JOE: *(Wincing.)* Oh that.

CORY: Yes, this.

JOE: *(Sheepishly.)* That's just the *Policeman's Gazette,* sir.

CORY: *(Looking at a picture.)* Is this a real corpse here, Joe? Or do you think they staged it?

JOE: *(Looking over Cory's shoulder.)* I think it's real, sir.

CORY: Then this must be real blood.

JOE: I think it is, sir.

CORY: *(Going deeper into the pile.)* Oh my gosh!…Oh good gravy! *(Looks at Joe.)* What's this, Joe?

JOE: *(Looking.)* What's what, sir?

CORY: *(Indicating picture.)* This magazine. Is she…are they… *(Looks at Joe.)* They're copulating, Joe.

JOE: *(Sheepishly.)* I know it, sir.

CORY: *(Looking at it again.)* This is something, Joe.

JOE: It's French, sir.

CORY: Oh. French. *(Shuts the paper.)* Do people buy this?

JOE: Yes, sir.

CORY: A lot of people?

JOE: A lot, sir.

CORY: Gosh. *(Pause.)* Well. Back to the *New York Times. (Pause.)* Good morning, Joe.

JOE: Good morning, Mr. Cory.

(Cory goes off. Joe turns to audience.)

JOE: Shame! I'm telling you, I felt real shame! I'm telling you, I felt I was caught in the act by Richard Cory. So I never sell that stuff no more. Not at my stand. You won't find it here. Never. Never on weekdays. Only on Saturdays. But never when Mr. Cory comes downtown.

AN ELEVATOR MAN: Going up, please. Elevator. Going up.

(A Young Woman named Louise enters hesitantly.)

ELEVATOR MAN: Hurry, miss. I'm holding it for you.

LOUISE: *(Glancing around.)* I'll wait for the next one, thank you.

ELEVATOR MAN: Suit yourself.

LOUISE: *(To audience, confidingly.)* Whenever I go to work, I always try to ride up on the elevator with Mr. Richard Cory. He shows up at five minutes to nine, almost exactly, almost on the dot.

(Cory comes in briskly, looks up as if at the elevator indicator, waits, reads his paper.)

LOUISE: Oh isn't he special! I've dreamed about him twice!

ELEVATOR MAN: Good morning, Mr. Cory.

CORY: Good morning, Frank.

ELEVATOR MAN: I'll take you right on up, sir.

CORY: Thanks, Frank. *(He faces front.)*

LOUISE: Wait, please. *(She walks with genteel dignity to the elevator.)*

ELEVATOR MAN: Thought you weren't coming, Tootsie.

LOUISE: My name is not Tootsie. *(She faces front, side by side with Cory.)*

(The Elevator Man pantomimes taking them up.)

CORY: *(To Louise.)* Good morning.

LOUISE: Good morning. *(She shivers; to audience.)* He's so…*clean!* He smells like soap. If you stand close to him, he smells like the soap at the men's counters in the department store.

CORY: Excuse me.

LOUISE: Yes?

CORY: Didn't we just pass your floor?

LOUISE: *(Glancing at indicator.)* Oh yes. It was.

CORY: That was this lady's floor, Frank. You missed her floor.

ELEVATOR MAN: Oh. Sorry. I'll let you off, sir, and then take her back down.

CORY: Take her down now.

ELEVATOR MAN: Yes, sir. *(He pantomimes controls.)*
   (Cory smiles at Louise.)
LOUISE: How'd you know that was my floor, sir?
CORY: You get off there every day.
LOUISE: *(Looking at him, smiling, nodding.)* I do, don't I?
ELEVATOR MAN: Here you are. *(He opens the door for her.)*
LOUISE: Thank you. *(She gets out, turns back to Cory.)* Good morning, sir.
CORY: Good morning. Enjoy the day.
LOUISE: *(With a curtsey.)* Don't mind if I do.
   (Elevator Man closes the gate, starts up the elevator, Louise stands where she got off and powders her nose.)
ELEVATOR MAN: *(To Cory.)* Nice little number, sir.
CORY: Hmmm?
ELEVATOR MAN: Nice little bit of fluff.
CORY: A charming young woman. Yes. *(He reads his* Times *till he gets to his floor.)*
LOUISE: *(Taking a deep breath.)* And I could still smell that soap, even after he was gone, and I kept wondering… I couldn't help it, I just kept wondering… *(Very confidingly.)* …how it would be in bed with Richard Cory. *(She runs off.)*
MRS. BAKER: Cory, Pierce, and Paine…One moment: I'll connect you.
   (Cory comes in.)
MRS. BAKER: Good morning, Mr. Cory.
CORY: Good morning, Mrs. Baker. Ask Eddie to come in, would you, please?
MRS. BAKER: Yes, sir.
   (Cory starts off, then stops.)
CORY: Mrs. Baker, I forgot to ask: how's your mother?
MRS. BAKER: Oh much better, thank you, sir. She's coming home from the hospital next week.
CORY: That's fine.
MRS. BAKER: And she still has the flowers you sent. Oh Mr. Cory, I really think those flowers did more good than the visit from the priest.
CORY: Thank you, Mrs. Baker. *(He goes to a desk, begins to settle in, as if in his office.)*
MRS. BAKER: *(Answering telephone.)* Cory, Pierce, and Paine…Good morning…One moment, I'll connect you.
   (The Young Man with tie, whose name is Eddie, comes into Cory's office deferentially.)
EDDIE: You wanted to see me, sir?

CORY: Yes, Eddie. I'm going to have to ask you to cancel my steamship tickets.

EDDIE: You're not going abroad this summer?

CORY: Not going abroad.

EDDIE: Your family?

CORY: No one's going, after all. *(Pause.)* I'm sorry. You were very efficient in getting them. I'm sorry.

EDDIE: Oh that's all right, sir. *(Starts out; then stops, turns.)* I hope everyone's well at home, sir.

CORY: Oh yes. Fine.

EDDIE: I hope there's no trouble, sir.

CORY: No, no. No trouble. *(He bends over his desk.)*

(Eddie moves again to leave.)

CORY: Except me. I'm the trouble.

EDDIE: Sir?

CORY: I just didn't want to go. *(Pause.)* There we were, all sitting around the living room, looking at travel books, and Cook's tours, and hotel advertisements, and I suddenly said, I don't want to go. I don't want to be there. I want to be here.

EDDIE: Here?

CORY: Here. Right here. Right downtown. I'm not getting any younger. I should know where I live.

EDDIE: Yes, sir.

CORY: So: The family will go up to the island, and I'll be here, and of course I'll join them weekends. And that will be that.

EDDIE: Yes, sir.

CORY: Now I think we both better get back to work.

EDDIE: Yes, sir. *(Starts out, turns once more.)* I'm glad you're going to be here, sir.

CORY: *(Waving him off.)* Thank you, Eddie.

(Eddie leaves the office.)

EDDIE: *(To audience.)* And it's true what I said. I wasn't just buttering him up. I'm glad he'll be here. Because I'm learning from him every day. He's an expert on trusts and estates. And he's shown me his will. It's beautiful. He's got a trust from his grandfather, and another from his father, and he's set one up for his children and even his *grand*children, though he doesn't have any yet.

MRS. BAKER: *(On telephone.)* Cory, Pierce, and Paine: good afternoon…

EDDIE: *(Continuing to audience.)* And he's got everything watertight. There's not a leak in the system. Oh Lord, when he first explained it to me, it was so perfect that I almost broke down and cried.

(Cory comes out.)

CORY: Good night, Mrs. Baker.

MRS. BAKER: Good night, Mr. Cory.

CORY: Good night, Eddie.

EDDIE: Good night, Mr. Cory. *(To audience.)* So I've signed up for law school at night. And I'll work here during the day. And someday, who knows, maybe I'll be a partner of Mr. Richard Cory!

ELEVATOR MAN: Going down.

CORY: *(Getting in.)* Good evening, Frank.

ELEVATOR MAN: Good evening, Mr. Cory.

(Louise gets on.)

CORY: Good evening.

LOUISE: Hello again.

(They ride down side by side. The Elevator Man slyly gooses Louise.)

LOUISE: *(Jumping.)* Ouch!

CORY: Some difficulty?

LOUISE: *(Controlling herself)* Nothing, sir.

ELEVATOR MAN: Ground floor.

LOUISE: *(To Cory; sweetly.)* Good-bye.

CORY: Good-bye.

(Cory goes off in one direction, Louise starts in the other. The Elevator Man calls to her.)

ELEVATOR MAN: I get off in half an hour. Want to wait around?

LOUISE: I've a good mind to report you to Mr. Cory. *(She goes off huffily.)*

ELEVATOR MAN: *(Calling after her.)* Hey Snooty! This is a democracy, remember?

JOE: Paper! Evening paper!

(Cory passes by; Joe hands him his paper.)

JOE: Here y'are, Mr. Cory.

CORY: *(Paying.)* Thank you, Joe.

JOE: Look at them A&P ads, sir. Look what they're asking for a piece of meat! Or even a loaf of bread!

CORY: *(Nodding vaguely.)* Does seem a little steep, Joe. *(Starts off.)*

JOE: *(Calling after him.)* People should be able to eat, sir! Everyone should be able to work and eat!

(Cory stops, looks at him.)

JOE: I mean, are we a democracy or what, sir?

CORY: *(Quietly.)* We're a democracy, Joe. Good night. *(He turns and goes off.)* *(Pause.)*

JOE: *(Looking after him.)* And Richard Cory, one calm summer night... *(He scratches his head, then calls out briskly.)* Paper! Morning paper! Leading citizen dead! Read all about it!

(Two women buy a paper from him; their names are Grace and Florence. Florence is older.)

FLORENCE: Who was it? I don't have my glasses.

GRACE: *(Reading avidly.)* Richard Cory.

(They enter a streetcar, a man gives up his seat, they sit back-to-back.)

FLORENCE: Hmm. How?

GRACE: A bullet through his head.

FLORENCE: Suicide?

GRACE: They don't say.

FLORENCE: *(Grimly nodding.)* Suicide. Used to have 'em regular. Four or five a year. Folks cutting their own throats. Burning themselves in barns. Hanging themselves in the fruit closet. Take anyone with him?

GRACE: No.

FLORENCE: Used to. Wanted company. Wife. Children. Dogs, sometimes. Cows…

(The man looks at her.)

GRACE: *(Reading.)* They don't give a reason.

FLORENCE: Hmmm?

GRACE: They don't say why.

FLORENCE: Don't have to.

GRACE: What do you mean?

FLORENCE: Only three reasons why: health, money, sex.

(The man looks at her again.)

GRACE: Really?

FLORENCE: Absolutely. Bad health, no money, too much sex.

GRACE: Not Richard Cory!

(They get up to get off.)

FLORENCE: You wait. It'll all come out. Health, money…

(She looks suspiciously at the man and flounces off, as a Nurse addresses the audience.)

NURSE: Whenever Richard Cory called the Doctor, we always did our best to squeeze him in…

(Cory comes on.)

CORY: Good morning.

NURSE: Good morning, Mr. Cory. Go right on in.

CORY: Thank you. *(Goes off.)*

(A Man with a foreign accent gets up from a chair.)

MAN: I thought I was next.

NURSE: I'm sorry.

MAN: I have to be at work.

NURSE: That was Richard Cory.

MAN: Well he's not the King of England.

NURSE: *(Sweetly.)* Come with me. I'll take your blood pressure.

MAN: It'll be too high now.

(The Nurse and Man go off as Cory comes back on with the Doctor.)

DOCTOR: So, Dick, what brings you here, bright and early?

CORY: You know.

DOCTOR: I'm afraid I don't, Dick.

CORY: I'm concerned about my health.

DOCTOR: Your health is fine, Dick. I told you that on the telephone.

CORY: I don't like telephones.

DOCTOR: They're a marvelous intervention. They simplify our lives.

CORY: *(Turning on him.)* You can't see a person on the telephone. You can't see their expression when they tell you things. *(Looks at the Doctor intensely.)* I want to see yours. Face-to-face.
    (Pause.)

DOCTOR: All right. I'll say it again. You are perfectly fine. *(Pause.)* You are in perfect shape. *(Pause.)* You are disgustingly healthy. It's almost unfair. *(Pause.)* You still don't believe me, do you?

CORY: I have this perpetual ache.

DOCTOR: There's nothing there.

CORY: This ache, deep inside.

DOCTOR: It's gas, air, nothing.

CORY: It's more than that.

DOCTOR: It's city life.

CORY: Sometimes my stomach *groans.*

DOCTOR: Start your vacation. Go up to your island and relax.

CORY: *(Shaking his head.)* It's worse up there.

DOCTOR: Then why not go to New York and see one of those new nerve specialists.

CORY: *(Smiling.)* Can you imagine me seeing one of them?

DOCTOR: No I can't, Dick.

CORY: Lying down on some couch? Spilling the beans? Can you imagine me doing that?

DOCTOR: No I can't, Dick.

CORY: *(Taking a deep breath.)* All right then. Thank you, John. I'll grin and bear it. *(Shakes his hand.)*

DOCTOR: Oh Good Lord, Dick, you *still* don't believe me!

CORY: I don't know… *(Smiles.)* It's embarrassing, this gas, this air. Last spring, at the opera, during a very quiet moment, during the *only* quiet moment, my stomach gave out this great ghastly groan. Everyone turned and looked at me.

DOCTOR: Learn how to fart, Dick. Try that.

(Cory looks at him, smiles.)

CORY: Oh very good, John. Thank you. Good-bye.

(A Minister sits down at his desk as if to write a sermon. Cory knocks.)

MINISTER: *(Calling out impatiently.)* Come in, come in. I'm in my study.

(He continues to write busily as Cory comes in.)

CORY: Reverend Davis?

(Davis looks up, jumps up.)

DAVIS: Richard Cory! I'm sorry! I was working on my sermon. *(Immediately officious.)* Please sit down. What brings you here on this summer afternoon?

CORY: I'm not sure.

DAVIS: Are you, as we say, in trouble, sorrow, sickness, need, or any other adversity?

CORY: No. *(Holds out an envelope.)* I want to give you this.

DAVIS: What is it?

CORY: A donation.

DAVIS: A donation?

CORY: A donation.

DAVIS: *(Not taking it.)* But dear man, you've already given. On behalf of your whole family.

CORY: I'm giving again. On behalf of myself.

(Davis takes the envelope.)

DAVIS: I'll put it toward the new stained-glass window.

CORY: No.

DAVIS: But it's almost totally funded. With Cory money. It will depict the entry into Jerusalem.

CORY: Give it to the poor.

DAVIS: The poor?

CORY: The poor, the poor. Give it to them.

DAVIS: But Richard, my friend. There are very few poor left in this parish.

CORY: Then give it to a parish downtown.

DAVIS: Downtown?

CORY: Downtown. Have it go for food.

DAVIS: Food?

CORY: Food: Meat. And bread.

DAVIS: *(Cowed.)* Very well. We will try. *(He puts the envelope, discreetly unopened, on his desk.)* You've been very generous over the years, Richard Cory.

CORY: I can afford to be. *(Notices the sermon on the desk.)* What's the sermon this Sunday?

DAVIS: *(His little joke.)* Oh well, I'm just warming something over for the summer.

(Cory doesn't laugh. Davis smiles; tries again.)

DAVIS: Actually, I should probably talk about the feeding of the five thousand. *(Pats the envelope.)* Loaves and fishes, eh?

CORY: You should talk about the rich man and the eye of the needle.

DAVIS: *(Smiling; wagging a finger at him.)* Oh ho. Very good. You've been dipping into your Bible. The eye of the needle, eh? *(Pause.)* No. I've tried that. It just confuses people. Christ seems to say that if you're a rich man, the case is hopeless.

CORY: Let's hope he's wrong. Good-bye. *(He walks out quickly.)*

DAVIS: *(Startled, calling after him.)* Good-bye. Good-bye, Richard. And thank you. *(Waits a moment, then hurries to the desk, rips open the envelope, hungrily takes out the check, looks at it.)* Good heavens! *(Looks where Cory has gone, then back at the check.)* This is much too much! The dear man has misplaced his decimal! *(Puts it back in the envelope.)* I'll send it right back. Care of *Mrs.* Cory. *(Goes off carrying the letter.)* Mr. Benbow, oh Mr. Benbow. I wonder if you'd do an errand for me straightaway!

(As Davis goes off, a woman named Charlotte settles herself at a table, a Waiter pulls out her chair for her.)

CHARLOTTE: *(To a Waiter.)* I'm waiting for someone.

(Cory appears across the room; she waves.)

CHARLOTTE: Ah. There he is…Dick! Oh, Dick.

(He sees her, sits down beside her.)

CHARLOTTE: See how eager I am! I got here first.

CORY: *(To Waiter.)* Tea, please.

(Waiter goes off.)

CHARLOTTE: *(Looking around.)* What a peculiar old spot.

CORY: I thought it might be better than meeting at my office. It's a little more—human.

CHARLOTTE: Absolutely. Where did you find it?

CORY: I used to come here with my grandmother. She'd taken me to a matinee, and then we'd have tea here afterwards.

CHARLOTTE: How sweet. And it's perfect. Way downtown. Perfect. *(She removes her gloves.)*

(The Waiter arrives with tea.)

CHARLOTTE: And here we are. Shall I pour? Did your grandmother do that?

CORY: Always.

CHARLOTTE: *(Fussing with the tea.)* I suppose I should state my business, shouldn't I? I mean I called you for professional help after all. Will you charge me by the hour, or what?

CORY: What's the difficulty, Charlotte?

CHARLOTTE: You should know, Dick…I've finally decided to divorce Ted.

CORY: Charlotte…

CHARLOTTE: My mind's made up. I have plenty of grounds—adultery, everything. I simply will not live with that man a day longer. And I want you, Dick. As my lawyer.

CORY: I can't take the case, Charlotte.

CHARLOTTE: Why not?

CORY: I know you both.

CHARLOTTE: You don't know Ted. You box with him at your club, you sail with him on weekends. You either pummel each other, or sit and grunt in that stupid boat. You don't know *him.* It's me, it's *me* you know.

CORY: All the more reason not to take the case.

CHARLOTTE: *(With a smile.)* Oh you dear man. I knew perfectly well you wouldn't do it. And frankly, between you and me and the bedpost, I'm glad you won't. Because then we would have had, what, a professional relationship. And who wants that? *(Pause.)* Do you suppose we could have something else here, or is there just tea?

CORY: What would you like?

CHARLOTTE: How about white wine? A Chablis or something? For the summer. *(Cory signals the Waiter.)*

CHARLOTTE: What should we have? A half-bottle? A bottle?

CORY: *(To Waiter.)* A glass of Chablis for the lady, please. *(To Charlotte.)* I'll stay with the tea.

CHARLOTTE: Oh Dick, I can't drink alone.

CORY: *(To Waiter.)* Two glasses, then. *(Waiter goes off.)*

CHARLOTTE: *(Leaning forward.)* Everyone says you've decided to stay in town all summer.

CORY: I'll go up to the island weekends.

CHARLOTTE: But during the week…

CORY: I'll be here.

CHARLOTTE: So will I. It's so dead up there, isn't it? There's so much more down here, isn't there? Or could be.

CORY: I hope so.

(Pause.)

CHARLOTTE: Do you know what finally made me make up my mind? About the divorce?

CORY: What?

CHARLOTTE: Hearing that you were going to be around.

CORY: Now Charlotte…

CHARLOTTE: It's true. That did it. That made me telephone you, and now here we are.

(The Waiter brings the wine; she takes a sip.)

CHARLOTTE: And when you said you wanted to meet here, I knew you were one step ahead of me.

CORY: I'm not one step—

CHARLOTTE: *(Taking a big sip.)* Oh Dick, let's not waste any more time. You know and I know that we are attracted to each other. Whenever you come in a room, I know you're there, and sooner or later we're making a beeline for each other. It's magnetism, Dick! It's there. It's there at every boring dinner party when you're seated next to me, and I can sense you shiver when my knee touches yours. It was there when you kissed me last summer. Oh Dick, it's there, and it's late in the day. We'll go away, we'll stay here, we'll ride down Main Street in an open carriage, I don't care—

CORY: Charlotte—

CHARLOTTE: No, let me finish. Let me say it out at long last. Dick, I know there are rooms upstairs in this tacky old barn. Let's get one. Please. Really. Let's. Now. Before I lose steam forever.

(Pause.)

CORY: *(Quietly, carefully.)* Charlotte, I have tremendous affection for you.

(She stares at him.)

CORY: And there's magnetism, as you say.

(She continues staring.)

CORY: But I think we've known each other too long.

(Pause. She sighs, gets up, calls out to the Waiter.)

CHARLOTTE: Oh waiter, would you bring the check, please. *(She pulls on her gloves.)* I've got to go. Ted will be wondering where I am.

CORY: *(Who has also stood up.)* Charlotte…

CHARLOTTE: *(Moving away from him.)* No really. I have to pack for the summer. Do I pay? Or will you?

(The Waiter has appeared, is totaling up the bill.)

CORY: Please, Charlotte…

CHARLOTTE: *(To Waiter.)* I really think you should hurry. Because Mr. Cory here has just lost the great love of his life, and after he's paid the bill, he plans to rush home and put a bullet through his head. *(She hurries out.)*

(The Waiter shakes his head, looks at Cory sympathetically.)

WAITER: Women…

CORY: *(Quietly.)* I'd like a double Scotch, please. *(Glances around.)* But not here. Bring it to the bar next door.

WAITER: Yes, Mr. Cory.

(Both go off, either way. People gather together, murmuring impatiently, to await an announcement: Reporters and bystanders. A Police Official comes out. They quiet down.)

OFFICIAL: I will read the following statement. *(He unfolds a piece of paper, reads carefully.)* Mr. Richard Cory, a leading citizen in this community, died last evening at his home on Holloway Hill.

(Amazed response from the group; the Official rides over it.)

OFFICIAL: A preliminary investigation leads us to conclude that the death was accidental, resulting from a bullet wound to the head, incurred while Mr. Cory was in the process of cleaning his gun.

(Skeptical response from the group; the Official rides over it.)

OFFICIAL: The Cory family has asked me also to announce that funeral services will be held at Trinity Church next Wednesday at four o'clock. Flowers are gratefully declined. Thoughts of sympathy may best be conveyed through donations to the several charitable organizations to which Mr. Cory lent his help. Thank you. *(He starts out.)*

REPORTER: *(Calling out.)* Did you look for indications of foul play?

OFFICIAL: We found none.

REPORTER: Nothing stolen? Broken? Missing?

OFFICIAL: Nothing at all.

ANOTHER: Who discovered the body?

OFFICIAL: The gunshot was heard by Mr. William Murdoch, the family coachman and retainer, who was living over the stable. He came to the house, found the body, and summoned the police.

ANOTHER: Was Mrs. Cory at home?

OFFICIAL: Mrs. Cory and the children were vacationing at the Cory summer home on Blue Island when the tragedy occurred.

ANOTHER: Was Mr. Cory depressed?

ANOTHER: Did he drink?

ANOTHER: Did you find a note?

ANOTHER: Were the Corys separated?

ANOTHER: Or estranged?

OFFICIAL: This conference is hereby concluded. *(He goes off.)*

(Max, a headwaiter at a restaurant, addresses the audience.)

MAX: *(To audience.)* Whenever Mrs. Cory went downtown,

We people on the pavement looked at her.

Her hair was gold, she wore a lovely gown,

And everywhere she went she made a stir.

(Emily enters, saying "Good morning" to people on the pavement. She enters the "restaurant.")

EMILY: Max…Oh Max…

MAX: *(Coming up, deferentially.)* Your usual table, Mrs. Cory?

EMILY: Not today, Max, thank you. We're on our way up to the island. But I had to stop by to put a bug in your ear.

MAX: A bug in my ear?

EMILY: I want you to start thinking about the last day of August. It's Mr. Cory's birthday, and I want to give him a spectacular party out at the house. I'm putting you in charge of the food department.

MAX: Ah. Thank you, Mrs. Cory.

EMILY: Now you know what he likes, Max. Serve all his favorite things! Plus a chocolate cake dripping with candles!

MAX: Of course, Mrs. Cory.

EMILY: And I'll get an orchestra from New York, and Japanese lanterns for the garden, and write all our favorite people. You should plan for at least fifty, Max, soup to nuts.

MAX: Very good, Mrs. Cory.

EMILY: And everything must be special, for a special man! *(She goes off.)*

MAX: Very good, Mrs. Cory. *(To audience.)* And so I thought we'd have oysters, followed by asparagus soup and then roast rack of lamb…

(Rose, a waitress in a cafe, comes on, calling off toward "the kitchen.")

ROSE: Hey, Mac, gimme Adam and Eve on a raft! Hold the spuds! *(Then to audience.)* Whenever Richard Cory came downtown,

He walked by our place on his way to work…

(A Man enters.)

MAN: Give me a roast beef sandwich, Rose.

ROSE: *(Calling off stage.)* One cow.

MAN: On rye.

ROSE: *(Calling off stage.)* Jewish cow.

MAN: With mayonnaise.

ROSE: *(Calling off stage.)* Grease the cow.

MAN: Potatoes on the side.

ROSE: *(Calling off stage.)* Make it Irish.

MAN: With lettuce and tomatoes.

ROSE: *(Calling off stage.)* Walk it through the garden.

MAN: What'll that set me back, Rose?

ROSE: Two bits.

MAN: How much without the beef.

ROSE: A dime.

MAN: I'll go without the meat.

ROSE: *(Calling off stage.)* Kill the cow. *(To audience.)* And every weekday morning, at, oh, about a quarter to nine, you could see Richard Cory waltzing by.

MAN: He got his newspaper over to Joe's…

ROSE: Joe comes in here, they all come in here…

(Another Man comes in.)

SECOND MAN: Morning, Rose. Who'd you go home with last night?

ROSE: William Howard Taft, what's it to you?

SECOND MAN: *(Settling onto a stool.)* Gimme a beer, Rose.

ROSE: *(As she gets it.)* Isn't it a little early?

SECOND MAN: That's what my wife said.

ROSE: And what did you say?

SECOND MAN: I said Rose'll give it to me any time I want.

(Laughter.)

ROSE: *(To audience.)* And so every day we'd see Richard Cory strutting by the window.

(Cory walks by; they watch him, after he goes:)

SECOND MAN: Want to take him home, Rose?

ROSE: A cat can look at a king, Charlie.

(Laughter.)

FIRST MAN: Take *me* home, Rose.

ROSE: You? You couldn't do it with a loaf of bread.

FIRST MAN: Oh yeah? Who do you think puts the holes in all them donuts?

(Everyone groans and laughs, Cory appears as if at the door; the laughter stops.)

CORY: Good morning. May I come in?

ROSE: Certainly, sir.

(The two men bury themselves in their coffee. Cory settles onto a stool.)

CORY: Black coffee, please.

ROSE: Black coffee. *(She fusses with the coffee.)*

(Cory holds up the Times, *begins to read. The life goes out of the place.)*

FIRST MAN: Hey, Rose. Where's my goddam sandwich?

ROSE: *(Sotto voce.)* Don't curse, Jack! For crying out loud!

(They look at Cory. Pause. The paper comes down slowly. Cory looks around.)

CORY: Please don't mind me.

ROSE: *(Under her breath.)* Dumb hicks!

CORY: I like vivid language.

ROSE: Stupid greenhorns!

(Pause. Cory returns to his paper. The other men huddle over their coffee. Finally, indicating his coffee.)

ROSE: Warm it up for you, sir?

CORY: No thank you.

ROSE: How about some toast, sir? We got fresh bread in today.

CORY: *(The paper comes down momentarily.)* No thank you.

ROSE: *(To others.)* The bread's good here, ain't it, fellas?

FIRST MAN: *(Mumbling.)* I dunno. I ain't tasted none yet.

ROSE: It's good bread.

CORY: *(The paper comes down again.)* I have to keep an eye on the old tum. *(Smiles, looks around, puts the paper up again. Suddenly putting his paper down.)* I wish you fellas would go on.

FIRST MAN: What d'ya mean?

CORY: I mean, you were telling jokes when I came in. I wish you'd go on.

SECOND MAN: You can't tell a joke twice, mister.

CORY: Maybe I could tell one. *(To Rose.)* May I tell a joke?

ROSE: Certainly, sir. Go right ahead.

FIRST MAN: *(Getting up.)* I gotta go.

SECOND MAN: Same. Back to work.

ROSE: What about your sandwich?

FIRST MAN: I'm not hungry. *(He leaves.)*

SECOND MAN: *(At door.)* The bread's lousy here anyway, Rose. It's lousy friggin' bread. *(He dashes out.)*

ROSE: *(Calling after them.)* Rubes! Clods! *(To Cory.)* They wouldn't appreciate your joke anyway, sir.

CORY: They might. I'll come back tomorrow and try again.

ROSE: Yes, sir. Try again.

CORY: *(Getting up.)* Well. Good morning. Thank you. *(Cory goes out.)*

ROSE: So long. *(She cleans off the counter.)* And I'm telling you, once he started coming in, the others started going out. He wasn't so good for business, Richard Cory, if you want to know. *(She lifts up his cup, finds a coin.)* But he always left a half-dollar under his cup, and I swear to God, during all the times he came in, I never once saw him put it there... *(She goes off.)*

MRS. BAKER: Cory, Pierce, and Paine. Good morning.
(Cory enters.)

CORY: Good morning, Mrs. Baker.

MRS. BAKER: Oh, Mr. Cory. Mr. Ted Babcock called and wants you to ride up to the island with him. He said if you met him at the station at noon, he'd have you onto the water by five-thirty and into a dry martini by seven.

CORY: Sounds like an accurate message from Ted Babcock. *(Pause.)* Thank him, but no.

MRS. BAKER: Really?

CORY: Just say no thank you.

MRS. BAKER: Oh, you should go, Mr. Cory. Your family's there. And it sounds so beautiful up there.

CORY: I'm sorry, Mrs. Baker, but I just don't seem to like islands any more. *(He goes off.)*

MRS. BAKER: *(At switchboard)* Give me Babcock and Beard, please. Mr. Babcock, please...Mr. Babcock? Mr. Cory says he can't.
(Louise has come out, and is waiting, as if on a street corner.)

LOUISE: Whenever Richard Cory went to lunch, he'd sometimes pass me on the corner of South and Main. Most days, I wait here for my girlfriend Jane who works at the new Sears and Roebuck. We have lunch over at the ice cream parlor...
(Elevator Man comes by.)

ELEVATOR MAN: *(To Louise.)* I'm off duty for lunch, beautiful.

LOUISE: Oh, go away!

ELEVATOR MAN: I'm also available at five-thirty and on weekends, sweetheart.
(He goes off.)
(Louise waits. Cory crosses past her.)

CORY: *(Automatically.)* Good morning.

LOUISE: *(Calling after him.)* It's not morning any more.

CORY: *(Stopping, turning.)* Good afternoon, then.

LOUISE: It's not that yet, either.

CORY: What is it, then?

LOUISE: It's noon. It's lunch time.

CORY: And what do I say then?

LOUISE: You could just say hello.

　　　(Pause.)

CORY: All right. Fair enough. Hello.

LOUISE: Hello there.

　　　(Cory smiles, starts off, stops, returns.)

CORY: Say.

LOUISE: Hm?

CORY: Would you like to join me?

LOUISE: Why? Are you coming apart?

　　　(Cory looks at her.)

LOUISE: That's a joke from the vaudeville.

CORY: Is it?

LOUISE: Yes. I go sometimes with my girlfriend. I'm waiting for her now, but it looks like I've been stood up.

CORY: People tend to change their plans in the summer.

LOUISE: Oh, is that it?

CORY: That can be it…People tend to be erratic in the summer.

LOUISE: Does erratic mean you have strong feelings?

CORY: No, that's erotic.

LOUISE: Oh.

　　　(Both laugh.)

CORY: Let's have lunch.

LOUISE: You're on.

　　　(They start off; then she stops and turns to him.)

LOUISE: I'm Louise.

CORY: I'm—John.

LOUISE: *(Wagging a finger.)* No, you're not.

CORY: *(With a slight sigh; then a bow, kissing her hand.)* Richard Cory. At your service.

LOUISE: Let's go, Richard Cory.

　　　(They go off, as Eddie, carrying a sheaf of papers, waits as if at the elevator. The Elevator Man opens the grate for him.)

ELEVATOR MAN: Up or down?

EDDIE: Down.

ELEVATOR MAN: Down it is.

> *(They ride down.)*

EDDIE: Oh it's down, all right. You know what he wants me to do now? He wants me to run down to the courthouse and put him on the list of court-appointed lawyers. He wants to handle criminal cases now.

ELEVATOR MAN: What do you mean?

EDDIE: I mean, the best tax man, the best estate man in town! Now suddenly he wants to defend every two-bit crook that comes along.

ELEVATOR MAN: Why?

EDDIE: I don't know. Says he wants to get his feet wet. Says he wants to get into things.

ELEVATOR MAN: I know a few things I'd like to get into.

EDDIE: Look, he's a good lawyer. Since when do good lawyers go to court? Answer me that.

ELEVATOR MAN: Ground floor.

> *(Eddie gets out, leaves, as Cory enters a library.)*

CORY: *(To Librarian, quietly.)* Good afternoon. Are you the head librarian?

LIBRARIAN: *(Hushed voice.)* Yes, sir. May I help you?

CORY: I discover I'll be at home in the evening this summer. And so I want to dig into some topic. I want to explore who we are, and where we came from, and what we all—all of us—have in common.

LIBRARIAN: Are you thinking of anthropology, sir?

CORY: That's it. Anthropology.

LIBRARIAN: Well that's in the basement, sir. Mr. Morris will help you down there.

CORY: *(Starting off.)* Thank you.

LIBRARIAN: Sir…

> *(Cory stops.)*

LIBRARIAN: Are you sure anthropology is what you want? It's hardly summer reading, sir. It's all about primitive rites, and strange ceremonies, and human sacrifices. It can be very raw.

CORY: *(With a smile.)* Sounds like just my meat.

> *(He goes off, as Alice, a young girl, comes over to the Librarian.)*

ALICE: Excuse me, Miss Emerson, but wasn't that Richard Cory?

LIBRARIAN: *(Fussing with books.)* I think it was, Alice. Yes.

ALICE: May I ask what book he wanted?

LIBRARIAN: He wanted a book downstairs, Alice.

ALICE: I'm bored with the Bobsey Twins. I'm going to see what Richard Cory reads. *(She goes off quickly.)*

LIBRARIAN: *(Following her off.)* Alice, you are not permitted down there! Alice! *(Ted Babcock comes out. Slip, a trainer, is boxing with him.)*

TED: *(To audience, as he boxes.)* Whenever Dick Cory was downtown, he used to stop by the Club on the way home. We'd go a couple of rounds to keep in shape, and have a steambath, and then old Slip here would give us a rubdown, and fix us a drink, and send us home feeling like a million dollars! Right, Slip?

SLIP: *(Scandinavian accent.)* Ya, ya.

TED: Say, I always got a kick out of sparring around with Dick Cory. I don't know. There's something about stripping down, and fighting it out, man to man—
(Cory comes on.)

TED: You're late, you bastard. Get ready. *(He shadow boxes with Cory.)*

CORY: No boxing tonight, Ted.

TED: Oh, come on. First you won't take a long weekend with me. Then, when I feel so guilty I stay down, you won't even go a couple of rounds.

CORY: I'll have a drink with you, Ted.

SLIP: Ya, ya. I get drinks. *(He starts off.)*

CORY: *(Calling after him.)* Slip, make one of those new martini cocktails. And put it all on my bill.

TED: What's the big occasion?

CORY: *(Helping him off with his gloves.)* I'm celebrating.
(Slip begins to shake up the martinis.)

TED: Celebrating what?

CORY: Coming downtown.

TED: Huh?

CORY: A new life, Ted.

TED: Balls.

CORY: I'm serious. I'm turning a corner. I might even run for office in the fall.

TED: You mean here at the Club?

CORY: I mean here down*town*.

TED: What office?

CORY: I don't know yet. Mayor maybe. I don't know.

TED: Richard Cory: I stand amazed.
(Slip serves them their martinis.)

CORY: Thank you, Slip.

TED: *(Raises his glass.)* Well. Here's to your big moment.

CORY: Thanks, Ted.

(*They sit down side by side.*)

TED: What does Emily say about all this?

CORY: Emily?

TED: Emily. You know. Your wife. We've got these wives, Dick. Yours is the pretty one. Her name is Emily.

CORY: I haven't told her yet.

TED: Saving it for the weekend, eh?

CORY: I'm not going up this weekend.

TED: Not going *up?*

CORY: I'm staying down.

TED: Jesus, Dick, I may have my troubles with Charlotte, but at least I show up weekends.

CORY: I'll telephone Emily.

TED: Thought you hated telephones.

CORY: Sometimes they're necessary.

TED: (*Half-serious.*) Tell you what, Dick. *I'll* tell her. I'll drop over this Saturday and put my arm around her shoulder and say, "Emily, Dick won't be around much this summer, sweetheart." Shall I do that, Dick?

CORY: It's a crucial summer for me, Ted. I know that.

(*Ted looks at him.*)

TED: Won't you put on the gloves? Just a round or two?

CORY: (*Getting up.*) No thanks. Got to go.

TED: Where? Or shouldn't I ask?

CORY: So long, Ted.

TED: Shouldn't have asked.

(*Cory waves and leaves. Slip rubs Ted's shoulders.*)

TED: I don't know, Slip. Seems to me he's walking away from it.

SLIP: Ya, ya.

TED: Just stepping out of the ring.

SLIP: Ya, ya.

TED: He's got the best left jab in town, too.

SLIP: Ya.

TED: And the prettiest wife on the island.

SLIP: Ya.

TED: (*With a sigh.*) Well, I guess I'll catch the train and go right on up then. Bring me a towel, will you, Slip? (*He goes off, after a final jab at Slip.*) (*Rose cleans off her counter.*)

ROSE: *(To herself)* So on we worked, and waited for— *(She stops, as she sees Cory standing in the door.)*

CORY: I thought maybe I might tell my joke.

ROSE: We're closed now, sir.

CORY: But I saw your light.

ROSE: That's for burglars, sir. It's getting tough down here at night.

CORY: Oh. *(Turns, starts off, stops, turns back.)* But you know, I was thinking: What if I had my birthday party right down here? What if we put tables out here, out here on the pavement. And had wine, not champagne, oh no, just good red wine. And you could serve it if you wanted to. And everyone would be invited. The whole town. Anyone who wanted to come. And we'd have music, and people could dance, or stroll around, it wouldn't matter. And what if it started the ball rolling. What if it began to happen, night after night. What if whenever anybody felt lonely he could come down here, and just *be* here, out in the light. And there'd be this *life* here, right here… *(Sings.)* "In the Good Old Summertime, in the Good Old Summertime…" *(He stops, embarrassed.)* I'm sorry. I've just had a martini cocktail.

ROSE: Yes. Well. Gotta catch my trolley.

CORY: Good night, then.

ROSE: Good night, sir.

(Cory starts off. Rose watches him go.)

ROSE: And Richard Cory, one calm summer night…

(William, the old coachman, sits repairing something leathery. A young Reporter approaches him.)

REPORTER: Are you Mr. William Murdock?

WILLIAM: Aye.

REPORTER: I'm doing an article on the Cory case. I understand you know something about the gun.

WILLIAM: Maybe.

REPORTER: What fascinates me is what it was doing there, in the first place? I mean, why did he have it? Where did he get it? That's what fascinates me. *(Pause. William continues to work.)*

REPORTER: Could you tell me anything about it?

WILLIAM: It was his grandfather's gun.

REPORTER: Ah. I see. He inherited it. It was a family gun.

WILLIAM: Aye.

REPORTER: But why did the grandfather have it?

WILLIAM: For the strikes.

REPORTER: You mean by the workers? Down at his factory?

WILLIAM: Aye.

REPORTER: But I still don't see…

WILLIAM: Said if they ever picketed, he'd pop 'em off, one by one.

REPORTER: Well, we won't put that in the paper. I assume the gun was never used.

WILLIAM: Aye.

REPORTER: Good God. By the grandfather?

WILLIAM: By the father.

REPORTER: Ah. Richard Cory's father actually used that gun.

WILLIAM: Aye.

REPORTER: *(Writing.)* For what?

WILLIAM: Thanksgiving.

REPORTER: Ah. He was a sportsman? He'd shoot the family turkey with that gun?

WILLIAM: Aye.

REPORTER: This is fascinating. From the capitalist to the sportsman. But wait a minute. How could he shoot a turkey with a pistol?

WILLIAM: He'd buy a live bird, put it in a crate, let its head stick out, back off, take a bead, shoot the head off.

REPORTER: *(Crossing off notes.)* I'd better not use that either. But then Richard Cory got the gun from his father.

WILLIAM: Aye.

REPORTER: And he kept it down at the office.

WILLIAM: Aye.

REPORTER: But for some reason he took it home to clean it the night he died.

WILLIAM: *(Looks up for the first time.)* Clean it? I cleaned that gun. That gun was clean as a whistle. Now run along, laddy, and let me be doing my work.

(The Reporter goes off, perplexed. Max, the headwaiter at the restaurant, addresses the audience.)

MAX: Each summer, Mrs. Cory left the town,
   The pavement got a little hot for her.
   But now and then she'd take the boat back down,
   When things came up she felt she couldn't defer…
   (Cory and his wife Emily come in.)

MAX: Good afternoon, Mr. Cory…Mrs. Cory…Right this way, please. *(He begins to lead them toward upstage.)*
   (Emily sees a table downstage.)

EMILY: Could we sit over there, please, Max?

MAX: *(A touch offended.)* Certainly, madam. *(He leads them to the table, seats them, hands out menus, leaves.)*

EMILY: He was going to put us right smack in the middle of the room.

CORY: That's because he wants to show you off.

EMILY: Oh please… *(Pause.)* I think we need a little privacy today, don't you?

CORY: I suppose.

MAX: Will you have an aperitif?

EMILY: Yes, please.

CORY: *(Simultaneously.)* No, thank you.

    (Pause. Max waits, pencil at the ready.)

EMILY: Dry sherry, please.

MAX: *(Writing.)* Dry sherry…And you, Mr. Cory?

CORY: Nothing, thanks.

MAX: Very good, sir. *(Goes off.)*

EMILY: Is this another change?

CORY: What?

EMILY: Not having a drink.

CORY: I've got to be in court this afternoon.

EMILY: Oh. Right. It's criminal law these days, isn't it? It's murder and mayhem all afternoon.

CORY: Em—

EMILY: What happens at five, when the courts close? Is that when you meet with politicians? How's your political career going? What are you running for? Mayor? President? King?

CORY: Come on, Em.

EMILY: You know what I miss most on the island? Those moments on the verandah before dinner. Alone with you. Without the children. When you'd have a drink. And I'd have one, too. Those were fun, those moments.

CORY: We'll do that again, Em.

EMILY: When? When will that be? When can we have the pleasure of your company?

CORY: Next weekend.

EMILY: Dick, you said that last weekend, and we all dashed down and waited for the ferry, for *two* ferries, and we had a roast of beef and corn on the cob, and you never even telephoned.

CORY: I telephoned that night.

EMILY: At midnight.

CORY: I was tied up.

EMILY: Doing what?

CORY: I was doing some reading.

EMILY: *Reading?*

CORY: This fascinating book!

EMILY: Just reading, Dick?

CORY: And other things...

EMILY: What other things?

(Max approaches.)

MAX: One dry sherry. *(Sets it down in front of Emily.)* May I take your orders now, please? We have an excellent crabmeat mousse.

CORY: Yes.

EMILY: *(Simultaneously.)* In a minute, please.

(Max bows and goes off. Emily takes a sip.)

EMILY: I had to practically threaten that Mrs. Baker of yours to get through to you this morning. It was a major effort to get you to have lunch.

CORY: You called so suddenly. I had other...

EMILY: I mean, what is going *on?* Reverend Davis returned all that money you gave the church, thank God. I mean, you have *children* to think of, Dick.

CORY: I know I have children.

EMILY: Then think of them, even if you won't think of me.

CORY: I think of you all, all the time. But I've got to do this.

(Max comes up to them again.)

MAX: Now the crabmeat mousse?

EMILY: Mr. Cory may want to order. He's a busy man.

CORY: *(Infinitely polite.)* Mrs. Cory isn't ready yet.

MAX: I'll be back, sir. *(He goes off.)*

EMILY: *(Suddenly.)* Is there a girl, Dick?

CORY: Hmmm?

EMILY: A girl! A girl! One of those things that middle-aged men become infatuated with?

CORY: I have lunch with a young lady occasionally.

EMILY: Were you supposed to have lunch with her today?

CORY: Yes.

EMILY: I knew that was it.

CORY: It's not it.

EMILY: What is it, then?

CORY: Give me this summer, Em. This one summer.

(Pause.)

EMILY: *(Finishing her sherry.)* All right. The summer's yours. Maybe it's just as well you're not on the island. All you do, lately, is make remarks about all our friends, anyway. *(Puts her glass down decisively, signals for Max.)*

MAX: *(Coming up, brightly, pencil poised.)* Ah, the mousse?

CORY: Yes, please.

EMILY: *(Simultaneously.)* Another sherry, please.

MAX: *(Taking glass off.)* Very good, madam.

EMILY: So. You can have your summer. *(Pause.)* Do you suppose I can have mine?

CORY: What do you mean?

EMILY: Well, I mean, just for example, that Ted Babcock has been hanging around just a little bit lately.

CORY: The son of a bitch.

EMILY: He asked me to join him on his boat for a cruise. Charlotte doesn't like to sail, so he asked me. I said, No, thank you. Maybe I should. Do you intend to sail this summer, Dick? May I join you on your boat?

CORY: Ted Babcock is a son of a bitch.

EMILY: I don't know. I think he's very attractive.

(Max returns with the drink.)

MAX: I regret to say we're all out of crabmeat mousse.

EMILY: I'll have the chef's salad and iced tea.

CORY: I'll have iced tea and a hot dog.

MAX: A frankfurter, sir? Very good. *(Goes off.)*

EMILY: *(Taking a sip.)* Do I get my summer, Dick?

(Pause.)

CORY: *(With a sigh.)* I guess that's fair.

EMILY: *(Coolly.)* All right, so what we have then is—what? An arrangement. Isn't that what people like us are supposed to have all the time, anyway? Arrangements? Isn't that what Charlotte and Ted have? So we're right in the swing now, aren't we, you and I?

CORY: Oh Em—

EMILY: Oh Dick. What do we do? Meet again in the fall and rearrange our arrangement? *(Suddenly leaning forward, reaching for his hand.)* Sweetie, come back with me to the island. We've done so well for eighteen years! We've been so good. We've loved each other, we've been decent to each other, we're bringing up such wonderful children! Oh, don't let's mess it up, Dick, sweetie, don't! When you break things like this, you can't put them back together, Dick. They're over, they're gone, they're never the same. Oh Dick, please, please, please, come back with me right now. We could make the two-thirty train.

(Pause.)

CORY: I can't, Em. Trust me on this. No. Don't even trust me. Just give me the benefit of the doubt.

EMILY: All right…Well. She tried. *(Downs her drink briskly.)* And: it's not a matter of life and death, anyway. *(Opens her purse.)* So: I brought down a list of things—other things—we have to talk about. *(Opens list.)* Ah. First of all, your son Chip.

CORY: What's he done now?

EMILY: Well the first thing he's done is break into the bar at the yacht club. That was just the first thing. And then, after I fixed *that* up, he…

(An Anarchist carrying a rumpled newspaper calls out to Passersby.)

ANARCHIST: Lies! All lies in this paper, people! Says a man can work if he wants to. That's a lie. I can't find work. They laid me off at the factory and put in a machine! That's not in this paper.

(A Mother and Child hurry by.)

CHILD: What's that man saying, Mother?

MOTHER: He's just a crackpot, dear. Next time we'll shop farther out.

ANARCHIST: *(Stopping someone else.)* And here's another lie. Look at what they say about Richard Cory. "Accidental death." That's a good one. That was no accident. That man was murdered, people.

A MAN: *(Hurrying by.)* Who done it, Sherlock?

ANARCHIST: I'll tell you who: The same ones who always do it. The bigwigs. The fat cats. Richard Cory liked the little man. He liked the people on the pavement. So the bigwigs killed him. Just like they killed Jesus and Abraham Lincoln and George Washington.

A MAN: *(Hurrying by.)* George Washington died of a cold, buddy.

ANARCHIST: You believe that? You really believe that? You really believe that *lie* that George Washington died of a cold?

(Follows him off as a Policeman brings on a criminal, Chester, in handcuffs.)

POLICEMAN: Wait here.

CHESTER: *(Jauntily.)* Where's my lawyer? Where's Richard Cory?

POLICEMAN: Conferring with the judge.

CHESTER: What do you think he'll get for me?

POLICEMAN: You lucky punk! Now you got Cory, you'll probably walk out of here scot-free!

CHESTER: Mr. Cory figured five years. I can live with five.

POLICEMAN: If I was Judge Howe, I'd give you the chair, you bum!

(Cory comes in, gestures for the Policeman to go. Chester smirks at the Policeman behind Cory's back.)

CORY: *(Taking a deep breath.)* Judge Howe is talking about fifteen years, Chester.

CHESTER: Fif*teen?*

CORY: He said it's the woman's testimony.

CHESTER: Fifteen YEARS?

CORY: They want to be tough these days. There's more crime. Immigrants coming in. Crowded cities.

CHESTER: Fifteen long ones! I can't deal with fifteen!

CORY: Now calm down. It's not over yet. I intend to cross examine the woman. We admit to breaking and entering, but her story about rape— that's the first we've heard of that. And I told Nat Howe I intend to break that one down this afternoon.

CHESTER: Fifteen. Sweet Jesus. Fifteen.

CORY: Chester, have you been listening to me? I said I intend to break her story down.

(Pause.)

CHESTER: How?

CORY: By asking her a series of very tough questions.

CHESTER: What if she answers them?

CORY: I imagine she'll find them very hard to answer.

(Pause.)

CHESTER: What if I did it?

(Pause.)

CORY: What if you—?

CHESTER: I did it.

CORY: You had—sexual relations with that woman when you broke into her room!

CHESTER: Uh huh.

CORY: You didn't tell me that.

CHESTER: Yeah well…

CORY: Why didn't you tell me that? I might have made an entirely different plea!

CHESTER: Yeah well…

CORY: I was just in there telling Nat Howe that we refused to accept the rape story! Why didn't you tell me?

CHESTER: I was…embarrassed.

CORY: Em*bar*rassed?

CHESTER: I didn't think you'd understand. A gentleman like you.

CORY: But I'm your lawyer! A lawyer is like a doctor! You see?

(Pause; Chester nods.)

CORY: So. Now. I'll go back to Nat Howe and tell him that I've discovered new elements to this case, and will need more time to— *(Stops; looks at Chester.)* Anyway, it wasn't the way she said it was, was it?

CHESTER: Huh? I don't get you.

CORY: I mean…She must have encouraged you. A man just can't—impose himself—on a woman. That's impossible. A man can't just—im*pose* himself.

(Pause.)

CHESTER: I did. *(Pause.)* I—imposed. *(Pause.)*

CORY: But—why?

CHESTER: Why?

CORY: Yes, why? You already had her money. Why go on and—arbitrarily do a brutal, violent thing like that?

(Chester stares at him for a moment.)

CHESTER: Could I have another lawyer? I want another lawyer. *(Calling off.)* Hey, I want another lawyer! I got a right to another court-appointed lawyer! *(He goes off.)*

(Cory goes off the opposite way, stunned. A group of local Party Workers begins to gather in a meeting room.)

PARTY WORKER: *(To audience.)* Whenever Richard Cory makes a speech, I'm always glad to hear the fellow out…

A PARTY BOSS: *(Skeptically.)* What's the story? What's he want?

PARTY WORKER: He thinks he might want to be mayor. If he gets our endorsement.

A WOMAN: Mayor? Oh he should win hands down. That handsome man. He has my vote right now.

ANOTHER: *(Shouting out.)* Here he is…Ladies and gentlemen, Mr. Richard Cory.

(Everyone claps as Cory comes in. They form an audience. He speaks easily and naturally, as if he were making an after-dinner speech.)

CORY: Thank you. Good morning.

(Everyone settles down to listen.)

CORY: I have been thinking about all of us. I have been reading books about you and me. I have been studying all summer how men and women have gotten together and made villages, towns, cities. Since the beginning of time, we have found that the family is not enough. Friendships are not enough. Ownership, leisure, recreation—none of these things is enough for a full life. We need places to celebrate ourselves. We need a center, we need downtown. *(Pause.)* And I have the sense that it's slipping away. The automobile is coming in, and we are going out. Money, clothes, possessions, machines are building up barriers between us. We're beginning to live on the edge of things. We're beginning to scatter, circling around our own lives like frightened birds. *(With increased passion.)* I must do something about this. I feel personally responsible. My grandfather helped build this town. My father helped it grow. It's my turn now to do what I can to keep it alive. Let me try. Thank you.

(Polite applause.)

CORY: And now I'd be delighted to meet and talk to you personally. Face-to-face.

(He steps into the crowd, tries to meet people, says, "How are you?" "Good to see you." People respond: "Good morning," "I've got to run," "I'm late for work." He is left standing alone. The Party Worker comes up to him, shakes his hand, claps him on the back.)

PARTY WORKER: Dick, fella. Fine speech, old buddy. *(He ushers Cory out.)*

CORY: *(As he goes.)* Thank you. Thank you very much.

(The Party Worker returns to confer with the Party Boss.)

PARTY WORKER: What do you think?

PARTY BOSS: What was he saying?

PARTY WORKER: Search me.

PARTY BOSS: Birds flying around. I don't get it.

PARTY WORKER: Who'll we put up as mayor?

PARTY BOSS: Me.

PARTY WORKER: You? You don't have any class.

PARTY BOSS: At least I talk clear. At least I talk meat and bread on the table.

(They both go out. Louise sits at a dressing table, combing her hair in a mirror.)

LOUISE: *(Into the mirror, to herself.)* Richard Cory. *(She stretches luxuriously.)* Richard Cory! *(She throws her head back and shouts, triumphantly.)* RICHARD CORY!

(Cory's voice is heard from offstage.)

CORY'S VOICE: I can't hear you.

LOUISE: *(Calling in.)* Doesn't matter!

(Cory comes in in an elegant bathrobe.)

CORY: I'm sorry.

LOUISE: All I said was "Richard Cory."

CORY: That's my name.

LOUISE: Richard Cory, Esquire. The first day I saw you, I wondered what you'd be like in bed.

CORY: Now you know.

LOUISE: Now I know. *(She smiles.)* My mother never told me.

CORY: Neither did mine.

(They laugh. He embraces her. Then she pulls away and looks at him.)

CORY: What's the matter? What are you looking at?

LOUISE: You.

CORY: Me?

LOUISE: You. I'm imagining you…

(Pause.)

CORY: What?

LOUISE: Stepping out of the bathtub.

CORY: Mmmm.

LOUISE: You looked like one of those Greek gods they have over at the museum. *(She pretends to read an inscription.)* "Richard Cory." By—some Greek.

CORY: I'm not a statue.

LOUISE: Well, at least you don't have your thingy cut off, like those other Greek gods.

CORY: I'm not a god, thank you. *(He starts back toward bathroom.)*

LOUISE: You going to take another bath?

CORY: No. Why?

LOUISE: Because I swear, Richard Cory, you're the only man I ever heard of who takes a bath both before and after.

CORY: Well if you can't keep the commandments, you can at least keep clean. *(He goes off.)*

(Louise talks to him as she gets dressed.)

LOUISE: No wonder you smell of soap. You are a clean man, Richard Cory. Clean and white. Like marble. You shine all over!

CORY'S VOICE: *(From within.)* I can't hear you. I'm brushing my teeth.

LOUISE: I wish I could tell people about you. When you come strutting down the street, I wish I could shout out to all the people on the pavement, "I've had that man. I made love with that man. I did it with Richard Cory."

(Cory comes back in, now dressed except for his tie.)

CORY: Please don't call me that all the time.

LOUISE: Call you what?

CORY: Richard Cory…Please call me Dick.

LOUISE: All right.

CORY: Or call me something else. What's the elevator man's name? Frank. Call me Frank. *(Pause.)* Or call me Chester.

LOUISE: *Ches*ter?

CORY: Or don't call me anything. Why do we have to have names? Why names things all the time? Say "hey you." Why not?

LOUISE: I'll try.

CORY: *(As he ties his tie in front of a "mirror. ")* Do you like this flat?

LOUISE: Oh yes. Whose is it? A friend's?

CORY: I rented it.

LOUISE: You rented it? Just for today?

CORY: For all of August.

LOUISE: You rented this place for all of August?

CORY: Certainly. You can leave things here. Clothes. Toothbrush. Anything you want. You can stay here at night. There's the key. Put it in your purse.

LOUISE: *(Looking at it, not taking it.)* Golly. A key.

CORY: So. We'll meet here tomorrow, then?

LOUISE: Tomorrow?

CORY: Yes. Or is that difficult for you?

LOUISE: No, no…

CORY: If it is, we can meet the day after.

LOUISE: Tomorrow's fine.

CORY: *(Looking at his pocket watch.)* I'll leave first. You follow in a few minutes. And don't worry about the bed or anything. I've got a woman coming in to clean every day.

LOUISE: Every *day?*

CORY: Of course. I don't want you to worry about a thing.

LOUISE: Oh.

(Pause.)

CORY: Good-bye, then.

LOUISE: Good-bye.

CORY: You're staring at me again.

LOUISE: I guess I just like to look at you.

(Cory suddenly crosses to her, takes her, and kisses her very passionately, she finally breaks loose.)

LOUISE: Ouch. That—hurt a little.

CORY: I'm sorry. Tomorrow, then. Don't forget your key. Good-bye.

LOUISE: Good-bye, Mr. Cory.

(He wheels on her almost threateningly, she cowers.)

LOUISE: I mean—just—good-bye.

CORY: Thank you. *(He goes out.)*

> *(She sits looking at the door. Then she finishes dressing hurriedly. She looks at the key, but does not pick it up. She goes to the door, opens it, turns back, surveys the flat, speaks quietly.)*

LOUISE: Good-bye, Richard Cory. *(She goes out.)*

MRS. BAKER: The last day Richard Cory came downtown …Cory, Pearce, and Paine…Good morning…

> *(Cory comes in.)*

MRS. BAKER: Oh Mr. Cory, there's someone waiting in your office.

CORY: Who?

MRS. BAKER: You'll see.

> *(Cory enters his office. His son, Chip, about seventeen, sits casually on Cory's desk, playing with an old revolver.)*

CORY: *(Standing at door.)* Chip!

CHIP: Hi, Dad. Look what I found in your desk drawer.

CORY: *(Hurrying to him.)* I'll take that, thank you. *(Takes it away quickly.)*

CHIP: It's not loaded. I checked.

CORY: It's still not a toy, Chip. *(Puts it away.)* Since when do we look in people's desks, anyway?

CHIP: When we're bored.

CORY: Why aren't you up at the island?

CHIP: Mother sent me down.

CORY: Why?

CHIP: She said she can't handle me, maybe you can.

> *(Pause.)*

CORY: You're in trouble again, Chip?

> *(Chip nods.)*

CHIP: They kicked me out of the yacht club.

CORY: And what did you do to get kicked out?

CHIP: I banged into Mr. Babcock's boat.

CORY: What were you drinking? Beer? Whiskey? What?

CHIP: Both.

CORY: Oh, Chip.

> *(Pause.)*

CHIP: We had words on the dock afterward, too.

CORY: Words? Were you fresh to him?

CHIP: I hit him.

CORY: You *hit* an older man?

CHIP: Well, he started shoving me.

CORY: Oh good God, Chip. You see? You see what happens? That comes from drinking! We don't hit older men, we don't drink in boats!

CHIP: There's nothing else to do up there.

CORY: There's everything to do up there. Tennis, riding, swimming, everything. It's *para*dise up there. There are thousands of poor people slaving away down here who'd give their eye*teeth* to be up there.

CHIP: It's just games up there.

CORY: Oh, Chip, I don't know. We send you to Saint Mark's, you get kicked out for smoking halfway through the first semester. We send you to Lawrenceville, and you lasted—how long, before you ran away?

CHIP: I lasted almost a year there, Dad.

CORY: Almost a year. We buy you your own boat, and you proceed to get into a row with a very good friend of mine, who happens to be Commodore of the yacht club. Did you hurt him?

CHIP: Naw.

CORY: Thank God.

CHIP: But I landed a good one, Dad. I decked him. I knocked him flat on his tail.

CORY: What? Ted Babcock? *(Starts to laugh.)* What did he say?

CHIP: Nothing. He was too surprised. And then everyone started gathering around, and I kind of shoved off.

CORY: *(Laughing.)* Oh God, oh God. I shouldn't laugh.

CHIP: It bores you, too, doesn't it, Dad? All that, up there.

CORY: Sometimes.

CHIP: Even Mother's bored up there.

CORY: Your mother adores it up there.

CHIP: She's bored, Dad. *(Impulsively.)* She's having an affair with Mr. Babcock, Dad. Everyone says so. That's really why I decked him.

CORY: That's enough, please.

CHIP: Well, it's true.

CORY: I'm not going to discuss your mother.

CHIP: It's *true,* Dad. Everyone's bored up there, and fooling around, and you won't go up there, and I don't want to go up there any more.

CORY: Maybe we haven't given it a fair shake, Chip.

CHIP: Oh Dad…

CORY: I'm serious. I've set a bad example. I've turned my back on my own people. And you've sensed that. And that's made you rebellious. Well I've been wrong, Chip. They're alive, aren't they? They're real. They're human. When you prick them, they bleed. When you hit them, they fall… *(He laughs again.)* Let's go up there and give it another try, Chip.

CHIP: You want to hit him, too, Dad?

CORY: No, no. But I want to reconnect. Come on. We'll grab the next boat, you and I.

CHIP: I don't want to go back, Dad.

CORY: Sure you do. Of course you do. *(Calls off to Mrs. Baker.)* Mrs. Baker! Please telephone my wife on the island. Tell her we've seen the light and we're on our way.

MRS. BAKER: Oh good, Mr. Cory. *(She goes to her switchboard.)*

CORY: *(To Chip.)* We have a few days of summer left!

CHIP: Dad…

CORY: *(Almost desperately.)* No, please, Chip. I'm finished down here. It's done, it's over, it didn't work. I want to be up there, with all of you. We'll have my birthday party up there, Chip. Just the family. We'll get together, be together, do things together once again.

(Mrs. Baker comes in.)

MRS. BAKER: Mr. Cory…

CORY: What did she say? What boat will she meet?

MRS. BAKER: She's not there, Mr. Cory.

CORY: Not there?

MRS. BAKER: I spoke to the cleaning woman. Mrs. Cory has gone on a cruise up the coast. And the children are all visiting. Even the maids are off. The house is empty, Mr. Cory. *(Pause.)*

CORY: Thank you, Mrs. Baker.

MRS. BAKER: Yes, sir. *(She goes out.)*

(Pause.)

CORY: *(Quietly.)* We could go up by ourselves, then, Chip. Just you and I.

CHIP: I think I should be on my own, Dad.

(Pause.)

CORY: Where would you go?

CHIP: Out West, maybe.

CORY: At seventeen? All alone?

CHIP: Great-grampa Cory came over at sixteen. All alone.

(Pause.)

CORY: You'll need money.

CHIP: I guess.

CORY: Here's what I've got. *(Gives him a wad.)*

CHIP: Thanks, Dad.

(They shake hands.)

CORY: Will I see you again?

CHIP: Oh sure, Dad.

CORY: I'll never see you again.

CHIP: Oh Dad.

CORY: Will you forget about me?

CHIP: I couldn't forget you if I tried, Dad.

CORY: Have I been that bad?

CHIP: No, sir! You've been that good. You've been perfect, Dad.

(Chip leaves. Cory looks after him, sighs, squares his shoulders, puts on his hat.)

CORY: *(To Mrs. Baker.)* Well Mrs. Baker. It's time to take a walk around town.

MRS. BAKER: Good, Mr. Cory. One of our last summer days.

(He starts out, then stops.)

CORY: By the way, how's your mother?

MRS. BAKER: Oh she's fine, Mr. Cory. She took a boat to Bermuda.

CORY: I should have sent flowers.

MRS. BAKER: You can't do everything, Mr. Cory.

CORY: You can try. Good-bye.

MRS. BAKER: Good-bye, Mr. Cory.

(He goes off. Rose comes on, as if in her cafe. She calls back into the kitchen.)

ROSE: Hey, Jake! Let's close early! There's no one around!

(Cory comes in, stands there.)

ROSE: Oh. Mr. Cory.

CORY: I never told my joke.

ROSE: Oh. Well. Um. Then tell it now. *(Calling off.)* Come out here, Jake. Mr. Cory's here and he wants to tell a joke.

(Jake comes out, wiping his hands on an apron. He and Rose stand deferentially.)

CORY: Well. This ostrich decided to go to an ostrich party, even though he hadn't really been invited. But the others saw him coming down the road. And being ostriches, they got nervous. Seeing a stranger. So they decided to hide. They stuck their heads in the sand, as ostriches do. And so when our ostrich arrived at the party, there they all were, all hiding, their rear ends sticking up, their tail feathers waving in the breeze. So what did he do? He looked around and said, "Where *is* everybody?"

(Pause; no one laughs.)

CORY: That's the joke. *(Pause.)* I wish I knew a better one.

ROSE: Oh that was a good one, sir. Just needs some thinking, that's all.

CORY: I see. Well. Thank you. *(He shakes hands with her.)* Thank you for listening to it, anyway. *(He shakes hands with Jake.)* Thank you. *(He starts
out, stops.)* He was an ostrich, too, you know. That was the joke. *(He goes
out.)*

JAKE: I still don't get it.

ROSE: It'll come, Jake. Just wait for the light.

(The Police Official enters and reads from a document.)

POLICE OFFICIAL: In response to continued rumor and speculation, the police
department has recently completed a thorough investigation of Mr.
Richard Cory's last day downtown. He left his office in mid-morning,
after bidding his son farewell on a trip west. He lunched alone. He
stopped by the courthouse to offer his legal services. He returned a book
to the library. He looked in briefly at a cafe to exchange pleasantries with
the waitress and the cook. Toward the end of the day, he returned to his
office to work on what we now know was his will.

(Cory enters, sits at his desk, begins to write.)

POLICE OFFICIAL: Among these activities we found none which would induce
a man to take his own life. We continue to view the Cory case as offi-
cially unresolved. *(Police Official goes off.)*

(Reverend Davis enters.)

DAVIS: The Richard Cory funeral packed our church.

And everything was beautifully done.

We prayed, we sang, I spoke appropriate words,

And afterwards, we lingered in the sun.

*(The crowd gathers in a knot. Louise comes down, and stands, as if waiting.
Frank, the elevator man, approaches her.)*

FRANK: Hey Tootsie. I saw you looking at me in there.

LOUISE: I was listening to the sermon. And my name's Louise.

FRANK: *(Taking her arm.)* Lemme buy you a beer, Louise.

LOUISE: Don't mind if I do. *(As they go.)* Say, what did that mean? That stuff
about the eye of the needle?

FRANK: *(Jauntily.)* Oh that just means, as we sew, so shall we reap new gar-
ments.

LOUISE: Oh.

(As they go off, Charlotte and Ted come down.)

CHARLOTTE: It was all very Cory, wasn't it? Emily being so brave. The children sitting in a row like soldiers.

TED: Goddam Dick Cory! What a crazy thing! It makes me furious!

CHARLOTTE: Why don't you go punch something, Ted? Or do you want to have another fight with Chip?

TED: I can think of other people I'd rather hit, Charlotte.

(He goes off as the Doctor comes up.)

CHARLOTTE: *(Covering.)* Ah. The good Doctor.

DOCTOR: Today was his birthday, you know. I got out his records.

CHARLOTTE: Oh stop, before I burst into tears.

DOCTOR: He thought he had an incurable disease. Did you know that?

CHARLOTTE: Nonsense. He did it because of me. But of course he knew that I'd never leave Ted.

(They go off either way. Eddie comes down. He wears his necktie. He is taken aside by a Reporter.)

REPORTER: Hey, I hear you're the guy that found the new will.

EDDIE: I can't comment on that.

REPORTER: They say he left a large portion of his estate to the community. For a park or something. Downtown.

EDDIE: That is a private family matter.

REPORTER: Well, it wasn't witnessed anyway. They'll probably never honor it.

EDDIE: Of course they'll honor it. He wrote it, didn't he? He signed his name. Of course they'll honor it!

(They go off separately as the Librarian comes out, followed by Alice, carrying a book.)

ALICE: Miss Emerson, Miss Emerson, look what I found down in anthropology.

LIBRARIAN: Not here, Alice. This is a funeral.

ALICE: But listen, it explains everything: *(She reads, quickly.)* "Sometimes, in more advanced tribes, a rich chieftain will have his property redistributed and then take his own life, so as to dramatize the limitations of wealth and to revive the communal spirit." *(Points to back of book.)* And look! He returned the book the day he died!

LIBRARIAN: *(Going off.)* Oh Alice, that's what you get when you go down to the basement!

ALICE: *(To herself)* I don't care! I'm going to work on it! *(She goes off.)*

(Cory stands up, looks out. His office is cleared away. Cory puts the gun neatly into his breast pocket, adjusts his coat, puts on his hat. The First Actor comes out with the Robinson book.)

FIRST ACTOR: *(Reading, as the stage is cleared.)*

So on we worked, and waited for the light,

And went without the meat, and cursed the bread,

And Richard Cory—

CORY: (*Stopping, tipping his hat, brightly.*) Good evening.

FIRST ACTOR: Good evening, Mr. Cory.

    (Cory goes off.)

FIRST ACTOR: And Richard Cory, one calm summer night,

    Went home and...

    (The First Actor looks off, slowly closes the book as the lights dim.)

The End

The Middle Ages
(1977)

AUTHOR'S NOTE

The Middle Ages has also had a chequered career. We tried it out first at a workshop at the Mark Taper Forum in Los Angeles, and then in a more elaborate production in Stamford, Connecticut, where it was roundly dismissed by most of the New York critics. It was revived five years later off-Broadway by several brave souls. This time, the *New York Times* decided to smile upon it, and the play went on to have a respectable run. I like its attempt to straddle forty years of American life without skipping a beat, but as with *Children,* its setting—in this case a restricted men's club in a decaying midwestern city—was off-putting to some and irrelevant to others. The play has had a good life around the country, and a continuous run of several years in Athens, Greece, of all places, where apparently the penultimate scene in Act I is given the full treatment.

ORIGINAL PRODUCTION

The Middle Ages was first produced at the Mark Taper Forum Lab in January, 1977, with the following cast:

Barney . . . . Cliff de Young
Eleanor. . . . . Kitty Winn
Charles. . . . . Keene Curtis
Myra . . . . Toni Lamonde
It was directed by Gordon Hunt.

It opened for a three-week run at the Hartman Theatre in Stamford, Connecticut, in January, 1978, with the following cast:

Barney. . . . . Peter Coffield
Eleanor. . . . . Swoosie Kurtz
Charles. . . . . Douglass Watson
Myra . . . . Patricia O'Connell
It was directed by Melvin Bernhardt, designed by John Lee Beatty, and lit by Dennis Parichy. The staging incorporated into this script is primarily from the latter production.

The Middle Ages was produced off-Broadway in March, 1983, by Alison Clarkson, Stephen Graham, Joan Stein, and The Shubert Organization at the Theatre At St. Peter's Church with the following cast:

Barney . . . . Jack Gilpin
Eleanor . . . . Ann McDonough
Charles . . . . Andre Gregory

Myra . . . . Jo Henderson

Setting by John Lee Beatty, Costumes by David Murin, Lighting by Frances Aronson, Stage Manager: M.A. Howard, The production was directed by David Trainer.

Original New York production by the Ark Theatre Company

CAST OF CHARACTERS
Barney
Eleanor
Charles, Barney's father
Myra, Eleanor's mother

SETTING
The action takes place in the trophy room of a men's club in a large city over a span of time from the mid-forties to the late seventies.

The trophy room: Victorian Gothic. Plenty of wood, plenty of leather, plenty of dusty old trophies on shelves. Upstage, a Gothic, mullioned window, with leaded glass, looking out over a gray cityscape. Branches of a tree or shrub intervene.

On the walls, above the wainscoting, are a number of stuffed heads of animals: moose, bear, mountain goat, gazelle; also several racks of guns, fishing rods, along with cases of flies and reels, and mounted game fish. Along shelves, in addition to the trophies, are plaques indicating who killed or caught what, who beat whom, and when. Old wooden tennis racquets, squash racquets, and polo mallets are crossed heraldically and mounted on the wall.

There's a cracked old leather couch, several chairs, and a large oaken table, displaying more trophies and prizes. The effect should be baronial, cluttered, and unused. This is a place where members of the club put things that they've won, or inherited, things they don't know quite what to do with.

Stage left, a wooden door leads to an old, rarely used bathroom; stage right, larger wooden double doors lead to a paneled hall and the main rooms of the club.

The Middle Ages

ACT I

Before Curtain: The sound of a piano playing a hymn: "Now the Day is Over." At Curtain: Barney stands at the window, back to the audience, looking out. Snow on the branches indicates winter, the light indicates late afternoon. He wears a gray flannel suit, and his sideburns are flecked with gray. After a long moment, the doors on the right open. The sound of the hymn is heard, louder, from offstage. Eleanor comes in, wearing a trim black dress, in the style of the late seventies. Barney turns at the noise. Eleanor closes the doors behind her, shutting out the sound Offstage. She is in her forties, lovely, well gotten up. They look at each other for a moment.

ELEANOR: I knew you'd be in here.

BARNEY: Where else would I be?

ELEANOR: *(Indicating the door.)* Out there. With the rest of us.

BARNEY: Doing what?

ELEANOR: Holding the fort, at least today.

BARNEY: I'll be out when they begin the service.

(He turns back to look out the window. She moves into the room.)

ELEANOR: Mother sent me to track you down.

BARNEY: She did, did she?

ELEANOR: She wants you to join the family.

BARNEY: She's not my mother.

ELEANOR: Well she's mine, Barney, and she's your father's widow, and we should do what she wants on this particular day.

BARNEY: I'll be out when I'm ready, El.

(Pause. She joins him by the window.)

ELEANOR: She's worried about you, Barney. She thinks you're upset.

BARNEY: She's right, for once.

ELEANOR: She thinks you're going to make some kind of speech.

BARNEY: Right again.

ELEANOR: Well she's nervous about that, Barney.

BARNEY: So am I. That's why I'm in here, thinking it out.

ELEANOR: No, but look, the thing is, everyone's pretty exhausted from the church. The feeling is here, here at the club, we should probably boil things down to a bare minimum. Your father would have hated dragging things out. He would have been the first to complain.

BARNEY: So?

ELEANOR: So here, after people arrive, all Mother wants to do is just sing his favorite hymn—

BARNEY: "A Mighty Fortress is Our God."

ELEANOR: I guess so, Barney, I don't know. The point is Billy will play it on the piano, and we'll all *sing* it. And then a few members of the club will get up and make some very brief remarks, and then we'll have a moment of silence, and then—over and out and into the bar. O.K.?

BARNEY: O.K. Got the picture.

ELEANOR: Good. Then I'll tell Mother… *(She starts for the door.)*

BARNEY: Tell her I'll be brief.

(Eleanor stops, turns back, takes a deep breath.)

ELEANOR: Please, Barney.

BARNEY: What's the matter?

ELEANOR: Mother doesn't want you to say anything at all.

BARNEY: Why?

ELEANOR: You know why.

BARNEY: Why can't I say a few words in memory of my own father?

ELEANOR: Because everybody's absolutely terrified, that's why.

BARNEY: Terrified? Of what?

ELEANOR: That you'll say something perfectly ghastly and ruin the whole goddamn day!

BARNEY: You think I'd do that?

ELEANOR: Oh, Barney.

BARNEY: You really think I'd do that?

ELEANOR: I think you might. Yes.

BARNEY: You really think I'd fuck up my own father's funeral?

ELEANOR: *(Defiantly.)* I really think you might. Yes.

BARNEY: Oh Christ, El.

ELEANOR: Well you've done it before.

BARNEY: What do you mean? He never *died* before.

ELEANOR: You know what I mean, Barney. Whenever people have gotten together around here, you've done something awful.

BARNEY: All because of you, El.

ELEANOR: *(Coming down from the balcony.)* That's a lie.

BARNEY: *(Following her.)* All because of you.

ELEANOR: That's not true, Barney.

BARNEY: Everything I've done is because of you.

ELEANOR: That is a big, fat *lie,* Barney.

BARNEY: You should have chosen me, El.

ELEANOR: That's enough, please.

BARNEY: Me, instead of my nice straight little brother.

ELEANOR: I said that's enough.

BARNEY: Of course you can still repair the damage.

ELEANOR: Please stop.

BARNEY: I'm still around. Still here. All you need to do is make your move.

ELEANOR: Barney, we are at a *funeral!* Honestly! *(Pause.)* Whatever went on between you and me is over. *(Pause.)* It was all back in the Middle Ages. *(Pause.)* Now. Are you going to make a speech? Or not?

BARNEY: I have things to say. *(He returns to the window.)*

ELEANOR: Well you just plain can't.

BARNEY: Why not?

ELEANOR: Only members can speak.

BARNEY: I'm a member.

ELEANOR: You are not, Barney. You're from out of town.

BARNEY: I am a permanent member of this club! I've been trying for thirty years to resign, they've been trying for thirty years to kick me out. It can't be done. It's against some fundamental rule. Once you're born into these things, you're doomed to lifetime membership.

ELEANOR: Not me. I'm not.

BARNEY: Well I am. And so was my father. Hell, this room—here's where we really live.

ELEANOR: Nobody ever comes in here, Barney.

BARNEY: Nobody dares. It's too much. It's the holy of holies, the inner sanctum, the castle keep.

ELEANOR: For you, maybe…

BARNEY: For everyone, if they'd just admit it. *(Looks around.)* Look. Here it all is. The weapons, the battle trophies, the sacred chronicles. Pick a book, any book. *(Takes a book from the shelf, blows off the dust, reads the title.)* Ivanhoe, by Sir Walter Scott. That's us, in three volumes. Heavy armor, extravagant crusades, endless tournaments. And a hero in love with the wrong woman.

ELEANOR: Barney, Mother's waiting.

BARNEY: So what? We're in the sanctuary, El. No one can touch us here. What's out there, anyway? The world, that's all. It doesn't mean much.

Because wherever we go, whatever we do, we carry all this with us. On our backs. In our heads. In our blood. Till we die. *(He falls on his knees.)*

ELEANOR: Get up, Barney.

BARNEY: Can't. I'm a prisoner in here. Tried to escape. Couldn't. Here I am. Caught. Doomed. Dead. Hell, bury me in here. Bury the old man. Bury us all. Stack us all up, body on top of body, generation on generation, and let us moulder in here forever.

(Pause.)

ELEANOR: Is that the speech you've been working on?

BARNEY: I've been working on it all my life. *(He gets up, brushes off his knees.)*

ELEANOR: Well now you've gotten it out of your system, suppose you just come and stand quietly next to Mother, and greet people as they arrive from the cemetery.

BARNEY: Just…stand?

ELEANOR: Stand, and even hug people occasionally, and then take Mother to her seat, and sit with her during the service.

BARNEY: Just…sit?

ELEANOR: Sit, and hold her hand for once in your life, and keep her from going to pieces.

BARNEY: And you and Billy?

ELEANOR: We'll be sitting on her other side.

BARNEY: Together?

ELEANOR: Together. For your father's sake, Barney. We can all close ranks for that.

BARNEY: Is Billy going to speak?

ELEANOR: Billy?

BARNEY: Billy. My younger brother. Is he going to speak?

ELEANOR: Now Barney—

BARNEY: Yes or no. Is he?

ELEANOR: Mother asked Bill to just say a few words, Barney.

BARNEY: Knew it!

ELEANOR: Oh dear.

BARNEY: Are you going back to him?

ELEANOR: Barney—

BARNEY: After the funeral, are you getting back together?

ELEANOR: Barney, people are beginning to ar*rive!*

BARNEY: *(Calling offstage.)* I don't give a SHIT! You're going back to him, aren't you?

ELEANOR: I'm not going *back,* Barney…

BARNEY: Sure you are.

ELEANOR: Here we go.

BARNEY: Damn right here we go! It's the story of my life! You get me all softened up and then you nail me with Billy!

ELEANOR: I think I'll scream!

BARNEY: O.K., baby, here's the thing: *(Takes an envelope out of his pocket.)* I've got something written down here, and I'm going to read it, *all* of it, out loud, out there, in front of the assembled multitude. You run and tell your mother that, O.K.? *(He sits defiantly on the couch.)*

ELEANOR: All right, Barney. I'll tell her that. *(She goes to the door, turns.)* But before I do, I want to tell you something. Just so you'll know. As soon as we get through this *day*, as soon as we put your father quietly to rest, I'm through, Barney! I'm through with this family, and this club, and this city! I've spent half my life running back and forth between you, and Billy, and Mother, and your father, and my*self,* and this is the last day I'm going to do it!

(She opens the door, the sounds of a group gathering can be heard.)

ELEANOR: All of you may be permanent members around here, Barney, but I'm not, and I can't wait to get the HELL out!

BARNEY: Oh Christ, I love you, El.

ELEANOR: Nuts to you, Barney. Just—nuts to you.

(She strides out, leaving the door open. Barney watches her, then goes to stand at the fireplace. The lights fade on the trophy room, except for on him and on the door. The funeral music comes up louder as Charles, Barney's father, appears in the doorway, shadowy and ghostly at first, wearing a dark suit. Barney remains lost in thought.)

CHARLES: Now, Barney: once again, once again I am obliged to excuse myself from a pleasant occasion in order to cope with my elder son. How many times, Barney, I'm asking you, how many times have I been called out of the office, off the golf course, away from a congenial gathering simply to deal with you.

(He closes the doors behind him. The music can no longer be heard. The lights begin to dim on Barney.)

CHARLES: It seems to me, Barney, that your only interest in this world is to interrupt those few rare moments of social intercourse which men and women have managed to create for themselves in this city. What is the difficulty, Barney? I'd appreciate an answer.

(Barney can no longer be seen. Charles addresses the audience, isolated in light.)

CHARLES: I'd appreciate advice from any quarter. Everything he's done has been disruptive. And it's been that way from the beginning. Why he was even born in the middle of a dinner party. His poor mother had to leave before the dessert. What's more, Doctor Russell tells me the first thing he showed the world was his rear end. And he's continued to show us very little else. When I think of Barney, I think of a whole history of unpleasant incidents. I think of nursemaids in tears because he refused to submit to the ducky chair. I think of cooks packing their bags because he peeked at them in the bathtub. I think of cleaning women huddled in corners while he covered them with a BB gun. I've tried to civilize him. I send him to kindergarten: the first thing he finds is the fire-alarm. The first thing he writes is a four-letter word. The first thing he draws is the male member. On Winnie-the-Poo. I send him to birthday parties: he pins the tail on the hostess. I send him to summer camp. They send him back. Apparently the only thing he learned was to break wind. At will. And put a match to it. I'm at a loss, my friends. He's a good dancer, but he was expelled from dancing school. For goosing people in the conga line. He's a good hockey player, but he spent half a game in the penalty box. For hiding the puck. In his athletic supporter. He's a good student, but he continually fails history. Why? Because he only will learn about riots, revolutions, and Franklin D. Roosevelt. I am at a loss, my friends.

(Charles goes to the door, opens it: we hear the sound of people singing around the piano, amateurishly but joyously "O Little Town of Bethlehem." Charles listens for a moment as the lights come up on the room. Barney is standing in the same place, now in a sweater and saddleshoes, and with the slicked-back hair of the mid-forties. Charles closes the doors and turns to him.)

CHARLES: And now this. This completely outrageous behavior at our first Christmas party since World War Two! How old are you, Barney? *(No response.)* I am asking you a question! How old are you?

BARNEY: *(Quickly joining him downstage.)* You know how old I am, Dad.

CHARLES: I want to hear it from you.

BARNEY: Sixteen.

CHARLES: Six-teen. Sixteen years old.

BARNEY: You knew that, Dad.

CHARLES: Never mind what I know and what I don't know. Do you consider yourself a man or a boy?

BARNEY: I consider myself—in the middle.

CHARLES: I see. And which do you want to be for the rest of your life?

BARNEY: A man.

CHARLES: And which do you think you were, out there, just now, during the Christmas party?

BARNEY: We were just hacking around, Dad.

CHARLES: Were you a man or a boy out there this afternoon?

BARNEY: All right, I was a boy.

CHARLES: You were a boy, all right. You were a baby. Your little brother, your brother Billy who is only fourteen, is playing the piano out there, and acting twice your age. Now there are families out there who haven't been together since the war. All they wanted to do was come down to this club and gather around the piano and sing some fine old Christmas music. That's all they wanted to do. But would you let them do that? Apparently not.

(Barney shrugs.)

CHARLES: My friends have suggested you miss your mother.

BARNEY: I hardly remember her, Dad.

CHARLES: I miss her.

BARNEY: I know you do, Dad.

CHARLES: Sometimes I miss her so much I almost—lose control.

BARNEY: I know, Dad.

CHARLES: But I hold on. I don't run around rooms causing trouble.

BARNEY: I know, Dad.

CHARLES: Then why do *you?*

BARNEY: Maybe I'm just—bad.

CHARLES: Nonsense.

BARNEY: You don't know me, Dad.

CHARLES: I know you perfectly well. And I know it's not too late to repair the damage.

BARNEY: How?

CHARLES: You can apologize.

(Pause.)

BARNEY: All right. I apologize.

CHARLES: Out there.

BARNEY: Out—?

CHARLES: There.

BARNEY: You mean, make a speech?

CHARLES: That's exactly what I mean.

BARNEY: What about the other boys?

CHARLES: You were the ringleader.

BARNEY: You mean I have to make a speech all by my*self?*

CHARLES: That's what I had to do when I spilled a cocktail on old Mr. Sidway.

BARNEY: But I'm not you, Dad.

CHARLES: You're my older son. And you've got to answer for it. *(He starts for the door.)*

BARNEY: Hey, Dad. Tell you what. Let's have a compromise. O.K.? You go back out there, and I'll go to the movies, O.K.?

CHARLES: I told you this morning. No.

BARNEY: But it's Errol Flynn in *Robin Hood,* Dad. They've brought it back.

CHARLES: Then you've already seen it.

BARNEY: I want to see it *again,* Dad. I could see it a thousand times! I love that movie.

CHARLES: No. I'm sorry. I'm not going to allow my elder son to go to a Hollywood movie in place of a Christmas party. Whose name is on these walls more than any other name?

BARNEY: *(With a sigh.)* Yours.

CHARLES: *Ours.* Who was the first president of this club?

BARNEY: My grandfather.

CHARLES: Your *great*-grandfather. Who—

BARNEY: *I know,* Dad. I know who shot that moose in Wyoming, and who dragged that poor fish out of some lake in the Adirondacks, and whose name is on that cup. *(He indicates cup, downstage left.)*

CHARLES: You scoff because you like to be fresh, but someday your name will be on it.

BARNEY: *Why?* Why will it?

CHARLES: Because you're my son. And you can't get away from it.

(Charles opens the door partway. The singing can be heard: "God Rest Ye, Merry Gentlemen.")

CHARLES: All right. Everything seems to have settled down. Now we will go out there, you and I, and I'll announce that you'd like to say a few words.

BARNEY: But what would I say, Dad?

CHARLES: Why you'd simply say you were sorry. For galloping through the halls. For sneaking into the pool when it was closed. For snapping towels in the locker room when someone could lose an eye or a testicle. For going off in the corner when the singing started, and whooping and giggling and catcalling like a bunch of hoodlums from the South Side.

BARNEY: Do I have to say all that?

CHARLES: You should find your own words, of course.

BARNEY: Can I say balls instead of testicles?

CHARLES: Now watch it.

BARNEY: But I can't *do* it, Dad.

CHARLES: Well you've got to.

BARNEY: *(Setting his jaw; carefully.)* Well I won't.

(*Pause. Charles turns to face him.*)

CHARLES: What did you say?

BARNEY: I said I won't.

(*Another pause. Charles stares at him. Barney holds his ground defiantly.*)

CHARLES: Then you'll stay in here until you do. Merry Christmas! *(He strides out of the room, slamming the doors behind him.)*

BARNEY: *(Calling after him.)* I still won't! *(Then louder.)* I'll never apologize! *(Even louder.)* NEVER! *(Pause; then tentatively.)* Screw you, Dad! *(Pause. More confidently.)* Go frig a pig, Dad! Go fuck a duck! *(He gives the door the finger; he gives the door his whole arm. He grabs a long polo mallet and gives that to the door. Then he gives it to the stuffed heads, one by one. Then he tosses it away and looks around for an escape. He sees the door at left, goes to it, opens it, goes in, comes out in a moment.)* Cripes!

(He slams the door, looks around, goes to the window, gets it open, climbs out on the sill, looks down, gets ready to jump as: The door to the hall opens, slowly, and Eleanor comes in. We hear singing behind her: "Bring the Torch, Jeanette, Isabella; Bring the Torch to the Stable Run." Eleanor looks about fourteen: she wears a dark velvet dress with a lace collar, long hair with a velvet ribbon in it, and black shoes. She comes in hesitantly as if looking for someone. Then suddenly she sees Barney poised on the window ledge. She screams.)

ELEANOR: Don't JUMP!

(Her scream startles him so that he loses his balance and almost falls. But he grabs onto a mullion and saves himself. He sees her, remains on the windowsill, halfway in, halfway out.)

BARNEY: Close the door!

ELEANOR: What? *(It's hard for her to hear since he's half outside and the music is behind her.)*

BARNEY: Close the goddamn door!

ELEANOR: Oh. *(She closes the door.)*

BARNEY: *(Standing on the sill.)* Otherwise, he'd try to prevent my escape.

ELEANOR: Who?

BARNEY: My father.

ELEANOR: Why?

BARNEY: He hates my guts.

ELEANOR: But why?

BARNEY: Because I'm not like him.

ELEANOR: Were you really going to jump?

BARNEY: Sure.

ELEANOR: Really?

BARNEY: *(Posing.)* Sometimes a man's got to risk his life for freedom.

ELEANOR: Gosh.

BARNEY: *(Standing at the railing.)* Who are you?

ELEANOR: Eleanor.

BARNEY: Eleanor who?

ELEANOR: *(Awkwardly holding out her hand.)* Eleanor Gilbert.

BARNEY: Never heard of you.

ELEANOR: *(Awkwardly letting her hand fall.)* We're visiting here.

BARNEY: Oh.

ELEANOR: We're guests of the Robbinses.

BARNEY: Never heard of them.

ELEANOR: Well I've never heard of you either.

BARNEY: That's because I haven't told you my name.

ELEANOR: Well what is it, then?

BARNEY: Barney Rusher.

ELEANOR: Never heard of you.

BARNEY: Well you better start, kid. My ancestors are plastered all over these walls.

ELEANOR: *(Indicating stuffed head.)* Is that one of them?

BARNEY: *(Laughing.)* Yeah, well, my father's president of this club. I can bowl here whenever I want, and play billiards even on weekends.

ELEANOR: Then why do you want to jump out the window?
   (Pause.)

BARNEY: Maybe I won't. *(He closes the window.)*

ELEANOR: *(Crossing to steps.)* Were you one of those noisy boys out there, during the singing?

BARNEY: Maybe.

ELEANOR: Yes you were. You were one of those rowdy boys off in the corner.

BARNEY: Maybe I was, maybe I wasn't.

ELEANOR: I was watching the whole thing. You were the ringleader.

BARNEY: All right. I was.

ELEANOR: You stood out like a sore thumb.

BARNEY: You were watching, huh?

ELEANOR: I watched your father throw you in here, too.

BARNEY: He didn't throw me in here.

ELEANOR: I saw him grab your arm.

BARNEY: I *walked* in here. He followed. *(Pause.)* Anyway he's not my real father. *(Pause.)* I'm an adopted child. *(He sits on railing.)*

ELEANOR: A what?

BARNEY: An adopted child. It's obvious. My mother had an affair with someone else. I'm not sure who, exactly, but I think it might have been Errol Flynn.

ELEANOR: Oh sure.

BARNEY: *(Jumping down from railing.)* Really. Oh my father forgave her. He probably got her to make a speech, and apologize.

ELEANOR: Oh sure. Any day.

BARNEY: It's true. And then they went on and had my brother Billy and my mother got so bored she died. *(He falls onto couch, downstage right.)*

ELEANOR: I just don't believe that.

BARNEY: *(Sitting up.)* Do you believe I'm adopted?

ELEANOR: I—don't know.

BARNEY: *(Jumping onto table.)* I must be. I'm so different. But I know that somewhere else in this world I have a twin, who's adopted too. And someday we'll meet, and recognize each other, and—click.
(Pause.)

ELEANOR: Would you do me a big favor?

BARNEY: Depends on what it is.

ELEANOR: Would you continue this conversation out there?

BARNEY: Why out there?

ELEANOR: Because I've got this mother. I'm supposed to meet people my own age, and I want her to see that I've done it.

BARNEY: Was that your mother standing by the piano?

ELEANOR: Yes.

BARNEY: That fussy lady?

ELEANOR: That was her—she—her. Do you want to meet her?

BARNEY: No thanks.

ELEANOR: Well you don't even have to. All you have to do is talk to me out there. If we run out of steam, you could introduce me to one of your friends.

BARNEY: *(Shaking his head.)* Uh-uh. Can't do it.

ELEANOR: Oh please. You don't know what it's like to be new some place. Everyone stares at you.

BARNEY: I like that.

ELEANOR: I just hate it. I could sink through the floor.

BARNEY: Maybe that's why I hack around all the time. So people will notice me.

ELEANOR: I noticed you, all right.

BARNEY: I saw you noticing. That made me do it all the more.

ELEANOR: I *thought* so. That's why I followed you in here. I thought you were the most exciting person there.

(*Pause; they look at each other.*)

BARNEY: What was your name again? I might give you a call and take you to the movies.

ELEANOR: Eleanor Goldberg.

BARNEY: *Gold*berg?

ELEANOR: *(Quickly.)* I mean, Gilbert.

BARNEY: Which is it?

ELEANOR: Gilbert.

BARNEY: Why'd you say Goldberg?

ELEANOR: We changed it to Gilbert.

BARNEY: Are you Jewish?

ELEANOR: *(Quickly.)* No.

BARNEY: My father says anything ending with berg is Jewish.

ELEANOR: My father is Jewish. My mother made him change his name.

BARNEY: Where's your father?

ELEANOR: Back in Harrisburg.

BARNEY: Harrisburg's Jewish.

ELEANOR: Well my mother comes from here, and she's High Episcopalian.

BARNEY: What's so hot about that?

ELEANOR: Nothing. It doesn't make any difference what you *are,* anyway.

BARNEY: Come on. We'll go to the movies.

ELEANOR: *(Backing away, left.)* I don't like prejudiced people.

BARNEY: I'm not prejudiced. *They're* prejudiced out there. That's why we should go to the movies.

ELEANOR: What do you mean?

BARNEY: If they find out you're a Jew, they'll kick you right out.

ELEANOR: I don't believe you.

BARNEY: They will. They don't allow Jews in here. I've heard them say it. *(Mimicking them.)* If you let one Jew in, they bring all their friends, and pretty soon, they're all over the place. In the squash courts, in the pool, in the bar…and you can't say anything without getting into an argument.

ELEANOR: You're prejudiced!

BARNEY: No I'm not.

ELEANOR: You most certainly *are!*

BARNEY: See? Argument!

ELEANOR: *(Walking away.)* Oh honestly.

BARNEY: *(Grabbing the polo mallet.)* Come on. Let's go to the movies. It's *Robin Hood.* I'll lead you down the back way, and if anyone tries to persecute you, I'll run him through. *(He protects her with his "sword.")* Come on. Got any money?

ELEANOR: Won't you please come out there with me?

BARNEY: Can't. If I did, I'd just end up one of them.

ELEANOR: What's so bad about that?

BARNEY: It'd kill me, that's all. I'd die.

(He falls melodramatically on his sword. The door bursts open. Charles puts his head in angrily.)

CHARLES: *(To Barney.)* I'll give you five more minutes! *(He sees Eleanor.)* Excuse me, young lady, but this boy has five more minutes! *(He turns, goes out, slamming the door.)*

ELEANOR: That was your father, wasn't it?

BARNEY: No. That was just someone I pay to tell me the time.

(Eleanor laughs in spite of herself.)

ELEANOR: You *are* kind of funny.

BARNEY: I got that joke from a movie.

ELEANOR: What did he mean, five more minutes?

BARNEY: *(Climbing the book ladder.)* Oh well, he just meant that in five more minutes, he's going to drag me out into that public square, and tie me to the piano, and light a fire under me, and burn me alive for being a heretic. And before I can surrender my soul to heaven, while my flesh is crackling like a leg of lamb, he's going to reach into the flames and grope around in my chest cavity, and hold up to the hooting multitude my warm, red, palpitating, human heart! And so… *(He reaches the top.)* To prevent that from happening… *(He jumps to the railing.)* To rob him of that obscene pleasure…. *(He grabs an old bell-pull.)* I have no choice but to bid you farewell!

(He swings to windowsill, jumps off, disappears. Eleanor screams and runs up to the window. Before she gets there, Barney's head pops up casually.)

BARNEY: It's O.K. There's a roof here.

ELEANOR: *(Embarrassed for showing concern.)* You *are* a show off, aren't you?

BARNEY: I sure am.

ELEANOR: Is that *all* you do? Just show off for people?

BARNEY: *(Looking at her.)* Oh no. I'm a very deep guy. Ug-glug glug.

(He holds his nose and disappears as if he were going under water. She rushes to the window, stands half-waving, romantically, looking after him, then closes the window. The door opens. Singing can be heard: "O Come, All Ye Faithful." Myra, Eleanor's mother, stylishly dressed, fortyish, and fussy, comes in. She stands looking at Eleanor for a long moment. Then she shakes her head and closes the doors.)

MYRA: Eleanor, dear love, what are you doing in this musty old room?

ELEANOR: I was just…

MYRA: I've been combing the woods for you. Are we playing Hide-And-Seek at the age of fourteen?

ELEANOR: Oh no. *(Proudly.)* I was talking to a boy, Mother.

MYRA: *(Looking around.)* Boy? What boy? I don't see any boy.

ELEANOR: *(Indicating window.)* He just…he… *(She looks at bell-cord, looks at window, looks at Myra, gives up with a sigh.)* Oh golly.

MYRA: *(Patiently.)* The boys are out *there,* Eleanor. Boys and parties happen to occur around pianos and people.

ELEANOR: I get so shy, Mother.

MYRA: That's part of your charm. You just don't realize. How could you, sitting around Harrisburg, playing chess with your father? Now go have fun!

ELEANOR: I'll try. *(She starts glumly for the door.)*

MYRA: Chin up, shoulders back, smile.

(Eleanor stiffens her shoulders, turns at the door with a ghastly fake smile.)

MYRA: That's it. The boys will gather like flies.

ELEANOR: What if they run away? *(Glances at window.)*

MYRA: Don't let them. Pretend you're having a perfectly marvelous time.

ELEANOR: *(Losing heart.)* I can't pretend…

MYRA: Of course you can. That's what growing up is. Pretend that party is for you.

ELEANOR: Oh not for me…

MYRA: As far as I'm concerned, that is your party. *(Leads her to the couch.)* My sweet lamb, you have only five more years, at the most, before everyone goes to college, and gets married, and scatters to the four winds. You've got to stake your claim, sweetie pie.

ELEANOR: Oh Mother…

MYRA: You do. This is the time and this is the place. In fact, I've decided to stay, dear.

ELEANOR: You mean, for supper?

MYRA: I mean…for supper. Now go find some *salle de bain* and comb your hair. And then you and I together will rejoin the human race.

(Eleanor gets up.)

MYRA: Go on. Shoo. There's still the shank of the evening to go.

(Eleanor goes to the door, opens it, turns, squares her shoulders, gives the ghastly forced smile, and goes out. The music is heard softly from the hall: "Deck the Halls with Boughs of Holly." Myra watches Eleanor go, then turns to the audience, leaving the door open.)

MYRA: Well I almost spilled the beans, didn't I? Couldn't help it. This place, this party. I was riding the crest of the wave. *(Comes downstage.)* Because I've finally decided to do it. I've decided to divorce Myron Gilbert. We have been at each other's throats since square one. This visit was a trial separation. I've tried. I'm separating. *(Glancing toward the party offstage.)* Eleanor will be fine. She can see her father any time she wants. But she won't want to. Not after she's lived here. Oh she'll be right in the swim of things before she knows it. She's lucky, actually. *(She takes a compact out of her purse, snaps it open, powders her nose, looks at herself in the compact mirror.)* When I was her age, my father changed his job, yanked us out of town, and dragged us around the country, not knowing a soul. Naturally I married the first man to look in my direction. What a life, wandering the face of the earth, chained to a stranger, frantically seeking out every second-rate bridge group and garden club and church supper, looking for some sense of connection. Never again! Not for me, not for her! We have come home. This is it. This club. This is the real thing. My mother told me about it, and it's true. Everything happens here: parties, dances, weddings. The whole life of this great city congeals right in this building. And that is why I paid sixty-three dollars for that velvet dress, and why I got Mimi Robbins to take us on, and why I want Eleanor out by that piano with everyone else. We'll stay here, and I'll launch her here, and she'll pick and choose and marry a man here, and she'll know what it means to be happy for the rest of her life!

(Charles comes in, looks around.)

CHARLES: Oh excuse me. I was looking for my son.

MYRA: I'm afraid there's nobody here but us chickens.

CHARLES: I'm sorry. Have you lost your way?

MYRA: *Au contraire.* I've found it, after fifteen long years. *(She holds out her hand.)* Myra Gilbert. We're with the Robbins.

CHARLES: *(Taking her hand; bowing.)* Charles Rusher.

MYRA: I know. You're the man we should thank for this spectacular *soirée.*

CHARLES: You're most welcome.

MYRA: I believe your son is out there, playing the piano.

CHARLES: That's my younger son, Bill. I was looking for Barney, the older.

MYRA: Well I don't know about him, but I do know the piano player is an absolute dream-boat. I have a daughter who's dying to meet him.

CHARLES: *(Offering her his arm.)* Then let's get them together.

MYRA: All right, let's. And maybe, after we've all struggled through a few more Christmas carols, we can talk people into some dancing!

CHARLES: Why not!

(They go out as the singing comes up loud: "O come ye, o come ye to Bethlehem." Then the music immediately modulates to a loud Lester Lanin-like dance tune from the early fifties, played by a party orchestra: something like "Green-Up Time." The lights from the hall spill into the trophy room. Through the window outside, we see the city lit at night. The branches in the foreground might have blossoms on them. Barney and Eleanor swirl into the room from the hall, dancing well together. Barney is in a black tuxedo, Eleanor in a long evening dress with white gloves. They do a couple of elegant spins to the music which wafts in, and then Barney, in a particularly deft turn, slyly kicks the doors closed as they spin by. The music becomes very faint, the only light is from the moon through the window.)

ELEANOR: Hey!

BARNEY: *(Sexily, still dancing.)* Hmmm?

ELEANOR: *(Breaking away from him.)* Open that door.

BARNEY: What's the matter?

ELEANOR: I said open that door, please.

BARNEY: Aw, El.

ELEANOR: I want that door open, please. Right now, Barney.

(Barney looks at her goes to the door, turns the key, locks the door, takes the key out, tosses it into the air, then puts it in his pocket.)

ELEANOR: Very funny, Barney. Ha, ha. Big joke.

BARNEY: *(Imitating Brando.)* You and I have had this date from the beginning, Blanche.

ELEANOR: I want to *dance,* Barney.

BARNEY: O.K. *(He opens an old air vent or the transom over the door, the music wafts in, faintly.)* See? *(He bows to her.)* Let's dance.

(They dance briefly, more passionately; then she breaks away.)

ELEANOR: No, seriously, Barney. Really. I don't like this. I was out there dancing with Billy, and you just grabbed me.

BARNEY: That's called cutting in.

ELEANOR: That was not cutting in. Cutting in is reasonably polite. You just grabbed. *(She goes to the door, tries it, turns.)* Give me the key, please.

BARNEY: Nope.

ELEANOR: Barney, I want the key to this door, please.

BARNEY: Nope.

ELEANOR: *(Turning on the lights; returning to him.)* Well what do we do then? Stand here, eyeing each other?

BARNEY: I've got a bone to pick with you, El.

ELEANOR: About what?

BARNEY: I've got a gripe with you.

ELEANOR: About WHAT?

BARNEY: How come you're going to Bermuda tomorrow with Billy for the rest of the spring vacation?
(Pause.)

ELEANOR: Who told you?

BARNEY: The word got out.

ELEANOR: Who told you?

BARNEY: *(Angrily.)* THE WORD GOT OUT, EL!

ELEANOR: You see? That's why it was a secret. Because you always yell bloody murder.

BARNEY: Damn right.

ELEANOR: Whoever told you was a big fat stinker.

BARNEY: You said it. It was your mother.

ELEANOR: Oh.

BARNEY: She told me I could just stop telephoning you after today.

ELEANOR: I'm going to Bermuda, Barney. A whole bunch of us are going.

BARNEY: She said you organized the whole goddamn thing! You didn't even ask me.

ELEANOR: Because I knew you wouldn't go.

BARNEY: *(Crossing downstage right.)* Damn right I wouldn't go. Frolicking around that crummy island with a bunch of superficial preppies!

ELEANOR: See? See the way you are? Well I want to go, and I'm going. I've had to babysit on the Cape for two summers to pay for it, and I can't stand it around here during the slush season, and I've seen all the movies with you, and I want to go to Bermuda.

BARNEY: Who's paying for Billy?

ELEANOR: I don't know and I don't care.

BARNEY: I know. My father's paying for him.

ELEANOR: Maybe he is.

BARNEY: He'd never pay for me.

ELEANOR: Well he's mad because you flunked out of college.

BARNEY: I didn't flunk. I left. Because they wouldn't let me on the fencing team.

ELEANOR: I don't blame them. You wanted to do it like Robin Hood.

BARNEY: Well Jesus. Who wants to just stand there?

ELEANOR: *(Sitting in chair.)* I don't know, Barney, but I want to go to Bermuda and have some fun.

BARNEY: You'll have fun, all right.

ELEANOR: I'm certainly going to try.

BARNEY: You'll get *laid* down there, El!

ELEANOR: Oh Barney.

BARNEY: You will! You'll get laid! I know that scene, El. All those blonde Ivy-League pricks running around in Madras shorts. They'll play volleyball with you, and then take you out on a motorbike, and get you all hotted up, and then you'll get *laid!*

ELEANOR: Barney, I promise…

BARNEY: You will! And then it'll be all over. *(He sinks onto the couch.)*

ELEANOR: Barney, trust me, for God's sake.

BARNEY: I don't trust *them.* They'll drag you into the poison ivy. They'll spill beer all over you. They'll get you all sandy. They'll barf! And then they'll go back to their grubby, sweaty, Greek-letter fraternities and stand around in the showers and scratch themselves and brag about you.

ELEANOR: I'll be with Billy.

BARNEY: *(Getting up.)* Then Billy will lay you, the sneaky little son-of-a-bitch! Oh gosh, El! Stay here with me.

ELEANOR: There's nothing to do here, Barney. The snow's gone. The skiing's over.

BARNEY: We could do it right, El.

ELEANOR: Do what?

BARNEY: It. IT. We could make it, El. Right here. Right now. You and me. We could—bang.

(Pause.)

ELEANOR: I could bang on that door, Barney, unless you give me that key.

BARNEY: No listen, El, really. Tonight's the night. And this is the place. You know we can't get into a hotel, and everyone says it's no fun in a car, and if we go to your place, your mother starts farting around, and if we go to mine, that son-of-a-bitch Billy hangs in there, so this is it, El, here, right here, where we first met.

(Eleanor looks at him, then runs to the door.)

ELEANOR: *(Pounding.)* Help!

(Barney grabs her arm, brings her back to couch.)

BARNEY: No, listen, El, *please.* Will you just *listen?* I've got it all figured out. Just give me two minutes, just *two,* and then if you don't like the idea, I'll open the door and take you back to Billy. O.K.?

(Pause.)

ELEANOR: O.K. *(She sits down on the edge of the couch, suspiciously.)*

BARNEY: O.K. Now. Here's what we do. *(He looks at his watch.)* It's late. Billy will think you were tired, I took you home.

ELEANOR: Hey, just a—

BARNEY: *(Sitting at her feet.)* Will you *wait?* Meanwhile, I've already moved my car around the corner, and I've called your mother and told her it broke down so you're sleeping over at Lucy Dunbar's. O.K.?

ELEANOR: *(Standing up.) Not* O.K.!

BARNEY: *(Forcing her to sit.)* Will you let me *finish?* Now Lucy's parents are in Florida, so her grandmother's there, who doesn't know diddly-squat, and I've told my father I'm staying over at a friend's, so everyone thinks we're somewhere else! We're covered, El! All the way! All the way down the line! We can stay here tonight, and bang, right on this couch, we can bang all we want, we can bang two or three times if we feel like it, El. What do you say? What do you say, El?

(Long pause. She looks at him, then gets up and starts pounding on the door.)

ELEANOR: Help! Somebody! Help!

BARNEY: *(Leaping over couch, grabbing her.)* Aw hell. *(He carries her downstage right.)*

ELEANOR: *(Shrieking.)* Help! Rape!

BARNEY: *(Kneeling at her feet, arms around her waist.)* Jesus, El. We're not kids anymore. You'll be in college next year, and I'll be drafted and sent to Korea to die! Oh this is it, El! I know it! If I don't get you tonight, I'll lose you forever!

(Eleanor looks down at him affectionately. Knocks are heard on the other side of the door.)

VOICES: Anybody in there?

(The handle is turned, the door rattled.)

VOICES: Anybody there?

(Eleanor continues to look at Barney.)

VOICES: It's locked. Guess no one's there. Maybe it was someone downstairs.

(Voices fade away.)

ELEANOR: *(Quietly.)* Barney, sweetie, I love you dearly, but Bermuda is all planned.

BARNEY: *(Bouncing up.)* So's this. This is planned. Look. *(He hurriedly drags a large suitcase out from the couch by the fireplace.)* Look what I smuggled in this afternoon!

ELEANOR: What's that?

BARNEY: Just wait. *(With a sweep, he clears the large oaken table downstage left of its sporting magazines.)* I'm going to make Bermuda look silly.

ELEANOR: *(Skeptical.)* Oh Barney.

BARNEY: *(Opening the suitcase.)* Just give me a *chance,* El! At least let me get into the game! *(He spreads an elaborate tablecloth on the table; quoting:)*
"Then by the bed-side, where the faded moon
Made a dim silver twilight, soft he set
A table, and, half-anguished, threw thereon
A cloth of woven crimson, gold, and jet…"
(To Eleanor.) That's from "The Eve of Saint Agnes." Did you read that in school?

ELEANOR: Yes.

BARNEY: *(Setting out silver candlesticks.)* I doubt it. It's a little raunchy for Miss Muff's in the Mountains or wherever it is you go. We had to memorize it. It's about this great love affair in the Middle Ages.

ELEANOR: I know what it's about.

BARNEY: Then you'll know that… *(He continues to set the table with silver dishes, quoting:)* "He, from forth a suitcase brought a heap…
Of candied apple, quince, and plum, and gourd
With jellies smoother than the creamy curd…"

ELEANOR: *(Taking up the poem.)* "…And lucent syrups, tinct with cinnamon; Manna and dates, in argosy transferred…"

BARNEY: *(Looking at her.)* Hey!

ELEANOR: We had to learn it, too…"From Fez"—

BARNEY: *(Joining her.)* "From Fez, and spiced dainties, every one, From silken Samarcand to cedared Lebanon."
(He has finished setting the table with goodies. From the air vent, music wafts in a romantic song from the early fifties.)

ELEANOR: Did you steal all that?

BARNEY: No.

ELEANOR: *(Eating a cookie.)* Mmmm. Toll House cookies. And the chocolate's still soft inside.

BARNEY: Made 'em myself. And there's banana ice cream, unless it's melted.

ELEANOR: Oh it's my favorite!

BARNEY: I know. And smoked oysters, which are supposed to be terrific for sex. *(He produces the oysters and ice cream side by side.)*

ELEANOR: Barney— *(She crosses downstage left.)*

BARNEY: The only thing I stole was this. *(Brings out a bottle of wine.)* From my father. *(Reads the label.)* Chateauneuf du Pape. *(Looks at her.)* Unless you prefer Mogen David.

ELEANOR: Just cut that out.

BARNEY: *(Going to table, taking the silver cup.)* We'll drink it from this. The Holy Grail. The citywide mixed doubles invitational tennis cup. Which my mother and father won in 1933. *(He kneels in front of her again.)*

ELEANOR: The only reason I'm going along with this, Barney, is to see what you'll do next.

BARNEY: *(Handing her matches and a corkscrew.)* Here. Light the candles. Open the wine. *(He looks at her, then turns.)* I've got to go pee. *(He goes into the bathroom.)*

ELEANOR: *(Calling after him.)* You're absolutely crazy, Barney! You know that, of course. *(She eats another cookie.)* Mmmm. These cookies are divine. I'll have a bite with you, Barney, because I can see you've worked hard over this. But that's that. *(She lights the candles.)* And if someone comes in, I'm going to sink through the floor.

BARNEY: *(From the bathroom.)* No one can come in. There's only one key.

ELEANOR: And I'm going to Bermuda, Barney. I'll have one glass of wine with you, for old time's sake, but if you try anything else, I'm going to scream my head off.

(Barney comes out of the bathroom wearing an exotic bathrobe.)

BARNEY: Hi.

ELEANOR: Oh my God.

BARNEY: It's my father's. What do you think?

ELEANOR: Oh Lord. What next?

BARNEY: This. *(From behind his back, he produces a black lacy negligée.)* Like it? I got it on sale.

ELEANOR: Help.

BARNEY: Put it on and we'll have a midnight supper.

ELEANOR: I'll stay as I am, thank you.

BARNEY: *(Hanging it by the fireplace.)* Suit yourself. I'll put it here for when you change your mind.

ELEANOR: I'll never change my mind, Barney.

(He goes back into the bathroom.)

BARNEY: *(From within.)* Sure you will.

ELEANOR: Never.

BARNEY: Wait till you see this. *(He comes back out with a huge protuberance in the front of his bathrobe.)* Stick 'em up.

ELEANOR: *(Shrieking.)* Oh HEAVENS!

BARNEY: That's just a preview of coming attractions! *(He pulls a toilet brush out from under his bathrobe, tosses it back into the bathroom.)*

ELEANOR: *(Bursting into laughter.)* Oh Barney, you absolute imbecile!

(She collapses onto the couch in laughter. He rushes to join her, sits down beside her, begins to kiss her. The music through the vent changes to "Goodnight, Sweetheart." Eleanor, sitting up.)

ELEANOR: The party's ending.

BARNEY: I know…

ELEANOR: Oh Barney, let's go out there.

BARNEY: *(Indicating his bathrobe.)* Like this?

ELEANOR: Let me go out there then.

BARNEY: *(Indicating the spread table.)* What about that?

ELEANOR: I don't know what to do.

BARNEY: When in doubt, dance.

(He pulls her up from the couch, they dance to the music very slowly, very affectionately.)

BARNEY: I love this push music.

ELEANOR: Barney, just shut up, please. Just shut your trap for once, O.K.?

(They rock together. Suddenly Barney shudders and freezes.)

BARNEY: Uh-oh.

ELEANOR: What?

BARNEY: Never mind.

ELEANOR: What's the trouble?

BARNEY: I said never *mind.*

ELEANOR: Well I mean—

BARNEY: I just had a little accident.

ELEANOR: You what?

BARNEY: *(Turning away.)* I had a little ACCIDENT!

(Pause.)

ELEANOR: *(Getting it.)* Oh. *(She carefully extricates herself. Pause.)* Well. That does it, doesn't it.

BARNEY: Not at all. I'll be right back.

(He goes into the bathroom, slams the door. The music ends. Through the vent, we hear the sounds of conversation. The party is breaking up.)

ELEANOR: *(Calling off to Barney.)* The party's over, Barney. Everyone's leaving. I want to leave too. I don't want to stay here tonight, sweetie. Really. I don't. *(She picks up a cookie, takes a bite, shakes her head, puts it down.)* I want my eight hours sleep. I want to go to Bermuda, Barney. I want to lie around in the sun with Billy and the whole gang. I want to play tennis and hear the Whiffenpoofs at the Elbow Beach Club. What's wrong with that, Barney? What's wrong with people having fun? I love all that, Barney. I love all those people. They're good-looking, and they play games, and they know all the lyrics to all the songs. *(Pause.)* You don't, Barney. You can't sing and your tennis is terrible. You're bad for me, Barney. Mother says so, and it's true. Every time I get with you, I get all mixed up. That's why I arranged Bermuda. You're too much for me, Barney. *(She blows out the candles.)* I don't love you, Barney. I love Billy. He was editor of the Year Book, and he's going to Princeton in the fall, and he wants to be a lawyer. You? You couldn't even stay in Franklin and Marshall. What kind of a future would I have with you? I want a home. I want a family. I've never had them. I'll never get them with you, Barney. Barney? Did you hear me, Barney?

(Silence. Then the sound of a shot from within the bathroom. Barney staggers out, stark naked except for a bloody towel clutched to his gut. He falls face down onto the couch by the fireplace. Eleanor screams, then sees the gun dangling from his hand. It's obviously a cap gun. Eleanor takes his hand, lets it fall.)

ELEANOR: Oh Barney! It's that same fake gun you used last summer. And probably the same ketchup. Jesus, Barney. Now you're even repeating yourself. Grow up!

(There a banging on the door.)

VOICES: *(From outside.)* What happened? Who's in there? Open the door.

ELEANOR: *(Whispering.)* Barney, get up! Please!

VOICES: Who's hurt? Somebody hurt in there?

(Eleanor frantically starts to clear the table, dumping the stuff back into the suitcase.)

ELEANOR: Barney, help! For God's sake!

BARNEY: *(Lifting his head.)* Only if you don't go to Bermuda.

ELEANOR: *(Defiantly.)* Never!

(Barney falls melodramatically back onto the couch.)

MYRA'S VOICE: *(From outside.)* Eleanor! It's your mother! Are you in there, dear?

ELEANOR: *(Frantically clearing.)* Barney, I'll never forgive you for this. Never!

CHARLES'S VOICE: *(From outside.)* Barney? I'm coming in there. *(To others outside.)* Wait. I think I've got a master key.

ELEANOR: *(Closing the suitcase, shoving it behind the couch.)* This is it, Barney. This is the END!

(A key is heard rattling in the door. Eleanor tosses the tablecloth to Barney, who covers himself. She turns bravely to face the door. The door bursts open. Myra and Charles come in, both in overcoats over their nightclothes, they take one look and turn back to the hall.)

CHARLES: *(As if to crowd in hallway.)* It's all right, everybody. Go home. I'll handle this.

(Eleanor has noticed the black nightie, still hanging by the fireplace. She quickly grabs it, shoves it under her dress. Charles and Myra close the doors behind them, enter the room.)

MYRA: *(Indicating the prone Barney, the defiant Eleanor.)* You see? You see why I telephoned you! Car breaking down, my eye!

CHARLES: *(Infinitely patient.)* What's the story, Barney?

MYRA: I might ask you the same question, Eleanor. With the door locked.

CHARLES: Barney, I am waiting for an answer.

BARNEY: *(Carefully.)* I got drunk. Took a shower. Passed out. She found me here and locked the door so I wouldn't be embarrassed.

CHARLES: *(Skeptically.)* They heard a shot. A scream.

BARNEY: I was goofing around with that old starter gun. *(To Eleanor.)* Sorry, El. *(Pause.)*

MYRA: Eleanor, Billy is out there, and I'm sure he'd be delighted to take you home.

(Eleanor looks at her, looks at Barney, and then walks slowly and stiffly out, the black nightie dragging behind her.)

CHARLES: Barney, get up, and go into that bathroom, and put your clothes on. You're coming home with me.

(Barney gets up, wrapping the tablecloth around him. Myra turns discreetly away. Barney goes into the bathroom and closes the door. Myra draws her overcoat around her ample bosom.)

MYRA: I don't think we heard the whole story, Charles. There was obviously some hanky-panky going on. But I think it's safe to say we nipped it in the bud.

CHARLES: You were right to telephone, Myra.

MYRA: I hope I didn't wake you up.

CHARLES: *(Covering up his pajamas.)* Not at all. I was reading in bed.

MYRA: Oh. So was I.

CHARLES: Really? What book?

MYRA: You'll laugh.

CHARLES: Not at all. Tell me.

MYRA: *The Black Rose.* By Thomas B. Costain. Am I hopelessly middle-brow?

CHARLES: No, no.

MYRA: Actually, it's quite risqué.

CHARLES: Is it?

MYRA: Yes. It tries to give an accurate picture of what went on in the Middle Ages.

CHARLES: What did?

MYRA: *(Looks at him; laughs flirtatiously.)* Won't tell.

CHARLES: *(Carefully.)* Well I imagine whatever went on then…still does.

MYRA: Oh yes. Oh yes. Absolutely.

    (Pause. He notices her bosom.)

CHARLES: *(Quickly calling off.)* Hurry up there, Barney.

MYRA: Of course, now, with all this confusion, I doubt if even a good book will do it.

CHARLES: Do it?

MYRA: Put me to sleep.

CHARLES: You might try an aspirin.

MYRA: Does that do it?

CHARLES: Sometimes. *(Pause. He glances again at her bosom. Then calls off.)* We're waiting, Barney.

MYRA: I must confess, sometimes I resort to a nightcap.

CHARLES: So do I.

MYRA: I always feel very sheepish, dipping into the Scotch, all by myself.

CHARLES: I know the feeling.

MYRA: Perhaps you'd like to stop by and join me?

    (Pause.)

CHARLES: But we'll have Barney.

MYRA: *(With a sigh.)* Oh. Yes.

CHARLES: And Eleanor will be there. With Bill.

MYRA: Yes. *(Pause.)* Of course, I intend to send her right to bed. She has to get up at the crack of dawn for Bermuda.

CHARLES: Yes. Bill should go to bed, too.

MYRA: Eleanor will go out like a light, of course. She sleeps like a top. *(Pause. Her overcoat has unaccountably fallen open again to reveal some magnificent cleavage.)*

CHARLES: I see. *(Suddenly calling off.)* Barney, we can't wait any longer! You'll have to get home by yourself. And don't wait up! I am having a night-cap with Mrs. Gilbert!

(He takes Myra's arm and quickly escorts her off, taking a good sidelong look at her bosom. They leave the door to the trophy room open. As they leave crowd sounds and music come up from off right; a piano, accordion and bass playing a bouncy version of "For Me and My Gal." The lights come up on the trophy room. It is a bright late afternoon in early summer. The curtains are open and through the windows we see blossoms on the branches. Eleanor comes in from the hall. She wears a white bridal gown in the style of the mid-fifties, carrying her train over one arm.)

ELEANOR: *(Softly; furtively.)* Barney? Are you in here, Barney? *(She looks behind the couch.)* Barney, where are you? *(She knocks on the bathroom door.)* Barney? *(She opens the bathroom door, looks in. Then she climbs to the balcony, goes to the window opens that, looks out.)* Barney? *(She leaves the window open, sighs, speaks to herself.)* Well I've done it, anyway, Barney. I've married Billy, and we're going to be happy, and there's nothing you can do about it now.

(Charles comes in, now dressed in a cutaway. The sounds of the wedding party come up loud behind him.)

CHARLES: When do I get a chance to dance with the bride?

ELEANOR: *(Brightly.)* Oh any time. Any time at all.

CHARLES: What brings you in here, of all places?

ELEANOR: I—I thought I might find Barney.

CHARLES: Barney?

ELEANOR: I thought he might be hiding.

CHARLES: Eleanor, sweetheart, he's in San Francisco.

ELEANOR: But he might just *arrive.*

CHARLES: How can he? The Navy wouldn't let him. His ship sails today for the Far East.

ELEANOR: I know, I know.

CHARLES: That's why we set this date!

ELEANOR: I just have this awful feeling…

(Charles looks at her, then closes the door behind him, shutting out the music.)

CHARLES: Let me show you something. *(He crosses to the cup, downstage left.)* You see this cup? My wife and I won this in 1933. Our names are right here.

ELEANOR: I know.

CHARLES: You've seen it?

ELEANOR: Someone showed it to me once.

CHARLES: It's been here forever. Look. Here's the dent from 1912 when old Mrs. Stevens grabbed it from the winning couple and threw it at her husband.

ELEANOR: Why did she do that?

CHARLES: She hated to lose. Everyone wanted to win in those days. My wife Helen and I tried every year after we were married. And never came close. Until 1933. When we won hands down.

ELEANOR: What made you win?

CHARLES: We found our rhythm. There wasn't a point we played that we weren't in tune. It was absolutely exhilarating.

ELEANOR: It sounds ideal.

CHARLES: It was. It was so ideal that I've never married again. I don't think I could ever find that rhythm with anyone else.

ELEANOR: Oh that's sad.

CHARLES: No, because we had a good thing going. And good things go. But I can remember it. And reflect on it. And recognize it in others. I see it in you and Bill.

ELEANOR: Our game has its problems.

CHARLES: That's what I'm saying. You have to practice, you have to play. And some day you and Bill will have your names on this cup.

ELEANOR: I hope so.

(Charles puts the cup back.)

ELEANOR: Do you think Barney will ever be on it?

CHARLES: I used to hope so.

ELEANOR: But not any more?

CHARLES: He doesn't have any staying power. He gets all wound up, but it doesn't last.

ELEANOR: *(Reminiscently.)* I know...

CHARLES: He leaves himself wide open. That's why Bill always beats him.

ELEANOR: Maybe he doesn't want to win.

CHARLES: Not at mixed doubles, anyway. But you wait. He'll come back from the Navy and turn into a champion—what? Bowler. He loves knocking things down. Now come on. Let me trot you around that dance floor.

ELEANOR: All right.

(The door bursts open. Myra comes in, all gussied up in a flowered dress, with hat and gloves.)

MYRA: Here you are. Eleanor, poor Billy is out there surrounded by old ladies.

ELEANOR: Oh, poor guy!

(She rushes out. Myra watches her go, then closes the door and turns to Charles.)

MYRA: Oh Charles, guess what just arrived.

CHARLES: What?

MYRA: A wedding present. Special delivery to the club.

CHARLES: From Barney?

MYRA: From your elder son.

CHARLES: I'm delighted he finally sent one.

MYRA: You won't say that when you hear what it was. I took the liberty of opening it.

CHARLES: Go on.

(Myra sits at the desk, downstage right. Charles follows.)

MYRA: It was a picture frame.

CHARLES: What's wrong with that?

MYRA: A silver picture frame. From Gump's.

CHARLES: What's wrong with Gump's?

MYRA: Nothing's wrong with Gump's. Gump's is one of the finest stores in San Francisco. It's what was in the frame that's wrong.

CHARLES: Well what was, Myra?

MYRA: His picture.

CHARLES: Barney's picture?

MYRA: Barney's picture was in that frame.

CHARLES: Well I think that's rather touching. I should have a picture of Barney in his sailor suit. I'll put it on the piano.

MYRA: He wasn't in his sailor suit.

CHARLES: Oh?

MYRA: He was in his birthday suit.

CHARLES: *(Exploding.)* Barney sent, as a wedding present, a picture of himself in the NUDE?

MYRA: Full front. Eleven by thirteen. In kodacolor.

CHARLES: Oh good Lord!

(He sits on couch, downstage right. Myra follows him.)

MYRA: And…

CHARLES: *And?*

MYRA: How do I say this?

CHARLES: How do you say WHAT?

MYRA: He had this great big white bow tied around his—dingy. *(She sits beside him on the couch.)*

CHARLES: *(Striking his head.)* Oh, oh, oh.

MYRA: And…

CHARLES: *(Anguished.)* AND? AND?

MYRA: There was a note.

CHARLES: SAYING WHAT?

MYRA: Saying "wish we could be there."

CHARLES: Oh God, oh God, oh God.

MYRA: Thank heavens he's a million miles away, Charles.

CHARLES: That's what I told Eleanor.

MYRA: Absolutely. And that's what I told those two sailors downstairs.

CHARLES: *(Looking at her.)* Sailors?

MYRA: Yes. Sailors. I think they were sailors. Except they wore leggings and armbands and carried nightsticks, like policemen.

CHARLES: *(Jumping up, grabbing her.)* Shore Patrol! What the hell did they want?

MYRA: They wanted Barney. So I said he was on his ship for the Far East. They asked if they could wait outside. I said there was no point, but they could. And I sent them each down a glass of champagne. Because they're defending us all against communism.

CHARLES: I'd better talk to them.

MYRA: All right Charles. *(Indicates bathroom.)* I'm going to powder my nose. The downstairs ladies room has been occupée all afternoon with tipsy bridesmaids. I'll see you on the dance floor.

(Charles hurries out as Myra crosses to the bathroom. After a moment Barney appears at the window in a white sailor suit. He climbs in stealthily, looks around. The party sounds waft in; the music might be playing "The Girl That I Marry." He watches the party for a moment. From the bathroom comes the sound of flushing. He starts, turns, hides. Myra begins to sing again, from within: "Ding, dong, the bells are gonna chime!" Barney gets an idea: he grabs an old gun from the gun racks on the wall. He hides behind the couch, right. The bathroom door opens, and Myra backs out, primping as if at a mirror, clucking, singing, "Get me to the church on time." She stops, adjusts her girdle, stops again, straightens a seam, stops again to brush off some lint. Then she is at center:)

BARNEY: *(Suddenly popping out with the gun.)* O.K., baby, reach!

MYRA: *(Jumps, gasps.)* Barney!

BARNEY: *(Waving the gun.)* One peep out of you, I'll plug you from your guzzle to your snatch!

MYRA: Oh Barney, no…

(Barney threatens her with the gun.)

BARNEY: Now. Go to the door, open it, and call your daughter in here.

MYRA: *(Pleading.)* Barney…

BARNEY: DO IT!

(She jumps. They sidle together to the door.)

BARNEY: Open it slowly.

(She does.)

BARNEY: Not too far.

(She has it open a crack. The sounds of the party come up. Barney stands behind her so he can't be seen.)

BARNEY: Can you see her?

MYRA: *(Weakly.)* She's dancing with Billy.

BARNEY: Call her.

MYRA: *(Weakly waving.)* Yoo-hoo. *(Turning to him.)* There's too much going on.

BARNEY: Get somebody to get her.

MYRA: *(Hastily, as if to someone in the hall.)* Oh Roger? Roger Bliss, would you ask Eleanor to come in here. I…I… *(She looks hopelessly over her shoulder at Barney.)*

BARNEY: You're drunk. You're sick. You've got the whirlies!

MYRA: *(To hallway.)* I'm—having trouble with my slip. Thank you, Roger.

BARNEY: Good. *(He closes door.)*

MYRA: *(Desperately backing toward center.)* Oh Barney, please, please, PLEASE leave her alone! Let her be happy, Barney, please!

BARNEY: She'll be happy with me.

MYRA: She's married, Barney. They've got furniture. They've got *lamps!*

BARNEY: She can return that crap.

MYRA: But she doesn't *want* to, Barney.

BARNEY: She can return Billy.

MYRA: She *loves* Billy.

BARNEY: Wrong! She loves me!

(The door opens. Eleanor comes in, sees Barney, quickly closes the door behind her.)

ELEANOR: Goddamn it, Barney. I knew it.

MYRA: He's got a gun, Eleanor.

(Barney goes through an elaborate gun drill.)

ELEANOR: *(Walking up to Barney.)* Give it to me, Barney.

(He hands it to her.)

ELEANOR: He's always playing with fake guns, Mother. *(Tosses the gun onto the couch.)*

BARNEY: *(To Eleanor.)* I have to see you.

ELEANOR: Let me talk to him, Mother.

MYRA: Eleanor, I'm not going to—

ELEANOR: I can handle it, Mother.

MYRA: Eleanor, I won't allow—

ELEANOR: *(Forcefully.)* Get *out* of here, Mother!

MYRA: *(Backing out.)* Yes. All right. Yes. *(She opens the door.)*

ELEANOR: And close the door after you, please. Tell Billy I'm fixing my dress. Period.

MYRA: Yes. Oh yes. Oh dear.

(Myra goes out, closing the door behind her. Eleanor faces Barney.)

BARNEY: *(Saluting her.)* Hi.

ELEANOR: Oh Barney. How'd you get here?

BARNEY: I went AWOL and grabbed a plane…let's go. *(Indicating window.)* I've got a Hertz-U-Drive-It hidden in back.

ELEANOR: Barney, I'm married to Bill!

BARNEY: Fair enough. He gets the wedding. I get the honeymoon…Come on!

ELEANOR: *(Backing away.)* You're on some ship.

BARNEY: Hell, that's halfway to Hawaii.

ELEANOR: Then you're a deserter!

BARNEY: No, no. I'm a conscientious objector. I object to Billy. You do the same!

ELEANOR: Oh I don't know where I am!

BARNEY: It doesn't matter, as long as you're not here. Come on. Out the window. We'll drive all night. We'll change clothes, change cars, change lives. We'll cross borders, El. Name your border, and we'll cross it. Skiing in Canada, swimming in Mexico, which do you want?

ELEANOR: It's like some movie…

BARNEY: *(Moving toward her.)* What's wrong with that? Here's what they do in the movies.

ELEANOR: *(Backing toward steps to balcony.)* Stay away from me.

BARNEY: I just want to kiss the bride.

ELEANOR: You just stay away.

BARNEY: Movies are better than ever.

(He corners her on the stairs. They kiss. She responds. The door bursts open. Charles rushes in, followed by Myra, who shrieks.)

CHARLES: *(To Myra.)* Close the door. Quickly.

(Myra does; Charles surveys Barney.)

CHARLES: Young Lochinvar out of the west, eh? About to sweep the bride off her feet, Barney?

BARNEY: We were just leaving, Dad.

CHARLES: Oh no you're not.

BARNEY: We are, aren't we, El?

ELEANOR: *(Anguished going to window.)* I don't know!

MYRA: Eleanor!

CHARLES: Nobody's leaving except you, Barney. And you are leaving quietly, down the backstairs, where the Shore Patrol is waiting to fly you back west.

ELEANOR: *(Turning from window.)* Shore Patrol?

MYRA: Two of the nicest boys. One's even a Negro.

CHARLES: Will you go, boy, or will you cause trouble?

BARNEY: I'm going out the window, and she's coming with me. Now stand back. *(He leaps to the windowsill holding Eleanor behind him as if she were Maid Marion.)*

ELEANOR: *(To Barney, breaking away.)* How'd the Shore Patrol know?

CHARLES: *(Going to door.)* All right, Barney. I'll bring them up here, and we'll have a very messy scene.

MYRA: Oh Charles, how ghastly!

ELEANOR: Wait! Please wait.

(Charles stops. She turns to Barney.)

ELEANOR: How'd they know you were here, Barney?

BARNEY: I don't know.

ELEANOR: What made them come here? Right to this club? Right in time for the reception?

BARNEY: I don't know.

ELEANOR: Did you tell someone you were coming here?

BARNEY: No. I—

ELEANOR: You told people, didn't you?

BARNEY: I just told—

ELEANOR: You told *every*one! You told your buddies, you told your captain…

BARNEY: I didn't tell the captain!

ELEANOR: You probably sent a wire to President Eisenhower, saying "Help, bring in the cavalry at the last minute!"

BARNEY: I might have told—

ELEANOR: Oh Barney, you left a trail a mile wide!

BARNEY: *(Looking at her; scratching his head.)* Maybe I did.

ELEANOR: You were just playing games, weren't you? You didn't even want to win.

BARNEY: Maybe I didn't.

ELEANOR: *(To Charles and Myra.)* He never wanted to. Ever.

BARNEY: Oh, El…

ELEANOR: *(Squaring her shoulders.)* O.K., Barney. You can keep on playing. You can play Robin Hood right now. You can have your Merry Men rush in here, and ruin my wedding. You can do that, Barney. Or you can grow up, and get the hell out of here, quietly, down the back way. Which is it, Barney?

(Pause.)

BARNEY: I'll go quietly.

MYRA: Then there is a God.

CHARLES: They said you could meet your ship in Hawaii, Barney.

(Barney goes to Charles, holds out his hand.)

BARNEY: Good-bye Dad.

(They shake hands.)

CHARLES: And I'll call someone in Washington. We'll get you off with a light punishment.

(Barney goes to Myra, holds out his hand.)

BARNEY: Good-bye, Mrs. Gilbert.

MYRA: *(Coldly, refusing to shake hands.)* Frankly, Barney, I think it will do you a lot of good if they put you in the clink or the jug or the mess or whatever it is they put you in.

(Barney shrugs, crosses to Eleanor, who is still on the balcony by the window.)

BARNEY: Good-bye, El.

(Eleanor holds out her hand for him to shake.)

ELEANOR: Good-bye, Barney.

(He takes her hand, then suddenly kisses it passionately.)

BARNEY: I still love you, El.

(Eleanor quickly withdraws her hand.)

CHARLES: *(Threateningly.)* Get going, Barney!

(Myra opens the door. Out he goes.)

MYRA: Eleanor, I think you and Bill should be changing for your wedding trip.

(Eleanor nods and starts for the door.)

CHARLES: And don't look so sad, Eleanor. The next time you see Barney, he'll be just another member of the family.

MYRA: Exactly. This sort of thing will never, never happen again.

ELEANOR: *(Turning in the doorway.)* Oh I know. That's what's so sad. *(She goes off.)*

MYRA: *(Crossing downstage center.)* How can she say a thing like that?

CHARLES: Because she'll miss him. So will I.

MYRA: He pointed a GUN at me, Charles!

CHARLES: Oh, Myra, he's harmless. Look, it's just one of those old things off the wall. Here. I'll put it back.

(He picks it up. It goes off with a bang, knocking down one of the stuffed heads. Myra screams, stands aghast. Charles looks at the gun, looks at Myra, looks at the door. The lights fade quickly.)

End of Act I

ACT II

The early sixties. Afternoon. The greenery outside the window indicates mid-summer. The window is open, the door is open. Through the door, we hear sounds of a baby crying and other children's voices, and the murmurs and laughter of a small gathering. Someone on the piano might be playing musical comedy selections. After a moment, Barney and Eleanor come in together from the hall, arm in arm. Eleanor wears a summer dress and carries a knitting bag, and Barney wears conventionally collegiate summer clothes: seersucker jacket, khakis, shirt and tie. He carries a gin and tonic.

ELEANOR: *(As they enter, indicating the room.)* See? Nothing's changed.

BARNEY: *(Remaining at door.)* Except us.

ELEANOR: Mmmm. Well come on *in*. We haven't had a chance to catch up.

BARNEY: *(Indicating door.)* Shall I…?

ELEANOR: Um. No. Better leave it open. Just in case.

BARNEY: In case what?

ELEANOR: In case the baby needs me. *(She sits on the couch downstage left.)*

BARNEY: Oh.

ELEANOR: You look marvelous. That California sun.

BARNEY: You look fine, too.

ELEANOR: Me? Oh I'm a cow. Since the baby. Since three babies. I'm two sizes larger. Upstairs.

BARNEY: Lucky baby.

ELEANOR: Now, now.

BARNEY: Lucky Billy.

ELEANOR: I said, now, now.

(Pause, she pats the couch. He sits beside her.)

ELEANOR: Barney, I want you to know how much I appreciate your coming all the way for the christening.

BARNEY: I wanted to. For my own godson, after all.

ELEANOR: But from San Francisco!

BARNEY: Oh I hitched a ride. With friends. It was O.K.

ELEANOR: Where'd you go after the church? We all got worried.

BARNEY: I just came right here.

ELEANOR: Here?

BARNEY: I was hot. I took a quick swim.

ELEANOR: You still like it here, then?

BARNEY: Can't stay away.

(Pause.)

ELEANOR: Thank you for the christening present, by the way.

BARNEY: That's all right.

ELEANOR: A silver spoon. It was lovely.

BARNEY: Well, you know. Born with it in his mouth. Might as well face up to these things.

ELEANOR: Mmm. Frankly, when I was opening it, I was a little nervous.

BARNEY: Really?

ELEANOR: Yes. I thought you might come up with something ghastly which would shock the pants off everybody.

BARNEY: Were you disappointed?

ELEANOR: *(Too insistently.)* No. Of course not. No. *(Pause.)* But I wanted you to be his godfather, Barney. I stuck to my guns on that.

BARNEY: Why?

ELEANOR: Oh...I don't know. My third child. Probably my last. I thought somebody in my family should have some connection with something outside these...walls.

BARNEY: That's why I came.

ELEANOR: What do you mean?

BARNEY: I needed some connection *in*side.

(Pause. They look at each other. From through the door, the sound of a baby crying.)

BARNEY: Don't you want to...?

ELEANOR: He just needs changing. Billy will do it. He's terribly helpful.

(The piano stops. The crying subsides.)

ELEANOR: See? *(Pause. Eleanor takes out her knitting.)* Now I want to hear all about you. It's been so long, Barney.

BARNEY: I took a second hitch in the Navy, I finished college on the G.I. Bill...

ELEANOR: Oh I know *that,* Barney. I want to hear the gory details. In the Navy, for example. Did you sew your wild oats?

BARNEY: I tried.

ELEANOR: I'll bet you did. Did you have any romantic adventures?

BARNEY: Sure.

ELEANOR: Can you talk about them?

BARNEY: Sure. Do you want to hear what happened one June, in Rangoon, during a monsoon, with a baboon?

ELEANOR: No thank you...so you won't talk about your adventures.

BARNEY: I'll talk about one.

ELEANOR: Go ahead.

BARNEY: I got married.

ELEANOR: *(Shocked.)* Barney!

BARNEY: Oh not legally. But married. She was Japanese.

ELEANOR: *(Flippantly.)* Oh gosh. *Madame Butterfly. Sayonara.* All that.

BARNEY: It was serious, El. I lived with her whenever we were in port. We had a little house. Made a little nest. I even mowed a little lawn.

ELEANOR: Just like me and Bill.

BARNEY: *(Looking at her.)* Right.

ELEANOR: Well what *hap*pened?

BARNEY: I wanted to bring her home. I went to the embassy, filled out the papers, everything…and then suddenly, I chickened out.

ELEANOR: Because of the club?

BARNEY: Because of you.

   (Pause.)

ELEANOR: Oh.

BARNEY: I was still playing *games!* That was just a Japanese's imitation of you and Bill. I was still competing with my brother, half-way around the world!

ELEANOR: Poor girl.

BARNEY: Poor *me.* I'll never love anyone, El.

ELEANOR: Oh phooey.

BARNEY: Never. I know that now. I'm doomed to live alone.

ELEANOR: You'll find someone.

BARNEY: Nope. It wouldn't be fair. I'd always be comparing her to you.

   (Pause.)

ELEANOR: Barney, tell you what: now you're back, why not stay? Bill and I have this marvelous house out in Fairview. We've fixed it all up. You could come out to dinner. Once a week, even. A regular thing. I'm a marvelous cook, Barney. We'll have these marvelous meals. And there's a guest room. You could spend the night. Any time. You'd be a breath of spring, out there, actually. Bill works his tail off, and I don't seem to get beyond the washer and the dryer, and the kids see nothing but green grass. You'll open us up, Barney. You'll be like one of those fabulous uncles in children's books—Uncle Wiggly, Doctor Doolittle. You'll take us where the wild things are. *(She sits on the edge of his chair ruffles his hair.)*

BARNEY: Um, no thanks, El. *(He gets up moves downstage left.)*

ELEANOR: Why not? We need you out there.

BARNEY: No. I'm going back to Berkeley.

ELEANOR: That's silly. You've finished school.

BARNEY: No. I've just started. I'm going to get my Ph.D.

ELEANOR: On what, for God's sake?

BARNEY: I want to work on the Middle Ages!

ELEANOR: The Middle *Ages?*

BARNEY: That's my area. I know it cold. *(He moves to the raised area by the window.)* The Middle Ages are very much like this.

ELEANOR: *(Following him up.)* This?

BARNEY: A quiet, dull life, punctuated by ceremony…

ELEANOR: Oh…

BARNEY: A closed universe, halfway between the last Roman Emperor… *(Indicates a portrait on the wall.)* …and a new way of life… *(He looks out the window.)*

ELEANOR: I see.

BARNEY: I know that world. I'm half in, half out. I can study it, write about it, teach it.

ELEANOR: Will you teach "The Eve of Saint Agnes"?

BARNEY: Hell no. That was just an adolescent version.

ELEANOR: *(Leaning against a pillar.)* I suppose…well. That's fine, Barney. Very sensible. Very mature.

BARNEY: *(Looking at her, carefully.)* I'm going to focus in on the idea of courtly love.

ELEANOR: Courtly love?

BARNEY: There was a whole movement. Of guys who were in love with married women. Courtiers, jesters, fools…

ELEANOR: And what did they do?

BARNEY: They wrote these fantastic love poems. They worshipped from afar.

ELEANOR: Is that all they did? Just—write poems?

BARNEY: They wrote, they went on quests—they sublimated.

ELEANOR: Didn't they ever just—come around?

BARNEY: Not much.

ELEANOR: Why not?

BARNEY: It was too dangerous.

(Long pause.)

ELEANOR: Well. I think we should be joining the others, don't you?

BARNEY: *(Getting up.)* Yes I do.

(Charles comes in hurriedly, closing the door behind him. He looks older, is dressed in a summer suit.)

CHARLES: I'm sorry to interrupt, but I've just had to call the police.

ELEANOR: The po*lice?*

CHARLES: There's trouble. Old Mr. Sidway went down to take his afternoon dip, and what did he find but three naked Negroes and a woman, all splashing around in the pool! They've obviously broken in, and the police will have to get them out.

BARNEY: They're my guests, Dad.

CHARLES: They're your WHAT?

BARNEY: I rode with them from Berkeley. They were hot.

(Charles stands looking at him, dumbfounded.)

ELEANOR: *(Quietly, exultantly.)* Welcome home, Barney.

(Pause. Charles looks from one to the other, then speaks with great restraint.)

CHARLES: Eleanor, I wonder if you'd tell the police we were mistaken.

ELEANOR: Yes. All right. *(She goes out quickly.)*

CHARLES: And Barney, I want you to go down to the pool, and ask your friends to put on their clothes, and come up to the main room, and raise a glass to my new grandson. Go on, Barney. Do it.

(Barney looks at him, then goes out. The lights begin to dim on the trophy room. Charles continues to, speak, as if to himself.)

CHARLES: I will greet them, I will shake their hands, I will see that they are made comfortable, because they're guests, and the cardinal rule of this club is hospitality. And if I hear one rude remark from anyone in the room about these—guests, then whoever makes it will feel my full fury. And then, when the party's over, when these guests have decided to depart, I am going to do something which I should have done ten years ago. *(Turning to audience.)* I am hereby blackballing my elder son! He is no longer welcome here, now or in the future. I will speak to Alice in the coatroom, and Fred in the bar, and John in the locker room, and if they see hide or hair of him, ever again, they should call me, or the police, or the National Guard! I want him OUT! Permanently and forever! *(He paces.)* We have always prided ourselves on our openness here. I like to think we are a democratic institution. In recent years, we have admitted many fine Jewish members, and there's talk that Walter Fay is partly Chinese. Fine. Good. But we are not ready for the invasion of naked barbarians. Poor old Mr. Sidway was profoundly disturbed by what he saw. He seems to have had a slight stroke. Fortunately, Doctor Russell was here. I told him to send Barney the bill. *(He sighs.)* Now I wish him well in Berkeley. I hope he works hard. I even hope he comes home, now and then, to visit. He's my son, after all, and I love him. But when he returns, he may not—repeat not—come to this club. If he wants to swim or play a game, let him seek out some public facility. If he wants to have a drink with old friends, let them meet in some gloomy saloon. If he wants to cash a check, let him stand in line at the bank. Oh we'll still break bread together, he and I. We'll still do that. But not here. Oh no. We will go out. To a restaurant. We will be shown to a dirty table in a dark corner by a cheap woman who chews gum. After an endless wait, she will bring us two watery cocktails, crackers wrapped in cellophane, call us "honey," and serve us lukewarm coffee with the main course. That's what democracy is these days. That's what Barney wants apparently. And I'm sorry. *(He crosses the stage to read a magazine, getting older by the step. The lights come up as Myra comes on in a pantsuit, also looking older. Her costume suggests the late sixties.)*

MYRA: *(Hesitantly.)* Charlie…

(He turns to her.)

MYRA: There was a telephone message at the desk. I told them I'd give it to you.

CHARLES: Yes?

MYRA: Long distance. From California. From you-know-who.

CHARLES: Go on.

MYRA: He needs money again.

CHARLES: Why?

MYRA: For bail. Again.

CHARLES: What did he do this time?

MYRA: What difference does it make? It's all the same. Marching without a permit, lying down in front of troop trains, picketing against poor Mr. Nixon.

CHARLES: How much does he need?

MYRA: It's higher this time.

CHARLES: How much?

MYRA: A thousand.

(Pause.)

CHARLES: What time do the banks close these days?

MYRA: Oh Charlie, you're not going to keep *doing* this.

CHARLES: He hasn't got a dime.

MYRA: Whose fault is that? He lost a perfectly good teaching job. Because he *stole,* Charles.

CHARLES: He didn't *steal,* Myra.

MYRA: He stole private property, Charles.

CHARLES: It was public property.

MYRA: He stole the university president's *car.* And drove it *around.*

CHARLES: He didn't keep it. He gave it to the poor.

MYRA: He gave it to Angela *Davis.*

CHARLES: Well Angela Davis is poor, Myra. Quite poor. I don't believe Angela Davis has a net worth of more than—

MYRA: Charlie, *honestly!*

CHARLES: *(With a sigh.)* Oh Myra, I'm suddenly very tired.

MYRA: So am I, Charlie. So am I. Tired of seeing you tear yourself apart over that boy. Charlie, he is simply *de trop.* Now you've got a wonderful, hardworking son and a lovely daughter-in-law, and three marvelous grandchildren—

CHARLES: They tire me too.

MYRA: Charlie!

CHARLES: They do. I don't like it out there. Those noisy meals, the television blaring away, the endless chatter about schools. I don't like it out there much.

MYRA: Why Charlie you're getting old.

CHARLES: That's it. Old. And I want to be with people my own age. *(He looks at her.)* Let's get married, Myra.

MYRA: Charlie!

CHARLES: Why not?

MYRA: I thought you were tired.

CHARLES: I am. Let's lean on each other in our autumn years.

MYRA: But Charlie...

CHARLES: Think about it. Take your time. I'll go see about that boy.

(He goes off. Myra looks after him, looks at audience, ponders very briefly, clears her throat.)

MYRA: After long and careful thought, I have decided to marry Mr. Charles Rusher, of this city. It will be a small, sober ceremony, family only, I probably won't even wear a hat. Then a few friends back here afterward for a quiet drink. A glass of champagne, maybe, French champagne, and I hope someone will get on his feet and make a toast. There might be music. I could bring in that accordion player from the Park Plaza who plays nothing but Fred Astaire. Which means someone might want to dance... *(She begins to sing, dance.)* "Heaven...I'm in Heaven..." *(Stops.)* And let there be food. Chicken in patties and peas. Oh hell, let's have a party! Let's have a biggie! Let's have the most spectacular get-together since the Cerebral Palsy Ball!

(Charles appears at the door.)

CHARLES: Myra…

MYRA: *(Swirling to him.)* Oh Charlie, yes, yes, YES!

CHARLES: *(Patting her hand.)* That's fine, dear. You make the arrangements. I've got to rush to the bank before they close.

(He goes out. She stands looking after him, then comes slowly downstage.)

MYRA: Make the arrangements, make the arrangements, Myra…Strange…my first husband used to say the same thing. Wouldn't drive, wouldn't carve, wouldn't…never mind what he wouldn't do. Oh why do I seem to attract such exhausted men? Or are they only exhausted when they get to me? *(She sits down.)* Why can't I be exhausted once in a while? What if I said No. I refuse. I am hereby *hors de combat. (She leans back, closes her eyes.)* Oh this is marvelous. *(She opens her eyes, sits up.)* But then who will move him out of that great barn of a house and into a nice apartment? And who will remind him to take his pills? And who will get him to think about his will, and the college education of three grandchildren? *(She stands up, squares her shoulders.)* Me! I'll do it! Myra Rusher will make the arrangements! I'll plan the trips and manage the meals and send out the Christmas cards year after year! And when things fall apart, I'll hold them together with Scotch Tape and Elmer's Glue and Gilbey's Gin! Somebody has to do these things! On my head be it! *Après moi, le déluge!* I'll arrange things until the day I die! Then I'll arrange my own funeral! Nobody else will bother, that's for sure!

(The lights come up on the trophy room. She defiantly takes a tape measure out of her pocket and begins to measure a chair, getting older with each move. Through the open doors we now hear the sounds of women's voices. After a moment Eleanor comes in, in a trim shirt and pants suggesting the early seventies. Through the window, the red and brown shrubbery now suggests early autumn, late afternoon.)

ELEANOR: *(Stands for a moment watching Myra.)* Mother. What are you doing?

MYRA: I am measuring this ratty old furniture. I plan to put slip covers on everything I can get my hands on.

ELEANOR: Why?

MYRA: Because no one else will.

ELEANOR: Not this room, Mother. Please. Leave it just the way it is.

MYRA: *(Huffily.)* All right. You're the boss, after all. This is your day.

ELEANOR: Oh not just mine, Mother. *(She goes to the window looks out.)*

MYRA: Well I mean, you fought for it. You won. It's primarily because of you that women now have the run of the club every Thursday.

ELEANOR: *(At the window; vaguely.)* We all fought.

MYRA: Well you were the leader. *(Looks at her.)* Why aren't you out there, enjoying it?

ELEANOR: I got a little bored, Mother.

MYRA: Well go bowl or play bridge or something! Go meet the new members. You can't just walk out on the whole she*bang!* I mean, if Charlie knew you were hiding in here after you fought tooth and nail for women to be out there, my God, he'd have *another* heart attack.

ELEANOR: *(Suddenly.)* He didn't even call me, Mother.

MYRA: Who?

ELEANOR: Barney.

MYRA: Oh Eleanor.

ELEANOR: I sat by the telephone all morning. He didn't even call.

MYRA: He was at the hospital, seeing his father.

ELEANOR: He still could have called.

MYRA: Eleanor, he's a busy man now. Or says he is. At least he seems to come and go every other minute.

ELEANOR: But he always calls.

MYRA: Well I can't stand here and sympathize with someone who doesn't receive a telephone call from a crazy brother-in-law. I've been sitting around hospitals for weeks. I'm going to try my hand at paddle tennis. *(She goes to the door, then turns.)* One thing sure. He can't come here! *(Myra goes out. Eleanor sighs, and turns back to look out the window. After a moment, a tall blonde woman backs into the room, wearing a raincoat and slacks. She closes the door stealthily behind her. Eleanor turns at the sound, faces her back.)*

ELEANOR: Yes? May I help you?

(The woman doesn't turn around.)

ELEANOR: I don't believe we've met. Are you a new member?

(The woman turns to face Eleanor. A long moment. It's Barney, of course, in a wig.)

BARNEY: No. I'm a guest. *(He tosses off the wig.)*

ELEANOR: *(With a shriek of joy.)* Barney!

BARNEY: Dad said it was woman's day, but faint heart ne'er won fair lady. *(He tosses off his raincoat, revealing a mod, mid-seventies outfit.)* So I bought a disguise. *(He puts the wig on a post of the balcony.)*

ELEANOR: Well it worked.

BARNEY: Oh boy, did it! One of the waiters tried to make a pass at me.

ELEANOR: *(Looks at wig.)* Wow. That must be a fifty-dollar wig.

BARNEY: That's O.K. I'm rich now.

ELEANOR: Doing what, Barney? Nobody can figure out what you do.

BARNEY: Oh I sell things, buy things.

ELEANOR: In San Francisco?

BARNEY: There, and New York. I've got apartments in both places.

ELEANOR: But what's your product?

BARNEY: Let's say I'm a middle man. As usual. As always. *(Looks at watch.)* And I'm in between planes. So fill me in on yourself.

ELEANOR: Oh. Me.

BARNEY: You. Dad says you're the high priestess around here now.

ELEANOR: Oh, I do my bit. I also have a part-time job. *(She comes down from the balcony.)*

BARNEY: Hey! Doing what?

ELEANOR: I'm a family counselor. I went back to school, like everyone else. Now I'm an expert in keeping families together on Mondays, Wednesdays, and Fridays.

BARNEY: Are you any good?

ELEANOR: Oh I'm terrific. We all get together in this hot, white room. And then we gripe, like mad. *(Pause.)* I gripe, too. *(Pause, she turns to him, hugs him.)* Oh Barney, it's so good to see you. If you hadn't come, I would have telephoned you, wherever you were.

BARNEY: Why?

ELEANOR: I got a vacation coming up. And I want to visit you.

BARNEY: Good God! With the whole gang?

ELEANOR: No, just me.

BARNEY: What about—Bill?

ELEANOR: Separate vacations are good occasionally, Barney. I've learned that much. He went duck-hunting with the boys last fall. The year before I visited my father. Now it's my turn again.

BARNEY: What about the kids?

ELEANOR: Oh. *(She laughs.)* They're big, Barney. They're huge. Bill can spoon out their spaghetti. Or they can do it themselves. No, I want *out* for a couple of weeks, Barney. I want to visit you.

BARNEY: Where?

ELEANOR: New York. I love New York. I'll come the next time you're there.

BARNEY: That might be a little tricky, El.

ELEANOR: Why? You could take me in tow. You probably have all these weird, wonderful New Yorky friends.

BARNEY: *(Mock-sophisticated.)* Oh I do, I do.

ELEANOR: Then— *(Looks at him.)* Ah-hah. *(Pause.)* You've got a girl there.

BARNEY: Right. *(He sits on the arm of the couch.)*

ELEANOR: She lives in your apartment.

BARNEY: Right.

ELEANOR: Do you love her?

BARNEY: No.

ELEANOR: But you *like* her.

BARNEY: When I'm there.

ELEANOR: And I might mess that up.

BARNEY: You might mess me up.

> *(Pause.)*

ELEANOR: Then I'll come to San Francisco.

BARNEY: El…

ELEANOR: You've got a girl there too.

BARNEY: Yes.

ELEANOR: Do you love *her?*

BARNEY: God, no…she's married.

ELEANOR: Then let me *visit* you. Send her back to her husband.

BARNEY: No.

ELEANOR: Why the hell not?

BARNEY: I'm also involved with the husband.

> *(Pause.)*

ELEANOR: What?

BARNEY: I like the husband, too.

> *(Pause.)*

ELEANOR: Oh God.

BARNEY: You asked.

ELEANOR: Oh Jesus, Barney. *(She turns away, comes downstage. Pause; then turns back to him, brightly.)* Who do you like the best?

BARNEY: I don't know. I like them all.

ELEANOR: I can't *stand* this. Do they know about each other?

BARNEY: Sure.

ELEANOR: They do?

BARNEY: Sure.

ELEANOR: Aren't they jealous of each other?

BARNEY: Not at all.

ELEANOR: Have they all *met* each other?

BARNEY: Sure.

ELEANOR: They *have?*

BARNEY: They've made it with each other.

ELEANOR: Oh no.

BARNEY: We've all made it together.

ELEANOR: Barney!

BARNEY: I told you I was a middle man.

ELEANOR: Yes. You told me.

BARNEY: And you might as well know what I do for a living.

ELEANOR: *(Walking downstage left.)* I don't want to hear.

BARNEY: *(Following her.)* I'm in the film business.

ELEANOR: Oh well, at least that's half decent.

> *(Pause.)*

BARNEY: Decent's not quite the word.

ELEANOR: You make *pornographic* movies.

BARNEY: I don't like that word, either.

ELEANOR: What are they then?

BARNEY: They are films about physical love.

ELEANOR: Are you *in* these things?

BARNEY: Hell no. I'm not good enough. *(Quickly.)* I mean, I'm good, but not that good…you should go to one.

ELEANOR: No thank you.

BARNEY: Billy goes.

ELEANOR: He does not.

BARNEY: He does. He told me. And Jackie Onassis goes. And the Unitarian Church shows them on retreats.

ELEANOR: Well I won't go.

> *(She moves away from him, he pursues her.)*

BARNEY: There's one you ought to see.

ELEANOR: I doubt it.

BARNEY: You ought to. It was my idea. We based it on *Robin Hood*. It's called *The Arrow and the Quiver*.

ELEANOR: Christ, Barney.

BARNEY: It's good. It's very artistic. We won a special prize at Cannes.

ELEANOR: *(Suddenly reeling on him.)* I think it's disgusting.

BARNEY: Oh yeah?

ELEANOR: I think your whole life sounds cheap and sad and disgusting.

BARNEY: Oh yeah? And what about you? What do you do now, in the swinging suburbs? Don't you all throw your car keys in the center of the rumpus room, and go home with whoever picks them up?

ELEANOR: No.

BARNEY: I'll bet.

ELEANOR: You think I'd do that?

BARNEY: How do I know? I've kind of lost touch with the middle class. Maybe you've got something different going with those dykes out in the main room.

(Eleanor looks at him, hauls off and slaps him, hard. He looks at her, then slaps her back.)

BARNEY: Equality of the sexes, friend. *(He strides upstage toward the door.)*

ELEANOR: Bastard!

(She hurls herself at him, begins to pummel him. He grabs her arms. They struggle. He holds her, then gives her a hard, passionate kiss. She struggles, then responds. Finally she breaks away, and goes to chair downstage left. Barney leans against the balcony railing, panting.)

BARNEY: The thing is…you don't realize this, but…by showing these films, we liberate people. There's a big connection between sex and politics…Open things up, spell things out, people will learn to be free…Hell, it's still Robin Hood, El…I'm still fighting the good fight.

ELEANOR: Do you really believe that?

(Pause.)

BARNEY: No.

ELEANOR: I didn't think so.

BARNEY: *(Indicating window.)* Out there, I believe it. *(Looks at her.)* In here, with you, it seems like a pile of crap.

ELEANOR: Glad to hear it.

BARNEY: Forget your vacation, El. Stick around here. It's a decent place.

(Pause.)

ELEANOR: Too decent for me, I'm afraid.

BARNEY: *(Coming down to her.)* That'll be the day.

ELEANOR: No, I mean it. Last summer, I almost had an affair.

BARNEY: Hey. Truth-telling time. Who with? *(He sits on the arm of her chair.)*

ELEANOR: You don't know him. Neither do I, really. He stopped by one time before supper, collecting for the Heart Fund. Bill wasn't home yet, the kids were hanging around some game, I was slapping a meal together before I went to a meeting. So in he came. I offered him a sherry. We got along. We decided to meet in town for lunch, and all that. So I got down my Sierra Club calendar and he got out his Mutual of Omaha appointment book, and we tried to arrange a day, but we never could get our schedules together. Finally I gave him a check. For twenty-five dollars. For the Heart Fund. And he left.

BARNEY: Just as well.

ELEANOR: I guess. But the family's not enough any more, Barney. At least, not for me. I thought I could make this club into a place where different people could get together.

BARNEY: Well it worked, didn't it? Ladies Day, Open Membership, all that?

ELEANOR: Oh I don't know. I wanted to turn it into a kind of camp, every summer, when people were away. You know: ghetto kids playing games, learning to swim. I mean it just *sits* here. But they voted me down.

BARNEY: What did you expect?

ELEANOR: I guess half the fun of clubs is keeping people out.

BARNEY: Mmm.

ELEANOR: Well. I got what I asked for, anyway, Barney. I got in.

BARNEY: And I got out. And now where are we?

ELEANOR: Nowhere.

BARNEY: *(Arm around her.)* I'll always count on you, El. You keep me honest.

ELEANOR: Yes. Between New York and San Francisco.

BARNEY: You're different, and you know it. I happen to love you.

ELEANOR: Whatever that means.

BARNEY: It means a lot, these days. *(Pause. He looks at her, looks at his watch.)* Oh my gosh. My plane leaves in forty-five minutes. *(Looks at her again.)* Want to come along?

ELEANOR: With you?

BARNEY: Sure.

(Long pause.)

ELEANOR: No.

(Pause.)

BARNEY: Thank God. I couldn't deal with you out there.

ELEANOR: Well I can't deal with you in here, Barney. *(Pause.)* So maybe you'd better go.

BARNEY: Uh…huh. *(He gets up.)* It's good-bye, then. *(He puts on his raincoat.)*

ELEANOR: *(Not looking at him.)* Yes it really is.

BARNEY: *(Brightly.)* I mean, so long.

ELEANOR: I mean good-bye.

(Pause.)

BARNEY: Christ… *(No response. He gets the wig and puts it on.)* Hey. I better wear this. Maybe I can still get it on with that waiter. *(No response. He goes to the door, turns.)* Someday something will happen, El. Right here in this room, where we first met. And you'll know it, and I'll know it, and it'll be absolutely fantastic.

(He opens the doors and minces out exaggeratedly as we hear the women's voices come up. Eleanor gets up, goes to balcony, looks out window as Myra bustles in.)

MYRA: *(Looking back down the hall.)* What a large woman that was. Do you suppose she's interested in bowling?

ELEANOR: She's from out of town.

MYRA: Oh. Well. Billy's on the phone, and he wants to know when he's supposed to put the pizza in the oven.

ELEANOR: Tell him I'll… *(Pause.)* Tell him… *(She starts to cry.)* Oh Mother, I don't want to go home.

MYRA: *(Rushing to hold her.)* Eleanor! Dear love!

(Eleanor sobs in her arms as the lights dim on the room. The lights come up on Barney, who is wheeling Charles into the room in a wheelchair. Charles looks old and weak, and is covered with a lap robe. Barney now wears a dark blue blazer.)

CHARLES: *(As he is being wheeled downstage center.)* Put me over there. Away from the draught… *(Looking around.)* I have the feeling I'm in this room for the last time.

BARNEY: Oh no, Dad. You're just having a bad day.

CHARLES: I'm all right. *(Pause.)* What brings you to town this time?

BARNEY: I just wanted to see you, Dad.

CHARLES: You need money?

BARNEY: No, Dad.

CHARLES: You won't get any more money from me.

BARNEY: I don't want money, Dad.

CHARLES: *(Indicating couch.)* Sit there.

BARNEY: *(Sitting on edge of chair.)* That's all right, Dad.

CHARLES: I said sit there.

BARNEY: *(Quickly.)* All right. *(He sits on the edge of the couch.)*

CHARLES: Will you see Eleanor this time?

BARNEY: No.

CHARLES: You sure?

BARNEY: I'm sure.

CHARLES: Thou shalt not covet thy brother's wife!

BARNEY: Neighbor's.

CHARLES: What?

BARNEY: It's "thy *neigh*bor's wife."

CHARLES: Doesn't matter. Nobody reads the Bible these days. *(Pause.)* They're separated now. You must know that. She's living in some miserable apartment. Can't make up her mind. Bursts into tears at parties. The children come and go. Billy sees another woman. It's very bad.

BARNEY: I'm sorry, Dad.

CHARLES: You damn well ought to be. You've been badgering the poor girl for thirty years!

BARNEY: Not any more, Dad.

CHARLES: She chose Bill.

BARNEY: I know, Dad.

CHARLES: You lost, Barney! You lost the game! Now get off the damn court! Do it! Promise me you'll leave her alone. We're not fooling around now. Promise.

(Pause.)

BARNEY: I promise I'll stay away, Dad.

CHARLES: Thank you.

BARNEY: Unless she comes to me.

CHARLES: Fair enough. *(Pause.)* I hear you've got a lot of money.

BARNEY: A little.

CHARLES: A lot. Myra told me how you made it. Peddling smut. *(Shakes his head.)* I can't discuss it.

BARNEY: I've sold out, Dad. I'm through.

CHARLES: What does it matter, anyway? There are only a few more apples in the barrel for me.

BARNEY: Oh no, Dad.

CHARLES: Oh yes. I'm going, it's all going. The club is going, did you know that?

BARNEY: I heard.

CHARLES: Oh yes. It's on the market. Nobody wants to keep it up any more. The waiters steal, the pool leaks. The men don't have time to stop by after work. The women don't bother with lunch. So it's up for sale. They plan to build some bubble in the suburbs. Held up by thin air.

BARNEY: It won't be the same, Dad.

CHARLES: I don't know who will buy this damn thing. Even the Catholics can't afford it any more. Probably some developer will break it up into doctors' offices. People will be getting rectal examinations right here in this room. *(Pause, looks at him.)* Not that you care. You never liked the club anyway.

BARNEY: I did, Dad. I always came back.

CHARLES: Just to cause trouble.

BARNEY: Not always.

CHARLES: Always.

BARNEY: Not this time, Dad. I want— *(Pause.)* I want your blessing, Dad.
(Pause.)

CHARLES: Do you know the story of the prodigal son? No, of course you
don't. Nobody reads the—

BARNEY: I know it, Dad.

CHARLES: A man has two sons, one good, one bad. The bad son comes home,
the father kills the fatted calf for him, even after all the trouble he's
caused.

BARNEY: I remember, Dad.

CHARLES: That father was a fool.

BARNEY: *(With a sigh.)* Yes, Dad.

CHARLES: Bill gets the fatted calf.
(Pause.)

BARNEY: Fair enough.

CHARLES: Well, he needs it, he has three children, he's stayed at the wheel all
these years.

BARNEY: O.K. Fine, Dad. I'm with you.

CHARLES: And all you've ever done is break up the party. Am I right? Am I
right, Barney?
(Pause. Myra appears at the door, in an older-looking dress.)

MYRA: Barney, your taxi's here.

BARNEY: Thanks.
(Myra goes off. Barney gets up.)

BARNEY: I'd better go. *(He gives his father a quick kiss on his head and starts for
the door.)* Good-bye, Dad.

CHARLES: Barney!
(Barney stops.)

CHARLES: Barney, there's a psychiatrist at the club, Jewish fella, I've forgotten
his name, who told me once that the trouble with the world is that
everyone wants to kill his father. Do you agree with that?

BARNEY: No.

CHARLES: And he said, if I understood him correctly, that's what you've been
trying to do all your life. Trying to kill me.

BARNEY: *(With a groan.)* Oh no, Dad!

CHARLES: Because if that's true, you've succeeded.

BARNEY: Oh Dad, PLEASE! *(He kneels by the wheelchair.)*

CHARLES: *(Looking at him tenderly.)* Did you really come to town just to see me?

BARNEY: To see you, Dad, I swear.

CHARLES: Oh Barney, why have you been so difficult all these years?

BARNEY: Maybe I wanted *you* to see *me*.

(*Charles stares at him for a long moment, touches him tenderly, then closes his eyes.*)

CHARLES: I'm very tired.

BARNEY: (*Getting up.*) Good-bye, Dad. (*Bends over, kisses him again and starts out.*)

CHARLES: Good-bye, Barney...thank you for stopping by.

(*Barney goes off as Myra comes in.*)

MYRA: Good-bye, Barney. (*To Charles.*) Now I think it's time for our nap. (*She begins to wheel him out.*) And then we'll have our blue pills, and one cocktail, and two poached eggs with Walter Cronkite.

CHARLES: I want to change my will, Myra.

MYRA: Oh Charles, not again.

CHARLES: I want to make things fair and square.

MYRA: We'll discuss it later, Charles.

CHARLES: He's a good boy.

MYRA: Billy's a good boy.

CHARLES: They're both good boys. We didn't do so badly after all, Helen.

MYRA: Helen? Charlie, I'm Myra. Really I must ask you to stop confusing me with your first wife.

(*She wheels him out as the lights darken. When they come up again, Barney is standing at the fireplace holding his speech, dressed in his gray suit as he was at the beginning. Eleanor comes in, in black again. A funeral prelude is heard.*)

ELEANOR: Now we really *are* ready to begin, Barney. (*No answer.*) I spoke to Mother, and she said yes, all right, read your speech. But please be brief. And respectful. (*No answer.*) Did you hear me, Barney?

BARNEY: (*Turning, passionately.*) I can't do it, El. I'd stand up there and cry like a goddamn baby.

ELEANOR: (*Moving toward him.*) Oh Barney...

BARNEY: (*Tossing the speech onto the fireplace couch.*) You do it.

ELEANOR: Me?

BARNEY: (*Moving away from her.*) Go on. I'm staying in here.

(*He goes to upstage center. Eleanor picks up envelope, opens it, looks at speech.*)

ELEANOR: This isn't a speech, Barney. This is some...document.

BARNEY: (*His back to her.*) It's a deed.

ELEANOR: It's a what?

BARNEY: *(Coming downstage.)* It's a deed, it's a DEED. I went and bought the place.

ELEANOR: Bought it?

BARNEY: Bought the whole frigging CLUB! With the proceeds of my pornography business.

ELEANOR: But what for?

BARNEY: I don't know. I don't even know. I wanted to give it to the old man. *(He comes downstage right.)*

ELEANOR: *(Following him.)* I think that's wonderful.

BARNEY: It was dumb. *(He tries to get away from her.)*

ELEANOR: I think it's fabulous.

BARNEY: It was just dumb. I'm a dumb clown. All my life making faces in front of the mirror. Still doing it, and the mirror isn't even here any more!

ELEANOR: I think it's the most fantastic thing. Oh Barney, I want to go out there and tell them.

BARNEY: Fine. Do that. And tell them to clear their smellies out of the locker room so I can have the place torn down. *(He crosses to chair left center, sinks into it.)*

ELEANOR: Tear it *down?* You wouldn't do that!

BARNEY: What else can I do with the damn thing?

ELEANOR: I don't know… *(Reaching for it.)* What would Robin Hood do?

BARNEY: Oh El, come off it.

ELEANOR: No really. What does he do, at the end of the movie?

BARNEY: I don't remember.

ELEANOR: *I* remember. He wins this great contest and gets his castle back.

BARNEY: That does not happen.

ELEANOR: It does. I know it does.

BARNEY: What does he do when he gets it? Sit around? And pay huge property taxes to the Sheriff of Nottingham?

ELEANOR: Um. No. What he does is…lower the drawbridge. And open the gates. Everyone rushes in. There's singing and dancing all over the place.

BARNEY: Oh sure.

ELEANOR: It's true! And you have the feeling he'll turn it into a wonderful place. *(Pause.)* And Maid Marion helps him.

BARNEY: Take a look at the latest version. Robin dies in battle. Maid Marion is a nun.

ELEANOR: That's not my version. In mine, they get together and start the Renaissance.

(Myra comes in, in black.)

MYRA: *(Looking from one to the other.)* Just what do you two think you're doing?

BARNEY: Dreaming.

ELEANOR: No. Planning.

MYRA: There happens to be a funeral going on. Eleanor, come with me. Billy's waiting.

ELEANOR: I'll come with Barney, Mother.

MYRA: Eleanor…

ELEANOR: And sit with him, too. In front of everyone. That's that.

MYRA: *(Taking a deep breath.)* This has been a long and difficult day. I have lost a husband. Now apparently I am losing a daughter. What can I say? *Tant pis.*

BARNEY: Watch your language.

(Myra turns and starts out huffily. Barney calls to her.)

BARNEY: Hey.

(Myra stops, looks at him stonily. He gets up, goes to her, touches her hand.)

BARNEY: I'm sorry.

MYRA: Thank you, Barney.

(She goes out. Barney goes to the balcony, looks out the window.)

ELEANOR: *(Carefully.)* I'll tell you something else Maid Marion does. When the service is over, she rides out to the supermarket, where she gets a box of Toll House cookies, a quart of banana ice cream, and some smoked oysters. Then she stops at the liquor store for some Chateauneuf du Pape. Then she returns to the castle, and opens the bottle, and pours it into this cup. *(She gets the cup from downstage left, places it on the table center.)* Then she just waits to see who walks through that door. *(Pause.)*

BARNEY: Do you think…after all these years…I could walk through that door?

ELEANOR: *(Eyes closed, anguished.)* Couldn't you?

BARNEY: Hell no! I'd come through the window!

(He opens the windows wide and then comes downstage to join her. Eleanor puts the deed in the cup, faces him. The funeral music begins offstage. People begin to sing: "A Mighty Fortress is Our God." Barney bows to Eleanor, offers her his arm. She takes it. They stride off joyfully, as if to their own wedding. The cup on the table catches the last of the light.)

The End

The Wayside
Motor Inn

(1977)

AUTHOR'S NOTE

The Wayside Motor Inn was also panned by the critics when it opened, and hasn't done very well since. I wrote it under a Rockefeller Playwright-in-Residency at the Manhattan Theatre Club, and I'm afraid my fascination with the play's complicated structure, coupled with my admiration for the English playwright Alan Ayckbourn, made it more a puzzle to be solved than a play to be performed. Some of its individual scenes may work up some steam, but for some reason when they are juxtaposed, they tend to cancel each other out. I keep suggesting to composers that the play's synchronicity might make it work as a musical or opera, but so far, no one has taken even that notion very far.

ORIGINAL PRODUCTION

The Wayside Motor Inn was first presented as a workshop production at the Manhattan Theatre Club, 321 East 73rd St., New York City, on November 3rd, 1977. It was produced by Lynne Meadow with the following cast:

Ray	Drew Snyder
Frank	Thomas Barbour
Jessie	Margaret Barker
Vince	John Braden
Mark	Richard Sale
Phil	Gary Cookson
Sally	Catherine Schreiber
Andy	Wayne Tippit
Ruth	Jill Andre
Sharon	Jill O'Hara

It was directed by Tony Giordano. Johnna Murray was the Production Stage Manager. David Potts designed the set, Kenneth M. Yount the costumes, Spencer Mosse the lighting, and George Hansen the sound.

TIME
The present

PLACE
A motel outside of Boston

CAST OF CHARACTERS

(In order of appearance)

Ray, early thirties, a sales representative for a large corporation
Frank, late sixties, a retired executive
Jessie, late sixties, his wife
Phil, early twenties, a student
Sally, early twenties, a student
Vince, early fifties, a businessman
Mark, late 'teens, his son
Andy, early forties, a doctor
Ruth, early forties, his wife
Sharon, thirties, a waitress

The play is composed of five separate subplots which take place simultaneously in one room of a suburban motor lodge outside of Boston during the late afternoon and early evening of a spring day in the late seventies.

The decor for this room is so-called "Early American": furniture stained to look like old pine or maple; busy Revolutionary War patterns on the wallpaper, bedspreads, and cushions; wastebaskets like drums, ashtrays like porringers, lamps like lanterns; cheap Currier and Ives prints on the walls.

The room is composed of the following general areas: Upstage, two double beds, separated by a telephone table, with a bureau, mirror, and chair nearby; an "executive area," containing a low round working table with an overhead hanging lantern-lamp, two chairs, and a TV nearby on a low stand; a writing-desk, again in colonial style, with a matching chair and having another telephone; a dressing area by the bathroom door, with two dressing stools, a mirror, and a closet full of rattly hangers; a small balcony, with a light, a portable chair, and a low railing.

While all the characters move from time to time around the entire room, most of them tend to have a particular area where they seem most at home. Ray settles by the executive area, with the phone and the TV; Frank needs his bed; Jessie putters about the dresser or the telephone table near him; Phil and Sally seem usually to be dressing or undressing by the closet; Mark is either in the bathroom or sprawled on the second bed; Vince likes to read out on the balcony; Andy hangs around the writing desk. Sharon and Ruth are less associated with a specific stage area.

NOTE

This play is about ten ordinary people who find themselves at the wayside of their lives, wondering which turn to take. Their difficulties and conflicts are commonplace, but I have attempted to give a dimension and resonance to their situations by presenting them side by side, and in some cases, simultaneously on stage. It is my hope that in this way we can make the ordinary seem somehow extraordinary, just as several simple melodies enhance each other when they are interwoven in a musical ensemble piece.

There are certain traps for actors here, however. Musicians can put down their instruments and rest at various moments in a work. Actors in this play can't. Whenever their scene is being interrupted or amplified by a concurrent scene, they must constantly maintain an organic sense of character, by feeling, being, or doing something appropriate. There must never be a "choral" tone to this play. Let the actors listen to the rhythms of their role and the roles of those acting with them, and all will be well. Otherwise, the play will have a stop-start, artificial, and mechanical tone to it.

The Wayside Motor Inn

ACT I

At curtain: The room is empty. It looks clean, neat, and bright in the late afternoon sun. After a moment, we hear the sound of a key in a lock, a door opening, a moment, a door closing. Then Ray, a sales representative, enters from the left. Ray enters with a procedure he has worked out from entering a million motels just like this one. He has his overnight bag in one hand, his working briefcase in the other, and because he has already stopped by the ice-dispenser at the end of the hall, he also carries a paper carton of ice cubes. He has his door key in his mouth. He drops his suitcase first, and then puts the ice container down on the low "executive" table. With his door key out of his mouth, he now can continue to chew his gum and hum a vague tune. He puts his briefcase neatly on the table. Then he turns on the television. It takes a moment to warm up. As it does, swinging his key, he checks the mattress and looks in the bathroom. Then he hangs his jacket neatly on a hanger in the open closet opposite the bathroom door. He continues his ritual of arrival. He puts his room key neatly down next to his briefcase. He takes his cigarettes and butane lighter out of a coat pocket and places them neatly next to the ashtray. From his inside pocket, he takes his address book and ballpoint pen and places them by his briefcase. Then he opens his suitcase, takes out a partially used bottle of bourbon, and places it by the ice. Then he puts his suitcase on the rack over the closet. He is like a hunter staking down his campsite at the end of the day. By now, the TV has warmed up and has been playing under Ray's activities. It is some late afternoon game show, where contestants are being humiliated for the sake of a prize. Ray doesn't pay much attention at first. He has turned it on more to fill up the loneliness of his room.

TV MC'S VOICE: Where you from, Shirley?
FEMALE CONTESTANT: Minerva, Ohio.
 (Applause from audience.)
TV MC'S VOICE: First time away from home, Shirley?
SHIRLEY'S VOICE: Yes. I'm here with my girlfriend.
 (More applause.)
TV MC'S VOICE: And do you like Hollywood, Shirley?

SHIRLEY'S VOICE: Oh we love it.

(Squeals and applause.)

TV MC'S VOICE: Well. Are you ready to play "You Name It"?

SHIRLEY'S VOICE: I hope I am.

TV MC'S VOICE: Then why don't you step into the booth.

(Creepy music. Giggles from audience.)

TV MC'S VOICE: ...And now Shirley is in—ha, ha—solitary confinement.

(Laughter from TV audience.)

TV MC'S VOICE: Let's speak to her over the intercom...can you hear me, Shirley?

SHIRLEY'S VOICE: *(Hollow sound.)* Yes.

TV MC'S VOICE: Can you see me, Shirley?

SHIRLEY'S VOICE: No.

TV MC'S VOICE: Can you see or hear our studio audience, Shirley?

SHIRLEY'S VOICE: No.

(Whoops of laughter from audience.)

TV MC'S VOICE: We will leave Shirley in solitary during this brief message.

(Soupy music is heard, perhaps advertising life insurance or retirement. Frank and Jessie come into their area. They are both exhausted, having been on the road all day. Their clothes are a little rumpled. Frank sits heavily on the edge of the first bed, and loosens his tie. Jessie stands looking at him. They don't see Ray, nor Ray, them. Ray goes off to the bathroom. By now, the TV is only subliminally audible.)

JESSIE: Are you all right?

FRANK: Fine.

(He reaches into his pocket for a bottle of pills. Jessie notices.)

JESSIE: You are not all right.

FRANK: I'm perfectly fine. *(He takes out a pill.)*

JESSIE: I'll get you some water.

FRANK: I'll get it. *(He gets up slowly.)*

JESSIE: Let me.

FRANK: I'll get it, Jess.

(He goes off into the bathroom, with his pills. Jessie fussily turns down the bed. The TV continues underneath almost inaudibly. It should never distract us from the stage events; the following TV dialogue is simply filler.)

TV MC'S VOICE: Now, Shirley, do you want to stay where you are, or do you want to escape?

SHIRLEY'S VOICE: I want to escape.

(Squeals from TV audience. Ray returns, carrying a tumbler from the bathroom,

still in it's sanitized wrapper. He uncovers the tumbler, holds open the wrapper, and neatly spits his gum into it. Then he folds the wrapper and puts it in a nearby wastebasket, which is probably shaped to imitate a Colonial drum.)

TV MC'S VOICE: Which door do you want us to open, Shirley? The red, the white, or the blue?

(Squeals from TV audience "The Red!" "The Blue!")

SHIRLEY'S VOICE: I don't know.

(Frank comes back from the bathroom carrying a tumbler of water and his pill bottle. He puts them both carefully on the bedside table, and sits down heavily again on the edge of the bed.)

JESSIE: *(Watching solicitously.)* How many did you take?

FRANK: Just one.

JESSIE: Tell me the truth.

FRANK: Just *one*, Jess.

TV MC'S VOICE: Now if you choose the red door, you stay with what you've got.

(Audience squeals "Stay," "Choose." Ray makes himself a drink with his bourbon and ice. He uses the melted water from the ice container to top it off.)

TV MC'S VOICE: And the white door is double or nothing.

(More audience squeals.)

JESSIE: You should have let me do the driving.

FRANK: Oh Jess.

JESSIE: At least part of the time.

FRANK: What about trucks?

JESSIE: I'm getting better about trucks.

FRANK: You clutch the dashboard every time they go by.

JESSIE: Well I've just got to learn to live with trucks, that's all.

(Jessie fusses at the bureau. Ray has made his drink by now. He taps himself out a cigarette, lights it briskly with a butane lighter, and settles back to watch TV.)

TV MC'S VOICE: And the blue door is something else entirely.

SHIRLEY'S VOICE: I just don't know what to do.

FRANK: *(Pulling at his collar.)* Is it hot in here?

JESSIE: Not especially.

FRANK: It feels hot.

JESSIE: I'll open these doors.

(She comes downstage to open the "sliding doors." Frank watches her, then surreptitiously takes another pill.)

SHIRLEY'S VOICE: I think…I think I'll choose the blue door!

(Squeals from the audience.)

TV MC'S VOICE: Are you sure, Shirley?

SHIRLEY'S VOICE: Yes. I'm sure. I want the blue.

(More squeals. TV suspense music.)

JESSIE: *(Trying to open the "sliding door.")* The doors don't open.

FRANK: Why not?

JESSIE: There's an air conditioner instead.

FRANK: I hate those things. *(He gets up heavily from the bed.)* I'll help you with those doors.

JESSIE: I'll *do* it, Frank.

FRANK: You'll need help.

(He puts on his glasses, looks at the lock. Meanwhile, Ray opens his work briefcase, takes out a series of documents which he arranges neatly and routinely in front of him. Then he takes out a pocket calculator, plugs it in, and begins to add up figures in columns. He occasionally smokes, occasionally sips his drink, occasionally glances at the TV, perfectly at home in this place. Frank gets the "door" open after a struggle.)

FRANK: There.

JESSIE: *(Looking at "doors.")* Why do they make things so difficult?

FRANK: *(Returning to the bed.)* That was a rape-lock.

JESSIE: A what?

FRANK: I read it somewhere. That's so people can't get in through the balcony and rape us.

JESSIE: *(Backing away.)* Mercy.

(Vince and Mark enter, from left. Vince is snappily dressed. He carries a bag, the key, and a stack of brochures and maps. A camera is slung over his shoulder. Mark, informally dressed, carries a knapsack.)

VINCE: *(Passing the balcony.)* Hey look! A balcony! With a view!

(Mark tosses his knapsack on the second bed and heads immediately into the bathroom.)

FRANK: *(Starting to take off his jacket.)* I think I might lie down for a minute.

JESSIE: *(Trying to help.)* Here. Let me.

FRANK: I can do it, Jess. I'm not an invalid. *(He gets his jacket off.)*

VINCE: *(Calling in to Mark as he hangs up his jacket.)* Hey I bet I can get some great shots from that balcony. *(He crosses back to the balcony with his camera.)*

JESSIE: *(Taking Frank's jacket.)* May I at least hang it up for you?

FRANK: Yes, love. You may do that.

(Jessie goes to the closet with his jacket. Frank takes off his shoes.)

VINCE: *(Calling to Mark from balcony.)* Hey, Mark! Come out here and get a load of this! We got the whole world spread out before us!

(Meanwhile, Ray's TV continues subliminally: loud squeals from audience.)

TV MC'S VOICE: Look what you got, Shirley! You got the Golden Door!

(More squeals.)

TV MC'S VOICE: Now, Shirley: if you open the Golden Door, you will either have to stay in solitary confinement *or* you will win a special ticket to FREEDOM. Why don't we let Shirley think about that during the following brief message?

(TV commercial.)

VINCE: *(Calling in again.)* You hear me? Come out here. Look at this, while it's still light. *(He gazes out at the view.)*

JESSIE: *(At closet.)* I'm having a terrible time with these hangers.

FRANK: *(Lying down; closing his eyes.)* Hmmm?

JESSIE: They have these nice wooden hangers, but I can't get them out.

FRANK: People steal them.

(Jessie gets his coat hung up, turns to him.)

JESSIE: People steal *hang*ers?

FRANK: I hear they do.

JESSIE: Oh my heavens. *(She returns to sit on the bed beside him.)*

TV MC'S VOICE: Now Shirley. Have you made up your mind?

SHIRLEY'S VOICE: Yes. I want to open the Golden Door!

(Pandemonium from TV audience, music, fanfare.)

TV MC'S VOICE: Open it, then. Open the Golden Door and let's see whether Shirley gets her ticket to freedom!

(Suspense music.)

JESSIE: Why would anyone want to steal a coat hanger?

(Ray watches the TV fascinated.)

JESSIE: I mean, you *get* hangers. Free. From the cleaners. Most people have too many hangers.

SHIRLEY'S VOICE: Oh I'm gonna die…I'm gonna die…

JESSIE: I suppose it's the wood, isn't it? It's really the wood they want. *(She ponders.)*

TV MC'S VOICE: *(Over fanfare music. Audience squeals.)* AND it's your ticket to freedom, Shirley: a nineteen seventy-eight Ford four-door LTD sedan, with AM-FM radio, interior color coordinated by a leading decorator, fully automatic—

(Ray shrugs, turns the TV off returns to working on his figures.)

VINCE: *(Calling in from balcony.)* Hey, Mark! Come out here! On the double! You ought to see this!

(Jessie looks at Frank, looks at the telephone on the table by the bed.)

JESSIE: I suppose I should call Joannie.

FRANK: In a minute.

JESSIE: She'll want to know we're here.

FRANK: In a minute, love.

(He closes his eyes. She sighs, waits patiently, holding his hand. Vince comes back into the room from the balcony.)

VINCE: *(Calling in toward bathroom.)* What's going on in there?

MARK: *(Coming out of the bathroom.)* I was in the bathroom.

VINCE: You just went to the bathroom. We had to stop in Springfield so you could go to the bathroom.

MARK: My stomach's acting up.

VINCE: Again?

MARK: I get nervous, Dad.

VINCE: You O.K. now?

MARK: I'm O.K.

(Vince leads him out onto the balcony.)

VINCE: *(Indicating the view.)* I just want you to see this. Look. It says in the brochure that three major arteries meet right here. See? One, two, and three. Learn something every day.

(Mark looks out; Vince reads from the brochure.)

VINCE: "…A major feat of highway engineering…first cloverleaf in the country…designed to eliminate the stop sign…" *(Looks out.)* See? Nobody stops.

MARK: Is that good?

VINCE: Sure it's good. Of course it's good.

(Looks at Mark. Mark looks out. Phil and Sally come in from left. They are a pair of young students, good-looking, informally dressed. They both carry knapsacks. Phil carries the key.)

PHIL: *(Unenthusiastically.)* What do you think?

SALLY: *(Unenthusiastically.)* I love it.

PHIL: Here's the bathroom. *(Looks in.)* Come on. Look at the bathroom. *(He goes into bathroom.)*

SALLY: *(Not looking.)* It's a beautiful bathroom. *(She sits on the second bed.)*

JESSIE: *(On the bed, nostalgically; to Frank.)* I remember the first time I came to Boston. With my mother.

VINCE: *(Reading again from the brochure.)* Listen to this: "The Wayside Motor Inn takes its name from the celebrated poem by Henry Wadsworth Longfellow." You read it?

MARK: Read what?

VINCE: The celebrated poem.

MARK: No.

VINCE: Neither have I.

PHIL: *(Coming out of bathroom.)* It's got everything. John, tub, shower. Look at all the towels.

SALLY: *(Not looking.)* Fabulous.

(Vince and Mark look out.)

JESSIE: We stayed at the Copley Plaza Hotel.

PHIL: And there's an infrared light in case you get cold. And that doo-dad there is for instant coffee.

SALLY: *(Trying to be excited.)* Wow.

JESSIE: I was meeting some boy for the Harvard game.

PHIL: *(Gesturing around the room.)* And color TV, and two double beds, and this one here has magic fingers.

SALLY: Magic what?

PHIL: Fingers. Fingers. You put a quarter in and the whole bed shakes. Automatically.

SALLY: Oh God, how gross!

PHIL: No, it's great! Got a quarter?

SALLY: No. *(She hangs up a jacket sulkily.)*

JESSIE: After the game, we had tea. My mother poured.

VINCE: You'll read that poem next year. "Tales from the Wayside Inn." They'll make you read it at Harvard.

MARK: I'm not there yet, Dad.

VINCE: You will be.

MARK: Maybe.

VINCE: Oh sure. You're on your way.

(They sit on the step and look out.)

JESSIE: And after tea, we went to the theatre: me, and the boy, and my mother.

PHIL: *(To Sally.)* What's the matter?

SALLY: Nothing.

JESSIE: And that was that. I said good night to the boy. And shook hands.

PHIL: Hey, come on. This is supposed to be special.

SALLY: It doesn't feel special.

PHIL: Look. It's been six whole months since we first got it on. It's our anniversary, Sal.

SALLY: It doesn't feel like an anniversary.

PHIL: You wait. It will. Just think: no roommates to barge in, no parents checking beds, no cold sleeping bags, no sand…oh my God, Sal. We can be together all night long! I'm so excited I've got to go pee! *(He goes back into the bathroom.)*

VINCE: *(Reading from brochure.)* "To the east, two mighty structures dominate the horizon: the Prudential and John Hancock Insurance buildings." *(He looks out.)* See, Mark? There they are!

(Sally makes up her mind about something, gets her knapsack, sits on the second bed.)

JESSIE: I think I should call Joannie.

FRANK: Not yet.

JESSIE: She'll begin to worry.

FRANK: I dread getting back into that car.

JESSIE: It's only about five more miles.

FRANK: I still dread it. How many years, Jess, have you and I spent sitting in cars, facing front, staring at some road?

JESSIE: We should have flown.

FRANK: Not on your life.

JESSIE: You used to like flying.

FRANK: Never. You will never get me into a plane again.

JESSIE: All right.

FRANK: Planes and hospitals. Never again.

JESSIE: All right, dear.

FRANK: Death traps, both of them. Walk into a plane or a hospital, you're a lamb going to slaughter.

JESSIE: All right, all right.

FRANK: Herding you through those tunnels, prodding you with those security things, strapping you down…

JESSIE: All right, dear.

SALLY: *(Who has found a small checkbook in her knapsack, calling towards bathroom.)* How much do I owe you?

PHIL'S VOICE: What?

SALLY: How much? I want to know. *(She gets out a ballpoint pen, poises it over her checkbook.)*

FRANK: Stewardesses and nurses bending over you, smiling, patronizing you, giving you bad food on trays—angels of death, that's what they are.

JESSIE: Yes dear. I get the picture. *(She shudders, goes to the bureau.)*

PHIL: *(Coming out of the bathroom.)* You don't owe me a thing.

SALLY: I want to make this fair and square. How much?

PHIL: My treat.

SALLY: I want to pay.

PHIL: Lookit, I got a birthday check from my grandmother. She said to buy something I liked.

SALLY: So you're buying *me*?

PHIL: I'm buying the night.

SALLY: *(Pen poised.)* Then so am I. How much?

PHIL: Sixteen.

SALLY: Six*teen? Dollars?*

PHIL: Thirty-two, altogether.

SALLY: Jesus.

PHIL: I asked for the best.

SALLY: *(Making out the check.)* All right. Sixteen.

FRANK: When I go, it won't be in a plane or a hospital. I want to be my own man.

JESSIE: Nobody's going anywhere, *please.*

SALLY: *(Handing Phil the check.)* There. Sixteen.

PHIL: I don't see why you're making such a big deal about paying.

SALLY: I don't want to feel obligated.

VINCE: *(To Mark; looking out.)* Isn't this something? Looking at cars. It kind of hypnotizes you. Everyone going every which way.

FRANK: At least in a car you're free.

SALLY: I want to be free.

PHIL: Free? To do what?

SALLY: Free to—I don't know.

VINCE: Look for Harvard. Maybe we can see Harvard.

PHIL: *(Going to Sally.)* So do you feel free now?

SALLY: Perfectly.

PHIL: Want to fool around?

SALLY: Now?

PHIL: Sure.

SALLY: *(Defiantly.)* All right.

(They start getting undressed by the closet.)

VINCE: *(Looking out; to Mark.)* Wouldn't it be something to live in a place like this?

MARK: Live *here?*

VINCE: I mean, with a view. So you could see the whole thing: where you've been...where you're going...

JESSIE: I've got to call Joannie.

FRANK: Next year they come to us.

JESSIE: Dearie, they can't. We don't have room anymore.

FRANK: I'll pay for their motel.

JESSIE: They still can't. They have too much equipment. My father used to say there are only two ways to travel. First class. Or with children. One's heaven, the other's hell.

FRANK: All travel is hell.

JESSIE: Well, I'm calling Joannie. *(She sits down next to phone at bedside table.)*

VINCE: *(Looking out.)* Hey! There's a white steeple. That must be it. That must be Harvard. A little to the left of the Prudential. There's *your* insurance, buddy. Harvard University. Come on, stand here. I'll take your picture with Harvard in the background. *(Vince poses Mark on the balcony.)*

MARK: Oh Dad...

SALLY: *(Stopping undressing.)* What did you tell them at the desk?

PHIL: *(Stopping undressing.)* Nothing.

SALLY: Did you say we were married?

PHIL: Hell no.

SALLY: Then what did you say? Do they think I'm a call girl?

PHIL: I just paid, Sal. They don't care as long as you pay.

(They continue getting undressed.)

VINCE: Smile.

(He takes Mark's picture. Mark starts in.)

VINCE: Hold it. Another, for Mom.

(Mark continues in.)

VINCE: Where you going?

MARK: In.

VINCE: You got diarrhea again?

MARK: I thought I'd watch TV.

VINCE: TV? Jesus, Christ, you get in the car, click, on goes the rock and roll. You arrive here, click, on goes the TV.

MARK: I just want to see what's going on, Dad.

VINCE: I'll tell you what's going on. *(Indicating the view.)* This is going on.

MARK: TV calms me down. O.K.?

VINCE: Read a *book* once in awhile. It'll help with Harvard.

MARK: O.K. Dad.

> *(He continues on in, lies down on the second bed, reads* Motor Trend Magazine. *Jessie is getting out her paraphernalia for telephoning: glasses, address book.)*

JESSIE: You'd think I'd know my own daughter's telephone number. But I refuse to clutter my brain with figures.

VINCE: *(Calling after Mark.)* Look in my bag. There's a package.

MARK: Huh?

VINCE: I got something for you in my bag!

> *(Vince returns to balcony to look at Harvard. Ray continues his work.)*

SALLY: *(Stopping undressing.)* By the way, have you done anything about next year?

PHIL: Next year?

SALLY: Have you told them?

PHIL: Told who what?

SALLY: Have you told your roommates to move out so I can move in?

PHIL: *(Stopping undressing.)* No.

SALLY: Knew it.

JESSIE: *(Fussing with telephone.)* I can't seem to get through here.

FRANK: *(Eyes closed.)* Hmmm?

> *(Jessie tries dialing again.)*

SALLY: Why haven't you?

PHIL: Haven't gotten around to it.

SALLY: You don't want to live with me.

PHIL: Come on, Sal.

SALLY: *(Sitting down on a dressing stool.)* You're avoiding it like the plague.

PHIL: It's a big decision.

SALLY: Maybe I should just stay in the dorm next year.

PHIL: Let's decide tomorrow.

SALLY: Why tomorrow?

PHIL: I mean, after tonight.

> *(Pause. She looks at him.)*

JESSIE: I *still* can't get through. I must be doing something very wrong.

FRANK: *(Eyes closed.)* Dial the desk.

JESSIE: All right. I'll try that.

SALLY: You mean everything depends on this one night?

PHIL: Why live together if we're sexually incompatible?

JESSIE: How do you dial the desk?

FRANK: Try dialing "0."

JESSIE: *(Reading dial.)* Oh yes. "0" says desk. Live and learn. *(She dials "0" carefully.)*

SALLY: Oh boy. Talk about laying a trip on someone.

PHIL: Listen, these things are important. Jim moved in with Nancy last year, and they discovered serious sexual difficulties.

SALLY: Such as?

PHIL: Never mind, but he got so upset, he flunked biochemistry.

SALLY: Poor Jim. *(She starts getting dressed.)*

JESSIE: Something's ringing, but nobody's answering.

PHIL: Yeah well I don't want to flunk. I want to get into medical school.

SALLY: And I want to get my master's in English, but that doesn't mean I have to take an exam in bed!

JESSIE: Ah! Success!…This is Room 404. Could you tell me how to dial out, please?

PHIL: What's the matter with you, Sal?

JESSIE: I want to dial my daughter in Sudbury. Would you get her for me?…No? All right. Then please tell me how.

SALLY: I refuse to be put on the line this way.

PHIL: Put on the *line?*

JESSIE: Nine. Thank you…good-bye. *(Hangs up.)* You dial nine.

FRANK: Sometimes it's eight.

JESSIE: Well it's nine here. *(She dials carefully.)*

SALLY: *(Getting dressed quickly.)* I'm sorry. Thank God I paid. Now I can leave without feeling one bit guilty.

PHIL: *(Starting to get dressed.)* You know what I think, Sal?

SALLY: No. What do you think, Phil?

PHIL: I think you wanted to walk out all along.

(She looks at him.)

PHIL: I think you paid so you could walk out.

JESSIE: *(On telephone; to Frank.)* Something's happening.

PHIL: I think you're basically scared of sexual relations.

(Sally looks at him.)

JESSIE: Yes, it's ringing…

SALLY: Well, I think you're scared of personal commitments.

PHIL: So what do we do?

(Ray is finishing his work. He arranges the results neatly in front of him,

pours himself another drink, lights another cigarette, and begins to dial the telephone. He dials briskly and efficiently, a long series of numbers.)

SALLY: I think we should talk it out.

PHIL: Fine.

SALLY: Not here. I feel trapped here.

PHIL: There's a bar down below. We could have a beer.

SALLY: I need something stronger, frankly.

JESSIE: Still ringing...how peculiar...

PHIL: Have what you want. It's a free country. *(He starts for the door.)*

JESSIE: *(On telephone.)* Darling! We're here!...Oh we're fine. Daddy's a little tired, but we're fine!...

RAY: *(On telephone; reciting automatically.)* Nine oh four...six five two...eight plus seven...holding...

JESSIE: What took you so long to answer?

SALLY: *(Following Phil.)* They'll probably ask for my I.D. Which I don't have.

PHIL: Nobody *cares,* Sal. I keep telling you. Nobody cares as long as you pay. Come on...

(He goes out left; she follows.)

JESSIE: *(On telephone.)* Oh how marvelous! *(To Frank.)* She was nursing the baby. *(To telephone.)* What? *(To Frank.)* She still *is!* *(To telephone.)* Oh I can't wait to get my hands on him!

RAY: *(On telephone.)* New England one three seven...Sales Rep nine five...request computer connection...

JESSIE: *(On telephone.)* Now listen, darling, Daddy's resting, so we'll be over in a little while...The Wayside? Oh yes. It's very convenient. A little— impersonal maybe, but very convenient all around.

RAY: *(On telephone; speaking extra clearly.)* Repeat: request computer connection.

JESSIE: All right, lovey. Good-bye.

(Hangs up. Mark finally gets up from the bed, rummages in the bag for Vince's present.)

RAY: *(On telephone.)* Hey!

JESSIE: She's feeding the children.

FRANK: Must be a madhouse.

JESSIE: Bob's still at work.

RAY: *(On telephone.)* Hey! *(He dials a couple of additional digits, angrily.)*

JESSIE: She was nursing the baby. On the telephone. Doesn't that sound marvelous?

FRANK: No, it sounds complicated.

JESSIE: Oh I wish I could be there, Frank.

FRANK: I don't.

JESSIE: That's because you're systematically turning into an old grump.

(Andy, about forty, comes in from left. He is informally dressed, but expensively so: a good sweater, good slacks, perhaps a parka. He carries an attaché case and a container of ice. He comes quickly to the desk, puts down his stuff, picks up the phone, then hesitates, and puts it down again. He sits at the desk, looking at the phone, then goes to hang up his parka.)

RAY: *(On telephone.)* Hey, Virginia, this is Ray. What's this? You put me on hold without telling me...new *policy?* Putting a man on hold without *tell*ing him?...Can't you just say we're putting you on hold?...I don't care about the music, you put a man on hold, you tell him...you say, "We have to put you on hold, sir"...O.K., O.K., Virginia, put me on hold...

(He smokes, drinks, does paperwork as he holds. Mark comes to the edge of the balcony carrying a cellophane-wrapped pink oxford-cloth button-down shirt.)

MARK: This?

VINCE: That's for you.

MARK: Me?

VINCE: For tonight and tomorrow.

MARK: I already got a shirt, Dad.

VINCE: Try it on.

MARK: This?

VINCE: Go on.

MARK: It's *pink,* Dad.

VINCE: So what?

MARK: I hate pink.

VINCE: It's what they wear.

MARK: Big deal.

VINCE: Put it on.

(Mark goes in skeptically; Vince calls after him.)

VINCE: There's a tie for you, too!

(Mark goes reluctantly to dressing area to try it on. Andy makes up his mind again, and dials the telephone quickly. Jessie gets up and goes to bureau.)

FRANK: *(Opening his eyes.)* Where're you going?

JESSIE: *(Getting car keys.)* I thought I'd do something about the bags.

ANDY: *(On telephone.)* Billy? Hi. It's Dad. Would you call Mom to the...Billy?

(Billy has hung up. Andy jiggles the receiver, then slams the phone down, thinks.)

FRANK: *(Slowly sitting up.)* I'd better help.

JESSIE: You stay right where you are.

FRANK: I'm not going to let you bring in the bags.

JESSIE: I'll find a bellboy.

FRANK: They don't have any bellboys.

JESSIE: *(Waving a dollar bill.)* I'll find someone.

FRANK: Be sure you do, Jess.

> *(Frank lies back down. Jessie goes out. Andy makes up his mind to dial once more. He dials angrily, and waits as it rings.)*

ANDY: *(On telephone, forcefully.)* Billy, I want to speak to your mother…may I speak to her, please ? Would you get her, please?…Would you get Mummy please?…Yes. Right now. *(He holds the phone, drumming his fingers impatiently on the desk.)*

RAY: *(On telephone.)* Request call back…request call back procedure…

ANDY: *(On telephone, coldly.)* Hi…I'm here…The Wayside…

RAY: *(On telephone.)* The Wayside Motor Inn…six one seven two four four five one six nine…over and out. *(Hangs up.)*

ANDY: Can I come over?

> *(Ray dials a single digit.)*

ANDY: Why the hell not?

RAY: *(On telephone.)* Gimme the coffee shop.

ANDY: How do we settle things then, Ruth?

RAY: *(On phone.)* Gimme room service.

ANDY: O.K. Fine. You come over here.

RAY: This is Room 302.

ANDY: Room 127.

RAY: Gimme a cheeseburger.

ANDY: I'll be here. Where else would I be?

RAY: Ketchup. The works.

ANDY: Lay off, Ruth. Just come over. All right? *(He hangs up angrily.)*

RAY: Salad go with that?…Gimme salad.

> *(Andy takes a bottle out of his attaché case, takes the ice container, and goes into the bathroom to make a drink.)*

RAY: Blue cheese extra here? What the hell, gimme blue cheese.

> *(Mark is now wearing the pink shirt and a knitted tie. The shirt is half tucked in and buttoned wrong, the tie poorly tied.)*

MARK: It doesn't fit, Dad.

VINCE: *(Looking up.)* Huh?

MARK: It doesn't fit.

VINCE: *(Going to Mark.)* No wonder. You got it on wrong. Here. *(He begins to struggle with unbuttoning and re-buttoning the shirt.)*

RAY: *(On phone.)* Whatcha got for pie? O.K. Give me apple.

VINCE: *(To Mark.)* Hold still while I do this.

RAY: What do I get for beverage?…O.K. Gimme coffee. And a beer…Room 302. Thanks, Sweetheart.

(Ray hangs up, begins to read Penthouse *magazine.)*

VINCE: *(Buttoning Mark's shirt.)* When I was at State, all the fraternity boys wore shirts like this.

MARK: Not pink.

VINCE: Sure, pink. I ought to know. I had the laundry concession. Every Monday, I picked up thirty, forty shirts like this, took 'em to the laundry, brought 'em back Friday, washed and ironed, ready for the parties…hold still…made a quarter a shirt.

MARK: Only a quarter?

VINCE: That's all right. It helped pay the freight. I was married. Even then. Don't get married in college, pal. Play the field.

MARK: You already told me that twenty times.

VINCE: Here's something I never told you…hold still. *(He begins to retie Mark's tie.)* I never told you this: once I got a shirt like this for myself. Bought it on the sly. Sneaked out one Saturday night. Told your mom I was going to the library. Went to a fraternity party. Put the shirt on in the men's room. Danced with a Vassar girl. Know what happened? Everyone started ribbing me. "Look at Vince, going Ivy League. Going white shoe on us." So I took it off. Went to the library after all. *(He almost strangles Mark, tightening the tie.)* Yeah well, now I've got a son going to Harvard. *(He claps Mark on the arm, stands back, looks at him admiringly.)* You wear that for Bill Baldwin tonight and the interview tomorrow.

MARK: I brought another shirt, Dad.

VINCE: What other shirt?

MARK: I got it with Mom before we left.

VINCE: Where? Sears? The five and ten?

MARK: It's a good shirt, Dad. Ask Mom.

VINCE: She's not here, pal.

MARK: I wish she was. She'd tell you it looks good.

VINCE: That's why she's not here. *(He goes back out onto the balcony.)*

MARK: *(Following him out.)* Did you tell her not to come?

VINCE: I told her it was boys' night out.

MARK: Why'd you tell her that?

VINCE: Because she's holding you back, buddy.

MARK: How? How is she?

VINCE: Oh look, pal. Your mom is a lovely lady on her own turf. But you've got to learn to say good-bye. To her. And then to me. I did. I said good-bye to my folks when I went to State. Didn't even say it in English. But it had to be said. That's what this country's all about. Moving. Up and away. Oh you'll come home for a while. Christmas, Thanksgiving. You'll bring a friend. First, a boy. Then a girl. And your mom and I will embarrass you. You'll say to yourself, "Who are these people? Who are these clods?" And then you'll stay away.

MARK: Never. I'll always come home.

VINCE: Hey, listen. You're in the major leagues now, friend. The best I can do now is shove you out on the field. Just think, pal. In one hour, you'll be having drinks right downstairs with Bill Baldwin. He's an important Harvard alumnus.

MARK: So I have to wear this.

VINCE: Sure. Wear it. Show him you're one of them. He'll write you a personal recommendation on executive stationery from Cabot, Cabot, and Forbes.

(Mark sighs, and looks out at the traffic. Jessie comes back into her room, carrying a dress bag.)

JESSIE: I'm furious.

(Frank opens his eyes.)

JESSIE: Oh I'm sorry.

FRANK: I was awake.

JESSIE: Well, I'm simply furious! I couldn't find anyone to bring in the bags.

(She crosses to the closet to hang up the bag, take out the dress.)

FRANK: Did you ask at the desk?

JESSIE: They said they don't provide that service.

FRANK: I'll get them later.

JESSIE: No you won't. Not with that heart.

FRANK: I put them in.

JESSIE: Well it's harder to take them out. *(Jessie returns to her chair by Frank's bed.)*

MARK: *(Looking out.)* What's so hot about Harvard, anyway?

VINCE: Huh?

MARK: What's so hot about Harvard?

VINCE: I keep telling you: you go to Harvard, you can write your own ticket.

MARK: Can you wear your own shirt?

VINCE: Wise guy.

MARK: I mean it, Dad. *(He goes back to the closet to put on his old shirt.)*

VINCE: *(Calling after him.)* Wise guy. *(Vince reads a brochure, shakes his head.)*

JESSIE: *(Crossing back to Frank's bed.)* They said they *might* be able to help, once things settle down.

(She takes out her knitting and works on something for the baby. Andy comes out of the bathroom with his drink. He goes to his desk, takes out his work from his attaché case, tries to concentrate on it. Ray puts down Penthouse *and dials a single digit.)*

RAY: *(On telephone.)* Collect call to my wife…area code 516…249… 3168… name's Ray…

JESSIE: Or that nice strong boy we saw with his father in the parking lot. *He* could bring in the bags. If I knew where he was.

RAY: *(On telephone.)* Hi, honey. You said to call, so I'm calling.

JESSIE: Or Bob can come over and do it. When he gets home. *If* he gets home.

RAY: *(On telephone.)* I'm not checking up. You said to call.

JESSIE: *(Stabbing angrily at her knitting.)* I'm just furious.

(Frank closes his eyes.)

RAY: *(On telephone.)* Look, are we married or not? I'm just calling home!…

(Mark, now wearing his old shirt, calls across to Vince.)

MARK: Dad…

RAY: *(On telephone.)* Who called the Ramada last night? Who's checking on who?

VINCE: *(From balcony, reading a brochure.)* Hmmm?

RAY: *(On telephone.)* I'm at the Wayside. Where else?

MARK: *(To Vince.)* Did Mr. Foley call you?

RAY: *(On telephone.)* Believe me, honey, that's where I am.

MARK: Dad…

RAY: *(On telephone.)* Sure I'm alone…

VINCE: *(Still reading.)* Who's Foley?

RAY: *(On telephone.)* I'm always alone, what d'you think?

MARK: You know who he is, Dad.

RAY: *(On telephone.)* How about you? Are you alone? Huh? Huh? How about that?

VINCE: That creep from your school?

MARK: He's not a creep. He's my guidance counselor.

VINCE: I think he's a creep.

RAY: *(On telephone.)* O.K., then just don't talk to me about being alone!

MARK: He said he'd *call* you, Dad. Did he?

VINCE: *(Putting down his brochure with a sigh, coming into the room.)* Yes. Mr. Foley called.

RAY: *(On telephone.)* O.K. So we're even. So what else is new? *(He begins to settle back, thumbing through his* Penthouse, *as his wife talks.)*

MARK: Did he tell you about delayed admissions?

VINCE: Delayed what?

MARK: About taking a year off.

VINCE: He gave me some double-talk. I don't remember.

MARK: What if I did that, Dad? Took a year off.

RAY: *(On telephone.)* Uh-huh.

VINCE: Don't give me that.

MARK: Lots of guys do it.

VINCE: Says who? Foley the counselor. Some counselor. Telling a kid to drop out.

MARK: Not *out,* Dad. Just *off.* Just for a year.

VINCE: And do what?

MARK: Work.

VINCE: Where?

MARK: At Vito's garage. He said he'd take me on.

VINCE: Working on *cars?* With that crook?

MARK: I love cars, Dad.

RAY: *(On telephone; bored.)* Uh huh, uh huh, uh huh…

VINCE: You'll love Harvard.

MARK: I'm not sure I'm ready, Dad.

VINCE: You gonna tell the interviewer that? "I don't want to study history, I want to fool around with Fords."

MARK: I know what I'm doing with cars, Dad.

VINCE: You'll fall behind. You'll never catch up.

RAY: *(On telephone.)* I gotta get back to work, honey.

MARK: Mr. Foley said a year off would help my colitis, Dad.

VINCE: Is he a doctor?

MARK: He's a registered psychologist.

VINCE: Counselors, psychologists…doesn't anybody teach any more?

RAY: *(On telephone.)* Hmm…hmm.

VINCE: What are our taxes for? So these creeps can tell our kids to drop out?

MARK: What if I don't get in, Dad?

VINCE: You'll get in.

MARK: My S.A.T. scores are down.

VINCE: They're fine.

MARK: They're *down*. 540 Math, 580 verbal. That's down.

VINCE: That's because you've been farting around with cars.

MARK: They're still down.

RAY: *(On telephone.)* Uh huh, uh huh.

VINCE: Yeah. Well give 'em other scores. Tell 'em your batting average in Little League.

MARK: Oh Dad...

VINCE: *Tell* 'em. Or I'll tell 'em. I ought to know. I was the coach. Want me to tell 'em?

MARK: No.

VINCE: Tell 'em how many votes you got for student council. Tell 'em how many slum kids you worked with last summer. Tell 'em those scores.

MARK: They don't *care,* Dad.

VINCE: Sure they care. Everybody cares when a kid like you comes down the pike! Now come on. Harvard is run by smart guys who know the real score. And the real score is who you are, and who you know, and how much your old man will cough up when they pass the hat.

RAY: *(On telephone.)* Got to say bye-bye, honey...I'm on computer call-back.

VINCE: And Bill Baldwin will tell 'em that. *(Arm around Mark.)* You'll knock 'em dead, Markie.

RAY: *(Eyes closed.)* Uh huh...uh huh...uh huh...

VINCE: Harvard, then maybe medical school. Why not?

JESSIE: *(At her knitting.)* I feel so useless here.

RAY: *(On telephone.)* Uh huh...uh huh...well bye, honey...

(Mark starts into the bathroom.)

VINCE: You feel O.K.?

MARK: I'll live. *(Goes in.)*

VINCE: *(Calling after him.)* Afterwards take your shower. We got about twenty minutes before Bill Baldwin. I'll go tell the desk to keep an eye out for him. *(Vince exits left.)*

JESSIE: Poor Joannie. Trying to feed the children all by herself.

RAY: *(On telephone.)* Bye honey...Love you, too...bye bye. *(Hangs up, rolls his eyes, then gets out an address book, starts thumbing through it.)*

FRANK: Why don't you go on over?

JESSIE: What?

(Andy moves to the balcony, stands looking out, holding his drink.)

JESSIE: I didn't hear what you said, Frank.

FRANK: I said why not go on over to Joan's?

JESSIE: Alone?

FRANK: Come back for me later.

JESSIE: I'm not going to leave you alone in a miserable motel room. Honestly. *(She jabs at her knitting.)* Besides, I don't even know how to get there.

FRANK: Ask at the desk.

JESSIE: Oh the desk, the desk. There's nobody there at the desk.

FRANK: Nobody there?

JESSIE: Just some teenager.

(Ray finds a number in his address book, dials.)

JESSIE: Fussing with the telephone. Handing out keys.

(Ray waits on the telephone.)

JESSIE: Sometimes I think the entire country is run by teenagers.

RAY: *(On telephone.)* Hi Marlene. This is Ray. What're you up to tonight?

JESSIE: Whatever happened to all those nice people who used to help us when we traveled?

RAY: No, Ray…I said, Ray…we met at the Marriott…

JESSIE: All those room clerks and gasoline attendants…

RAY: You sure this is Marlene?

JESSIE: And nice polite waitresses. Where did they all go? *(She broods.)*

RAY: *(Checking his book.)* No, I'm wrong. It wasn't the Marriott. It was Ho-Jo's cocktail lounge. You brought me a stinger…yeah, and then we went out, Marlene…we talked, we danced, we did a lot of things…what d'ya mean, you don't remember?…Yeah well *I* remember, sweetheart. I remember you were a lousy screw! *(He slams down the phone.)* Bitch! *(He picks up* Penthouse *again.)*

JESSIE: I keep thinking about those people…

FRANK: What people, dear?

JESSIE: All those people who gave a hand along the way. Where are they now? Well, we're a democracy, aren't we? Maybe they all earned enough money. Maybe they're all sitting in motels, waiting to see their grandchildren.

FRANK: Go on over, Jess.

JESSIE: How can I, without you?

FRANK: Take the car.

JESSIE: Oh Frank, let's both go. Right now. Let's get out of this miserable place. We could stay with Joannie.

FRANK: They don't have room, love.

JESSIE: Of course they do.

FRANK: Three kids? One bathroom?

JESSIE: They asked us. They bought a couch for the den.

FRANK: I don't like couches.

JESSIE: It's a Castro Convertible.

FRANK: I don't like Castro.

JESSIE: I'm serious. You don't like anything any more.

FRANK: I like you, Jess.

JESSIE: Sometimes I wonder.

FRANK: Oh Jess. *(He reaches for her hand.)*

JESSIE: *(Crossing to bedside telephone.)* Then get me out of here. Let's tell them at the desk we made a mistake. We should be with our family. I could be helping. Bob could be bringing in the bags. You could be taking a nice long nap.

FRANK: I could be taking a nap right now, Jess.

(Pause. She looks at him. Then speaks coldly.)

JESSIE: Is there a roadmap in the car?

FRANK: Of course.

JESSIE: Then I just might go by myself.

FRANK: All right.

(Jessie starts out, stops, turns.)

JESSIE: Next year, I'll come alone. I'll fly down and sleep in the den and stay as long as I want!

(Frank lies back, closes his eyes. She gets a sense of premonition, goes to him, kisses him.)

JESSIE: Oh sweetie, I'm sorry. It's been a long day.

FRANK: Get going, Jess. Before it's dark.

JESSIE: *(Covering him up with a bedspread.)* For some reason, I'm frantic to see that baby.

FRANK: Watch out for trucks.

(She looks at him again, waves, then goes out quietly. A buzzer rings off left. Andy, on the balcony, starts, puts his glass on his desk, goes off to answer it. In a moment, he returns, preceded by Ruth. She is good-looking, around forty, informally dressed in a slightly Bohemian way. They remain standing, around the desk.)

RUTH: *(Looking around.)* This is kind of nice, isn't it?

ANDY: Nice?

RUTH: Well I mean it's just your meat. Very clean. Very organized.

ANDY: It's a place to stay.

RUTH: *(Looking at desk.)* Even a desk. *(She glances at his papers.)* I see you brought your work. What do you do, now you're running a hospital? Budgets? Medicaid reports?

ANDY: Lots of that.

RUTH: Do you ever see a patient now?

ANDY: Of course I do.

RUTH: I hope so. You were a good doctor.

ANDY: Still am, I hope.

RUTH: I mean, the human touch. The bedside manner. All that's important.

ANDY: I think so too.

    (Pause.)

RUTH: Do you have a nice apartment in Pittsburgh?

ANDY: It's fine.

RUTH: Big?

ANDY: Tiny. Actually, it's sort of like this.

RUTH: A balcony and everything?

ANDY: A little one. And a kitchenette.

RUTH: And neat, I'll bet.

ANDY: As a pin.

    (Both smile, remain standing.)

RUTH: I never could be neat. I tried. I never could be.

ANDY: *(Looking at his watch.)* Ruth—

RUTH: *(Quickly.)* Oh, I thought it would be a good idea if I came over, and we talked ahead of time, so we don't start bickering in front of the children.

ANDY: Good idea.

RUTH: I mean things have been so civilized so far…

ANDY: Right…

RUTH: It would be a shame to have them suddenly degenerate.

ANDY: I couldn't agree more.

RUTH: My lawyer says it's a mistake even to see each other. He's dead against it, but what the hell. I'm brave if you are.

ANDY: Lawyers…

RUTH: Exactly. This will be a good test. Dividing a few things up. Without fighting.

ANDY: I don't want much, actually.

RUTH: And I don't want to hold onto anything that's yours.

ANDY: Ditto.

RUTH: And if we start tearing away at each other, at least the children won't be around to see the blood.

ANDY: That won't happen.

RUTH: I was just joking, Andy.

ANDY: Some joke.

RUTH: *(Walking away.)* Oh Lord. This is hell.

ANDY: Want a drink? I brought a bottle.

RUTH: No thanks. Make yourself one if you want.

ANDY: How about coffee? There's a gismo here for instant—

RUTH: No thanks.

ANDY: I think I will have another drink.

RUTH: Fine.

ANDY: Please sit down.

> *(He goes off to the bathroom with his glass. Ruth stands uneasily at the balcony, looking out. Phil and Sally come back in from left, giggling profusely.)*

PHIL: What was that second thing you had?

SALLY: That was called a Rum Runner.

PHIL: Do you think that did it?

SALLY: I think the Minute Man Marguerite did it.

PHIL: Whatever.

> *(They kiss in center of the room. Andy returns, carrying another drink. Ruth turns to him.)*

RUTH: *(Brightly.)* Well. So. What do you plan to take?

ANDY: My camera, for one thing.

RUTH: I thought you took your camera.

ANDY: No. It's still there.

RUTH: Where? I haven't seen your camera.

ANDY: I think it's still hanging in my closet.

RUTH: Well maybe.

PHIL: *(Coming out of the kiss; tenderly.)* How about it?

SALLY: Why not?

> *(They move to the dressing area, begin to undress.)*

ANDY: My suit should be there, too.

RUTH: What suit?

ANDY: My good gray suit.

RUTH: I thought you took all your clothes.

ANDY: I think I left my good gray suit.

RUTH: If it's there, it's yours.

ANDY: Fair enough.

SALLY: *(Suddenly giving a little shriek, covering herself.)* Oh!

PHIL: What's the matter?

SALLY: *(Indicating mirror.)* I thought someone was looking at me.

PHIL: That's just a mirror.

SALLY: I know what it is. Now.

RUTH: *(To Andy.)* Frankly I haven't been in your closet.

SALLY: *(Looking around.)* I've never seen so many mirrors…

RUTH: *(To Andy.)* I suppose you need your suit for all sorts of fancy parties in Pittsburgh.

ANDY: Not so many.

SALLY: Mirrors everywhere.

PHIL: All the better to see you with…

RUTH: All sorts of fancy do's. Head of a hospital, living in a snappy apartment, overlooking a river…

ANDY: I don't go out much.

RUTH: I'll bet.

ANDY: I don't.

RUTH: I'll bet.

SALLY: All I know is these mirrors make things terribly…

PHIL: What?

SALLY: Clinical. I feel I'm in a hospital or something.

RUTH: Have you found someone yet?

ANDY: No. How about you?

RUTH: Still free and clear.

PHIL: *(Rummaging in his knapsack.)* Hey.

SALLY: What?

PHIL: I got something for you.

SALLY: What?

   (Phil rummages.)

ANDY: Have you gone out with anyone?

RUTH: Yes.

ANDY: Have a good time?

RUTH: Yes. *(Pause.)* No. Not very. It was like going back fifteen years. To some—blind date.

ANDY: Mmm.

RUTH: It's tough. Starting again. From scratch.

ANDY: I know.

PHIL: *(Finding a couple of joints in his knapsack.)* Here it is. Grass.

SALLY: Oh.

PHIL: Want some?

SALLY: Not now.

PHIL: I think I will.

   (He lights one nervously. Sally fusses with her shoes.)

RUTH: *(To Andy.)* Have you been out?

ANDY: Yes.

RUTH: With a nurse, I'll bet.

ANDY: Right.

RUTH: Was she terrific in bed?

ANDY: No.

PHIL: *(Taking a book out of his knapsack.)* Oh. I brought this, too.

SALLY: What?

PHIL: Take a look. *(Hands her the book.)*

RUTH: Better than me, though.

ANDY: No.

SALLY: *(Flipping through book.)* Jesus, Phil…

ANDY: Sex was never our problem.

RUTH: Glad to hear it.

SALLY: *(Reading title.) The Joy of Sex?* That's gross!

ANDY: We've got five kids to prove it.

SALLY: *(Handing it back.)* Really gross.

RUTH: They prove something. I don't know what they prove. But they prove something.

SALLY: *(Sitting down on a dressing stool.)* You certainly putting on the pressure tonight, Phil. Pot, dirty books…

PHIL: Not dirty. I got it right in Harvard Square…

RUTH: What *was* our problem, by the way?

ANDY: Oh, Ruth…

PHIL: It was right on the counter. Next to Julia Child.

RUTH: Why can't we discuss it, now we've had time to think?

PHIL: So I picked it up. Nothing heavy.

SALLY: I think it's heavy.

ANDY: You kicked me out. That was the problem.

RUTH: You walked out. On the whole shebang.

ANDY: I got a better job, and you guys wouldn't come with me.

RUTH: You wouldn't even wait till the end of the school year.

ANDY: I couldn't. They wanted me immediately.

RUTH: Well I couldn't yank five kids out of school!

ANDY: I'm talking about my *job,* Ruth. What I *do!*

RUTH: Well I have a job, too!

ANDY: Part-time.

RUTH: And that doesn't count? The kids don't count?

ANDY: This counted more.

RUTH: Apparently.

PHIL: What's wrong with a book? My parents have a book.

SALLY: Mine don't.

PHIL: How do you know? How do you know what your parents are into?

ANDY: It's more than just a job. I was drowning here.

PHIL: *(Thumbing through book.)* It's a good book…

ANDY: Drinking too much, working all hours…I was going under. Down there, I can breathe…

RUTH: Down there, we sink. You swim.

PHIL: Tasteful illustrations…look.

SALLY: No thanks.

PHIL: Recommended by doctors…

SALLY: Doctors don't know everything.

ANDY: Well. We've been all through it.

RUTH: Yes. What else do you want?

ANDY: My chair.

SALLY: *(Rummaging in her bag.)* Well I brought my own book.

RUTH: Which chair?

PHIL: What book?

ANDY: The one I sat in, Ruth.

RUTH: You sat in a great many chairs, Andy.

SALLY: *(Rummaging.)* You'll see.

ANDY: My reading chair.

RUTH: Oh. Your "reading" chair. So that's what it was. A "reading" chair.

SALLY: *(Finding the book.)* Jane Eyre.

PHIL: *Jane Eyre?*

SALLY: *(Flopping onto bed.)* I have to write a paper on *Jane Eyre*.

RUTH: Of course you can have it. That's your chair, all right, as we all were reminded often enough.

PHIL: *(To Sally.)* What's the matter with you?

RUTH: *(To Andy.)* What else?

ANDY: The old sailing print my mother gave me.

RUTH: Yours. Sold to American. Take it away.

PHIL: Hm? What's the matter?

(Sally flips a page angrily, continues reading.)

RUTH: What else?

ANDY: The coffee table.

RUTH: The coffee table? The *liv*ing-room coffee table?

PHIL: Will you at least move over? Will you at least do that?

(Sally slides over on the bed, continues to read. Phil lies down, reads the sex book beside her.)

ANDY: I made it, Ruth.

RUTH: You made it for me.

ANDY: I made it for the family.

RUTH: I thought it was for me. For my birthday.

PHIL: Thirty-two bucks for a study date, Sal?

SALLY: Ssssh. I'm reading.

ANDY: *(Carefully.)* You want it, then? You want to keep the coffee table?

RUTH: No, it's yours.

ANDY: If you really want the thing...

RUTH: It's yours, Andy. I said it was yours. That's that. What else do you want?

ANDY: *(Reaching into his pocket.)* Just odds and ends. Actually I've got a list.

RUTH: Oh good God, a list.

ANDY: Just a short one.

RUTH: Oh Andy, I know your lists. Of things for people to do. Well, hand it over. Let's see your little list.

(Andy hands it to her.)

PHIL: *(Looking at a sex illustration.)* Hey wow! Look at this!

SALLY: *(Pointedly reading aloud.)* "...she loved the garden, where she could be alone..."

(Phil groans.)

RUTH: *(Reading list.)* What's this?

ANDY: What's what?

RUTH: This. I can't read your writing.

ANDY: Books.

RUTH: That's a B?

ANDY: That's a B.

RUTH: No wonder people can't read your prescriptions.

ANDY: We're talking about books, Ruth.

RUTH: Don't worry about books. I've made three piles of books. The ones I like, the ones you like, the ones we both like. *(She sits at the desk, takes out a pencil and paper.)*

ANDY: Won't be many of those.

RUTH: Exactly. I'm writing these things down. *Leg*ibly. For my lawyer.

ANDY: Is that necessary?

RUTH: I think it is.

ANDY: All right.

PHIL: *(Indicating sex book.)* Can't we just try a couple of things out?

SALLY: No.

PHIL: Can't we at least try?

　　(Sally reads. Phil closes the book, groans, lies back.)

RUTH: *(Finishing copying.)* There. You see? I'm not completely helpless.

ANDY: I see that.

RUTH: How will you get all this stuff down to Pittsburgh?

ANDY: I've got a U-Haul-It.

RUTH: A what?

ANDY: A U-Haul-It. Attached to my car.

RUTH: Oh Lord. One of those.

ANDY: It seemed the easiest thing.

RUTH: Why don't you just back up a whole truck?

ANDY: What do you mean?

RUTH: Instead of your U-Haul-It.

ANDY: I'm not taking much, Ruth.

RUTH: Oh Andy… *(She waves the list at him.)*

ANDY: Keep what you want.

RUTH: No. I'll go along with this list.

ANDY: Good.

RUTH: That was simple, wasn't it?

ANDY: Very civilized.

RUTH: So. I'll keep this, you keep yours, and both lawyers get copies.

ANDY: I'll get mine typed.

RUTH: *(Reaching for it.)* I'll do it when we get home.

ANDY: *(Holding onto it.)* No, thanks. My secretary will do it.

RUTH: Oh. Your secretary.

　　(Vince comes in, carrying a Harvard catalogue. He calls toward Mark, who is still in the bathroom.)

VINCE: They'll ring the room when Baldwin arrives.

RUTH: *(Looking at her copy of the list.)* I think you forgot something.

ANDY: What did I forget?

VINCE: Hey, I picked up the Harvard catalogue from the car. We can go over it while we're waiting.

RUTH: *(After checking her list again.)* You forgot the stereo.

ANDY: I didn't forget the stereo.

RUTH: It's not on your list, Andy.

ANDY: It's not supposed to be on my list, Ruth.

RUTH: It's your favorite thing.

ANDY: I'll pick up another stereo.

RUTH: We thought it was yours.

ANDY: It's everyone's stereo.

RUTH: Everyone's! Oh boy. *(She laughs.)*

ANDY: What's so funny?

RUTH: Who was always putting on opera records, and taking off the rock and roll?

ANDY: The stereo stays.

RUTH: Fine. Wonderful. I'm absolutely delighted.

ANDY: So that's that.

RUTH: Tell me something, Andy…how do I say this so you won't get mad?

ANDY: Just say it, Ruth.

RUTH: How come…

(She pauses. Phil tries to embrace Sally on the bed.)

SALLY: Don't. Please. Not now.

ANDY: Go on.

RUTH: How come you can listen to opera, full blast, everyone screeching away at one time, and you can't even stand a houseful of your own children?

(Andy looks at her.)

PHIL: *(To Sally.)* Jesus, you're a drag.

ANDY: I love my children. *(Pause.)* That's all I'm going to say. *(He starts for the bathroom.)* Now you go. I'll wash up.

RUTH: I'll wait.

ANDY: I'll be a minute.

RUTH: I'll still wait.

ANDY: *(Turning at bathroom door.)* I think of the kids all the time. I have a whole stack of presents for the kids.

RUTH: Where? In your U-Haul-It?

(Andy looks at her, then goes into the bathroom. Ruth paces around the room, speaks half to him, half to herself.)

RUTH: By the way, maybe you'd like to haul away all the dining room furniture. Chairs, sideboard, table, everything. Who needs a dining room anyway? The dinner party is dead, friend! No more slaving away in the kitchen for your macho medical friends! No sir. I'll turn the dining room into a family room, you hear me, Andy? Put the TV in there, a few old bean bag chairs. It won't be neat, it'll be grubby as hell, but people will *use* it.

PHIL: *(To Sally.)* You are. You're a real drag. *(He sits on the edge of the bed.)*

RUTH: *(Calling in to Andy.)* I might even knock down the wall to the kitchen.

I'll make everything one big room, where we can finally have some common life together. I'll put the stereo in there. The children will be thrilled they can keep it.

(Andy has come out of the bathroom and is grabbing his parka from the closet.)

ANDY: What did you say?

RUTH: I said the children will be thrilled about the stereo.

(Andy stares at her.)

RUTH: What's the matter?

ANDY: You *told* them I'd take the stereo.

RUTH: I assumed you would.

ANDY: Those kids think I'd walk out with the stereo?

RUTH: It's all right, Andy.

ANDY: It's *not* all right.

RUTH: We've all started saving for another.

ANDY: Shit, Ruth. What a thing to let them think.

RUTH: I just wanted to prepare them.

ANDY: No wonder they've been so shitty on the phone.

RUTH: I just assumed…

ANDY: Well let's go, goddammit. So I can repair the damage. *(He starts off left.)*

RUTH: *(Following him.)* Fine. Bring your U-Haul-It.

ANDY'S VOICE: Jesus. The stereo. I can't get over that.

RUTH'S VOICE: Well please try.

(The door is heard slamming.)

PHIL: *(Suddenly getting up.)* Yeah, well I'm getting something to eat. *(He starts to get dressed.)*

SALLY: *(Closing her book.)* There. I've finished the chapter.

(A buzzer rings, off left. Ray looks up, quickly closes his Penthouse, *turns on the TV, crosses to answer the door. The TV is on very faintly until the end of the act.)*

VINCE: *(Crossing toward bathroom, calling in to Mark.)* Hey Mark. You can take whatever you want to Harvard. Even as a Freshman. Computer Science, Colonial History, anything…

PHIL: *(To Sally.)* I don't know, Sal. You kind of turned me off.

(He continues to get dressed. Ray comes back in, followed by Sharon. She wears a corny, updated Pilgrim uniform and carries a tray.)

RAY: *(Indicating his table.)* Put it over there.

SHARON: *(Stopping; horrified.)* There?

RAY: Sure. Right there.

SHARON: Isn't that sort of close to the TV?

RAY: I want it close so I can switch channels.

SHARON: O.K. They're your gamma rays, not mine.

RAY: What d'you mean, gamma rays?

SHARON: You get gamma rays from those things.

RAY: Naaa.

SHARON: You do. They send out gamma rays. Give you cancer of the colon.

RAY: I'll turn it off while I eat.

SHARON: They still give out rays. All over the food.

RAY: *(Indicating a spot farther away.)* O.K. Put it over there.

SHARON: Smart man. *(She begins to unload.)*

VINCE: *(Sitting at desk; continuing to read catalogue.)* They have a special biology course for pre-meds, Mark.

RAY: *(To Sharon.)* You look familiar.

SHARON: Maybe I served you before.

RAY: No, it was somewhere else.

SHARON: I used to work at the Ramada.

RAY: No. It wasn't there.

SALLY: *(To Phil; from bed.)* I'm sorry, Phil.

RAY: Do I look familiar?

SHARON: Sure.

RAY: Yeah?

SHARON: You phone things into a computer, right?

RAY: Right.

SHARON: You look like all the other guys who do that.

RAY: Thanks.

(Sharon makes out the check.)

VINCE: *(Calling in.)* They have a good baseball team, too, Mark. Last year: nine wins, two losses.

SHARON: I'm putting down milk instead of beer.

RAY: Milk?

SHARON: Most companies don't pay for the beer.

RAY: Mine does.

SHARON: They let beer go through their computer?

RAY: Put down beer.

SHARON: Suit yourself.

(Writes down beer, hands him the check. He looks it over.)

SALLY: Really, Phil. I'm sorry. *(She goes to him.)*

PHIL: *(Tying his shoes.)* Yeah, well I'm still hungry.

SHARON: Could I have my tip in cash?

RAY: Why?

SHARON: They hold out on me in the office.

RAY: Come on.

SHARON: They do. They hold out at the Ramada, too.

RAY: O.K. Cash…here. *(He hands her a dollar.)*

SHARON: Thanks. *(She pockets the money; smiles at him.)*

PHIL: *(To Sally, who is now nuzzling him.)* Cut it out, Sal. I can't find my shoe.

SALLY: *(Huffily; sitting back on the bed.)* I said I was sorry.

RAY: I know I've seen you before.

SHARON: Maybe it was the Sonesta.

RAY: You worked there, too?

SHARON: I work where there's work.

RAY: Never tried the Sonesta.

SHARON: Don't bother. It's the pits.

    (Ray starts to eat; Sharon starts out.)

VINCE: *(Flipping through catalogue.)* Art…Music Appreciation…what I'd give to take courses like this…

SHARON: *(Stopping; turning.)* Go easy on that cheeseburger.

RAY: *(Mouth full.)* Why?

SHARON: It's bad.

    (Ray stops chewing.)

SHARON: I mean, they put crap in it.

RAY: *(Trying to swallow.)* What do you mean, crap?

SHARON: They put everything in hamburgers these days…

VINCE: …History…

SHARON: Tails, ears, eyeballs…

VINCE: Philosophy…

SHARON: Testicles…and then they douse it with monosodium glutamate. Drink lots of liquid. Beer's O.K. They put crap in it, but at least it's natural crap.

    (Ray takes a big swig of beer.)

SHARON: Actually, it's the same stuff that puts foam in our urine.

    (Ray sputters, slams down his glass.)

RAY: I could get you fired. I could pick up this phone.

SHARON: Oh don't.

RAY: Bad-mouthing the food, knocking the management…

SHARON: I'm sorry. I'll shut up.

RAY: It's happened before, hasn't it?

SHARON: Getting fired?

RAY: At the Ramada, at the Hyatt Regency…maybe you ought to find another line of work.

SHARON: That's kind of hard these days.

RAY: Then why screw things up?

SHARON: *(Grimly.)* I just can't let things go by.

SALLY: You were putting such pressure on me, Phil.

PHIL: *(Tying shoes.)* Yeah? Well I'm a man. I have needs.

RAY: *(After looking Sharon over.)* Well I'll let you off the hook.

SHARON: Thanks.

RAY: Just relax, O.K.?

SHARON: It's kind of hard to relax when we're slowly being poisoned to death.

RAY: I'll show you how to relax. Stop by when you finish.

SHARON: I don't visit the rooms, thanks.

RAY: Well I can't leave. I'm expecting a call.

SHARON: I don't mean to be rigid, but I don't know you.

RAY: We met. I swear. Stop by, and we'll figure it out.

SHARON: Let me think about it.

RAY: Think about relaxing, too. O.K.?

SHARON: I'll try. *(She goes out left.)*

VINCE: *(Closing catalogue; to himself.)* And Foley the counselor tells him not to go… *(Shakes his head, goes back to the balcony.)*

SALLY: I'm relaxed now, Phil.

PHIL: *(Angrily brushing his hair.)* Look, I'm not a machine. You can't just turn me on and off like the TV.

(Sharon comes back in.)

SHARON: Shall I take back the pie?

RAY: No, I want the pie.

SHARON: You're going to *eat* that pie?

RAY: What's wrong with the pie?

SHARON: That apple pie there?

RAY: That good old American apple pie. What's wrong with it?

SHARON: That pie there is just crap in a crust.

RAY: What's your name?

SHARON: Sharon.

RAY: Get out of here, Sharon.

SHARON: It's true about the pie.

RAY: Everything's bad, what's good? How about sex? Is sex bad, Sharon?

SHARON: Actually I think sex is one of the few healthy things left in this country. Sex and jogging. I'm in favor of both. *(She goes out left again.)*

RAY: *(Calling after her.)* Then stop by, Sharon!

(He returns to his table, his TV, and his meal. Phil crosses toward the door.)

PHIL: I'll be in the coffee shop.

SALLY: You won't even wait?

PHIL: I'll wait down there.

SALLY: You'll just leave me alone? In this…room?

PHIL: You won't be alone. You'll have *Jane Eyre*. *(He starts off left again.)*

SALLY: If you walk out that door, I'm leaving, Phil.

PHIL: Fine. Perfect. That's what you wanted all along.

SALLY: How will I get back to town? You've got the car.

PHIL: *(Reaching into pocket, tossing her the keys.)* Here. Feel free. *(He goes out.)*

SALLY: *(Calling after him.)* Phil?…Phil!

(The door is heard slamming. She starts to get dressed angrily. Ray eats, watches his TV, which remains only subliminally audible. Vince gets up, crosses to dressing area, calls in to Mark, who is still in the bathroom.)

VINCE: *(Looking in.)* Hey Mark. Aren't you dressed yet?

(Frank tosses and turns in his bed. Vince reads to Mark from another brochure.)

VINCE: Listen to this: It says here there used to be an old inn where these roads meet. Are you listening? This is education. This is history.

(Frank sits up, turns on the light by the bed. Mark comes out of the bathroom, shirtless, toweling his hair. Vince continues reading to him.)

VINCE: It says here "Travelers to Boston used to scrape the mud from their boots and gather around an open hearth, sharing a pipe, a glass of rum, and a hearty New England stew…" How's that?…"Perhaps after dinner everyone would compete as to who could tell the best tale"…Sounds good, huh? I'd tell 'em about your home run last week, Markie. Bases loaded, top of the ninth.

(Mark puts on his shoes. Frank sits on the edge of the bed, feels his pulse, looking at his watch.)

VINCE: Hey, and listen…"Then they would retire, sometimes to sleep two or three to a bed"…What do you think, Mark? Maybe two hundred years ago, you and me would of shared a bed with the farmer's daughter, huh?

(Sally is angrily getting dressed, packing her knapsack to leave. Frank is taking his own pulse.)

VINCE: Well, if I couldn't get you into Harvard, maybe I could get you in there, pal.

(Mark winces, Vince pats him on the shoulder.)

VINCE: Sorry. That was a cheap shot. *(Vince moves away from him, back to the balcony.)* Don't tell Mom I said that, O.K.? That was a bush league thing to say. *(He sits down out on the balcony.)*

FRANK: *(On telephone, having dialed a single digit.)* This is room 404...I wonder...do you have such a thing as a house doctor?...Then is there a doctor nearby you might recommend?

MARK: *(Calling to Vince.)* Dad...what if I went to State?...Closer to home?

VINCE: Hurry up and get dressed. Baldwin's never late.

FRANK: *(On telephone.)* No, no. Nothing serious. I just want someone to listen to my heart.

(Vince returns to his reading)

FRANK: Could you give me that number, please.

(Sally, all packed, hoists her knapsack on her back and crosses to the door carrying car keys. She stops, reflects, in the middle of the room, looking at the car keys. Frank finds pencil writes down number.)

FRANK: 344-2198. Thank you. *(He hangs up, dials again carefully. On telephone.)* May I speak to the doctor, please? Then is there some other doctor who's taking his calls?...I see...what do you mean, "beep" him?...You mean he's gone to the Red Sox game?

VINCE: *(Looking up from his brochure, calling toward Mark, who has not yet put on a shirt.)* Hey. Listen to this.

FRANK: *(On telephone.)* I see. No, it's not that important...

VINCE: *(Calling to Mark.)* It says they had some big battles around here in the Revolutionary War.

FRANK: *(On telephone.)* No ambulances...no hospitals...no...thank you. Good-bye.

(He hangs up, remains seated on the edge of the bed. Sally changes her mind. She crosses to closet, takes off her knapsack, hangs up her coat.)

VINCE: *(Calling to Mark.)* Listen "Rebel troops challenged the forces of tyranny at several key points in this area..."

(Frank picks up the telephone again, dials a single digit.)

VINCE: A lot of blood was spilled around here...

FRANK: *(On telephone.)* This is room 404 again. I wonder...would you by any chance have a doctor registered here in the motel?

VINCE: *(Calling to Mark.)* Yeah, well. That's over. Now everyone's got a car. See? Nobody even has to stop.

FRANK: *(On telephone.)* Would you mind ringing it for me, please?...Thank you.

(Andy's phone begins to ring. Frank waits on telephone. Sally crosses to leave for the coffee shop, carrying her wallet. Frank, jiggling receiver.)

FRANK: Desk? Desk?...I guess there's no one there.

(Andy's telephone stops ringing. Frank lies back on his bed. Vince reads his guidebook on his balcony, sips a drink. Mark sits disconsolately on the edge of his bed. Ray eats, watches TV, which now becomes audible.)

RAY'S TV: *(Announcer's voice.)* Now stay tuned for "City Streets," where Bart Mason gets more than he bargains for when he traces a stolen car. *(Hectic TV music. Slow blackout.)*

End of Act I

ACT II

Fifteen minutes later. Frank is still lying down. Vince is on the balcony still reading. Mark has the pink shirt out on the bed. He stands looking down at it, anguished about wearing it. Ray is finishing his pie. His TV is still audible. It is the middle of a detective story.

TV WOMAN: How could Mike have been in two places at the same time, Bart?

TV DETECTIVE: He couldn't, Laura. Unless…

TV WOMAN: Unless he changed cars on 64th Street…

TV DETECTIVE: Now you're cooking…

(The TV continues to play under the scenes, but now, as before, it becomes only barely perceptible. What we should hear is occasional tough dialogue, city sounds, hectic jazzy music, automobile horns, tires screeching, gunshots. But never so that it distracts from the play. Meanwhile, Mark has picked up the pink shirt and is trying it on in front of the mirror. He hates what he sees. The telephone at the desk rings. Mark starts, hurries to answer it. Vince looks up from his reading.)

MARK: *(On telephone.)* Yes?…O.K. I'll tell him. *(He calls to Vince.)* He's waiting in the bar.

VINCE: Bill Baldwin?

MARK: *(Crossing to dressing area.)* They said he's waiting.

(Vince, on the balcony, stacks up his brochures. Mark comes to a quick decision. He takes off the pink shirt, shoves it into the bag, and takes out a blue work-shirt from his bag. He buttons it hurriedly in front of the mirror.)

VINCE: Let's make our move. *(He comes into room, sees the shirt that Mark is putting on.)* What's that you're wearing?

MARK: My shirt.

VINCE: Where's the shirt I got you?

MARK: *(Indicating bag.)* In there.

VINCE: *(Carefully.)* Uh huh. I see. Want to wear a work-shirt, huh?

MARK: It's clean, Dad.

VINCE: Want to embarrass me down there, huh?

MARK: I feel easier in it.

VINCE: Want to embarrass me? When I introduce you, what'll I say? My son, the hood? My son, the mechanic?

MARK: I hate the pink one, Dad.

VINCE: Uh huh. I see, I see.

MARK: I don't feel right in it.

VINCE: So that's it, is it?

MARK: I'm just not the type, Dad.

VINCE: That's what you said about Little League.

MARK: I never liked Little League.

VINCE: Oh yeah? Leading hitter, two years running?

MARK: I still didn't like it, I don't like Harvard, Dad.

VINCE: You haven't *seen* Harvard.

MARK: It's too much for me, Dad.

VINCE: Uh huh. I see. And so you want to crawl under cars? I see. You got that shirt for crawling under cars.

MARK: Just for a year, Dad.

VINCE: Your mother in on this?

MARK: No.

VINCE: Oh sure; she wants you home till the day she dies!

MARK: *I* want to do it. *Me.*

VINCE: She doesn't know what college *means!*

MARK: Leave Mom out of this!

VINCE: Don't tell *me* who to leave out!

MARK: *(Crossing toward door, his shirt on.)* Then don't tell me what to wear!

VINCE: Go easy now.

MARK: It's a free country, Dad.

VINCE: You're letting me down, pal.

MARK: Why can't I do what I want, and go where I want, and wear what I want without you leaning on me all the time?

VINCE: *Lean*ing on you?

MARK: Breathing down my neck, like a goddam umpire!

VINCE: Hey. I'm your dad. I know what's best.

MARK: Mr. Foley knows more than you.

VINCE: Foley?

MARK: I can talk to him. About anything!

VINCE: Foley, the counselor? Telling you to drop out…

MARK: He says you're the cause of my colitis, Dad.

VINCE: Me?

MARK: That's what he said.

　　(Pause.)

VINCE: Get that shirt off.

MARK: *(Grimly.)* I bought it, I like it, I'm wearing it.

VINCE: Get it OFF!

MARK: Make me.

VINCE: What did you say?

MARK: *(Frightened, hovering by the balcony.)* Make me.

> *(Vince strides up to him as if to hit him. Mark holds his ground. Vince grabs the shirt and rips it down the front.)*

VINCE: Now change that fucking shirt and meet us down in the Minute Man bar.

> *(Vince strides out left, angrily. Mark, fighting back the tears, falls into the chair on the balcony. He stays there, looking out. Ray's buzzer rings. He looks up, puts down his coffee, turns off his TV and goes to answer the door. After a moment, Sharon marches in grimly, with the tray.)*

RAY: Glad you came back.

SHARON: I have to pick up the dishes before they close.

RAY: I didn't finish my coffee.

SHARON: They want the dishes.

RAY: Jeez. First you foul up my meal, then you won't let me finish it.

SHARON: *(Looking at him, then smiling.)* Finish your coffee.

> *(She crosses her arms and waits. Ray starts to drink his coffee, then stops, looks at it, looks at her.)*

RAY: What's the story on coffee, Sharon?

SHARON: You'll get me fired.

RAY: Naaa. Come on. What does it give you? Cancer? Athlete's foot?

SHARON: Actually, it's very bad for your heart.

RAY: Ah hah!

SHARON: But that's not my gripe with coffee. *(She starts to pile her tray.)*

RAY: What's your gripe with coffee, Sharon?

SHARON: Want to know?

RAY: I want to know.

SHARON: *(Stopping piling.)* Coffee is controlled by an international cartel.

RAY: Come off it.

SHARON: Coffee is controlled by a huge multinational conglomerate. That's my gripe with coffee.

RAY: Gotcha.

SHARON: We should be paying no more than six cents a cup. Oh I'm sorry. I forgot. Your company pays. So what do you care?

RAY: I care. Really, I care.

> *(Jessie comes quietly back in. She looks haggard. She puts down an overnight bag by the bureau.)*

SHARON: You want to know why we have to take back the trays?

RAY: They give out gamma rays.

SHARON: No. People steal.

(Jessie stands by the balcony, looking out.)

SHARON: Cups, plates, glasses…people steal even the trays.

FRANK: *(Opening his eyes.)* How's Joan?

JESSIE: Oh, you're awake.

SHARON: *(Stacking the tray.)* Towels, sheets, blankets…

FRANK: How's Joannie?

JESSIE: Never got there.

FRANK: Never got there?

JESSIE: I got lost.

SHARON: They just pile stuff into the car and drive off.

FRANK: Poor Jess. *(He gets up heavily, joins her at the balcony.)*

JESSIE: Somehow I got onto the Turnpike again. And couldn't get off.

SHARON: People with vans take tables and chairs.

RAY: Naw.

SHARON: They do.

JESSIE: I drove for miles.

FRANK: Oh Jess.

JESSIE: A nice man at a toll booth got me turned around.

SHARON: Once I caught a fella taking apart a bed.

RAY: No.

SHARON: Yes!

JESSIE: I've just been driving around in one great big circle.

SHARON: *(Wiping off the table.)* Some day I'll walk into a completely empty room.

(Jessie and Frank sit at the edge of the bed.)

JESSIE: *(Holding Frank's hand.)* One full circle. Well, it seems to apply. Here we've spent forty years raising children and getting them out of the nest, and now all I want is to get my hands on a baby again.

SHARON: Do you know why people steal?

RAY: No. Why do people steal, Sharon?

SHARON: People steal because we're in the last stages of the capitalistic system. You tell people that owning things is such a big deal, they end up stealing them. I read an article. *(She is hoisting up the tray.)*

JESSIE: I brought in the overnight bag, by the way. I'm not completely helpless. *(She begins to unpack a few toilet articles.)*

RAY: *(Suddenly; to Sharon.)* Now I know where we met.

(Sharon stops.)

RAY: Fort Devons, Massachusetts!

SHARON: *(Putting down the tray.)* Where?

RAY: Fort Devons, 1968. I was being inducted into the Army and you were marching around with a bunch of hippies.

SHARON: That's—possible.

RAY: Sure. You came right up to me in line, and said "Don't go."

SHARON: And what did you do?

RAY: I went.

(Frank has lain down again on the bed.)

JESSIE: *(Unpacking; her back to him.)* How about you? Are you all right?

FRANK: I'm fine.

SHARON: You and everyone else.

RAY: But I remember you. As I went in the gates, I looked back. There you were, still marching around, hair blowing in the wind, no bra, carrying a sign saying "Hell no, don't go." Am I right?

SHARON: It's quite possible.

RAY: Sure. That was you. I couldn't get you out of my mind. When I got my first pass, I looked for you. But you weren't there.

SHARON: We moved on.

JESSIE: *(Unpacking.)* I never know whether to believe you or not, Frank.

RAY: You remember me?

SHARON: No.

RAY: You came right up.

SHARON: It was a long time ago.

RAY: Well I remember you, Sharon.

SHARON: Much good it did. You went in. I went in.

RAY: What do you mean? I'm out! I work for a private corporation.

SHARON: Same thing. I'll bet your company is owned by another, and another owns that, and if you trace it on out, it's the same multinational conglomerate that got us into the war.

RAY: That's a load.

SHARON: It's true. They own everything. I've read books.

RAY: Naaa.

SHARON: They own this place.

RAY: Naaa.

SHARON: They own the Wayside Motor Inn!

RAY: They don't own—

SHARON: They own the Wayside, they own Wonderbread, they own movie studios...

RAY: They don't.

SHARON: They *do*. Did you see *Jaws*?

RAY: Sure I saw *Jaws*.

SHARON: They made *Jaws*. They made the pie you just ate. They own the Minnesota Vikings. *(She empties the ashtray.)*

FRANK: I had a slight attack.

JESSIE: Oh Frank.

FRANK: Nothing serious. I'm fine.

JESSIE: Oh Frank. Should we call a doctor?

SHARON: The only thing they don't own is our own bodies.

FRANK: I tried.

JESSIE: You tried?

SHARON: Otherwise they own the whole world.

FRANK: I couldn't get one.

JESSIE: Couldn't *get* one?

FRANK: I couldn't get one, Jess.

RAY: They don't own me.

JESSIE: *(Crossing around bed to telephone.)* I'm going to get one.

SHARON: Oh yeah? You're tied to that phone, and that phone is tied to a computer and that computer is tied—

RAY: I can leave any time I want.

JESSIE: I'm going to call Joannie.

SHARON: I doubt it. *(She crosses left with the tray, to leave.)*

JESSIE: Joannie will know a good doctor.

RAY: *(Getting up, moving partway toward her.)* Come on. Let's go out.

FRANK: Joannie's got her hands full.

RAY: Come on. You finish up, I'll shower, then away we go.

JESSIE: *(Sitting on bed, by telephone.)* Nonsense. I'm calling her.

SHARON: What about your call?

RAY: We'll go out, whether they call or not.

FRANK: Please, Jess.

JESSIE: I'm sorry. I am. *(She gets out her glasses and memo book again.)*

SHARON: It's a deal.

FRANK: She won't find a doctor.

JESSIE: She can try. People can try.

RAY: So get ready, O.K.

SHARON: *(Delighted.)* I read an article once…

JESSIE: Now first you dial nine…

SHARON: It said things will never change until the middle class changes.

RAY: *(Enthusiastically.)* Right on!

FRANK: You'll just worry her.

JESSIE: Can't be helped.

SHARON: I thought you were hopelessly middle-class. *(She exits left, excitedly.)*

RAY: *(Calling after her.)* The name's Ray, Sharon. Call me Ray.

FRANK: Tell her I just want someone to listen to my heart.

> *(Ray rubs his hands delightedly, then goes to the rack for his suitcase, and takes it into the bathroom with him.)*

JESSIE: It's ringing… *(On telephone.)* Darling, we're still here. Your father doesn't feel very well.

FRANK: I'm perfectly fine.

JESSIE: I think he should see a doctor.

> *(Andy comes back in carrying several photograph albums which he carries to Ray's table. He sits, and begins to go through them nostalgically.)*

JESSIE: What hospital?

FRANK: No hospital.

JESSIE: He won't go to the hospital.

FRANK: Never again.

JESSIE: He just won't. He thinks they're too impersonal.

FRANK: And too expensive.

JESSIE: Do you know a doctor?

FRANK: I just want someone…

JESSIE: *(On telephone.)* He just wants someone to listen to his heart…would you try, dear? Family doctor, someone…there must be someone…

FRANK: *(Getting up, wandering around.)* Hospitals…

JESSIE: *(On telephone.)* Oh that would be wonderful…

FRANK: Bedpans…nurses waking you up to put you back to sleep…

JESSIE: *(On telephone.)* We'll be right here, sweetheart. Room 404. Just ring when you arrive. You're a godsend, darling. *(Hangs up, to Frank.)* Bob's home. They'll get a sitter for the kids and come right over. They know a good doctor.

FRANK: He'll be at the Red Sox game.

JESSIE: Nonsense…how do you feel?

FRANK: Fine. *(He sits on the edge of the bed.)*

JESSIE: Oh Frank, I think we should move.

FRANK: Where?

JESSIE: Near them.

FRANK: No.

JESSIE: Why not? What's left at home?

FRANK: Home's home.

JESSIE: It's not, any more. Half our friends are dead, the rest are staggering around Florida. Here's where our family is.

FRANK: They don't want us, Jess.

JESSIE: They do. I could lend a hand.

FRANK: Jess, haven't you ever heard a good old American mother-in-law joke?

JESSIE: I don't care. We're all in this thing together.

FRANK: We're all on our own, in the end. *(He lies down.)*

JESSIE: *(Moving around the room.)* That's not true. I don't believe that. I believe the most important things in the world have to do with other people. I don't like what we've done—selling the house, moving into an apartment, getting rid of the dog. I don't like it. I don't like sitting around watching television and fussing with the burglar alarm. I hate that. It's just like this. Waiting around in a strange motel room. What are we doing here? We should be with our family. No wonder you're flat on your back, feeling perfectly miserable. You've asked for this, Frank. You've turned away from life. You've painted yourself into a corner. This is what you get when you do that. *(Pause.)* Frank?

FRANK: *(Quietly.)* I didn't get rid of the dog.

JESSIE: You had him put away.

FRANK: He wanted to go. He wouldn't even come in at night. Not even in November. He dug a place in the leaves. It was instinct. He didn't want...

JESSIE: What didn't he want?

FRANK: People fussing around.

(Jessie looks at him, goes to bureau, gets some powder and cold cream, crosses to dressing area, then turns.)

JESSIE: I'm not talking about dogs.

FRANK: Neither am I.

JESSIE: *(Taking her fresh dress into the bathroom.)* I'm going to take a bath.

(She goes in. Frank lies back. A loud insistent knocking is suddenly heard off left. Andy looks up, then stacks the albums carefully, and puts them on his desk as he crosses to answer the door. Ruth storms into the room. She see the albums on the desk immediately.)

RUTH: I knew it, you son of a bitch.

ANDY: What's the matter?

RUTH: *(Pointing at the albums.)* Those! Those are the matter, you son of a bitch. You swiped those.

(She moves toward them; he blocks her.)

ANDY: Nobody swiped anything...

RUTH: You must have sneaked them into your goddam U-Haul-It when I was in the kitchen, scrambling you some eggs!

ANDY: Nobody sneaked…

RUTH: I should have watched you like a hawk. *(Looks around the room.)* What else did you take? God, and I thought everybody was being so civilized.

ANDY: *(Standing by the albums.)* Look, these are mine.

RUTH: Yours? That's a good one! Yours!

ANDY: Who owned the camera? Who took the pictures year after year?

RUTH: I bought the albums! I pasted them in!

ANDY: You got the kids…

RUTH: The pictures stay *with* them.

ANDY: Come on, Ruth.

RUTH: Why do you think I had them out? The children look at them. All the time.

(She reaches for them; he moves away.)

ANDY: They can look at them when they visit me.

RUTH: Oh no.

ANDY: Why the hell not?

RUTH: The pictures belong with the family.

ANDY: I'm family, too.

RUTH: Not any more, Andy. Not any more.

(She makes another move. He keeps his distance, moving behind Ray's table.)

ANDY: *(Grimly.)* I'm keeping them, Ruth.

RUTH: We'll see what the lawyers say.

ANDY: No lawyer is going to get these pictures out of me.

RUTH: So what'll we do?

(Ruth makes another step for the albums. Andy blocks her way.)

ANDY: Maybe you ought to go.

RUTH: Not without the pictures!

ANDY: I'll get copies.·

RUTH: I don't believe you.

ANDY: I'll have every picture copied.

RUTH: I just don't believe you, Andy. I'll never see those pictures again.

ANDY: Ruth…

RUTH: Never! Never again!

ANDY: Oh, Ruth…

RUTH: What about my wedding pictures? Can't I at least have my own wedding pictures?

(Pause.)

ANDY: All right. *(Tosses a white album to the floor.)* Here. Take the wedding.

RUTH: *(Stooping to pick it up.)* Thanks so much.

ANDY: Now so long.

RUTH: *(She goes to telephone at desk.)* I'm calling my lawyer. Right now. *(She slams open the desk drawer, takes out a telephone book, begins flipping through it.)*

ANDY: *(Walking away.)* Call the police, I'm still keeping them.

RUTH: We'll see about that.

> *(She searches for number. Vince comes in, looks around, sees Mark still sitting in the balcony chair; Mark notices him and turns his back on him. Ruth finds the number, dials out; dials the number.)*

VINCE: *(To Mark; awkwardly.)* The man left...Bill Baldwin left...we had one drink and then he left.

> *(Ruth holds the telephone impatiently.)*

VINCE: He had to meet his wife. For dinner or something. Those type guys are always meeting their wives.

> *(Ruth slams down the telephone.)*

ANDY: Even lawyers go home, Ruth.

RUTH: Then I'll call him at home. *(She flips through telephone book again.)*

VINCE: *(To Mark; earnestly.)* Hey. Not to worry, though. I covered for you. I said you were asleep.

ANDY: If you call your lawyer, I'll call mine, Ruth.

RUTH: I don't care who you call. *(She searches for the number.)*

VINCE: I told him you were tired. I said you played a full game yesterday and I didn't have the heart to wake you up. He said "Fine." Those guys love games.

RUTH: *(Slamming down the telephone.)* He must be unlisted!

ANDY: I don't blame him. Now get the hell out!

VINCE: *(To Mark.)* So he still wants to meet you, kid.

RUTH: *(To Andy.)* What about the trip to Disneyland?

ANDY: What about it?

RUTH: I took all those pictures. You weren't even there, Andy.

ANDY: Thank God.

VINCE: I'll bring you by his office. After the interview. Cabot, Cabot, and Forbes, Mark.

RUTH: Can I have Disneyland then?

ANDY: I'll mail them.

RUTH: I'll bet. I'll bet you'll mail them.

ANDY: I will.

RUTH: Any day.

VINCE: So no harm done. O.K.?

ANDY: O.K. I'll give you Disneyland. *(He flips through an album.)*

VINCE: I crowed, I *crowed* about you! He thinks you're a real wheel!

ANDY: *(Flipping through an album.)* Disneyland…Disneyland…where's Disneyland?

VINCE: I told him all your accomplishments. Grades, scores, batting average…

MARK: *(Suddenly getting up.)* Did you tell him you purposely tore my good shirt? *(He strides past Vince toward the dressing area.)*

ANDY: Here's Disneyland. *(He tears the pages out of the album.)*

VINCE: *(Following Mark in.)* No. I didn't tell him that.

MARK: You should've told him that.

ANDY: *(Tossing Ruth the pages.)* There's Disneyland.

VINCE: Of course I didn't tell him that.

RUTH: *(Picking them up off the floor.)* Thank you.

ANDY: Now so long. O.K.?

VINCE: How could I tell him that?

RUTH: I'm calling my lawyer first thing, Andy. *(She starts out.)*

VINCE: *(Moving toward Mark.)* Come on, Mark. Shake? Friends? Pals?
(Holds out his hand. Mark moves away.)

ANDY: *(Calling to Ruth.)* Hey!
(She stops; Andy indicates album.)

ANDY: There's a picture here of your parents. Several pictures. When they visited. Want them?
(Ruth stands looking at him, Andy rips the page out of the album; holds it out. She doesn't take it. He drops it.)

ANDY: Here. Your parents.
(It flutters to the floor. She stands looking at it, then at him.)

VINCE: I'll get the shirt fixed, Mark. It can be sewn up. O.K.?

RUTH: *(Stooping down to pick up the picture of her parents.)* You're such a bastard, Andy. *(She starts out again.)* Such a bastard.

VINCE: Mom can sew it when we get back.

ANDY: *(Flipping through album angrily.)* Wait, Ruth. Here's our trip to Bermuda. Our second honeymoon. So-called. Want it? I don't want it. Take it. It's yours.
(He rips the pages out of the album, holds them out to her tantalizingly. She stands looking at them.)

MARK: I don't *want* her to sew it.

VINCE: Aw, Mark.

MARK: I want to wear it tomorrow.

VINCE: Aw, Markie...

MARK: And when they ask how come I'm wearing this torn shirt, I'll say my own Dad ripped it. On purpose.

(Ruth grabs the Bermuda pictures, starts tearing them up.)

VINCE: Aw, Jesus, Mark.

MARK: That's what I'm going to say to Harvard, Dad!

ANDY: *(Looking at her grimly, then sitting down at his desk, spreading the albums in front of him.)* O.K....O...K...Let's see: what else would you like? *(He begins to go through them.)*

VINCE: Aw come on, Markie. What can I do?

ANDY: *(Flipping through albums.)* Young married days...skiing with the MacKenzies... *(Rips out the page.)*

VINCE: Huh?

MARK: *(Taking off his shirt, throwing it at him.)* You tore it, you fix it!

ANDY: Climbing Mount Monadnock...

VINCE: *(Catching the shirt.)* I'll check if they have tailor service.

ANDY: Crane's Beach...the trip to the Vineyard...want these?

RUTH: No.

ANDY: Neither do I. *(Tears up the pages, tosses the scraps at her.)*

MARK: I want you to fix it! Yourself!

ANDY: *(Who has been flipping through the album.)* And here come the babies... oh hell, take the whole thing...the babies were yours. *(He tosses the album at her feet.)* I'll just keep this last one. When they started growing up. And acting like human beings. *(He flips through it, loose pictures fall out.)* You didn't do much organizing by this time. You got your job! *(He shuffles through the pictures.)* Things were beginning to fall apart.

VINCE: I don't sew, Mark. *(He looks helplessly at the torn shirt in his arms.)*

RUTH: *(Picking the baby album up from the floor.)* You're such a bastard, Andy.

MARK: You should of watched Mom some time, Dad.

RUTH: Healer of the sick. That's a good one.

VINCE: I don't even have a needle, Mark.

RUTH: *(Picking up other pictures.)* You took the hyprocritic oath, that's what you took, Andy!

MARK: *(Starting in to bathroom.)* Then you better get one, Dad. Pretty quick!

VINCE: Where you going? You sick again?

MARK: *(Coming out of bathroom.)* Hell no. I'm going to watch TV!

VINCE: TV! Always TV! Never a book!

MARK: *(Grimly.)* I'm going to watch TV until you fix my shirt!

(Mark turns on the TV defiantly. It blasts out, preferably gunshots and violent sounds. Vince storms out of the room, carrying the shirt. Mark looks after him, immediately turns TV off, and throws himself face down on the second bed.)

RUTH: *(Bitterly; to Andy.)* The man in white; the good doctor! Bullshit!

ANDY: *(Stiffly; to Ruth.)* I don't see why you say these things, Ruth. I do a great deal of good in Pittsburgh. *(He moves away from the desk.)* I was drowning here. Too many patients, too many hours, too many kids—

(Ruth makes a sudden lunge for the remaining album, grabs it, backs away from Andy.)

ANDY: Give me that.

RUTH: *(Clutching it.)* Sorry.

ANDY: I want that one.

RUTH: So do I.

ANDY: Give it to me, or I'll...

RUTH: You'll what?

ANDY: Take it.

(He makes move toward her. Ruth suddenly drops to the floor.)

RUTH: You take one more step toward me, and I'll—

ANDY: You'll what?

RUTH: You'll see. I'll take every one of these pictures, and I'll tear...I'll tear...

(She starts to tear up all the pictures, frantically.)

ANDY: *(Grabbing her shoulders; shaking her.)* Oh stop!

(Pictures fly all over the place.)

ANDY: Oh God.

(She screams. He is suddenly embracing her.)

ANDY: Oh Jesus, what are we doing?

RUTH: *(Burying her head in his chest; crying.)* I don't know, I don't know, I don't know.

(They remain huddled together on floor, surrounded by torn pictures. After a moment, Phil and Sally come into their dressing room area, somewhat happier.)

PHIL: Some meal. They wouldn't even let us have dessert.

SALLY: They were closing.

(They sit at Ray's table. Phil takes out a joint.)

SALLY: We couldn't stay down there forever, anyway arguing. At some point, we had to come back here.

PHIL: I wanted the pie.

SALLY: It wouldn't have been any good.

PHIL: Why not?

SALLY: They bring it in.

PHIL: How do you know?

SALLY: The waitress told me. She said it was crap in a crust.

> *(He offers her a drag on his joint. Ruth breaks away from Andy but remains on the floor. Sally, taking a drag.)*

SALLY: I'm not sure this will do it, Phil. *(She hands him back the joint.)*

PHIL: *(Taking a drag.)* Give it a chance. O.K.?

SALLY: *(Huddled into herself.)* I don't know whether it's the thirty-two bucks, or your book, or this *room,* but I'm beginning to think if you and I don't come up with one huge simultaneous Fourth of July orgasm, someone will put us in jail.

PHIL: Big joke. Ha, ha.

RUTH: *(Idly piecing together a torn picture.)* Remember this?

ANDY: Yep.

> *(They begin to gather up the pieces around them.)*

SALLY: Everyone has to be so sexy all the time in this country. I think it's brutal.

PHIL: Don't get paranoid. O.K.?

ANDY: *(Looking at picture.)* Where was this?

RUTH: That? That was Round Hill. That picnic.

ANDY: Oh. Right.

> *(They continue to sort pictures. Jessie comes out of the bathroom, fresh from her bath, in a different dress.)*

JESSIE: *(To Frank.)* Don't you want to change before they come?

FRANK: Yes. All right.

> *(He gets up, with some effort. She tries to help.)*

FRANK: I can *do* it, Jess.

SALLY: Emerson says we're all Puritans at heart. Maybe that's why we can't deal with sex.

PHIL: I can deal with it. I can deal.

JESSIE: *(Getting things from overnight bag.)* Here's a clean shirt, and some socks.

FRANK: Thank you. *(He takes them, goes off to the bathroom.)*

SALLY: I once saw this movie, Polish or Russian or something, where this young couple spends their entire time trying to find a place to be alone. And here we've got it, easy as pie, and we're all hung up. You can't win.

PHIL: I wish I had my records. *Fleetwood Mac* would do it.

SALLY: Nothing will *do* it, Phil.

RUTH: *(Looking at a picture.)* I'd forgotten this.

ANDY: What?

RUTH: That Teddy was terrified of the water. Look at him. He's terrified.

ANDY: *(Looking at picture.)* Oh yes.

RUTH: How'd we get him over that?

ANDY: It took time.

(They go through the pictures.)

JESSIE: *(Calling off to Frank.)* There's a thing there for instant coffee. Shall I make you some?

FRANK'S VOICE: I don't want instant anything.

JESSIE: *(Patiently.)* All right, dear. *(She knits in her chair.)*

SALLY: *(Slightly stoned.)* Next year, we should live in a commune.

PHIL: Oh God.

SALLY: Seriously. Not just with people our own age. We'd have old people, and middle-aged people, and teenagers, and babies, and dogs. There'd be doctors and hard hats and hippies. And everyone would help each other out.

PHIL: We'd last about a week.

SALLY: I don't think so.

PHIL: We'd all be at each other's throats.

SALLY: I don't think so. We'd be like one big family. *(Pause.)* We'd work it out.

ANDY: *(To Ruth; indicating picture.)* Here's when we had the vegetable garden. Remember that project?

RUTH: We had gorgeous vegetables. I remember that.

SALLY: Oh Phil, let's just leave.

PHIL: And lose thirty-two bucks?

SALLY: I'll pay you the other sixteen, if we just leave.

PHIL: Where would we go?

SALLY: I don't know. My dorm. Your place.

PHIL: What about roommates?

SALLY: It's better than this. This is like playing tennis without a net.

PHIL: I want the whole night.

SALLY: I want more.

PHIL: How can we have more if we can't last the night?

SALLY: Maybe we can't.

PHIL: Then maybe we're lucky we found it out.

(A knocking off left. Jessie gets up, calls to Frank.)

JESSIE: Someone's at the door, Frank. I'll get it. *(She goes off to answer it.)*

PHIL: *(Taking another drag.)* One thing I know. Here's where it happens. Here or nowhere. We can't go back. No way.

(He hands her the joint. Jessie comes back in, followed by Vince, who carries his torn shirt.)

JESSIE: You've come to the right place, sir. I always carry a needle and thread. *(Calling to Frank.)* It's only a fellow-traveler, dear. *(She pokes through her bag.)*

VINCE: *(Awkwardly.)* They didn't have one at the desk.

JESSIE: *(Fussing in the bag.)* Oh the desk, the desk...

VINCE: I heard your voice. I figured a woman...

JESSIE: Here it is. Right here. *(Hands him a needle and thread.)*

VINCE: *(Taking it.)* I'll bring it back.

JESSIE: Oh heavens. There's more where that came from.

VINCE: *(Holding out the shirt.)* My son wants to wear this for his interview at Harvard.

JESSIE: Mercy! I'd sew it for you, but... *(Whispering.)* my husband likes his privacy.

VINCE: That's O.K. I'll figure it out.

JESSIE: That's right. Live and learn. Good-bye.

(Vince goes off. Jessie settles into the chair by the telephone, works on her knitting.)

ANDY: *(Indicating a picture to Ruth.)* You want this?

RUTH: *(Looking at it.)* Thanksgiving dinner? Don't you?

ANDY: We both want it then. *(He puts it aside.)*

SALLY: *(Musingly.)* The Wayside Motor Inn...

PHIL: *(Singing sadly, to the tune of the "Yellow Submarine.")* We all lived at the Wayside Motor Inn...

SALLY: *(Now quite stoned.)* What does the Bible say? Some seeds fell by the wayside, and the birds devoured them.

PHIL: Which means?

SALLY: Which means we can't take root here. We can't grow.

PHIL: Want another joint?

SALLY: *(Getting up.)* No. I want something else.

PHIL: What?

SALLY: Water.

PHIL: Water?

SALLY: I want to take a bath. *(She goes in.)*

PHIL: *(Calling after her.)* Think you'll grow in the bathtub, Sal?

SALLY'S VOICE: At least I'll feel clean.

RUTH: *(Looking at a picture.)* Now this is yours. Climbing Mount Washington. You and the boys. Except I want it.

(Andy looks over her shoulder. Unconsciously he rubs his cheek against hers. Ruth moves away.)

RUTH: Don't Andy.

(Andy tries to kiss her cheek.)

RUTH: I said don't.

(Andy moves away.)

RUTH: Maybe we should make a pile. Of the ones we both want.

(She puts it with the Thanksgiving picture. A buzzer from off left. Ray comes out of the bathroom, zipping up his fly. He wears an exotic colored shirt and double-knit pants, no shoes or socks. He looks himself over in the mirror, opens his Penthouse *to a particularly suggestive photograph which he places conspicuously on his table. Then he dances to answer the door. Phil goes to the bathroom door, looks at Sally in the bathtub. After a moment, Ray comes back in followed by Sharon, who now wears blue jeans and a T-shirt saying "Save the Whales.")*

SHARON: Ready or not, here I am.

RAY: *(Looking her over.)* Hey. I like the civilian clothes.

SHARON: *(Standing at door.)* Let's go.

RAY: *(Indicating telephone.)* They'll call in five minutes.

SHARON: Remember our deal.

RAY: Just five. *(He goes to his table to put on his shoes.)* I could lose my job.

SHARON: I already lost mine.

RAY: Huh?

SHARON: Some customer complained.

RAY: Bastard.

SHARON: All I did was tell him about the pie.

RAY: You poor kid.

SHARON: That's all right. They always need help at the Holiday Inn. *(She sits uneasily on the edge of Frank's bed.)*

RAY: *(Pouring a drink.)* You need a drink.

SHARON: I don't drink.

RAY: Mind if I do?

SHARON: No, no. Go ahead.

(He takes a drink.)

SHARON: If you have to.

RAY: I don't have to.

SHARON: If you knew the alcohol consumed in this place…if you saw the bottles tossed out in the trash… *(Gets up.)* Come on. I'll show you the trash.

RAY: Sit down. I swear. They'll call any minute. *(Ray lights a cigarette.)*

SHARON: I wish you wouldn't smoke. It's my lungs, too.

RAY: Sorry. *(He tries to wave away the smoke.)*

SHARON: The reason I'm waiting is I'm trying not to be so rigid.

RAY: Oh yeah?

SHARON: Do you think I'm a rigid person?

RAY: Naw.

SHARON: My ex-husband said I was rigid as a rail. Do you agree?

RAY: Oh no, no, no.

SHARON: Well, I'm trying not to be. I'm trying to relate one on one.

RAY: Thanks. *(Looks at her; crosses to her; sits on the bed beside her.)* Me, too. You know, sometimes I'd like to chuck all this. Wife, job, the whole scene. Sometimes I dream of running off to the woods with a gorgeous hippy like you, Sharon. *(Makes a quick drink.)*

SHARON: Might be better than sitting here every night. Waiting to be called by some machine.

RAY: *(Angrily.)* Yeah, and you know, they got guys like me stacked up all over the country.

(He crosses gloomily back, sits at his table, looks angrily at the phone. Vince comes in carrying the torn shirt and the needle and thread. He goes to Mark, who is facedown on the bed. Mark gives no response. Vince sighs, goes out onto the balcony, sits in the chair, begins to sew the shirt.)

PHIL: *(Toward the bathroom; to Sally.)* You look terrific.

SALLY'S VOICE: *(Splashing.)* What?

PHIL: You look great.

SALLY'S VOICE: At least I'm more relaxed.

PHIL: Can I come in?

SALLY'S VOICE: I'm taking a *bath.*

PHIL: Can I take one too?

SALLY'S VOICE: All right. Come on in.

PHIL: *(Peeling off his clothes as he goes in.)* O.K. I'm coming in.

(Ray has nervously lit another cigarette. Sharon notices.)

SHARON: Please…

RAY: Sorry. *(Again puts out cigarette, again tries to get rid of smoke.)*

RUTH: *(Looking at a picture.)* Here's one of your friend Grace in a bathing suit. I suppose you want it.

ANDY: Nope.

RUTH: *(Putting it aside.)* Well Lord knows I don't.

SHARON: *(Crossing to Ray's table.)* Why don't you call *them?*

RAY: Fat chance.

PHIL'S VOICE: *(Over loud splashing.)* Wow! That's too hot!

SALLY'S VOICE: I'm sorry! I'll put in some cold!

(Mark sits up, watches Vince trying to sew. Vince doesn't see him.)

SHARON: Why don't you try?

RAY: They'll just put me on hold.

SHARON: I'm getting nervous here. Tell them you're in a hurry.

RAY: Tell who? After five now they put us on automatic hold. All we get is music.

RUTH: *(Indicating pile to Andy.)* This is quite a pile.

ANDY: Fourteen years.

SHARON: Music?

RAY: You want to hear the love theme from *Doctor Zhivago?*

SHARON: Oh boy! They make you sit in a car all day long, peddle your papers, stay in a crummy place like this, and all you get at the end is *Doctor Zhivago.*

RAY: Actually I like *Doctor Zhivago.*

SHARON: They *own Doctor Zhivago…*

RAY: Knock it off.

SHARON: They're paying themselves money for putting it on.

RAY: Knock it off, O.K.

PHIL'S VOICE: Where's the soap?

SALLY'S VOICE: Here's the soap…I said, *here's the soap,* Phil!

RUTH: *(To Andy, indicating pile.)* What will we do with them?

ANDY: I don't know.

SHARON: *(To Ray.)* Let's get out of here. They don't know you're alive.

(Ray looks at telephone.)

SALLY'S VOICE: Now what are you doing?

PHIL'S VOICE: Washing your back.

SALLY'S VOICE: That's not my back, Phil. *(Giggles and squeals.)*

RAY: If we left, where would we go?

SHARON: Anywhere but that lousy, stinking Ramada.

RAY: Name a place, then.

SHARON: And I don't want to sit around some smoky bar, with a lot of drunken salesmen, and the TV blaring away.

RAY: You're kind of hard to please, Sharon.

SHARON: I know it.

RAY: You live around here. Think of a place.

SHARON: *(Sitting on the edge of a chair.)* I'm thinking…

ANDY: *(Stacking photographs, giving them to Ruth.)* Oh hell. Take them home. *(He gets up off the floor, brushes himself off.)*

RUTH: Thank you, Andy. *(She prepares to leave.)*

SHARON: *(To Ray.)* We could go to the movies.

RAY: What movie?

SHARON: Not *Jaws*.

RAY: How about *The Swinging Stewardesses?*

SHARON: Never.

RAY: Let's skip the movies.

MARK: *(Calling over to Vince.)* That's O.K., Dad.

VINCE: Huh?

MARK: That's O.K.

VINCE: *(Struggling with sewing.)* I can do it.

RUTH: *(With photographs, purse, and jacket.)* I'll be going then. *(She starts left.)*

ANDY: Ruth…
    (Ruth stops.)

ANDY: Can I come home tonight?
    (Ruth looks at him.)

SHARON: *(To Ray.)* Do you like to bowl?

RAY: Naw.

SHARON: Neither do I.

RUTH: *(To Andy.)* Just tonight?

ANDY: I don't want to stay here, Ruth.

RUTH: It'll just stir up the kids.

RAY: Do you like discos?

SHARON: No.

RAY: Too bad.

RUTH: If you come home, Andy, I want more than one night.

PHIL'S VOICE: *(Singing from bathroom, more joyfully.)* "We all lived at the Wayside Motor Inn…"

ANDY: There's my job, Ruth.

RUTH: And there's mine. And the kids. And our friends. And the house…

SHARON: I know where there's a party.

RAY: *(Getting up.)* Let's go.

SHARON: It's to raise money for mental health.

RAY: *(Sitting down.)* Let's not.

RUTH: We should talk about all these things.

ANDY: We have.

RUTH: We haven't. Not really. Ever.

ANDY: What more is there to say?

RUTH: *(Clutching photographs.)* I don't know. All I know is I don't see how two people, who obviously feel strongly about each other, can just throw away fourteen perfectly good years.

(Pause. Andy looks at her, then grabs his parka and briefcase. They go out together. Mark moves down to the edge of the balcony.)

MARK: Really, Dad. That's O.K.

VINCE: *(Determinedly.)* I can do this thing.

(He sews grimly. Mark sits on the edge and watches.)

SHARON: *(Making up her mind, standing up.)* Oh what the hell. Want to come home?

RAY: Home?

SHARON: Where I live.

RAY: Sure. I'll go home with you.

SHARON: I'll give you homemade bread.

RAY: I hope that's not all you'll give me.

SHARON: I'll get wine. Wine's O.K. I'll give you wine.

RAY: Bread and wine and what else?

SHARON: *(After a pause.)* My mother's there.

RAY: Your mother?

SHARON: Who do you think sits with my kid?

RAY: O.K. I'll drive your mother home. You put the kid to bed.

SHARON: She lives there.

RAY: Your mother?

SHARON: She helps with the rent.

RAY: Does she have her own room?

SHARON: Sure.

RAY: Does she go to bed? Does she sleep?

SHARON: She might get up.

(Ray starts to light another cigarette.)

SHARON: Please don't smoke. Please.

(Ray shakes out the match.)

RAY: I'll be quick. I'll leave.

SHARON: I don't like that idea.

RAY: Why not?

SHARON: I just don't.

RAY: You're middle-class too, huh, Sharon?

SHARON: I guess I am.

(Jessie's telephone rings. She answers it quickly.)

JESSIE: Yeah?…Oh hello, darling…

RAY: Why not stay here?

SHARON: Here? At the Wayside?

JESSIE: Oh good…

RAY: Sure.

JESSIE: Oh fine.

SHARON: I wouldn't stay here if you paid me.

RAY: It's the only place left, Sharon.

JESSIE: Oh wonderful. Wait out front, and I'll get your father…

SHARON: I'd feel right under their thumb, staying here.

JESSIE: Good-bye, darling. *(Jessie hangs up.)*

SHARON: Tell you what: you come home and say hello, and maybe next time…

JESSIE: Frank. They're here, sweetheart.

FRANK'S VOICE: *(From bathroom.)* Good.

JESSIE: *(Grabbing a shawl.)* I'll just run down for a minute. *(She goes off left.)*

RAY: How about this: you stay here, and next time, I come home and say hello.

MARK: I'm hungry, Dad.

VINCE: Let me finish this damn thing…

SHARON: I'm beginning to think it's hard for two people to get together around here.

RAY: You make it hard.

SHARON: So do you.

(Loud splashings from bathroom.)

SALLY'S VOICE: *(Singing.)* "Rubber Ducky, I love you…"

(Phil joins her. More laughing and splashing is heard.)

SHARON: You're the first man I've asked home in years, and you won't even come.

RAY: How can I risk a good job, just to meet somebody's mother?

SHARON: All right. If I stay, what happens tomorrow?

RAY: *(After a pause.)* I've got this wife.

SHARON: *(Turning toward door.)* I guess I'll go.

RAY: What's wrong with just tonight?

SHARON: *(Turning back by the doorway.)* I happen to want a more personal relationship.

RAY: *(Coming to her.)* Oh yeah? Personal? *(He kisses her, then steps back.)* You don't even know my name. *(He stands back, lights a cigarette.)*

SALLY AND PHIL'S VOICE: *(From bathroom.)* Oh wow!…Oh my God!

THE WAYSIDE MOTOR INN 217

SHARON: Sure I do. It's…it's…

MARK: *(Impatiently.)* Come on, Dad.

VINCE: I'm almost there, Markie.

RAY: The name's Ray, Sharon.

SHARON: So long, Ray.

RAY: So long, Sharon.

> *(She goes out. Ray returns to his table, picks up* Penthouse.*)*

VINCE: *(Finishing his sewing.)* There? See? Your old man can still fix a thing or two. My grandfather used to sew. Back in the old country. Pretty good, eh? *(Holds out a miserably repaired shirt.)* Try it on.

MARK: *(Taking the shirt.)* That's all right, Dad.

VINCE: I fixed your shirt, didn't I?

MARK: Uh huh.

VINCE: Not as good as your mom. But fixed, huh?

MARK: Right, Dad.

VINCE: Does Foley sew shirts? Huh?

MARK: No.

VINCE: Your Dad, your DAD sews your shirt for you.

MARK: Right, Dad.

VINCE: So. You're gonna wear it for your interview, huh?

MARK: No.

VINCE: What? All my work…

MARK: Sorry, Dad.

> *(Pause.)*

VINCE: You gonna wear the pink one?

MARK: No.

> *(Pause.)*

VINCE: You gonna tell them you want delayed admissions?

MARK: I don't think so.

VINCE: I'll buy you a shirt tomorrow in Harvard Square.

MARK: I'll pick it out.

VINCE: But I'll pay. O.K.? I'll pay.

MARK: O.K.

> *(Pause.)*

VINCE: So. Want to go eat?

MARK: *(Getting up.)* O.K. *(He gets his jacket from the closet.)*

VINCE: *(Following him in.)* How's your stomach?

MARK: Fine.

VINCE: Sure?

MARK: Really, Dad. It's fine.

VINCE: *(Carefully.)* Want to check it out with Foley first?

MARK: No. *(Pause.)* Do you want to check it with Bill Baldwin?

(Pause.)

VINCE: Touché, pal.

(Pause.)

MARK: Let's just go, Dad.

VINCE: Right. Let's go.

(They go out left. Frank comes out of the bathroom, buttoning his shirt. He goes to his bed, begins slowly to put on his shoes. Jessie comes hurriedly in from left.)

JESSIE: Oh please, sweetie. Hurry. They brought the baby. Wait till you see him.

FRANK: *(Putting on his shoes.)* I'll be right there.

JESSIE: *(Kneeling; trying to help with his shoes.)* And they found this nice doctor who'll see you right in his own home.

FRANK: I can still tie my own shoes, Jess!

JESSIE: *(Getting up, going to closet, getting his coat.)* And then, we'll all go get something to eat.

(Frank stands up, ties his tie in the mirror over the bureau. Jessie brings him his coat.)

JESSIE: They got a sitter for the other kids, but Joan said the baby might want to nurse. Isn't that marvelous, just bringing him along? Here, darling. *(She holds out his coat.)*

FRANK: Stop fussing, Jess. I can do things myself! *(He decides to retie his tie.)*

JESSIE: *(Hurt.)* All right. *(She lays his coat on the bed.)*

FRANK: *(Turning; coming to her.)* Jess. Forgive me, Jess. *(He kisses her on the cheek.)*

JESSIE: *(Smiling.)* At least I can hold the baby.

(She goes out left. Frank sighs, and continues dressing. Ray turns on his TV. A family sitcom is in progress. We hear it as Frank continues to get dressed.)

TV SON: Gee, Dad. If I don't get the car tonight, I'll be nowhere.

(Canned laughter.)

TV FATHER: Sonny, if you get the car tonight, *I'll* be nowhere.

(Canned laughter.)

TV MOTHER: Let him have the car, Morris. What's a car between friends?

TV FATHER: Who says we're friends?

(Canned laughter. Frank by now is dressed. He has turned off the light by his bed, and pocketed his pills. Suddenly, by the edge of the bed, he has an

other attack. He sits on the bed, reaches into his pocket, takes a pill. Ray's TV continues.)

TV MOTHER: Why do you want the car anyway, Morris?

TV SON: He wants to see his psychiatrist.

(Laughter.)

TV MOTHER: He wants to see his secretary.

(Laughter.)

TV FATHER: I want to see my mother.

(Frank sits on the edge of the bed, recovering. Sally and Phil come out of the bathroom, draped in towels.)

SALLY: Jesus, Phil. In the *bath*tub!

PHIL: *(Proudly.)* What the hell.

SALLY: I dunno. I feel kind of kinky.

PHIL: I like it.

SALLY: Gosh. In the bathtub. Is that what happens next year? We have to do it in the bathtub?

(Phil embraces her. Ray's telephone rings. He turns off the TV and quickly answers it, as he organizes his work in front of him.)

RAY: Yo. Roger. Two zero one. Ready.

(He begins to read figures into the phone.)

RAY: Hyannis, seventeen…New Bedford, twenty-two…Wakefield, four…

(These figures continue on through to the end of the play. Phil is whispering something to Sally.)

SALLY: Again?

PHIL: Why not?

SALLY: O.K. But in bed.

PHIL: I'll get the light.

(He turns off the light in the dressing area. Both slip into bed. Lights remain on Ray's table and on the balcony.)

SALLY: *(On bed.)* I'm old-fashioned. I like beds.

PHIL: Shall I turn on the magic fingers?

SALLY: God NO!

(Frank seems to be all right. He gets up, starts for the doorway, then suddenly stops, leans against the wall.)

FRANK: *(Calling toward off left.)* Jessie!

RAY: *(Continuing to recite figures into the phone.)* Somerville, thirteen minus the two…Newton, twenty-seven…Weston, six, plus the two…Wayland, three plus fifteen…Sudbury, two and the twelve…

(Frank staggers back to his bed, sits on the edge, breathing heavily. Ray, continuing.)

RAY: Quincy, fifteen…Cohasset, three plus nine…Hingham, ten…Lowell, twenty, plus the six…

PHIL: *(In bed.)* Oh boy! Here we go again!

SALLY: Slow down. We've got all night.

(Jessie hurries in from left, carrying an infant wrapped in her shawl.)

JESSIE: *(Exuberantly.)* Oh Frank, look what I found outside!

(Frank looks at her, unable to move, alone in his pain. She looks at him, at the baby in her arms, at the door, as the lights begin to dim.)

RAY: *(On telephone, concurrently.)* Lexington, seven oh two…Concord, nine plus five…Salem, four plus fourteen…Charlestown, six…Plymouth, ten minus the two…

(The lights are out by now.)

The End

The Dining Room
(1982)

AUTHOR'S NOTE

The Dining Room was commercially successful enough to enable me to leave my teaching job at M.I.T. in Boston, and devote full time to writing plays in New York. It brings together in a single resonant space the fragmented, mosaic structure I had explored in *Scenes from American Life, Richard Cory,* and *The Wayside Motor Inn.* Like *Children,* it takes place over the course of one day, yet like *The Middle Ages,* it leaps through a number of years. The play opened in a tiny theatre at Playwrights Horizons on 42nd Street, and became popular enough to settle into a long run off-Broadway. Since then, it has been done all over the country and all over the world. Its setting may still be elitist, but its form is certainly democratic, and I hope that its subject matter, in the sense that all families want to sit down and eat together, is universal. I owe a debt to Thornton Wilder for this one, particularly his short play, *The Long Christmas Dinner.*

ORIGINAL PRODUCTION

The Dining Room was first produced at the Studio Theatre of Playwrights Horizons, in New York City, opening January 31, 1982, with the following cast:

1st Actor:	Remak Ramsay
2nd Actor:	John Shea
3rd Actor:	W.H. Macy
1st Actress:	Lois de Banzie
2nd Actress:	Ann McDonough
3rd Actress:	Pippa Pearthree

It was directed by David Trainer. Loren Sherman designed the set, Deborah Shaw the costumes, and Frances Aronson the lighting. The production stage manager was M. A. Howard. Eternal thanks to them all.

CASTING SUGGESTIONS

If a cast of six is used, and there are strong arguments for using this number, the following casting of the roles has proved to be workable and successful:

1st Actor: Father, Michael, Brewster, Grandfather, Stuart, Gordon, David, Harvey, and Host

2nd Actor: Client, Howard, Psychiatrist, Ted, Paul, Ben, Chris, Jim, Dick, and Guest

3rd Actor: Arthur, Boy, Architect, Billy, Nick, Fred, Tony, Standish, and Guest

1st Actress: Agent, Mother, Carolyn, Sandra, Dora, Margery, Beth, Kate, Claire, Ruth

2nd Actress: Annie, Grace, Peggy, Nancy, Sarah, Harriet, Emily, Annie, and Guest

3rd Actress: Sally, Girl, Ellie, Aggie, Winkie, Old Lady, Helen, Meg, Bertha, and Guest

SETTING

The play takes place in a dining room—or rather, many dining rooms. The same dining room furniture serves for all: a lovely burnished, shining dining room table; two chairs, with arms, at either end; two more, armless, along each side; several additional matching chairs, placed so as to define the walls of the room. Upstage somewhere, a sideboard, with a mirror over it.

Upstage, left, a swinging door leads to the pantry and kitchen. Upstage, right, an archway leads to the front hall and the rest of the house. But we should see no details from these other rooms. Both entrances should be masked in such a way as to suggest a limbo outside the dining room.

There should be a good, hardwood floor, possibly parquet, covered with a good, warm oriental rug.

A sense of the void surrounds the room. It might almost seem to be surrounded by a velvet-covered low-slung chain on brass stanchions, as if it were on display in some museum, many years from now.

Since there are no walls to the dining room, windows should be suggested through lighting. The implication should be that there are large French doors downstage, and maybe windows along another wall.

Since the play takes place during the course of a day, the light should change accordingly.

The play requires a cast of six—three men, three women—and seems to work best with this number. Conceivably it could be done with more, but it would be impossible to do with fewer. The various roles should be assigned democratically; there should be no emphasis on one particular type of role. It might be good to cast the play with people of different ages, sizes, and shapes, as long as they are all good actors.

It would seem to make sense to end the play with the same actors playing Ruth, Annie, and the Host as played Mother, Annie, and Father in the breakfast scene in Act I.

For costumes, it is suggested that the Men wear simple, conservative suits, or jackets and slacks, which can be modified as required. For more informal scenes, for example, an actor might appear in shirt sleeves, or a sweater. Women's costumes might seem to pose a more complicated problem but again the best solution turns out to be the simplest: each actress may wear the same simple, classically styled dress—or skirt and blouse—throughout, with perhaps an occasional apron when she plays a maid. There is hardly enough time between scenes for actors to fuss with changes or accessories, and there is an advantage in being as simple and straightforward as possible.

The place mats, glassware, china, and silverware used during the course of the play should be bright, clean, and tasteful. We should only see used what is absolutely necessary for a particular scene. Actual food, of course, should not be served. The thing to remember is that this is not a play about dishes, or food, or costume changes, but rather a play about people in a dining room.

The blending and overlapping of scenes have been carefully worked out to give a sense of both contrast and flow. When there is no blending of scenes, one should follow another as quickly as possible. The play should never degenerate into a series of blackouts.

The Dining Room

No one on stage. The dining room furniture sparkles in the early morning light. Voices from off right. Then a woman real estate Agent and her male Client appear in the doorway. Both wear raincoats.

AGENT: …and the dining room.

CLIENT: Oh boy.

AGENT: You see how these rooms were designed to catch the early morning light?

CLIENT: I'll say.

AGENT: French doors, lovely garden, flowering crabs. Do you like gardening?

CLIENT: Used to.

AGENT: Imagine, imagine having a long, leisurely breakfast in here.

CLIENT: As opposed to instant coffee on Eastern Airlines.

AGENT: Exactly. You know this is a room after my own heart. I grew up in a dining room like this. Same sort of furniture. Everything.

CLIENT: So did I.

AGENT: Then here we are. Welcome home.

> *(Pause.)*

CLIENT: What are they asking again?

AGENT: Make an offer. I think they'll come down.

> *(Another pause.)*

CLIENT: Trouble is, we'll never use this room.

AGENT: Oh now.

CLIENT: We won't. The last two houses we lived in, my wife used the dining room table to sort the laundry.

AGENT: Oh dear.

CLIENT: Maybe you'd better show me something more contemporary.

AGENT: That means something farther out. How long have we got to find you a home?

CLIENT: One day.

AGENT: And how long will the corporation keep you here, after you've found it?

CLIENT: Six months to a year.

AGENT: Oh then definitely we should look farther out. *(She opens the kitchen door.)* You can look at the kitchen as we leave.

CLIENT: You shouldn't have shown me this first.

AGENT: I thought it was something to go by.

CLIENT: You've spoiled everything else.

AGENT: Oh no. We'll find you something if we've got all day. But wasn't it a lovely room?

CLIENT: Let's go, or I'll buy it!

(They both exit through the kitchen door as a Brother comes in from the hall, followed by his Sister. Both are middle-aged. His name is Arthur, hers is Sally.)

ARTHUR: The dining room.

SALLY: Yes…

ARTHUR: Notice how we gravitate right to this room.

SALLY: I know it.

ARTHUR: You sure mother doesn't want this stuff in Florida?

SALLY: She hardly has room for what she's got. She wants us to take turns. Without fighting.

ARTHUR: We'll just have to draw lots then.

SALLY: Unless one of us wants something, and one of us doesn't.

ARTHUR: We have to do it today.

SALLY: Do you think that's enough time to divide up a whole house?

ARTHUR: I have to get back, Sal. *(He looks in the sideboard.)* We'll draw lots and then go through the rooms taking turns. *(He brings out a silver spoon.)* Here. We'll use this salt spoon. *(He shifts it from hand to hand behind his back, then holds out two fists.)* Take your pick. You get the spoon, you get the dining room.

SALLY: You mean you want to start here?

ARTHUR: Got to start somewhere.

(Sally looks at his fists. Annie, a Maid, comes out from the kitchen to set the table for breakfast. She sets placemats at either end and two coffee cups, with saucers. Sally and Arthur take no notice of her. Annie then leaves.)

SALLY: *(Not choosing.)* You mean you want the dining room?

ARTHUR: Yeah.

SALLY: What happened to the stuff you had?

ARTHUR: Jane took it. It was part of the settlement.

SALLY: If you win, where will you put it?

ARTHUR: That's my problem, Sal.

SALLY: I thought you had a tiny apartment.

ARTHUR: I'll find a place.

SALLY: I mean your children won't want it.

ARTHUR: Probably not.

SALLY: Then where on earth…?

ARTHUR: Come on, Sal. Choose.

(He holds out his fists again. She chooses. Arthur lowers his hands. Annie comes in from the kitchen, bringing the morning paper. She puts it at the head of the table and then leaves.)

ARTHUR: You don't want it.

SALLY: Of course I want it!

ARTHUR: I mean you already have a perfectly good dining room.

SALLY: Not as good as this.

ARTHUR: You mean you want two dining rooms?

SALLY: I'd give our old stuff to Debbie.

ARTHUR: To Debbie?

SALLY: She's our oldest child.

ARTHUR: Does Debbie want a dining room?

SALLY: She might.

ARTHUR: In a condominium?

SALLY: She might.

ARTHUR: In Denver?

SALLY: She just might, Arthur.

(A Father comes in from the right. He settles comfortably at the head of the table, unfolds his newspaper importantly.)

ARTHUR: *(Shuffling the spoon behind his back again. Then holding out his fists.)* I don't want to fight. Which hand?

(Sally starts to choose, then stops.)

SALLY: Are you planning to put it in storage?

ARTHUR: I might.

SALLY: I checked on that. That costs an arm and a leg.

ARTHUR: So does shipping it to Denver. *(He holds out his fists.)*

FATHER: *(Calling to kitchen.)* Good morning, Annie.

SALLY: *(Almost picking a hand, then stopping.)* I know what will happen if you win.

ARTHUR: What?

SALLY: You'll end up selling it.

ARTHUR: Selling it?

SALLY: That's what will happen. It will kick around for a while, and you'll end up calling a furniture dealer.

(Annie comes out with a small glass of "orange juice" on a tray.)

ARTHUR: I am absolutely amazed you'd say that.

SALLY: I don't want to fight, Arthur.

ARTHUR: Neither do I. Maybe we should defer the dining room. *(He starts for door, right.)*

SALLY: *(Following him.)* Maybe we should.

ANNIE: Good morning, sir.

FATHER: Good morning, Annie.

ARTHUR: Selling the dining room? Is that what you told Mother I'd do?

SALLY: *(Following him.)* I told her I'd give you the piano if I can have the dining room…

ARTHUR: I'll be lucky if I keep this spoon.

SALLY: I'll give you the piano and the coffee table if I have the dining room. *(Arthur and Sally exit into the hall.)*

FATHER: Annie…

(Annie is almost to the kitchen door.)

ANNIE: Yes sir…

FATHER: Did I find a seed in my orange juice yesterday morning?

ANNIE: I strained it, sir.

FATHER: I'm sure you did, Annie. Nonetheless I think I may have detected a small seed.

ANNIE: I'll strain it twice, sir.

FATHER: Seeds can wreak havoc with the digestion, Annie.

ANNIE: Yes, sir.

FATHER: They can take root. And grow.

ANNIE: Yes, sir. I'm sorry, sir. *(Annie goes out.)*

(Father drinks his orange juice carefully, and reads his newspaper. A little Girl sticks her head out through the dining room door.)

GIRL: Daddy…

FATHER: Yes, good morning, Lizzie Boo.

GIRL: Daddy, could Charlie and me—

FATHER: Charlie and I…

GIRL: …Charlie and I come out and sit with you while you have breakfast?

FATHER: You certainly may, Lizzikins. I'd be delighted to have the pleasure of your company, provided—

GIRL: Yippee!

FATHER: I said, PROVIDED you sit quietly, without leaning back in your chairs, and don't fight or argue.

GIRL: *(Calling off.)* He says we *can!*

FATHER: I said you *may,* sweetheart.

(The Girl comes out adoringly, followed by a Little Boy.)

GIRL: *(Kissing her father.)* Good morning, Daddy.

BOY: *(Kissing him too.)* Morning, Dad.

(*They settle into their seats. Annie brings out the Father's "breakfast."*)

ANNIE: Here's your cream, sir.

FATHER: Thank you, Annie.

ANNIE: You're welcome, sir. *(Annie goes out.)*

(*The children watch their father.*)

BOY: Dad…

FATHER: Hmmm?

BOY: When do we get to have fresh cream on our shredded wheat?

GIRL: When you grow up, that's when.

FATHER: I'll tell you one thing. If there's a war, no one gets cream. If there's a war, we'll all have to settle for top of the bottle.

GIRL: Mother said she was thinking about having us eat dinner in here with you every night.

FATHER: Yes. Your mother and I are both thinking about that. And we're both looking forward to it. As soon as you children learn to sit up straight… *(They quickly do.)*

FATHER: …then I see no reason why we shouldn't all have a pleasant meal together every evening.

BOY: Could we try it tonight, Dad? Could you give us a test?

FATHER: No, Charlie. Not tonight. Because tonight we're giving a small dinner party. But I hope very much you and Liz will come down and shake hands.

GIRL: I get so shy, Dad.

FATHER: Well you'll just have to learn, sweetie pie. Half of life is learning to meet people.

BOY: What's the other half, Dad?

(*Pause. The Father fixes him with a steely gaze.*)

FATHER: Was that a crack?

BOY: No, Dad…

FATHER: That was a crack, wasn't it?

BOY: No, Dad. Really…

FATHER: That sounded very much like a smart-guy wisecrack to me. And people who make cracks like that don't normally eat in dining rooms.

BOY: I didn't mean it as a crack, Dad.

FATHER: Then we'll ignore it. We'll go on with our breakfast.

(*Annie comes in.*)

ANNIE: *(To Girl.)* Your car's here, Lizzie. For school. *(Annie goes out.)*

GIRL: *(Jumping up.)* O.K.

FATHER: *(To Girl.)* Thank you, Annie.

GIRL: Thank you, Annie... *(Kisses Father.)* Good-bye, Daddy.

FATHER: Good-bye, darling. Don't be late. Say good morning to the driver. Sit quietly in the car. Work hard. Run. Run. Good-bye.

(Girl goes off. Father returns to his paper. Pause. Boy sits watching his father.)

BOY: Dad, can I read the funnies?

FATHER: Certainly. Certainly you may.

(He carefully extracts the second section and hands it to his son. Both read, the Son trying to imitate the Father in how he does it. Finally:)

FATHER: This won't mean much to you, but the government is systematically ruining this country.

BOY: Miss Kelly told us about the government.

FATHER: Oh really. And who is Miss Kelly, pray tell?

BOY: She's my teacher.

FATHER: I don't remember any Miss Kelly.

BOY: She's new, Dad.

FATHER: I see. And what has she been telling you?

BOY: She said there's a depression going on.

FATHER: I see.

BOY: People all over the country are standing in line for bread.

FATHER: I see.

BOY: So the government has to step in and do something.

(Long pause. Then:)

FATHER: Annie!

ANNIE: *(Coming out of kitchen.)* Yes, sir.

FATHER: I'd very much like some more coffee, please.

ANNIE: Yes, sir. *(Annie goes out.)*

FATHER: You tell Miss Kelly she's wrong.

BOY: Why?

FATHER: I'll tell you exactly why: if the government keeps on handing out money, no one will want to work. And if no one wants to work, there won't be anyone around to support such things as private schools. And if no one is supporting private schools, then Miss Kelly will be standing on the bread lines along with everyone else. You tell Miss Kelly that, if you please. Thank you, Annie.

(Annie comes in and pours coffee. Father returns to his paper. Annie has retreated to the kitchen. Boy reads his funnies for a moment. Then:)

BOY: Dad...

FATHER: *(Reading)* Hmmm?

BOY: Could we leave a little earlier today?

FATHER: We'll leave when we always leave.

BOY: But I'm always late, Dad.

FATHER: Nonsense.

BOY: I am, Dad. Yesterday I had to walk into assembly while they were still singing the hymn.

FATHER: A minute or two late…

BOY: Everyone looked at me, Dad.

FATHER: You tell everyone to concentrate on that hymn.

BOY: I can't, Dad…

FATHER: It's that new stoplight on Richmond Avenue. It affects our timing.

BOY: It's not just the new stoplight, Dad. Sometimes I come in when they're already doing arithmetic. Miss Kelly says I should learn to be punctual.

FATHER: *(Putting down paper.)* Miss Kelly again, eh?

BOY: She said if everyone is late, no one would learn any mathematics.

FATHER: Now you listen to me, Charlie. Miss Kelly may be an excellent teacher. Her factoring may be flawless, her geography beyond question. But Miss Kelly does not teach us politics. Nor does she teach us how to run our lives. She is not going to tell you, or me, to leave in the middle of a pleasant breakfast, and get caught in the bulk of the morning traffic, just so that you can arrive in time for a silly hymn. Long after you've forgotten that hymn, long after you've forgotten how to factor, long after you've forgotten Miss Kelly, you will remember these pleasant breakfasts around this dining room table.

(Mother glides into the room from the right.)

FATHER: And here is your mother to prove it.

MOTHER: *(Kissing Father.)* Good morning, dear. *(Kissing Charlie.)* Good morning, Charlie.

FATHER: *(Remaining seated.)* I know people who leap to their feet when a beautiful woman enters the room.

(Charlie jumps up.)

MOTHER: Oh that's all right, dear.

FATHER: I also know people who rush to push in their mother's chair.

(Charlie does so.)

MOTHER: Thank you, dear.

FATHER: And finally, I know people who are quick to give their mother the second section of the morning paper.

CHARLIE: Oh! Here, Mum.

MOTHER: Thank you, dear.

FATHER: Now Charlie: take a moment, if you would, just to look at your lovely mother, bathed in the morning sunlight, and reflected in the dining
room table.

MOTHER: Oh Russell…

(Charlie looks at his mother.)

FATHER: Look at her, Charlie, and then ask yourself carefully, Which is worth
our ultimate attention? Your Mother? Or Miss Kelly?

MOTHER: Who is Miss Kelly?

FATHER: Never mind, dear. Which, Charlie?

CHARLIE: My Mother.

FATHER: Good, Charlie. Fine. *(He gets up; taking his section of the paper.)* And
now, I think you and I should make a trip upstairs before we say good-
bye, and are on our way.

*(Mother smiles sweetly. Charlie gives his Mother a kiss. Father and Son leave
the room. Annie enters, carrying coffee server.)*

MOTHER: Good morning, Annie.

ANNIE: Good morning, Mrs.

MOTHER: Tell Irma I'll have poached eggs this morning, please, Annie.

ANNIE: Yes, Mrs.*(Annie goes out.)*

*(Mother sits sipping coffee, reading her section of the paper. A Youngish
Woman—call her Ellie—comes out of the kitchen. Her arms are stacked
with a small portable typewriter, papers, several books and notebooks. She
finds a place at the table and begins to spread things out around her. Mother
pays no attention to her. A Man called Howard, carrying a briefcase, appears
at right.)*

HOWARD: Hey!

ELLIE: Ooooops. I thought you had gone.

HOWARD: I forgot my briefcase…What's going on?

ELLIE: I have to get this term paper done.

HOWARD: In here?

ELLIE: Where else.

HOWARD: You're going to *type?*

ELLIE: Of course I'm going to type.

HOWARD: In here? At that table?

ELLIE: Why not?

HOWARD: You're going to sit there, banging a typewriter on my family's dining room *table?*

ELLIE: Why not?

HOWARD: Because it wasn't designed for it, that's why!

ELLIE: *(Sighing)* Oh, Howard...

HOWARD: Lucky I came back. Next thing you know, you'll be feeding the dog off our Lowestoft china.

ELLIE: It's got rubber pads under it. I checked. *(Gets up, goes to sideboard.)* And I'll get something else, if you want. *(She takes out a couple of place mats.)*

HOWARD: You're not going to use those place mats?

ELLIE: I thought I would. Yes.

HOWARD: Those are good place mats.

ELLIE: We haven't used them in ten years.

HOWARD: Those are extremely good place mats, Ellie. Mother got those in Italy.

ELLIE: All *right*.

(She puts the place mats back in the sideboard rummages around finds a couple of hot pads. He watches her carefully.)

ELLIE: I'll use these, then. Mind if I use these? We put pots on them. We can certainly put a typewriter.

(She carries them to the table, puts them under the typewriter, continues to get things set up. Howard watches her. Meanwhile, Mother, impatient for her poached eggs, puts down her paper and rings a little silver bell on the table in front of her. Annie comes out of the kitchen.)

ANNIE: Yes, Mrs?

MOTHER: I wonder if anything might have happened to my poached eggs, Annie.

ANNIE: Irma's cooking two more, Mrs.

MOTHER: Two more?

ANNIE: The first ones slid off the plate while she was buttering the toast.

MOTHER: *(Standing up.)* Is she drinking again, Annie?

ANNIE: No, Mrs.

MOTHER: Tell me the truth.

ANNIE: I don't think so, Mrs.

MOTHER: I'd better go see...A simple question of two poached eggs. *(She starts for the kitchen.)* Honestly, Annie, sometimes I think it's almost better if we just do things our*selves*.

ANNIE: Yes, Mrs.

(Mother goes out into the kitchen; Annie clears the Mother's and Father's places, leaving a glass and plate for the next scene. Annie exits.)

ELLIE: *(To Howard, who is standing at the doorway, still watching.)* Don't you have a plane to catch? It's kind of hard to work when your husband is hovering over you, like a helicopter.

HOWARD: Well it's kind of hard to leave when your wife is systematically mutilating the dining room table.

ELLIE: I'll be careful, Howard. I swear. Now good-bye.

(She begins to hunt and peck on the typewriter. Howard starts out, then wheels on her.)

HOWARD: Couldn't you *please* work somewhere else?

ELLIE: I'd like to know where, please.

HOWARD: What's wrong with the kitchen table?

ELLIE: It doesn't work, Howard. Last time the kids got peanut butter all over my footnotes.

HOWARD: I'll set up the bridge table in the living room.

ELLIE: I'd just have to move whenever you and the boys wanted to watch a football game.

HOWARD: You mean, you're going to leave all that stuff *there?*

ELLIE: I thought I would. Yes.

HOWARD: All that shit? All over the dining room?

ELLIE: It's a term paper, Howard. It's crucial for my degree.

HOWARD: You mean you're going to commandeer the *din*ing room for the rest of the *term?*

ELLIE: It just sits here, Howard. It's never used.

HOWARD: What if we want to give a dinner party?

ELLIE: Since when have we given a dinner party?

HOWARD: What if we want to have a few people *over,* for Chrissake?

ELLIE: We can eat in the kitchen.

HOWARD: Oh Jesus.

ELLIE: Everybody does these days.

HOWARD: That doesn't make it right.

ELLIE: Let me get this done, Howard! Let me get a good grade, and my Master's degree, and a good job, so I can be *out* of here every day!

HOWARD: Fine! What the hell! Then why don't I turn it into a *tool* room, every night? *(He storms out.)*

(Ellie doggedly returns to her work, angrily hunting and pecking on the typewriter. Grace enters from right. She sits downstage left, and begins to work on her grocery list. Carolyn, a girl of fourteen, enters sleepily a moment later.)

CAROLYN: Why did you tell Mildred to wake me up, Mother?

GRACE: Let me just finish this grocery list.

CAROLYN: I mean it's Saturday, Mother.

GRACE: *(Finishing the list with a flourish.)* Sshh…There. *(Puts down the list.)*

I know it's Saturday, darling, and I apologize. But something has come up, and I want you to make a little decision.

CAROLYN: What decision?

GRACE: Start your breakfast, dear. No one can think on an empty stomach.
(Carolyn sits at the table.)

GRACE: Now. Guess who telephoned this morning?

CAROLYN: Who?

GRACE: Your Aunt Martha.

CAROLYN: Oh I love her.

GRACE: So do I. But the poor thing hasn't got enough to do, so she was on the telephone at the crack of dawn.

CAROLYN: What did she want?

GRACE: Well now here's the thing: she's got an extra ticket for the theatre tonight, and she wants you to join her.

CAROLYN: Sure!

GRACE: Now wait till I've finished, dear. I told her it was your decision, of course, but I thought you had other plans.

CAROLYN: What other plans?

GRACE: Now think, darling. Isn't there something rather special going on in your life this evening?
(Pause.)

CAROLYN: Oh.

GRACE: Am I right, or am I right.

CAROLYN: *(Grimly.)* Dancing school.

ELLIE: Shit. *(She begins to gather up her materials.)*

GRACE: Not dancing school, sweetheart. The first session of the Junior Assemblies. Which are a big step beyond dancing school.

ELLIE: I can't work in this place! It's like a tomb! *(She goes out into the kitchen.)*

GRACE: I told Aunt Martha you'd call her right back, so she could drum up someone else.

CAROLYN: I thought it was my decision.

GRACE: It is, sweetheart. Of course.

CAROLYN: Then I'd like to see a play with Aunt Martha.
(Pause.)

GRACE: Carolyn, I wonder if you're being just a little impulsive this morning. You don't even know what the play is.

CAROLYN: What is it, then?

GRACE: Well it happens to be a very talky play called *Saint Joan*.

CAROLYN: Oh we read that in school! I want to go all the more!

GRACE: It's the road company, sweetheart. It doesn't even have Katherine Cornell.

CAROLYN: I'd still like to go.

GRACE: To some endless play? With your maiden aunt?

CAROLYN: She's my favorite person.

GRACE: Well then go, if it's that important to you.

CAROLYN: *(Getting up.)* I'll call her right now. *(She starts for the door.)*

GRACE: Carolyn…

(Carolyn stops.)

GRACE: You realize, of course, that on the first Junior Assembly, everyone gets acquainted.

CAROLYN: Really?

GRACE: Oh heavens yes. It starts the whole thing off on the right foot.

CAROLYN: I didn't know that.

GRACE: Oh yes. It's like the first day of school. Once you miss, you never catch up.

CAROLYN: Oh gosh.

GRACE: You see? You see why we shouldn't make hasty decisions.

(Pause.)

CAROLYN: Then maybe I won't go at all.

GRACE: What do you mean?

CAROLYN: Maybe I'll skip all the Junior Assemblies.

GRACE: Oh Carolyn.

CAROLYN: I don't like dancing school anyway.

GRACE: Don't be silly.

CAROLYN: I don't. I've never liked it. I'm bigger than half the boys, and I never know what to say, and I'm a terrible dancer. Last year I spent half the time in the ladies room.

GRACE: That's nonsense.

CAROLYN: It's true, Mother. I hate dancing school. I don't know why I have to go. Saint Joan wouldn't go to dancing school in a million years!

GRACE: Yes, and look what happened to Saint Joan!

CAROLYN: I don't care. I've made up my mind.

(Pause.)

GRACE: Your Aunt Martha seems to have caused a little trouble around here this morning.

CAROLYN: Maybe.

GRACE: Your Aunt Martha seems to have opened up a whole can of worms.

CAROLYN: I'm glad she did.

GRACE: All right. And how do you propose to spend your other Saturday nights? I mean, when there's no Aunt Martha. And no Saint Joan? And all your friends are having the time of their life at Junior Assemblies?

CAROLYN: I'll do something.

GRACE: Such as what? Hanging around here? Listening to that stupid Hit Parade? Bothering the maids when we're planning to have a party?

(Aggie, a Maid, comes out of the kitchen, sits at the table, begins to polish some flat silver with a silver cloth.)

CAROLYN: I'll do some thing, Mother.

GRACE: *(Picking up Carolyn's breakfast dishes.)* Well you're obviously not old enough to make an intelligent decision.

CAROLYN: I knew you wouldn't let me decide.

GRACE: *(Wheeling on her.)* All right, then! Decide!

CAROLYN: I'd like to—

GRACE: But let me tell you a very short story before you do. About your dear Aunt Martha. Who also made a little decision when she was about your age. She decided—if you breathe a word of this, I'll strangle you—she decided she was in love with her riding master. And so she threw everything up, and ran off with him. To Taos, New Mexico. Where your father had to track her down and drag her back. But it was too late, Carolyn! She had been…overstimulated. And from then on in, she refused to join the workday world. Now there it is. In a nutshell. So think about it, while I'm ordering the groceries. And decide. *(She goes out left, carrying Carolyn's glass and plate.)*

(Aggie polishes the silver. Carolyn sits and thinks. She decides.)

CAROLYN: I've decided, Mother.

GRACE'S VOICE: *(From the kitchen.)* Good. I hope you've come to your senses.

CAROLYN: *(Getting up.)* I've decided to talk to Aunt Martha. *(She goes out.)*

GRACE: *(Bursting through the kitchen door.)* You've got a dentist appointment, Carolyn! You've got riding lessons at noon—no, no, well skip the riding lessons, but—Carolyn! Carolyn!

(She rushes out through the hall as Michael comes in through the kitchen. He is about twelve.)

MICHAEL: *(Sneaking up on her.)* Boo!

AGGIE: Michael! You scared me out of my skin!

MICHAEL: I wanted to.

(Pause. He comes a little more into the room. Aggie returns to her polishing.)

AGGIE: Your mother said you was sick this morning.

MICHAEL: I was. I am.

AGGIE: So sick you couldn't go to school.

MICHAEL: I *am*, Aggie! I upchucked! Twice!

AGGIE: Then you get right straight back to bed.

(He doesn't.)

MICHAEL: How come you didn't do my room yet?

AGGIE: Because I thought you was sleeping.

MICHAEL: I've just been *lying* there, Ag. Waiting.

AGGIE: Well I got more to do now, since Ida left. I got the silver, and the downstairs lavatory, and all the beds besides.

(He comes farther in.)

MICHAEL: My mother says you want to leave us.

(She polishes.)

AGGIE: When did she say that?

MICHAEL: Last Thursday. On your day off. When she was cooking dinner. She said now there's a war, you're looking for a job with more money.

(Aggie polishes.)

MICHAEL: Is that true, Ag?

AGGIE: Maybe.

MICHAEL: Money isn't everything, Aggie.

AGGIE: Listen to him now.

MICHAEL: You can be rich as a king and still be miserable. Look at my Uncle Paul. He's rich as Croesus and yet he's drinking himself into oblivion.

AGGIE: What do you know about all that?

MICHAEL: I know a lot. I eat dinner here in the dining room now. I listen. And I know that my Uncle Paul is drinking himself into oblivion. And Mrs. Williams has a tipped uterus.

AGGIE: Here now. You stop that talk.

MICHAEL: Well, it's *true,* Ag. And it proves that money isn't everything. So you don't have to leave us.

(Pause. She works. He drifts around the table.)

AGGIE: It's not just the money, darlin'.

MICHAEL: Then *what,* Ag? *(No answer.)* Don't you like us any more?

AGGIE: Oh, Michael…

MICHAEL: Don't you like our family?

AGGIE: Oh, Mikey…

MICHAEL: Are you still mad at me for peeking at you in the bathtub?

AGGIE: That's enough now.

MICHAEL: Then what *is* it, Ag? How come you're just leaving?

(Pause.)

AGGIE: Because I don't... *(Pause.)* I don't want to do domestic service no
more.

MICHAEL: Why?

AGGIE: Because I don't like it no more, Mike.

(He thinks.)

MICHAEL: That's because Ida left and you have too much to do, Ag.

AGGIE: No darlin'...

MICHAEL: *(Sitting down near her.)* I'll help you, Ag. I swear! I'll make my own
bed, and pick up my towel. I'll try to be much more careful when I pee!

AGGIE: *(Laughing.)* Lord love you, lad.

MICHAEL: No, no, really. I will. And I'll tell my parents not to have so many
dinner parties, Ag. I'll tell them to give you more time off. I'll tell them
to give you all day Sunday.

AGGIE: No, darlin'. No.

MICHAEL: I'm *ser*ious, Ag.

AGGIE: I know, darlin'! I know.

(Two Men come in from right; an Architect and a prospective Buyer.)

ARCHITECT: O.K. Let's measure it out then.

*(The Architect has a large reel tape measure and a roll of blueprints. They
begin to measure the room systematically, the Architect reading the figures
and recording them in a small notebook, the Buyer holding the end of the
tape. They first measure the downstage length.)*

MICHAEL: When will you be going then, Ag?

AGGIE: As soon as your mother finds someone else.

MICHAEL: She can't *find* anyone, Aggie.

AGGIE: She will, she will.

MICHAEL: She says she *can't.* They keep showing up with dirty fingernails and
dyed hair!

ARCHITECT: *(Reading measurements, writing them down.)* Twenty-two feet, six
inches.

BUYER: Fine room.

ARCHITECT: Big room.

MICHAEL: So you *got* to stay, Ag. You can't just leave people in the *lurch.*

BUYER: Look at these French doors.

ARCHITECT: I'm looking. I'm also thinking. About heat loss.

(They measure more.)

AGGIE: I'll stay till you go away for the summer.

ARCHITECT: *(Measuring width of "French doors.")* Eight feet two inches.

(Michael gets up and comes downstage, looks out through the French doors, as the Architect goes upstage, to record his notes on the sideboard.)

MICHAEL: You gonna get married, aren't you, Ag?

AGGIE: Maybe.

MICHAEL: That guy you told me about from church?

AGGIE: Maybe.

MICHAEL: You gonna have children?

(Aggie laughs.)

MICHAEL: You will. I know you will. You'll have a boy of your own.

ARCHITECT: Hold it tight now.

MICHAEL: Will you come back to see us?

AGGIE: Oh my yes.

MICHAEL: You won't, Ag.

AGGIE: I will surely.

MICHAEL: You'll never come back, Ag. I'll never see you again! Ever!

ARCHITECT: *(Now measuring the width.)* Twelve feet four inches…

AGGIE: *(Holding out her arms.)* Come here, Mike.

MICHAEL: No.

AGGIE: Come here and give Aggie a big hug!

MICHAEL: No. Why should I? No.

AGGIE: Just a squeeze, for old time's sake!

MICHAEL: No! *(Squaring his shoulders.)* Go hug your own kids, Agnes. I've got work to do. I've got a whole stack of homework to do. I'm missing a whole day of school. *(He runs out of the room.)*

AGGIE: Michael! *(She resumes polishing the last few pieces of silver.)*

ARCHITECT: *(Reeling in his tape with professional zeal.)* O.K. There's your dining room, Doctor.

BUYER: *(Who is a psychiatrist.)* There it is.

ARCHITECT: Big room…light room…commodious room…

PSYCHIATRIST: One of the reasons we bought the house.

ARCHITECT: And one of the reasons we should consider breaking it up.

PSYCHIATRIST: Breaking it up?

ARCHITECT: Now bear with me: What say we turn this room into an office for you, and a waiting room for your patients?

PSYCHIATRIST: I thought we planned to open up those maid's rooms on the third floor.

ARCHITECT: Hold on. Relax.

(He begins to spread a large blueprint out on the table, anchoring its corners

with his tape measure and centerpiece. Aggie has finished polishing by now. She gathers up her silver and polishing stuff and leaves.)

ARCHITECT: The patient trusts the psychiatrist, doesn't he? Why can't the psychiatrist trust the architect? *(He begins to sketch on the blueprint, with a grease pencil.)* Now here's the ground plan of your house. Here's what you're stuck with, for the moment, and here, with these approximate dimensions, is your dining room.

PSYCHIATRIST: I see.

ARCHITECT: *(Drawing with his grease pencil.)* Now suppose…just suppose…we started with a clean slate. Suppose we open this up here, slam a beam in here, break through here and here, blast out this, throw out that, and what do we have?

PSYCHIATRIST: I'm not quite sure.

ARCHITECT: Well we don't have a dining room anymore. That's what we don't have.

PSYCHIATRIST: But where would we eat?

ARCHITECT: Here. Right here. Look. I'm putting in an eating area. Here's the fridge, the cooking units, Cuisinart, butcher-block table, chrome chairs. See? Look at the space. The flow. Wife cooks, kids set the table, you stack the dishes. All right here. Democracy at work. In your own home.

PSYCHIATRIST: Hmm.

ARCHITECT: Now, lets review your day. You come down to breakfast, everybody's fixing his or her own thing. *(He goes out through the hall, reappears through the kitchen door.)* Eggs, cornflakes, pop-tarts, whatever. You eat, chat, read the paper, say good-bye, come in here to go to work, Do you have a nurse or a receptionist?

PSYCHIATRIST: No, no. I'm just a humble shrink.

ARCHITECT: *(Beginning to move around the room.)* Well, you come in here to the reception room, maybe adjust the magazines on a table, here, maybe add your newspaper to the pile, then you go through a soundproof door into your office. You turn on your stereo-console here, maybe select a book from a wall-unit here, and then settle behind your desk module here. You read, you listen to music. Soon—buzz—a patient arrives. You turn off the music, put aside your book, and buzz him in through the soundproof doors. He flops on the couch here, *(He creates the couch with two upstage chairs.)* tells you his dream, you look out the window here, he leaves, you write him up, buzz in the next. Soon it's time for lunch. You go in here, have lunch with the wife, or one of the kids, and maybe stroll back in here for a nap. More buzzes, more patients, and soon it's time for a good easy cooperative supper with your family.

PSYCHIATRIST: But not in the dining room.

ARCHITECT: No. Not in the dining room.

PSYCHIATRIST: This room has such resonance.

ARCHITECT: So does a church. That doesn't mean we have to live in it.

PSYCHIATRIST: Mmm.

ARCHITECT: Look, I know whereof I speak: I grew up in a room like this.

PSYCHIATRIST: Oh, yes?

ARCHITECT: Oh sure. This is home turf to me.

PSYCHIATRIST: Really.

ARCHITECT: Oh God yes. My father sat in a chair just like that...

PSYCHIATRIST: *(Beginning to lookout the window.)* Mmmm.

ARCHITECT: And my mother sat here. And my sister here. And I sat right here. *(He sits.)* Oh, it all comes back...

PSYCHIATRIST: *(After a pause.)* Do you want to tell me about it?

ARCHITECT: It was torture, that's all. Those endless meals, waiting to begin, waiting for the dessert, waiting to be excused so they couldn't lean on you any more.

PSYCHIATRIST: *(Almost by rote.)* Was it that bad?

ARCHITECT: Man, it was brutal. I remember one time I came to the table without washing my hands, and my father— *(He stops.)*

PSYCHIATRIST: Go on.

ARCHITECT: *(Snapping out of it, getting up.)* Never mind. The point is, Doctor, it's time to get rid of this room. *(He begins to roll up his plans.)* Tell you frankly, I'm not interested in screwing around with any more maid's rooms. I can do that in my sleep.

(Peggy comes out of the kitchen, carrying a large tray, loaded with paper plates, napkins, hats, and favors for a children's birthday party. She begins to set the table.)

ARCHITECT: What I want is the chance to get in here, so I can open up your whole ground floor! Now what do you say?

PSYCHIATRIST: I'll have to think about it.

ARCHITECT: O.K. Fine. Take your time. *(He starts out.)* Tell you what. I'll send you my bill for the work I've done so far.

PSYCHIATRIST: Good. And I'll send you mine.

(They are out. Peggy, meanwhile, is finishing setting the birthday table. She surveys it, then goes to the doorway, right, and calls off.)

PEGGY: All right, Children! We're ready!

(She is almost bowled over by a moiling, shrieking mob of children coming in to celebrate the birthday party. They scream, yell, scramble over chairs, grab for favors, wrestle, whatever. Peggy claps her hands frantically.)

PEGGY: Children, children, CHILDREN!

(They subside a little.)

PEGGY: This is a *dining* room! This is *not* the monkey house at the zoo!

(They all start imitating monkeys. Peggy shouts them down.)

PEGGY: All right then. I'll just have to tell Roberta in the kitchen to put away all the ice cream and cake.

(The noise subsides. There is silence.)

PEGGY: Good. That's much better. Now I want everyone to leave the table…quietly, QUIETLY…

(The children begin to leave.)

PEGGY: And go into the hall, and then come back in here in the right way. That's it. Go out. Turn around. And come in. Come in as if you were your mummies and daddies coming into a lovely dinner party.

(Children come back in much more decorously, unconsciously parodying their parents.)

PEGGY: No, no. Let Winkie go first, since it's her birthday and she's the hostess…That's it. Good. Good. You sit at the head of the table, Winkie… Good…No, no? Billy, you sit next to Winkie…It should be boy-girl, boy-girl…That's it. Yes. Very good.

(Children are making a concerted effort to be genteel, though there are occasional subversive pokings, hitting, and gigglings.)

PEGGY: Now what do we do with our napkins?…Yes. Exactly. We unfold them and tuck them under our chins…And then we put on our party hats…

A LITTLE BOY: *(Named Brewster.)* Can the boys wear their hats in the house?

PEGGY: Yes they can, Brewster, because this is a special occasion. And sometimes on special occasions, the rules can change.

(Children explode. Ray! Yippee! Peggy has to shout them down.)

PEGGY: I said *some*times. And I meant some of the rules.

ANOTHER LITTLE BOY: *(Named Billy: pointing toward the hall.)* There's my Daddy.

PEGGY: *(Quickly.)* Where, Billy?

(Ted comes on from the hall; she tries to be casual.)

PEGGY: Oh. Hi.

TED: Hi. *(Waves to son.)* Hi, Bill.

(Party activity continues, the children opening favors. Peggy and Ted move downstage to get away from the noise.)

PEGGY: What brings you here?

TED: Have to pick up Bill.

PEGGY: I thought Judy was picking him up.

TED: She asked me to.

PEGGY: You're a little early. We haven't even had our cake.

TED: She told me to be early.

(A Little Girl calls from the table.)

A LITTLE GIRL: *(Named Sandra: fussing with favor.)* I can't get mine to work.

PEGGY: Help her, Brewster. Little boys are supposed to help little girls.

TED: Where's Frank?

PEGGY: Playing golf. Where else?

TED: On Winkie's birthday?

PEGGY: Don't get me started. Please.

(Winkie calls from the head of the table.)

WINKIE: Can we have the ice cream now, please.

PEGGY: In a minute, dear. Be patient. Then you'll have something to look forward to.

(The children whisperingly begin to count to sixty.)

TED: Judy must have known he'd be playing golf.

PEGGY: Judy knows everything.

TED: She knows about us, at least.

PEGGY: About us? How?

TED: She said she could tell by the way we behaved.

PEGGY: Behaved? Where?

TED: At the Bramwell's dinner party.

PEGGY: We hardly spoke to each other.

TED: That's how she could tell.

(The children's counting has turned into a chant: "We want ice cream! We want ice cream!")

PEGGY: They want ice cream. *(She starts for the kitchen.)*

TED: *(Holding her arm.)* She says she'll fight it, tooth and nail.

PEGGY: Fight *what?* We haven't done anything.

TED: She wants to nip it in the bud.

CHILDREN: Ice cream! Ice cream!

PEGGY: All right, children. You win.

(Cheers from children.)

PEGGY: Now Roberta is very busy in the kitchen because she also has a dinner party tonight. So who would like to help bring things out?

(Hands up, squeals: "Me! Me!")

PEGGY: All right. Tell you what. Billy, you get the ice cream, and Sandra, you bring out the cake!

("Ray! Yippee!")

PEGGY: Careful, careful! Walk, don't run! And be polite to Roberta because she's working very hard. And Brewster and Winkie, you'll have other responsibilities!

(Sandra and Billy go out into the kitchen.)

PEGGY: For instance, Brewster: when Billy and Sandra reappear through that door, what will you do?

(Long pause.)

BREWSTER: Sing the song.

PEGGY: Good, Brewster. Now be very quiet, and watch that door, and as soon as they come out, start singing.

(The children watch the door. Peggy hurries back to Ted)

PEGGY: So what do we do?

TED: She says she's thinking of telling her father about us.

PEGGY: Her *father?*

TED: He'd fire me. Immediately.

PEGGY: What if he did?

TED: I'd be out of a job, Peggy.

PEGGY: You could get another.

TED: Where? Doing what?

(The dining room door opens. Billy and Sandra come out carefully carrying a cake platter and an ice cream bowl. Everyone starts singing a birthday song, probably out of tune. Peggy helps them along. Billy puts the cake down in front of Winkie, who takes a deep breath to blow out the candles.)

PEGGY: No, no, sweetheart. Wait. Always wait. Before you blow out the candles, you have to make a wish. And Mummy has to make a wish. See? Mummy is putting her wedding ring around one of the candles. Now we both close our eyes and make a wish.

WINKIE: I wish I could have—

PEGGY: No, no. Don't tell. Never tell a wish. If you do, it won't come true. All right. Now blow.

(Winkie blows out "the candles." The children cheer.)

PEGGY: Now Winkie, would you cut the cake and give everyone a piece, please. And Brewster, you pass the ice cream.

(The children organize their food as Peggy joins Ted downstage. There is a kind of cooing hum of children eating which punctuates their dialogue.)

TED: What did you wish for?

PEGGY: Won't tell.

TED: Do you think it will come true?

PEGGY: No.

(Pause.)

TED: She'd make it so messy. For everyone.

PEGGY: Judy.

TED: She'd make it impossible.

PEGGY: So would Frank.

TED: I thought he didn't care.

PEGGY: He'd care if it were messy.

(Pause.)

TED: We could leave town.

PEGGY: And go where?

TED: Wherever I find another job.

PEGGY: Yes…

TED: I've got an uncle in Syracuse.

PEGGY: Syracuse?

TED: We could live there.

PEGGY: Is it nice? Syracuse?

TED: I think it's on some lake.

PEGGY: Syracuse…

TED: You'd have Winkie. I'd get Bill in the summer.

PEGGY: In Syracuse.

TED: At least we'd be free.

(They look at their children.)

PEGGY: Winkie, wipe your mouth, please. *(She goes to Winkie.)*

TED: Billy.

BILLY: What?

TED: Would you come here a minute, please?

(Billy does. Ted takes him aside.)

TED: Do you have to go the bathroom?

BILLY: No.

TED: Then don't do that, please.

BILLY: Don't do what?

TED: You know what. Now go back and enjoy the party.

(Billy returns to his seat. Ted rejoins Peggy.)

TED: Sorry.

PEGGY: I grew up here.

TED: Who didn't?

PEGGY: To just pick up stakes…

TED: I know.

PEGGY: I mean, this is where I *live*.

TED: Me, too. *(Touching her.)* We'll just have to behave ourselves, then.

PEGGY: Oh Ted…

TED: Be good little children.

PEGGY: Oh I can't stand it. *(She takes his hand and presses it furtively to her lips.)*

TED: And if we're seated next to each other, we'll have to make a conscious effort.

PEGGY: Oh we won't be seated next to each other. Judy will see to that.

TED: For a while any way.

PEGGY: For quite a while.

> *(The children are getting noisy. Winkie comes up.)*

WINKIE: Everyone's finished, Mummy.

PEGGY: Thank you, sweetheart.

WINKIE: And here's your ring. From the cake.

PEGGY: Good for you, darling! I forgot all about it! *(She puts the ring back on.)*

TED: Time to go, then?

PEGGY: I've planned some games.

TED: Want me to stay?

PEGGY: It would help.

TED: Then I'll stay.

PEGGY: *(To children.)* Into the living room now, children. For some games.

BREWSTER: What games?

PEGGY: Oh all kinds of games! Blind Man's Bluff. Pin the Tail on the Donkey…

CHILDREN: Yippee! Yay! *(The children run noisily Offstage.)*

> *(Peggy begins putting the mess back onto the tray.)*

TED: I'll get them started.

PEGGY: Would you? While I propitiate Roberta.

TED: I'll be the donkey.

PEGGY: Oh stop.

TED: I'll be the ass.

PEGGY: Stop or I'll scream.

> *(He is about to kiss her, over the tray, when Winkie appears at the door. They break away.)*

WINKIE: Come *on*, Mummy! We're waiting!

PEGGY: We're coming, dear.

(Winkie disappears into the hall. Ted and Peggy go off different ways as a Grandfather enters from the hall. He is about eighty. He sits at the head of the table, as a maid, Dora, comes out of the kitchen and begins to set a place in front of him. After a moment, his grandson Nick breathlessly appears in the doorway from the hall. He is about thirteen or fourteen.)

NICK: *(Panting, frightened.)* Grampa?

GRANDFATHER: *(Looking up.)* Which one are you?

NICK: I'm Nick, Gramp.

GRANDFATHER: And what do you want?

NICK: To have lunch with you, Gramp.

GRANDFATHER: Then you're late.

NICK: I went down to the club.

GRANDFATHER: Who said I'd be at the club?

NICK: My parents. My parents said you always eat there.

GRANDFATHER: Lately I've been coming home.

NICK: Yes, sir.

GRANDFATHER: Don't know half the people at the club any more. Rather be here. At my own table. Dora takes care of me, don't you, Dora?

DORA: Yes, sir.

GRANDFATHER: *(To Nick.)* Well you tracked me down, anyway. That shows some enterprise. *(Indicates a place.)* Bring him some lunch, Dora.

DORA: Yes, sir. *(She goes out.)*

NICK: *(Sitting opposite him at the other end of the table.)* Thank you, Gramp.

GRANDFATHER: So you're Nick, eh?

NICK: Yes. I am.

GRANDFATHER: You the one who wants to go to Europe this summer?

NICK: No, that's Mary. That's my cousin.

GRANDFATHER: You the one who wants the automobile? Says he can't go to college without an automobile?

NICK: No, that's my brother Tony, Gramp.

GRANDFATHER: What do you want then?

NICK: Oh I don't really want...

GRANDFATHER: Everyone who sits down with me wants something. Usually it's money. Do you want money?

NICK: Yes, sir.

GRANDFATHER: For what?

NICK: My education, Gramp.

GRANDFATHER: Education, eh? That's a good thing. Or can be. Doesn't have to be. Can be a bad thing. Where do you want to be educated?

NICK: Saint Luke's School, in Litchfield, Connecticut.

GRANDFATHER: Never heard of it.

NICK: It's an excellent boarding school for boys.

GRANDFATHER: Is it Catholic?

NICK: I don't think so, Gramp.

GRANDFATHER: Sounds Catholic to me.

NICK: I think it's high Episcopalian, Gramp.

GRANDFATHER: Then it's expensive.

NICK: My parents think it's a first-rate school, Gramp.

GRANDFATHER: Ah. Your parents think…

NICK: They've discussed all the boarding schools, and decided that this is the best.

GRANDFATHER: They decided, eh?

NICK: Yes, sir.

GRANDFATHER: And then, they decided you should get your grandfather to pay for it.

NICK: Yes, sir.

(Dora has returned, and set a place mat and a plate for Nick.)

GRANDFATHER: Another one leaving the nest, Dora.

DORA: Yes, sir. *(She waits by the sideboard.)*

GRANDFATHER: And taking a piece of the nest egg.

DORA: Yes, sir.

(Pause.)

GRANDFATHER: Why don't you stay home?

NICK: Me?

GRANDFATHER: You.

NICK: Oh. Because I want to broaden myself.

GRANDFATHER: You want to what?

NICK: I want to broaden my horizons. My horizons need broadening.

GRANDFATHER: I see.

NICK: And I'll meet interesting new friends.

GRANDFATHER: Don't you have any interesting friends here?

NICK: Oh sure, Gramp.

GRANDFATHER: I do. I have interesting friends right here. I know a man who makes boats in his basement.

NICK: But…

GRANDFATHER: I know a man who plays golf with his wife.

NICK: But I'll meet different types, Gramp. From all over the country. New York…California…

GRANDFATHER: Why would you want to meet anyone from New York?

NICK: Well they're more sophisticated, Gramp. They'll buff me up.

GRANDFATHER: They'll what?

NICK: My mother says I need buffing up.

GRANDFATHER: Do you think he needs buffing up, Dora?

DORA: No, sir.

GRANDFATHER: *(To Nick.)* Dora doesn't think you need buffing up. I don't think you need buffing up. You'll have to give us better reasons.

NICK: Um. Well. They have advanced Latin there…

GRANDFATHER: I see. And?

NICK: And an indoor hockey rink.

GRANDFATHER: Yes. And?

NICK: And beautiful grounds and surroundings.

GRANDFATHER: Don't we? Don't we have beautiful surroundings? Why do we have to go away to have beautiful surroundings?

NICK: I don't know, Gramp. All I know is everyone's going away these days.

GRANDFATHER: Everyone's going away? Hear that, Dora? Everyone's going away.

NICK: *(Desperately.)* An awful lot of people are going away!
    (Pause.)

GRANDFATHER: I didn't go away.

NICK: I know, Gramp.

GRANDFATHER: Didn't even go to Country Day. Went to the old P.S. 36 down on Huron Street.

NICK: Yes, Gramp.

GRANDFATHER: Didn't finish, either. Father died, and I had to go to work. Had to support my mother.

NICK: I know that, Gramp.

GRANDFATHER: My father didn't go to school at all. Learned Greek at the plow.

NICK: You told us, Gramp.

GRANDFATHER: Yes well I didn't do too badly. Without a high Episcopal boarding school, and an indoor hockey rink.

NICK: But you're a self-made man, Gramp.

GRANDFATHER: Oh is that what I am? And what are you? Don't you want to be self-made? Or do you want other people to make you? Hmmm? Hmmm? What've you got to say to that?

NICK: *(Squashed.)* I don't know…

GRANDFATHER: Everyone wants to go away. Me? I went away twice. Took two vacations in my life. First vacation, took a week off from work to marry your grandmother. Went to Hot Springs, Virginia. Bought this table. Second vacation: Europe. 1928. Again with your grandmother. Hated the place. Knew I would. Miserable meals. Took a trunkload of shredded wheat along. Came back when it ran out. Back to this table. *(Pause.)* They're all leaving us, Dora. Scattering like birds.

DORA: Yes, sir.

GRANDFATHER: We're small potatoes these days.

DORA: Yes, sir.

GRANDFATHER: This one wants to go to one of those fancy New England boarding schools. He wants to play ice hockey indoors with that crowd from Long Island and Philadelphia. He'll come home talking with marbles in his mouth. We won't understand a word, Dora.

DORA: Yes, sir.

GRANDFATHER: And we won't see much of him, Dora. He'll go visiting in New York and Baltimore. He'll drink liquor in the afternoon and get mixed up with women who wear lipstick and trousers, and whose only thought is the next dance. And he wants me to pay for it all. Am I right?

NICK: No, Gramp! No I don't! I don't want to go! Really! I never wanted to go! I want to stay home with all of you!

GRANDFATHER: Finish your greens. They're good for your lower intestine.

(They eat silently. From left a man named Paul enters. He's in his mid-thirties and wears a sweater. He starts carefully examining the dining room chairs along the left wall, one by one, turning them upside down, testing their strength. Finally; with a sigh; to Nick.)

GRANDFATHER: No. You go. You've got to go. I'll send you to Saint Whoozies and Betsy to Miss Whatsie's and young Andy to whatever-it's-called. And Mary can go to Europe this summer, and Tony can have a car, and its all fine and dandy.

(He gets slowly to his feet. Nick gets up too.)

GRANDFATHER: Go on. Enjoy yourselves, all of you. Leave town, travel, see the world. It's bound to happen. And you know who's going to be sitting here when you get back? I'll tell you who'll be sitting right in that chair. Some Irish fella, some Jewish gentleman is going to be sitting right at this table. Saying the same thing to *his* grandson. And your grandson will be back at the *plow! (Starts out the door, stops, turns.)* And come to think of it, that won't be a bad thing either. Will it, Dora?

DORA: No, sir.

(*He exits. Dora starts clearing off. Nick stands in the dining room.*)

DORA: Well, go on. Hurry. Bring him his checkbook before he falls asleep.

(*Nick hurries off right, Dora goes off with plates left. Paul begins to check the table. A Woman, about forty, call her Margery, appears in the hall doorway. She watches Paul.*)

MARGERY: What do you think?

PAUL: (*Working over a chair.*) You're in trouble.

MARGERY: Oh dear. I knew it.

PAUL: It's becoming unglued.

MARGERY: I know the feeling.

PAUL: Coming apart at the seams.

MARGERY: Do you think it's hopeless?

PAUL: Let me check the table. (*He crawls under the table.*)

MARGERY: It shakes very badly. I had a few friends over the other night, and every time we tried to cut our chicken, our water glasses started tinkling frantically. And the chairs creaked and groaned. It was like having dinner at Pompeii.

PAUL: (*Taking out a pocket knife.*) I'm checking the joints here.

MARGERY: It's all very sad. How things run down and fall apart. I used to tell my husband—my *ex*-husband—we have such lovely old things. We should oil them, we should wax them, we should keep them up. But of course I couldn't do everything, and he wouldn't do anything, and now here you are to give us the *coup de grace*.

PAUL: (*Still under table.*) Hey look at this.

MARGERY: What?

PAUL: Look under here.

MARGERY: I don't dare.

PAUL: I'm serious. Look.

MARGERY: Wait till I put on my glasses. (*She puts on her glasses which are hanging from a chain around her neck; then she bends down discreetly.*) Where? I can't see.

PAUL: Under here. Look. This support. See how loose this is?

MARGERY: I can't quite…Wait. (*She gets down on her knees.*)

PAUL: Come on.

MARGERY: All right. (*She crawls under the table.*)

PAUL: See? Look at this support.

MARGERY: I see. It wiggles like mad.

(*They are both crawling around under the table now.*)

PAUL: *(Crawling around her.)* And look over there. I'll have to put a whole new piece in over here. See? This is gone.

MARGERY: *(Looking.)* I see.

PAUL: *(Crawling back.)* And…excuse me, please…this pedestal is loose. Probably needs a new dowel. I'll have to ream it out and put in another…

MARGERY: Do you think so?

PAUL: Oh sure. In fact your whole dining room needs to be re-screwed, re-glued, and re-newed. *(His little joke. He comes out from under.)*

MARGERY: Hmmmm. *(She is still under the table.)*

PAUL: What's the matter?

MARGERY: I've never been under a table before.

PAUL: Oh yeah?

MARGERY: It's all just…wood under here, isn't it?

PAUL: That's all it is.

MARGERY: *(Fascinated.)* I mean you'd think a dining room *table* was something special. But it isn't, underneath. It's all just…wood. It's just a couple of big, wide…boards.

PAUL: That's right.

MARGERY: *(Peering.)* What's this, here?

PAUL: What's what?

MARGERY: Well you'll have to come back under here, to see. There's some writing here, burned into the wood.

PAUL: *(Crawling under.)* Where?

MARGERY: Right here. *(She reads, carefully.)* "Freeman's Furniture. Wilkes-Barre, Pa. 1898."

PAUL: *(Under the table.)* Oh that's the manufacturer's mark.

MARGERY: 1898?

PAUL: That's what it says.

MARGERY: But that's not so old.

PAUL: Not if it was made in 1898.

MARGERY: That's not old at all. It's not even an antique. *(Pause.)* It's just…American.

PAUL: There's a lot of these around. They used to crank them out, at the end of the 19th century.

MARGERY: Now, aren't I dumb? For years, we've been thinking it's terribly valuable.

PAUL: Well it is, in a sense. It's well made. It's a solid serviceable copy. Based on the English.

MARGERY: Well I'll be darned. You learn something every day.

(They are both sitting side by side, under the table. She looks at him.)

MARGERY: You know a lot about furniture, don't you?

PAUL: I'm beginning to.

MARGERY: Beginning to. I'll bet your father was a cabinetmaker or something.

PAUL: My father was a banker.

MARGERY: A *bank*er?

PAUL: And I was a stockbroker. Until I got into this.

MARGERY: I don't believe it.

PAUL: Sure. I decided I wanted to see what I was doing. And touch it. And see the results. So I took up carpentry.

MARGERY: I am amazed. I mean, I *know* some stockbrokers. *(Embarrassed pause. She looks at the strut.)* Is this the support that's bad?

PAUL: That's the one.

MARGERY: What if you put a nail in here?

PAUL: Not a nail. A screw.

MARGERY: *(Crawling over him.)* All right. And another one over here. Or at least some household cement.

PAUL: Well, they have these epoxy glues now…

MARGERY: All right. And maybe cram a matchbook or something in here.

PAUL: Not a matchbook.

MARGERY: A wedge then. A wooden wedge.

PAUL: Good idea.

MARGERY: See? I can do it too.

(In her intensity, she has gotten very close to him physically. They both suddenly realize it, and move away, crawling out from under the table on either side, and brushing themselves off.)

MARGERY: So. Well. Will you be taking the table away? Or can you fix it here?

PAUL: I can fix it here. If you want.

MARGERY: That might make more sense. My husband used to ask for written estimates. Materials and labor.

PAUL: I'll write one up.

MARGERY: Suppose I helped. On the labor.

PAUL: I've never worked that way…

MARGERY: I should learn. I shouldn't be so helpless.

PAUL: O.K. Why not?

MARGERY: Besides, it's not an antique. If I make a mistake, it's not the end of the world, is it?

PAUL: Not at all.

MARGERY: When could we start?

PAUL: Today. Now, if you want.

MARGERY: Then we're a partnership, aren't we? We should have a drink, to celebrate.

PAUL: O.K.

(From off right, we hear voices singing the Thanksgiving hymn: "Come Ye Thankful People, Come.")

MARGERY: What'll we have? Something snappy? Like a martini?

PAUL: No, I gave them up with the stock market. How about a beer?

MARGERY: Fine idea. Good, solid beer. If I've got it.

(They go off into the kitchen, as Nancy, in her thirties, comes out, carrying a stack of plates and a carving knife and fork. She calls back over her shoulder.)

NANCY: I've got the plates, Mrs. Driscoll. You've got your hands full with that turkey. *(She sets the plates and carving utensils at the head of the table and calls toward the hall.)* We're ready, everybody! Come on in!

(The singing continues as a Family begins to come into the dining room, to celebrate Thanksgiving dinner. The oldest son Stuart has his Mother on his arm. She is a very vague, very old Old Lady.)

STUART: …Now, Mother, I want you to sit next to me, and Fred, you sit on Mother's left, and Ben, you sit opposite her where she can see you, and Nancy and Beth hold up that end of the table, and there we are.

(Genial chatter as everyone sits down. The two Sons push in their Mother's chair. After a moment the Old Lady stands up again, looks around distractedly.)

STUART: What's the matter, Mother?

OLD LADY: I'm not quite sure where I am.

STUART: *(Expansively; arm around her; seating her again.)* You're *here,* Mother. In your own dining room. This is your table, and here are your chairs, and here is the china you got on your trip to England, and here's the silver-handled carving knife which Father used to use.

OLD LADY: Oh yes…

(Genial laughter; ad-libbing: "She's a little tired…It's been a long day…" The Old Lady gets up again.)

OLD LADY: But who are these people? I'm not quite sure who these people are. *(She begins to wander around the room.)*

STUART: *(Following her around.)* It's me, Mother: Stuart. Your son. And here's Fred, and Ben, and Nancy, and Beth. We're all here, Mother.

NANCY: *(Going into the kitchen.)* I'll get the turkey. That might help her focus.

STUART: Yes. *(To Old Lady.)* Mrs. Driscoll is here, Mother. Right in the kitchen, where she's always been. And your grandchildren. All your grandchildren were here. Don't you remember? They ate first, at the children's table, and now they're out in back playing touch football. You watched them, Mother. *(He indicates the French doors.)*

OLD LADY: Oh yes...

(She sits down again at the other end of the table. Nancy comes out from the kitchen, carrying a large platter. Appropriate Oh's and Ah's from Group.)

STUART: And look, Mother. Here's Nancy with the turkey...Put it right over there, Nancy...See, Mother? Isn't it a beautiful bird? And I'm going to carve it just the way Father did, and give you a small piece of the breast and a dab of dressing, just as always, Mother. *(He sharpens the carving knife officiously.)*

OLD LADY: *(Still staring out into the garden.)* Just as always...

STUART: *(As he sharpens.)* And Fred will have the drumstick—am I right, Fred?—and Beth gets the wishbone, and Ben ends up with the Pope's nose, am I right, Ben?

(Genial in-group laughter.)

NANCY: Save some for Mrs. Driscoll.

STUART: I always do, Nancy. Mrs. Driscoll likes the second joint.

OLD LADY: This is all very nice, but I think I'd like to go home.

STUART: *(Patiently, as he carves.)* You are home, Mother. You've lived here fifty-two years.

BEN: Fifty-four.

BETH: Forever.

STUART: Ben, pass this plate down to Mother...

OLD LADY: *(Getting up.)* Thank you very much, but I really do think it's time to go.

NANCY: Uh-oh.

STUART: *(Going to her.)* Mother...

BETH: Oh dear.

OLD LADY: Will someone drive, me home, please? I live at eighteen Summer Street with my mother and sisters.

BETH: What will we do?

STUART: *(Going to Old Lady.)* It's not there now, Mother. Don't you remember? We drove down. There's a big building there now.

OLD LADY: *(Holding out her hand.)* Thank you very much for asking me...Thank you for having me to your house. *(She begins to go around the table, thanking people.)*

FRED: Mother! I'm Fred! Your son!

OLD LADY: Isn't that nice? Thank you. I've had a perfectly lovely time... Thank you...Thank you so much. *(She shakes hands with Nancy.)* It's been absolutely lovely...Thank you, thank you.

STUART: Quickly. Let's sing to her.

BETH: Sing?

STUART: She likes singing. We used to sing to her whenever she'd get upset...Fred, Ben. Quickly. Over here.

OLD LADY: *(Wandering distracted around.)* Now I can't find my gloves. Where would my gloves be? I can't go out without my gloves.

BEN: What song? I can't remember any of the songs.

STUART: Sure you can. Come on. Hmmmmm.

(He sounds a note. The others try to find their parts.)

BEN & FRED: Hmmmmmmmmm.

OLD LADY: I need my gloves, I need my hat...

STUART: *(Singing.)* "As the blackbird in the spring...

OTHERS: *(Joining in.)* 'Neath the willow tree...

Sat and piped, I heard him sing,

Sing of Aura Lee...

(They sing in pleasant, amateurish, corny harmony. The Old Lady stops fussing, turns her head, and listens. The other women remain at the table.)

MEN: *(Singing.)* Aura Lee, Aura Lee, Maid of Golden Hair...Sunshine came along with thee, and swallows in the air."

OLD LADY: I love music. Every person in our family could play a different instrument. *(She sits in a chair along the wall, downstage right.)*

STUART: *(To his brothers.)* She's coming around. Quickly. Second verse.

MEN: *(Singing with more confidence now; more daring harmony.)*

"In thy blush the rose was born,

Music, when you spake,

Through thine azure eye the morn

Sparkling seemed to break.

Aura Lee, Aura Lee, Maid of Golden Hair,

Sunshine came along with thee, and swallows in the air."

(They hold a long note at the end. The Old Lady claps. Everyone claps.)

OLD LADY: That was absolutely lovely.

STUART: Thank you, Mother.

OLD LADY: But now I've simply got to go home. Would you call my carriage, please? And someone find my hat and gloves. It's very late, and my mother gets very nervous if I'm not home in time for tea. *(She heads for the hall.)*

STUART: *(To no one in particular.)* Look, Fred, Ben, we'll drive her down, and show her everything. The new office complex where her house was. The entrance to the Thruway. The new Howard Johnson's motel. Everything! And she'll see that nothing's there at all.

FRED: I'll bring the car around.

STUART: I'll get her coat.

BEN: I'm coming, too.

STUART: We'll just have to go through the motions.

(The brothers hurry after their mother. Nancy and Beth are left alone onstage. Pause. Then they begin to stack the dishes.)

NANCY: That's scary.

BETH: I know it.

NANCY: I suddenly feel so…precarious.

BETH: It could happen to us all.

NANCY: No, but it's as if we didn't exist. As if we were all just…ghosts, or something. Even her own sons. She walked right by them.

BETH: And guess who walked right by *us*.

NANCY: *(Glancing off.)* Yes… *(Pause.)* Know what I'd like?

BETH: What?

NANCY: A good stiff drink.

BETH: I'm with you.

NANCY: I'll bet Mrs. Driscoll could use a drink, too.

BETH: Bet she could.

NANCY: *(Deciding.)* Let's go out and ask her!

BETH: Mrs. Driscoll?

NANCY: Let's!

(Pause.)

BETH: All right.

NANCY: Let's go and have a drink with Mrs. Driscoll, and then dig into this turkey, and help her with the dishes, and then figure out how to get through the rest of the goddamn day!

(They go off, into the kitchen. The table is clear, the dining room is empty.)

End of Act I

ACT II

The dining room is empty. The light suggests that it is about three in the after-noon. After a moment, a Girl's voice is heard off right, from the front hall.

GIRL'S VOICE: Mom? MOM? Anybody home? *(Silence; then more softly.)* See? I told you. She isn't here.

(Sarah appears in the doorway, with Helen behind her.)

HELEN: Where is she?

SARAH: She works. At a boutique. Four days a week. And my father's away on business. In Atlanta. Or Denver or somewhere. Anyway. Come on. I'll show you where they keep the liquor.

HELEN: My mom's always there when I get home from school. Always.

SARAH: Bummer.

HELEN: And if she isn't, my grandmother comes in.

SARAH: The liquor's in the pantry.

(Sarah goes out through kitchen door, left. Helen stays in the dining room.)

HELEN: *(Taking in the dining room.)* Oh. Hey. Neat-o.

SARAH'S VOICE: *(From within.)* What?

HELEN: This *room.*

SARAH'S VOICE: *(Over clinking of liquor bottles.)* That's our dining room.

HELEN: I know. But it's viciously nice.

SARAH: *(Coming out of kitchen, carrying two bottles.)* Which do you want? Gin or vodka?

HELEN: *(Wandering around the room.)* You decide.

SARAH: *(Looking at bottles.)* Well there's more gin, so it's less chance they'll notice.

HELEN: Gin, then.

SARAH: But the reason there's more gin is that I put water in it last week.

HELEN: Vodka, then.

SARAH: Tell you what. We'll mix in a little of both. *(She goes into the kitchen.)*

HELEN: O.K...Do you *use* this room.

SARAH: Oh sure.

HELEN: Special occasions, huh? When the relatives come to visit?

SARAH'S VOICE: Every night.

HELEN: Every NIGHT?

SARAH'S VOICE: Well at least every night they're both home.

HELEN: Really?

SARAH: *(Coming in, carrying two glasses.)* Oh sure. Whenever they're home, my father insists that we all eat in the dining room at seven o'clock. *(Hands Helen her drink.)* Here. Gin and vodka and Fresca. The boys are bringing the pot.

HELEN: *(Drinking.)* Mmmm…It must be nice, eating here.

SARAH: *(Slouching in a chair.)* Oh yeah sure you bet. We have to lug things out, and lug things back, and nobody can begin till everything's cold, and we're supposed to carry on a decent conversation, and everyone has to finish before anyone can get up, and it sucks, if you want to know. It sucks out loud.

(They drink.)

HELEN: We eat in the kitchen.

SARAH: Can you watch TV while you eat?

HELEN: We used to. We used to watch the local news and weather.

SARAH: That's something At least you don't have to talk.

HELEN: But now we can't watch it. My mother read in *Family Circle* that TV was bad at meals. So now we turn on the stereo and listen to semi-classical music.

SARAH: My parents said they tried eating in the kitchen when I went to boarding school. But when I got kicked out, they moved back in here. It's supposed to give me some sense of stability.

HELEN: Do you think it does?

SARAH: Shit no! It just makes me nervous. They take the telephone off the hook, so no one can call, and my brother gets itchy about his homework, and when my sister had anorexia, she still had to sit here and *watch,* for God's sake, and my parents spend most of the meal bitching, and the whole thing bites, Helen. It really bites. It bites the big one. Want another?

HELEN: No thanks.

SARAH: I do…You call the boys and tell them it's all clear. *(Sarah goes back into the kitchen.)*

HELEN: *(Calling toward kitchen.)* Sarah…

SARAH'S VOICE: *(Within.)* What?

HELEN: When the boys come over, can we have our drinks in here?

(Kate, a woman in her mid-forties, comes. out. She carries a small tray containing a teapot, two teacups, sugar and creamer. She sits at the table and watches the teapot.)

SARAH'S VOICE: *(Within.)* In the *din*ing room?

HELEN: I mean, wouldn't it be cool, sitting around this shiny table with Eddie and Duane, drinking gin and Fresca and vodka?

SARAH: *(Coming out from the kitchen.)* No way. Absolutely no way. In here?

I'd get all up tight in here. *(She heads for the hall.)* Now come on. Let's call them.

(Helen starts after her.)

SARAH: Having *boys* in the *din*ing room? Jesus, Helen. You really are a wimp sometimes.

(They go out, right, Helen looking back over her shoulder at the dining room.)

KATE: *(Calling toward hallway.)* I'm in here, Gordon. I made tea.

(Gordon comes in from the hall. He is about her age. He is buttoning his shirt, carrying his jacket and tie slung over his shoulder.)

GORDON: Tea?

KATE: Tea.

GORDON: Why tea?

KATE: Because I like it. I love it. *(Pause.)* Or would you like a drink?

GORDON: No thanks.

KATE: Go ahead. Don't worry about me. I'm all over that. We even have it in the house, and I never touch it.

GORDON: No thanks, Kate.

KATE: Then have tea. It's very good. It's Earl Gray.

GORDON: I ought to be getting back.

KATE: Gordon, please. Have tea.

(Pause.)

GORDON: All right.

KATE: Thank you. *(She begins to pour him a cup.)*

GORDON: *(Ironically.)* Tea in the dining room.

KATE: Where else? Should we huddle guiltily over the kitchen table?

GORDON: No.

KATE: Then tea in the dining room…What would you like? Lemon or milk?

GORDON: Whatever.

KATE: Gordon.

GORDON: Milk, then. No sugar.

KATE: Milk it is. *(She hands him a cup.)* Well sit down, for heaven's sake.

GORDON: *(Not sitting.)* I thought I heard a sound.

KATE: Oh really? And what sound did you hear? A distant lawn mower? A faulty burglar alarm?

GORDON: I thought I heard a car.

KATE: What? A car? On this godforsaken street? Should we rush to the window? Cheer? Wave flags?

GORDON: Go easy, Kate.

KATE: Well I doubt very much that you heard a car.

GORDON: *(Listening.)* It stopped.

KATE: The sound?

GORDON: The *car.* The car stopped.

KATE: All right, Gordon. You heard a car stop. But it's not Ed's car, is it? Because Ed, as you and I well know, is in Amsterdam, or Rotterdam, or who-gives-a-damn until next Tuesday. *(Reaching for his hand.)* Now sit *down.* Please. Let's have tea, for heaven's sake.

(He sits on the edge of his chair.)

KATE: Now when can we meet again?

GORDON: *(Jumping up.)* I heard a car door slam.

KATE: Oh really. That's because cars have doors. And people when they get really frustrated feel like slamming them.

GORDON: I'm going.

KATE: I see how it is—a quick tumble with the bored wife of your best friend.

GORDON: Someone's at the front door.

KATE: No…

GORDON: Yes. Someone with a key!

(Kate jumps up, They listen.)

KATE: *(Whispering.)* Now you've got to stay.

(Gordon quickly puts on his coat. A boy's voice is heard calling from the hall.)

BOY'S VOICE: Mom!

KATE: Lord help us.

BOY'S VOICE: I'm home, Mom!

KATE: *(Grimly to Gordon.)* Now you've got to have tea.

BOY'S VOICE: Mom?

KATE: *(Calling out.)* We're in the dining room, dear.

(Chris slides into view from right. He is about seventeen, carries a dufflebag. Kate goes to him effusively.)

KATE: Darling! How'd you get here?

CHRIS: I took a cab from the bus station.

(Kate embraces him. He looks at Gordon.)

KATE: You look marvelous! Taller than ever! Say hello to Uncle Gordon.

GORDON: Hi, Chris. Welcome home.

CHRIS: *(Coolly.)* Hi.

KATE: What's this? Is this what they teach you at Deerfield? Not to shake hands? Not to call people by name?

CHRIS: Hello, Uncle Gordon.

(They shake hands.)

GORDON: Hi, Chris.

KATE: But what brings you home, my love? I expected you Saturday.

CHRIS: I got honors.

KATE: Honors?

CHRIS: You get two days early if you get an over-eighty-five average.

KATE: But then you should have telephoned.

CHRIS: I wanted to surprise you.

    (Pause.)

GORDON: I ought to go.

KATE: Nonsense. Have more tea. Chris, would you like tea? I was taking a nap, and Gordon stopped by, and we thought we'd have tea. Have some tea, dear. Or a Coke. Have a Coke. Or shall I get you a beer? How about a beer for a big boy who gets honors?

CHRIS: No, thanks.

GORDON: I'd really better go.

KATE: You won't have more tea.

GORDON: Can't. Sorry.

KATE: All right, then. Good-bye.

GORDON: *(Shaking hands with her stiffly.)* Good-bye...Good-bye, Chris. *(He tries to shake hands with Chris.)*

CHRIS: *(Turning away.)* Good-bye.

    (Gordon goes, quickly, right. Kate starts to put the tea things back on the tray.)

KATE: He wanted to talk to me about stocks. I inherited some stock he thinks I should sell, and so he stopped by—

CHRIS: Where's Dad?

KATE: He's in Europe, darling. As I think I wrote you. He'll be home Tuesday. *(She starts for the kitchen with the tray.)*

CHRIS: Oh Mom.

KATE: *(Stopping, turning.)* And what does that mean, pray tell? "Oh Mom." *(He turns away.)*

KATE: I'd like to know, please, what that means? *(He shakes his head.)*

KATE: I happened to be having *tea,* Christopher. It happens to be a very old custom. Your grandmother used to have tea at this very table with this same china every afternoon. All sorts of people would stop by. All the time. I'd come home from school, and there she'd be. Serving tea. It's a delightful old custom, sweetheart. *(He starts for the hall.)*

KATE: Where are you going? I asked you a question, please. We don't just walk away.

(Chris walks out of the room. Kate calls after Chris.)

KATE: Chris, I am talking to you. I am talking to you, and I am your mother, and the least you can do is…

(She follows him out into the hall, still carrying the tray. A Young Man named Tony comes in from the kitchen, decked out with a camera and various pieces of photographic equipment. He begins to test the room with his light meter. He finds an area by a chair which pleases him. He calls toward the kitchen.)

TONY: Would you mind setting up over here, Aunt Harriet? I want to get you in the late afternoon light.

(Aunt Harriet, a woman of about sixty, appears at the kitchen door, carrying another tray, glittering with old china and crystal.)

AUNT HARRIET: *(Beaming proudly.)* Certainly, Tony. *(She goes to where he indicates, puts down her tray, and begins to set a place at the table.)* Now I thought I'd use this Irish linen place mat with matching napkin, that my husband—who was what? Your great uncle—inherited from his sister. They have to be washed and ironed by hand every time they're used.

(She places the place mat; he photographs it.)

AUNT HARRIET: And then of course the silver, which was given to us as a wedding present by your great-grandmother. You see? Three prong forks. Pistol-handled knives. Spoon with rat tail back. All Williamsburg pattern. This should be polished at least every two weeks.

(She sets a place as he photographs each item. She becomes more and more at home with the camera.)

AUNT HARRIET: And then this is Staffordshire, as is the butter plate. All of this is Bone. The wine glasses are early Steuben, but the goblets and finger bowls are both Waterford. None of this goes in the dishwasher, of course. It's all far too delicate for detergents. *(The place is all set. She surveys it proudly.)*

TONY: Finger bowls?

AUNT HARRIET: Oh yes. Our side of the family always used finger bowls between the salad and the dessert.

TONY: Would you show me how they worked?

AUNT HARRIET: Certainly, dear.

(He continues to snap pictures of her as she talks.)

AUNT HARRIET: You see the maid would take away the salad plate—like this— *(She puts a plate aside to her right.)* And then she'd put down the finger bowls in front of us. Like this. *(She does.)* They would be filled approximately halfway with cool water. And there might be a little rose floating in it. Or a sliver of lemon…Now of course, we'd have our napkins in our laps—like this. *(She sits down, shakes out her napkin, puts it discreetly in her lap.)* And then we'd dip our fingers into the finger bowl…gently, gently…and then we'd wiggle them and shake them out…and then dab them on our napkins…and then dab our lips…then, of course, the maids would take them away… *(She moves the finger bowl aside.)* And in would come a nice sherbet or chocolate mousse!

(She beams at the camera, at last used to it. He snaps her picture.)

TONY: Thanks, Aunt Harriet. That was terrific. *(He begins to pack up his photographic gear.)*

AUNT HARRIET: You're welcome. Now, Tony, dear, tell me again what all this is for. I didn't quite understand over the telephone.

TONY: This is a classroom project. For Amherst.

AUNT HARRIET: Oh, my. A project. *(She stands up.)* In what, pray tell.

TONY: Anthropology, actually.

AUNT HARRIET: Anthro*polo*gy. Heavens! *(She starts to return items to her tray.)* What does that have to do with this?

TONY: Well you see we're studying the eating habits of various vanishing cultures. For example, someone is talking about the Kikuyus of Northern Kenya. And my roommate is doing the Cree Indians of Saskatchewan. And my professor suggested I do a slide show on us.

AUNT HARRIET: Us?

TONY: The Wasps. Of Northeastern United States.

(Pause.)

AUNT HARRIET: I see.

TONY: You can learn a lot about a culture from how it eats.

AUNT HARRIET: *(With increasing coldness.)* Such as what?

TONY: Well. Consider the finger bowls, for example. There you have an almost neurotic obsession with cleanliness, reflecting the guilt which comes with the last stages of capitalism. Or notice the unnecessary accumulation of glass and china, and the compulsion to display it. Or the subtle hint of aggression in those pistol-handled knives.

AUNT HARRIET: I think I'll ask you to leave, Tony.

TONY: Aunt Harriet…

AUNT HARRIET: I was going to invite you to stay for a cocktail, but now I won't.

TONY: Please, Aunt Harriet… *(He begins to gather up his equipment.)*

THE DINING ROOM 267

AUNT HARRIET: Out! Right now! Before I telephone long distance to your mother!

(Tony backs toward the hallway.)

AUNT HARRIET: Vanishing culture, my eye! I forbid you to mention my name in the classroom! Or show one glimpse of my personal property! And you can tell that professor of yours, I've got a good mind to drive up to Amherst, with this pistol-handled butter knife on the seat beside me, and cut off his anthropological balls!

(Tony runs hurriedly from the room. Harriet returns to her tray proudly, and carries it back into the kitchen, As she goes, an Older Man, called Jim, comes in from the hall, followed by his daughter, Meg. He is in his late sixties, she is about thirty.)

MEG: Where are you going now, Daddy?

JIM: I think your mother might want a drink.

MEG: She's reading to the children.

JIM: That's why she might want one.

MEG: She wants no such thing, Dad.

JIM: Then I want one.

MEG: Now? It's not even five.

JIM: Well then let's go see how the Red Sox are doing. *(He starts back out, right.)*

MEG: Daddy, *stop!*

JIM: Stop what?

MEG: Avoiding me. Ever since I arrived, we haven't been able to talk.

JIM: Good Lord, what do you mean? Seems to me everybody's been talking continuously and simultaneously from the moment you got off the plane.

MEG: Alone, Daddy. I mean *alone*. And you *know* I mean alone.

JIM: All right. We'll talk. *(Sits down.)* Right here in the dining room. Good place to talk. Why not? Matter of fact, I'm kind of tired. It's been a long day.

MEG: I love this room. I've always loved it. Always.

JIM: Your mother and I still use it. Now and then. Once a week. Mrs. Robinson still comes in and cooks us a nice dinner and we have it in here. Still. Lamb chops. Broilers—

MEG: *(Suddenly.)* I've left him, Daddy.

JIM: Oh well now, a little vacation…

MEG: I've left him permanently.

JIM: Yes, well, permanently is a very long word…

MEG: I can't live with him, Dad. We don't get along at all.

JIM: Oh well, you may think that now...

MEG: Could we live here, Dad?

JIM: Here?

MEG: For a few months.

JIM: With three small children?

MEG: While I work out my life.

(Pause. Jim takes out a pocket watch and looks at it.)

JIM: What time is it? A little after five. I think the sun is over the yardarm, don't you? Or if it isn't, it should be. I think it's almost permissible for you and me to have a little drink, Meg.

MEG: Can we stay here, Dad?

JIM: Make us a drink, Meggie.

MEG: All right. *(She goes into the kitchen; the door, of course, remains open.)*

JIM: *(Calling to her.)* I'd like Scotch, sweetheart. Make it reasonably strong. You'll find the silver measuring gizmo in the drawer by the trays. I want two shots and a splash of water. And I like to use that big glass with the pheasant on it. And not too much ice. *(He gets up and moves around the table.)*

MEG'S VOICE: *(Within.)* All right.

JIM: I saw Mimi Mott the other day...Can you hear me?

MEG'S VOICE: *(Within.)* I can hear you, Dad.

JIM: There she was, being a very good sport with her third husband. Her third. Who's deaf as a post and extremely disagreeable. So I took her aside—can you hear me?

MEG'S VOICE: *(Within.)* I'm listening, Dad.

JIM: I took her aside, and I said, "Now Mimi, tell me the truth. If you had made half as much effort with your first husband as you've made with the last two, don't you think you'd still be married to him?" I asked her that. Point blank. And you know what Mimi said? She said, "Maybe." That's exactly what she said. "Maybe." If she had made the effort.

(Meg returns with two glasses. She gives one to Jim.)

MEG: That's your generation, Dad.

JIM: That's every generation.

MEG: It's not mine.

JIM: Every generation has to make an effort.

MEG: I won't go back to him, Dad. I want to be here.

JIM: *(Looking at his glass.)* I wanted the glass with the pheasant on it.

MEG: I think the kids used it.

JIM: Oh. *(Pause. He drinks, moves away from her.)*

MEG: So can we stay, Dad?

JIM: I sleep in your room now. Your mother kicked me out because I snore. And we use the boys' room now to watch TV.

MEG: I'll use the guest room.

JIM: And the children?

MEG: They can sleep on the third floor. In the maid's rooms.

JIM: We closed them off. Because of the oil bills.

MEG: I don't care, Dad. We'll work it out. Please.

> *(Pause. He sits down at the other end of the table.)*

JIM: Give it another try first.

MEG: No.

JIM: Another try.

MEG: He's got someone else now, Dad. She's living there right now. She's moved in.

JIM: Then fly back and kick her out.

MEG: Oh, Dad…

JIM: I'm serious. You don't know this, but that's what your mother did. One time I became romantically involved with Mrs. Shoemaker. We took a little trip together. To Sea Island. Your mother got wind of it, and came right down, and told Betty Shoemaker to get on the next train. That's all there was to it. Now why don't you do that? Go tell this woman to peddle her papers elsewhere. We'll sit with the children while you do.

MEG: I've got someone too, Dad.

> *(Pause.)*

JIM: You mean you've had a little fling.

MEG: I've been going with someone.

JIM: A little fling.

MEG: I've been living with him.

JIM: Where was your husband?

MEG: He stayed with his girl.

JIM: And your children?

MEG: Oh they…came and went.

JIM: It sounds a little…complicated.

MEG: It is, Dad. That's why I needed to come home.

> *(Pause. He drinks.)*

JIM: Now let's review the bidding, may we? Do you plan to marry this new man?

MEG: No.

JIM: You're not in love with him?

MEG: No. He's already married, anyway.

JIM: And he's decided he loves his wife.

MEG: No.

JIM: But you've decided you don't love him.

MEG: Yes.

JIM: Or your husband.

MEG: Yes.

JIM: And your husband's fallen in love with someone else.

MEG: He lives with someone else.

JIM: And your children…my grandchildren…come and go among these various households.

MEG: Yes. Sort of. Yes.

JIM: Sounds extremely complicated.

MEG: It is, Dad. It really is.

(Pause. He drinks, thinks, gets up, paces.)

JIM: Well then it seems to me the first thing you do is simplify things. That's the first thing. You ask the man you're living with to leave, you sue your husband for divorce, you hold onto your house, you keep the children in their present schools, you—

MEG: There's someone else, Dad.

(Pause.)

JIM: Someone else?

MEG: Someone else entirely.

JIM: A third person.

MEG: Yes.

JIM: What was that movie your mother and I liked so much? *The Third Man?*

(He sits, downstage left.)

MEG: It's not a man, Dad.

(Pause.)

JIM: Not a man.

MEG: It's a woman.

JIM: A woman.

MEG: I've been involved with a woman, Dad, but it's not working, and I don't know who I am, and I've got to touch base, Daddy. I want to be here.

(She kneels at his feet.)

(Pause. Jim gets slowly to his feet. He points to his glass.)

JIM: I think I'll get a repair. Would you like a repair? I'll take your glass. I'll get us both repairs. *(He takes her glass and goes out to the kitchen, leaving the door open.)*

MEG: *(Moving around the dining room.)* I'm all mixed up, Dad. I'm all over the ball park. I've been seeing a Crisis Counselor, and I've taken a part-time job, and I've been jogging two miles a day, and none of it's working, Dad. I want to come home. I want to take my children to the Zoo, and the Park Lake, and the Art Gallery, and do all those things you and Mother used to do with all of us. I want to start again, Dad. I want to start all over again.

(Jim comes out from the kitchen, now carrying three glasses.)

JIM: I made one for your mother. And I found the glass with the pheasant on it. In the trash. Somebody broke it *(He crosses for the doorway, right.)* So let's have a nice cocktail with your mother, and see if we can get the children to sit quietly while we do.

MEG: You don't want us here, do you, Dad?

JIM: *(Stopping.)* Of course we do, darling. A week, ten days. You're most welcome.

MEG: *(Desperately.)* I can't go back, Dad!

JIM: *(Quietly.)* Neither can I, sweetheart. Neither can I. *(He shuffles on out.)* *(Meg stands for a moment in the dining room, then hurries out after him as Emily, a woman of about thirty-five comes in and looks at the table.)*

EMILY: *(Distractedly.)* I don't know whether to eat, or not. *(Her son David comes in. He's about fourteen.)*

DAVID: What's the trouble, Mother?

EMILY: I don't know whether to eat or not. Your father and I were sitting in the living room, having a perfectly pleasant cocktail together, when all of a sudden that stupid telephone rang, and now he's holed up in the bedroom, talking away. *(She closes the kitchen door.)*

DAVID: Who's he talking to?

EMILY: I don't know. I don't even know. I think it's someone from the club. *(Claire, her daughter, comes on. She's about sixteen.)*

CLAIRE: Are we eating or not?

EMILY: I simply don't know. *(Bertha, the Maid, sticks her head out of the kitchen door.)*

EMILY: I don't know whether to go ahead or not, Bertha. Mr. Thatcher is still on the telephone.

CLAIRE: Couldn't we at least start the soup?

EMILY: I don't know. I just don't know. Oh, let's wait five more minutes, Bertha.

BERTHA: Yes, Mrs.

(Bertha disappears. Emily, David, and Claire sit down.)

EMILY: Honestly, that telephone! I could wring its neck! It should be banned, it should be outlawed, between six and eight in the evening.

(The Father comes in hurriedly from the hall. His name is Standish.)

STANDISH: I've got to go.

EMILY: *(Standing up.)* Go? Go where?

STANDISH: Out.

(Bertha comes in with the soup tureen.)

EMILY: You mean you can't even sit down and have some of Bertha's nice celery soup?

STANDISH: I can't even finish my cocktail. Something very bad has happened.

EMILY: Bertha, would you mind very much putting the soup back in a saucepan and keeping it on a low flame. We'll call you when we're ready.

BERTHA: Yes, Mrs.

(Bertha goes out, Standish takes Emily aside, downstage left.)

EMILY: *(Hushed tones.)* Now what on earth is the matter?

STANDISH: Henry was insulted down at the club.

EMILY: Insulted?

CLAIRE: *(From the table.)* *Uncle* Henry?

STANDISH: *(Ignoring Claire; to Emily.)* Binky Byers made a remark to him in the steam bath.

EMILY: Oh no!

DAVID: What did he say, Dad?

CLAIRE: Yes, what did he say?

STANDISH: I believe I was speaking to your mother.

(Pause. The children are quelled.)

STANDISH: Binky made a remark, and apparently a number of the newer members laughed. Poor Henry was so upset he had to put on his clothes and leave. He called me from Mother's.

EMILY: Oh no, oh no.

STANDISH: I telephoned the club. I spoke to several people who had been in the steam bath. They confirmed the incident. I asked to speak to Binky Byers. He refused to come to the phone. And so I've got to do something about it.

EMILY: Oh dear, oh dear.

DAVID: Won't you tell us what he said to Uncle Henry, Dad?

STANDISH: I will not. I will not dignify the remark by repeating it.

DAVID: Oh come on, Dad. We're not babies.

EMILY: Yes, Standish. Really.

STANDISH: He said— *(Checks himself.)* Claire, I want you to leave the room.

CLAIRE: Why? I'm older.

EMILY: Yes. She should know. Everybody should know. These are different times.

(Bertha comes out.)

EMILY: We're not quite ready yet, Bertha.

(Bertha goes right back in.)

EMILY: Now go on, Standish. Be frank. This is a family.

STANDISH: *(Hesitatingly; looking from one to the other.)* Mr. Byers…made an unfortunate remark…having to do with your Uncle Henry's…private life. *(Pause. The children don't get it.)*

EMILY: I'm afraid you'll have to be more specific, dear.

STANDISH: *(Taking a deep breath.)* Mr. Byers, who had obviously been drinking since early afternoon, approached your Uncle Henry in the steam bath, and alluded in very specific terms to his personal relationships.

CLAIRE: What personal relationships?

STANDISH: His—associations. In the outside world.

(Pause.)

DAVID: I don't get it.

EMILY: Darling, Mr. Byers must have made some unnecessary remarks about your Uncle Henry's bachelor attachments.

DAVID: You mean Uncle Harry is a *fruit?*

STANDISH: *(Wheeling on him.)* I WON'T HAVE THAT WORD IN THIS HOUSE!

DAVID: I was just…

EMILY: He got it from school, dear.

STANDISH: I don't care if he got it from God! I will not have it in this house! The point is my own *brother* was wounded at his *club!*

(Pause.)

EMILY: But what can you do, dear?

STANDISH: Go down there.

EMILY: To your mother's?

STANDISH: To the *club!* I'll demand a public apology from Binky in front of the entire grille.

EMILY: But if he won't even come to the telephone…

STANDISH: I'll have to fight him.

EMILY: Oh, Standish.

STANDISH: I have to.

CLAIRE: Oh, Daddy…

STANDISH: I can't let the remark stand.

DAVID: Can I come with you, Dad?

STANDISH: You may not. I want you home with your mother. *(He starts for the door.)*

EMILY: Standish, for heaven's sake!

STANDISH: No arguments, please.

EMILY: But Binky Byers is half your age! And twice your size!

STANDISH: It makes no difference.

EMILY: I think he was on the boxing team at Dartmouth!

STANDISH: No difference whatsoever.

EMILY: What about your bad shoulder? What about your hernia?

STANDISH: I'm sorry, I imagine I shall be seriously hurt. But I can't stand idly by.

CLAIRE: *(Tearfully.)* Oh, Daddy, please don't go.

(Bertha comes out of the kitchen.)

BERTHA: The lamb will be overdone, Mrs.

EMILY: And it's a beautiful *lamb,* Standish!

STANDISH: *(Shouting them down.)* Now *listen* to me! *All* of you!

(Bertha has been heading back to the kitchen.)

STANDISH: And you, too, Bertha!

(He points toward a chair downstage left. Bertha crosses, as everyone watches her. She sits on the edge of the chair. Everyone turns back to Standish.)

STANDISH: There is nothing, nothing I'd rather do in this world, than sit down at this table with all of you and have some of Bertha's fine celery soup, followed by a leg of lamb with mint sauce and roast potatoes. Am I right about the sauce and the potatoes, Bertha?

BERTHA: Yes, sir.

STANDISH: There is nothing I'd rather do than that. But I have to forego it. My own brother has been publicly insulted at his club. And that means our family has been insulted. And when the family has been insulted, that means this table, these chairs, this room, and all of us in it, including you, Bertha, are being treated with scorn. And so if I stayed here, if I sat down with all of you now, I wouldn't be able to converse, I wouldn't be able to laugh, I wouldn't be able to correct your grammar, David, I wouldn't be able to enjoy your fine meal, Bertha. *(Turning to Emily.)* I wouldn't even be able to kiss my handsome wife goodbye. *(He kisses her. It's a passionate kiss.)* Good-bye, dear.

EMILY: Good-bye, darling.

(He kisses Claire.)

STANDISH: Good-bye, Winkins.

CLAIRE: Good-bye, Daddy.

(He shakes hands with David.)

STANDISH: Good-bye, David.

DAVID: So long, Dad. Good luck.

STANDISH: Good-bye, Bertha.

BERTHA: Good-bye, sir. God bless you.

STANDISH: Thank you very much indeed. *(He goes out.)*

(Pause.)

EMILY: *(Now all business.)* Of course we can't eat now, Bertha. Have something yourself, and let people raid the icebox later on.

BERTHA: Yes, Mrs.

EMILY: And the children can have lamb hash on Saturday.

BERTHA: Yes, Mrs. *(Bertha goes off.)*

EMILY: David: you and I will drive down to the club, and wait for the outcome in the visitor's lounge.

DAVID: O.K., Mother.

EMILY: So get a book. Get a good book. Get *Ivanhoe*. We could be quite a while.

DAVID: O.K. *(He goes out.)*

EMILY: And Claire: I want you to stay here, and hold the fort.

CLAIRE: All right, Mother.

EMILY: Get on the telephone to Doctor Russell. I don't care whether he's having dinner or in the operating room. Tell him to be at the club to give your father first aid.

CLAIRE: All right, Mother.

EMILY: And then study your French.

CLAIRE: All right. *(She starts out, then stops.)* Mother?

EMILY: *(Impatiently in the doorway.)* What, for heaven's sake?

CLAIRE: Is it true about Uncle Henry?

EMILY: Well it may be, sweetheart. But you don't say it to *him*. And you don't say it at the *club*. And you don't say it within a ten-mile radius of your *father*. Now good-bye.

(Emily rushes off, right, followed by Claire. An Old Man and his middle-aged son come on from right. The Old Man is Harvey, his son is Dick. The light is dim in the dining room now, except downstage center, by the "French doors".)

HARVEY: *(As he enters.)* We'll talk in here. No one will disturb us. Nobody comes near a dining room any more. The thought of sitting down with a number of intelligent, attractive people to enjoy good food, well cooked and properly served...that apparently doesn't occur to people any more. Nowadays people eat in kitchens, or in living rooms, standing around, balancing their plates like jugglers. Soon they'll be eating in bathrooms. Well why not? Simplify the process considerably.

DICK: Sit down somewhere, Pop.

HARVEY: *(Coming well downstage, pulling a chair down, away from the table.)* I'll sit here. We can look out. There's a purple finch who comes to the feeder every evening. Brings his young.

(Dick pulls up a chair beside him. Behind, in the dim light, three Women begin to set the table, this time for an elaborate dinner. A great white tablecloth, candles, flowers, the works. The process should be reverential, quiet, and muted, not to distract from the scene downstage. Taking an envelope from his inside pocket.)

HARVEY: Now. I want to go over my funeral with you.

DICK: Pop—

HARVEY: I want to do it. There are only a few more apples left in the barrel for me.

DICK: You've been saying that for years, Pop.

HARVEY: Well this time it's true. So I want to go over this, please. You're my eldest son. I can't do it with anyone else. Your mother starts to cry, your brother isn't here, and your sister gets distracted. So concentrate, please, on my funeral.

DICK: All right, Pop.

HARVEY: *(Taking out a typewritten document.)* First, here is my obituary. For both newspapers. I dictated it to Miss Kovak down at the office, and I've read it over twice, and it's what I want. It's thorough without being self-congratulatory. I mention my business career, my civic commitments, and of course my family. I even touch on my recreational life. I give my lowest score in golf and the weight of the sailfish I caught off the Keys. The papers will want to cut both items, but don't you let them.

DICK: O.K., Pop.

HARVEY: I also want them to print this picture. *(He shows it.)* It was taken when I was elected to chair the Symphony drive. I think it will do. I don't look too young to die, nor so old it won't make any difference.

DICK: All right, Pop.

HARVEY: *(Fussing with other documents.)* Now I want the funeral service announced at the end of the obituary, and to occur three days later. That will give people time to postpone their trips and adjust their appointments. And I want it at three-thirty in the afternoon. This gives people time to digest their lunch and doesn't obligate us to feed them dinner. Notice I've underlined the word *church*. Mr. Fayerweather might try to squeeze the service into the chapel, but don't let him. I've lived in this city all my life, and know a great many people, and I want everyone to have a seat and feel comfortable. If you see people milling around the door, go right up to them and find them a place, even if you have to use folding chairs. Are we clear on that?

DICK: Yes, Pop.

(By now the table has been mostly set behind them. The Women have gone.)

HARVEY: I've listed the following works to be played by Mrs. Manchester at the organ. This Bach, this Handel, this Schubert. All lively, you'll notice. Nothing gloomy, nothing grim. I want the service to start promptly with a good rousing hymn—"Onward Christian Soldiers"—and then Fayerweather may make some brief—underlined *brief*—remarks about my life and works. Do you plan to get up and speak, by the way?

DICK: Me?

HARVEY: You. Do you plan to say anything?

DICK: I hadn't thought, Pop…

HARVEY: Don't, if you don't want to. There's nothing more uncomfortable than a reluctant or unwilling speaker. On the other hand, if you, as my eldest son, were to get on your feet and say a few words of farewell…

DICK: *(Quickly.)* Of course I will, Pop.

HARVEY: Good. Then I'll write you in. *(He writes.)* "Brief remarks by my son Richard." *(Pause; looks up.)* Any idea what you might say?

DICK: No, Pop.

HARVEY: You won't make it sentimental, will you? Brad Hoffmeister's son got up the other day and made some very sentimental remarks about Brad. I didn't like it, and I don't think Brad would have liked it.

DICK: I won't get sentimental, Pop.

HARVEY: Good. *(Pause; shuffles documents; looks up again.)* On the other hand, you won't make any wisecracks, will you?

DICK: Oh, Pop…

HARVEY: You have that tendency, Dick. At Marcie's wedding. And your broth-er's birthday. You got up and made some very flip remarks about all of us.

DICK: I'm sorry, Pop.

HARVEY: Smart-guy stuff. Too smart, in my opinion. If you plan to get into that sort of thing, perhaps you'd better not say anything at all.

DICK: I won't make any cracks, Pop. I promise.

HARVEY: Thank you. *(Looks at documents; looks up again.)* Because you love us, don't you?

DICK: Yes, Pop.

HARVEY: You love us. You may live a thousand miles away, you may have run off every summer, you may be a terrible letter-writer, but you love us all, just the same. Don't you? You love me.

DICK: *(Touching him.)* Oh yes, Pop! Oh yes! Really!

(Pause.)

HARVEY: Fine. *(Puts his glasses on again; shuffles through documents.)* Now at the graveside, just the family. I want to be buried beside my brothers and below my mother and father. Leave room for your mother to lie beside me. If she marries again, still leave room. She'll come back at the end.

DICK: All right, Pop.

HARVEY: Invite people back here after the burial. Stay close to your mother. She gets nervous at any kind of gathering, and makes bad decisions. For example, don't let her serve any of the good Beefeater's gin if people simply want to mix it with tonic water. And when they're gone, sit with her. Stay in the house. Don't leave for a few days. Please.

DICK: I promise, Pop.

(Annie, the Maid from the first scene, now quite old, adds candlesticks and a lovely flower centerpiece to the table.)

HARVEY: *(Putting documents back in the envelope.)* And that's my funeral. I'm leaving you this room, you know. After your mother dies, the table and chairs go to you. It's the best thing I can leave you, by far.

DICK: Thanks, Pop.

(Annie exits into the kitchen.)

HARVEY: Now we'll rejoin your mother. *(He gets slowly to his feet.)* I'll put this envelope in my safe deposit box, on top of my will and the stock certificates. The key will be in my left bureau drawer. *(He starts out, then stops.)* You didn't see the purple finch feeding its young.

DICK: *(Remaining in his chair.)* Yes I did, Pop.

HARVEY: You saw it while I was talking?

DICK: That's right.

HARVEY: Good. I'm glad you saw it *(He goes out slowly.)*

(Dick waits a moment, lost in thought, and then replaces the chairs. The lights come up on the table, now beautifully set with white linen, crystal goblets, silver candlesticks, flowers, the works. Annie begins to set plates as a Hostess—Ruth—comes in from right.)

RUTH: *(Surveying the table.)* Oh Annie! It looks absolutely spectacular.

ANNIE: Thank you, Mrs.

RUTH: *(As she begins to distribute place cards carefully around the table.)* Now make sure the soup plates are hot.

THE DINING ROOM 279

ANNIE: I always do, Mrs.

RUTH: But I think we can dispense with butter-balls. Just give everyone a nice square of butter.

ANNIE: I'll do butter-balls, Mrs.

RUTH: Would you? How nice! And keep an eye on the ashtrays, Annie. Some people still smoke between courses, but they don't like to be reminded of it.

ANNIE: I know, Mrs.

RUTH: And let's see…Oh yes. Before people arrive, I want to pay you. *(She produces two envelopes from the sideboard.)* For you. And for Velma in the kitchen. It includes your taxi. So you can both just leave right after you've cleaned up.

ANNIE: Thank you, Mrs.

RUTH: There's a little extra in yours, Annie. Just a present. Because you've been so helpful to the family over the years.

ANNIE: Thank you, Mrs.

RUTH: And now I'd better check the living room.

ANNIE: Yes, Mrs.

(Ruth starts out right, then stops.)

RUTH: Oh Annie. I heard some strange news through the grapevine.

(Annie looks at her.)

RUTH: Mrs. Rellman told me that you won't be available any more.

ANNIE: No, Mrs.

RUTH: Not even for us, Annie. We've used you more than anyone.

ANNIE: I'm retiring, Mrs.

RUTH: But surely special occasions, Annie. I mean, if we're desperate. Can I still reach you at your nephew's?

ANNIE: He's moving away, Mrs.

RUTH: But then where will you go? What will you do?

ANNIE: I've got my sister in Milwaukee, Mrs.

RUTH: But we'll be lost without you, Annie.

ANNIE: You'll manage, Mrs.

RUTH: *(Indicating the table.)* But not like this. We'll never match this.

ANNIE: Thank you, Mrs.

RUTH: I think I heard the bell.

ANNIE: I'll get it, Mrs.

RUTH: Women's coats upstairs, men's in the hall closet.

ANNIE: Yes, Mrs. *(Annie starts out.)*

RUTH: Annie!

(Annie stops. Ruth goes to her and hugs her. Annie responds stiffly.)

RUTH: Thank you, Annie. For everything.

ANNIE: You're welcome, Mrs. *(Annie goes off right, to answer the door.)*

(Ruth goes to the sideboard, gets a book of matches. She lights the two candles on the table as she speaks to the audience.)

RUTH: Lately I've been having this recurrent dream. We're giving this perfect party. We have our dining room back, and Grandmother's silver, before it was stolen, and Charley's mother's royal blue dinner plates, before the movers dropped them, and even the finger bowls, if I knew where they were. And I've invited all our favorite people. Oh I don't mean just our old friends. I mean everyone we've ever known and liked. We'd have the man who fixes our Toyota, and that intelligent young couple who bought the Payton house, and the receptionist at the doctor's office, and the new teller at the bank. And our children would be invited, too. And they'd all come back from wherever they are. And we'd have two cocktails, and hot hors d'oeuvres, and a first-rate cook in the kitchen, and two maids to serve, and everyone would get along famously!

(The candles are lit by now.)

RUTH: My husband laughs when I tell him this dream. "Do you realize," he says, "what a party like that would cost? Do you realize what we'd have to pay these days for a party like that?" Well, I know. I know all that. But sometimes I think it might almost be worth it.

(The rest of the Cast now spills into the dining room, talking animatedly, having a wonderful time. There is the usual gallantry and jockeying around as people read the place cards and find their seats. The Men pull out the Women's chairs, and people sit down. The Host goes to the sideboard, where Annie has left a bottle of wine in a silver bucket. He wraps a linen napkin around it, and begins to pour people's wine. The conversation flows as well. The lights begin to dim. The Host reaches his own seat at the head of the table, and pours his own wine. Then he raises his glass.)

HOST: To all of us.

(Everyone raises his or her glass. As their glasses go down, the lights fade to black. The table is bathed in its own candlelight. Then the two downstage actors unobtrusively snuff the candles, and the play is over.)

The End

Suggested Ideas for Small Talk at the End of the Play

FIRST ACTRESS (HOSTESS):

1. Come in, come in. Are you famished? I hope so. We've got four courses tonight, and I don't want to hear any talk about diets or calories or cholesterol.

2. I've even put place cards. I've arranged it so husbands and wives can't sit together. With six it's easy. My mother used to spend hours arranging the seating for a dinner of twelve.

3. Do you like the candelabra? Do you think they're too much? I dug them out of the attic. They belonged to my great-grandmother, and I thought tonight we'd really splurge.

4. Now be kind to me on the food. I bought the new Julia Childs cookbook, and decided to go whole hog. Thank God for Annie. I don't think there's anyone else in the city who knows how to serve.

SECOND ACTRESS:

1. This does it! I give up! From here on in, it's hamburgers in the kitchen for me. Ruth, you should go to Washington. They should set you up at the White House. They should make you Secretary of Dinner Parties.

2. Place cards yet! Now where am I sitting? I didn't bring my glasses. Here? Really? *(To Second Actor.)* For some strange reason, I'm sitting next to you.

3. *(To Second Actor.)* Now I want to hear all about you. I hear you've done very well. Do you think the company will move you? No? You mean you'll be here? Well that's lucky. No, I mean it. I'm really very glad you're going to be here.

4. *(To Second Actor.)* Oh Lord, here comes the wine. Now stop me if I drink too much. I feel like going overboard tonight. My children are sleeping over at my mother's, and so I'm on my own. Keep an eye on me, for God's sake, so I don't say and do things I'll be sorry for later.

THIRD ACTRESS:

1. Oh my what a lovely table. How do you do it, Ruth? I try and try, but it never comes out like this. Someone should take a picture. I should have brought my camera. This should be preserved for posterity.

2. Now where do I sit? Ah, right here. You know I used to sit at this place when I was a little girl. Right next to my Daddy. Oh God, what memories. It's my favorite spot. Ruth you put me at my favorite place.

3. I wish my children could see this table. They have no idea what a good table looks like. We've tried to tell them, but they don't care. They don't know what they're missing.

4. What kind of wine is that? It looks like lovely wine. I'm just beginning to learn about wine. I've bought books on it. It's a whole science. We're thinking of going to France just to taste wines.

FIRST ACTOR (HOST):

1. And here we are! Come in, come in! Ruth, you've outdone yourself. I don't know how she does it. She was out all afternoon doing something for the Art Gallery, and then suddenly she produces this. It just seems to appear. Like magic.

2. Now find your seats, everyone. Ruth has all that figured out very carefully. I stay out of that department. All I know is that I'm sitting next to the two loveliest women in town.

3. Now the wine I do know something about. I won't tell you what it is, but I had quite a discussion with Simmons down at the liquor store. It's a special shipment from the Loire Valley, and Ruth and I got the name of it when we were there last spring. So let's try it, and discuss it, and if we don't like it, I'll bring out something else.

4. Now is everybody seated? Is everybody happy? Then let me simply raise my glass: "To all of us."

SECOND ACTOR:

1. Good God, this is too much. It's like a dream. What was that movie? *The Discreet Charm of the Bourgeoisie.* Did you see that? That's where we are. We're in that movie.

2. *(To Second Actress)* I hope I'm sitting next to you. Yep. Here we are. Good old Ruth. Do you think she's trying to match us up?

3. How are things going by the way? Are you getting along since your husband left? Are the kids O.K.? Do you like your job? Any chance we could have lunch some day? We've got a lot to talk about.

4. Ah the wine. You always get good wine in this house. I don't know whether it's French or Californian, but it's the best. Most people don't pay much attention to the wine but here, they do.

THIRD ACTOR:

1. Wow, what a spread! What is this? Versailles? This is incredible. Ruth, I haven't seen anything like this for years.

2. I actually flew back from Denver for this party. Grabbed an earlier plane. Wouldn't have missed it. I figured you were putting on the dog, and I wanted to get in on it. My God, I should have worn my tuxedo.
3. Can't wait to see what's on the menu. You're the best cook in town, Ruth. I still remember that soufflé thing we had the last time we were here.
4. I hope you noticed I held off on the hors d'oeuvres. I was trying to save room. Except for those bacon things. You should have kept them away from me. I must have eaten ten. No matter. I'll play three sets of tennis tomorrow, and work them off.

What I Did Last Summer

(1983)

AUTHOR'S NOTE

What I Did Last Summer had a terrible childhood, but seems to have finally landed on its feet. It was first produced in a troubled tour on the Westport summer circuit, and then was remounted with a different director and cast at Circle Rep in New York. This production, too, was plagued by difficulty, and finally opened a week late, with no director listed and a last-minute replacement valiantly coping with a main part. On opening night, a chair collapsed and a member of the audience fell headlong onto the stage. Meanwhile, the plumbing in the restrooms had backed up noticeably. The critics predictably responded to the evening without enthusiasm. Since then, however, the play has found a substantial life in schools, colleges, and community theatres, and I have to say that I've always had a special fondness for it.

ORIGINAL PRODUCTION

What I Did Last Summer was first produced as a play-in-progress at the Circle Repertory Company in New York City in November, 1981, directed by Porter Van Zandt. It was similarly done at the Seattle Repertory Company in February, 1982, directed by Daniel Sullivan.

Its first full production opened at the Cape Playhouse in Dennis, Massachusetts, on August 9, 1982, with the following cast:

Charlie	Mark Arnott
Ted	Tod Waring
Grace	Barbara Feldon
Elsie	Ellen Parker
Bonny	Eve Bennett-Gordon
Anna Trumbull	Eileen Heckart

Melvin Bernhardt was the director, Loren Sherman the designer, Scott Lehrer did the sound, and Denise Romano the costumes. James B. McKenzie was the Executive Producer, Jack V. Booch, the Artistic Producer.

It opened in New York at the Circle Repertory Company on February 6, 1983, with the following cast:

Charlie	Ben Siegler
Ted	Robert Joy
Grace	Debra Mooney
Elsie	Christine Estabrook
Bonny	Ann McDonough
Anna Trumbull	Jacqueline Brookes

John Lee Beatty designed the set, Jennifer Von Mayrhauser the costumes, Craig Miller the lighting, and Chuck London the sound. The production stage manager was Suzanne Fry.

CAST

Charlie, fourteen*
Ted, sixteen, Charlie's friend.*
Grace, Charlie's mother
Elsie, nineteen, Charlie's sister*
Bonny, fourteen*
Anna Trumbull

* The young people in this play may be played by actors older than these indicated ages. In this way, we will have more of the sense of actors enacting their roles. Indeed, throughout this play, we should be aware of things in the process of being fabricated or made: the characters by actors; the setting by the manipulation of simple scenic elements; the play itself by its obviously traditional and presentational form.

TIME
Summer, 1945

PLACE
A summer "colony" on the Canadian shore of Lake Erie, near Buffalo, New York.

SET
Simple and presentational. Wooden and wicker furniture, sun-bleached and sandworn, as indicated in ground-plan; a simple wooden glider might serve as a central element, becoming occasionally the front seat of a car. Plenty of sunlight, blue sky, and occasional green shade.

PROPS
As indicated. In other words, only when it seems simpler to use them than not. For example, the clay in Act I probably is helpful, but plates and glasses for the supper scene probably are not.

COSTUMES
To be changed or adjusted only when indicated.

What I Did Last Summer

ACT I

Before Curtain: Music: an old Bing Crosby recording such as "Swinging on a Star." Charlie comes in in khakis, T-shirt, and old sneakers, as a fourteen-year-old.

CHARLIE: *(To audience.)* This is a play about me when I was fourteen, back during the war, when we had this house at a place called Rose Hill, on the Canadian shore of Lake Erie, near Buffalo, New York, where I was born…That was the summer I planned to sit around the house… *(He sits.)* And study Latin, which I flunked in June…and sail my dad's catboat in the races every Wednesday and Saturday…or practice driving my mother's car in the driveway… *(The bench might momentarily become a car. He mimes driving.)* or play tennis on the Wilsons' clay court… *(He is up by now, miming an elaborate serve.)* Pow! and then after a game, me and my friend Ted Moffatt…

(Ted runs across the stage, in old clothes.)

TED: Bombs away! *(He exits downstage right, whistling like a bomb.)*

CHARLIE: *(Watching him.)* …would run down the bank to the beach, jumping over the patches of poison ivy, and then dash over the hot sand, and charge through the water out to the sandbar, where you could dive in, and open your mouth, and drink in half the lake, if you wanted to!

TED: *(Shouting, from offstage.)* Come on, Charlie!

CHARLIE: *(Starting to take off his sneakers.)* Prepare to attack! Look out below! *(Grace comes on from upstage left.)*

GRACE: Charlie, you stay right where you are! *(She is in her late thirties, attractive, in a simple summer dress.)* Nobody's going near that water until they've picked up their room! It's an absolute pigsty!

CHARLIE: *(Holding his sneakers.)* Later, Mom.

GRACE: Right now, Charlie!

TED: *(Offstage.)* Zowie! The water's great!

CHARLIE: Mom, Ted's waiting! *(He dashes off, dropping his sneakers onstage.)*

GRACE: Charlie, I'm warning you…Charlie, I am issuing an ultimatum!… Charlie!

(But he's gone. Elsie, Charlie's sister, comes on from upstage left. She is nineteen,

wears rolled-up blue jeans and a baggy man's shirt. She carries a large copy of War and Peace.)

ELSIE: He wouldn't get away with that if Daddy were here.

GRACE: Well Daddy's not here, as we all well know, and so we'll just have to do the best we can without him… *(She peers out at the lake.)* Oh now honestly.

ELSIE: What?

GRACE: *(Peering.)* Are those boys…wearing…their bathing suits?

ELSIE: *(Looking out.)* Oh God.

GRACE: Are they? Or not. I can't tell. *(She shades her eyes.)*

ELSIE: Wouldn't you know.

GRACE: What?

ELSIE: They're playing "When the Moon Comes Over the Mountain."

GRACE: They're playing what?

ELSIE: They're *mooning,* Mother. They think it's an absolute riot. They take everything off, and roll their rear ends around in the waves.

GRACE: Oh don't be silly.

ELSIE: They *do,* Mother. Wait, I'll get the binoculars.

GRACE: That's not necessary, Elsie. *(She stares out.)* Why on earth would they want to do a thing like that?

ELSIE: They like to tease the baby-sitters on the beach. Who think it's a perfect scream.

GRACE: Well I don't think it's funny at all.

ELSIE: Neither do I, Mother. And lately do you know what else they've been doing?

GRACE: I'm not interested, thank you. *(She starts to pick up the sneakers, stops.)* What?

ELSIE: They fill their athletic supporters full of stones, and then march up and down. All the way to the public beach. With these great bulges in their fronts.

GRACE: Oh honestly.

ELSIE: That's what they do! And it's repulsive, Mother. With women and children around? No one even knows where to look.

GRACE: I'll speak to him.

ELSIE: And here it is just the beginning of summer. Lord knows what he'll be up to by Labor Day. *(She settles down to read* War and Peace *"in the chair.")*

GRACE: We'll just have to think up some projects for him, that's all. We'll have to make a good, long list. Repairing the steps, painting the terrace furniture…

ELSIE: Oh God, I can see it now. Paint dripping all over the house…

GRACE: Now that's enough, Elsie. I don't see you killing yourself this summer.

ELSIE: Mother!

GRACE: And I think *your* room could stand a little more attention.

ELSIE: Mother, I am busy all the *time*. I'm collecting money for Bundles for Britain, I've started *War and Peace* for summer reading…

GRACE: Well all I know is I don't get much help with the errands.

ELSIE: That's because I can't *drive,* Mother.

GRACE: You *can* drive, Elsie. You've even got your license. You just won't, that's all.

ELSIE: I get nervous, Mother.

GRACE: Well you're not too nervous to pick on your brother every other minute.

ELSIE: But he's so imma*ture,* Mother.

GRACE: Yes well, we all have a little growing to do, now don't we.

ELSIE: Oh, Mother, what a snide thing to say!

GRACE: Yes well…

ELSIE: I mean it! I just wish Daddy were here, that's all! That's all I wish ! *(She storms off upstage left.)*

GRACE: *(Looking after her with a sigh.)* So do I. Oh boy. So do I. *(She picks up Charlie's sneakers as she speaks to the audience.)* This is also a play about me, trying to run a house, trying to run two houses, one here, one in town, trying to keep things clean, trying to keep things going, trying to give two children a good healthy summer, away from the city, away from the polio scare, even during the war, with gas coupons, and meat rationing, and you name it, while my husband is away, overseas for eighteen and a half months, somewhere in the Pacific, cooped up on a destroyer escort, when any minute some Kamikaze pilot could dive down and blow him to smithereens!…*that's* what this play is about, if you ask me! And if it isn't, it should be.

(Grace strides off, upstage left, carrying Charlie's sneakers, as Charlie and Ted come on from downstage right, snapping towels at each other, as if they were duelists in a movie. They duel all over the stage, peppering their attacks with expressions from comic books.)

CHARLIE: Shazam!

TED: Pow!

CHARLIE: Ooof!

TED: Whammo!

CHARLIE: Banzai!

TED: Die, Yankee dog!

CHARLIE: Take that...and that...and that, you Canuck bastard!

(Ted, suddenly serious, grabs Charlie's towel.)

TED: What did you say?

CHARLIE: I just said—

TED: You called me a Canuck.

CHARLIE: What's wrong with that? You're Canadian, aren't you?

TED: *(Shoving him.)* I'm not a Canuck, Charlie!

CHARLIE: *(Shoving him back.)* Hey now watch it...

(And suddenly they are wrestling in earnest, puffing and grunting. Ted forces Charlie to the ground, and tries to pin him. Charlie writhes and heaves to get out from under. Bonny comes on quickly from upstage left. She is pretty and young, wearing an informal summer dress.)

BONNY: Oh *no!* What *now?*

(The boys continue to struggle.)

BONNY: I thought you two were best friends!

TED: Not when he insults a guy.

CHARLIE: *(Still struggling.)* He can't even take a joke!

BONNY: Let him UP, Ted. He's younger.

TED: First he's got to apologize.

CHARLIE: *(Struggling.)* That'll be the day.

BONNY: Oh you're both so juvenile!

TED: *(Trying to pin him.)* Come on, Charlie, unconditional surrender!

CHARLIE: Never! You Canuck!

(More intense struggling.)

BONNY: *(Sitting down.)* All right. I just wanted to know who could crew for me this afternoon.

(The boys stop fighting and look at her.)

BONNY: My father's playing golf, so I get to skipper the Snipe.

(Ted and Charlie jump up.)

TED & CHARLIE: *(Simultaneously.)* I'll do it...Let me...

BONNY: *(To Ted.)* I thought you had to cut people's grass this summer, Ted. I thought you had a job.

TED: I'll take the afternoon off.

BONNY: You will?

CHARLIE: Yeah, but I know more about sailing. My dad taught me.

BONNY: That's true. Oh help. I'm terrible about making decisions. Hmmm.

(She makes the most of the moment.) Tell you what...This time I'll take Ted.

CHARLIE: How *come?*

BONNY: Because he's a working man, Charlie. You're free any time, all summer.

CHARLIE: I'm not. I'm working. I work, too.

TED: Yeah sure. For your mother.

CHARLIE: Well you work for your father.

BONNY: It's not the same thing, Charlie. Ted is personally responsible for a large number of lawns.

CHARLIE: That's because his father is caretaker around here. He gave him the job.

TED: I'd better go check out with him, by the way. *(He starts off, downstage left.)*

CHARLIE: *(Calling after him.)* If my dad were home, I'd have a regular job, too. In the city, maybe. We'd drive in together every day. We'd commute!

TED: *(Returning.)* Hey, Charlie, why don't you get a job with the Pig Woman? She's got a notice up in Brodie's drugstore.

CHARLIE: Maybe I will.

TED: I hear she doesn't wear any underpants. Might give you a charge.

BONNY: Don't get grubby, please.

CHARLIE: Maybe I will work for her.

TED: Sure. Work for the Pig Woman. Of course, I hear she pays peanuts. Or maybe it's acorns. *(He goes off laughing.)*

BONNY: Ted's getting very sarcastic this summer.

CHARLIE: Does the Pig Woman really have a notice up in Brodie's?

BONNY: I don't know, Charlie. You shouldn't work for her anyway.

(They sit down, side by side, on the glider.)

CHARLIE: Why not?

BONNY: My mother says she's an immoral woman.

CHARLIE: What do you mean, immoral?

BONNY: She used to be somebody's mistress.

CHARLIE: No kidding.

BONNY: She *was!* She was the mistress of some doctor. He kept his wife in town, and brought the Pig Woman out here. And left her that place when he died.

CHARLIE: Ted says she's part Indian.

BONNY: She is! She's got mixed blood. And she's an artist manquée.

CHARLIE: A what?

BONNY: Artist manquée. It means she gives art lessons but nobody takes them.

CHARLIE: Then how can she pay? I mean, if I decide to work for her.

BONNY: I don't know, Charlie. Mother says she's just hanging on, with no visible means of support. *(She gets up.)* And now I've got to go sail. *(She starts off, right.)*

CHARLIE: *(Getting up.)* Yeah well thanks a bunch for picking Ted.

BONNY: I tried to be fair, Charlie.

CHARLIE: Yeah fair. Uh huh fair. You didn't even let us draw lots.

BONNY: He has a *job,* Charlie. He needs rest and recreation.

CHARLIE: I think you picked him because he's got his driver's license.

BONNY: Oh stop it.

CHARLIE: I do. I think you want to neck with him. In his car.

BONNY: Oh just grow UP, Charlie. Please! *(She goes off, upstage right.)*

CHARLIE: *(Shouting after her.)* That's what I *think,* Bonny.

(Elsie comes on from upstage left carrying her War and Peace.*)*

ELSIE: Charlie, Mother's driving to the village, and she needs someone to help with the groceries. *(She takes his towel from him.)*

CHARLIE: Why don't you go?

ELSIE: Because I've made other PLANS, Charlie. *(She spreads the towel out on the platform, downstage right, and lies down.)* Now hurry! She's waiting in the car!

(Charlie starts shuffling off.)

ELSIE: God, you're a slob.

CHARLIE: *(Turning, giving her the finger.)* Perch and rotate, Elsie. Perch, and systematically rotate, please. *(He goes off, upstage left.)*

ELSIE: Oh Jesus, you're disgusting.

(The lights dim on Elsie reading, as Grace comes on from upstage right, briskly, carrying a paper bag. She stops, looks over her shoulder.)

GRACE: *(To audience.)* Now where'd he go? I left him right by the cash register.

(Charlie comes on from upstage right, carrying another grocery bag.)

CHARLIE: I dropped the eggs.

GRACE: Oh, Charlie.

CHARLIE: It's O.K. They gave me more.

GRACE: Well let's get things into this car before the ice cream melts.

(They unload the groceries into the "trunk" of the glider.)

GRACE: Where'd you go earlier? I thought you wanted to pick out the cookies.

CHARLIE: I just went to Brodie's, Mom.

GRACE: To read the funny books?

CHARLIE: No, not to read the "funny" books, Mom. I don't read "funny" books any more.

GRACE: Then what was that I found under your bed?

CHARLIE: That was Classic *Comics,* Mom. For school. *A Tale of Two Cities.*

GRACE: Well I don't consider it a tale of two anything. I threw it out.

CHARLIE: Oh boy. You would.

(They close the "trunk," come around either side, to get into the "car." They talk over the "top.")

GRACE: Did you at least stop by the post office?

CHARLIE: Of course.

GRACE: Anything?

CHARLIE: I would have told you, Mom.

GRACE: Oh dear.

CHARLIE: It's been five weeks since we heard.

GRACE: Oh well now we mustn't brood. He's on a ship. You wait. Soon there'll be a great stack of letters. For all of us.

(They get into the "car." Grace sits for a moment before starting it.)

GRACE: I have a bone to pick with you.

CHARLIE: What?

GRACE: When Mr. McAlister came up by the cash register, you were very rude.

CHARLIE: Who? Boris?

GRACE: Mr. McAlister to you, please.

CHARLIE: He looks like Boris. Of Karloff fame.

GRACE: Well for your information, he happens to be one of the most attractive men in Buffalo.

CHARLIE: He's always hanging around you.

GRACE: Don't be silly.

CHARLIE: He is. He's always coming up.

GRACE: He's a very lonely man.

CHARLIE: Yeah yeah.

GRACE: You just don't know, Charlie. His son was killed in Italy. His wife is in the hospital with a nervous breakdown—

CHARLIE: Well all I know is he's all over you like a tent.

GRACE: Oh, Charlie…

CHARLIE: He's a son of a beech…

(Grace wheels on him.)

CHARLIE: …nut tree.

(Grace starts the "car," and mimes driving, very simply. No gear-shifting or foot-pedaling is necessary. Using the "wheel" should be enough. The glider might rock back and forth very simply.)

CHARLIE: By the way, I might get a job this summer.

GRACE: We'll think up plenty of jobs.

CHARLIE: I mean a real job.

GRACE: We'll think up a big project.

CHARLIE: I don't mean working for my mother.

GRACE: What did you have in mind then, Charlie?

CHARLIE: There's a notice on Brodie's bulletin board: "Man wanted. Odd Jobs."

GRACE: All right. Try that. Where?

CHARLIE: Black Point.

GRACE: How will you get there? With gas rationing? I can't chauffeur you all over the lakeshore.

CHARLIE: I'll ride my bike.

GRACE: Now that's good, Charlie. That's very enterprising. Daddy would be proud.
  (They drive.)

GRACE: Whom will you be working for, by the way?

CHARLIE: Huh?

GRACE: Don't say "huh," Charlie. Cavemen say "huh."

CHARLIE: I didn't hear your question, Mother dear.

GRACE: I said, whom will you be working for?

CHARLIE: The Pig Woman.

GRACE: Who?

CHARLIE: Anna Trumbull. The Pig Woman. It's her notice up in Brodie's.
  (Pause.)

GRACE: I don't think so, Charlie.

CHARLIE: Why not?

GRACE: I don't think that's a good idea. At all.

CHARLIE: Would you mind telling me why the hell not?

GRACE: Don't swear, please, Charlie. *(Pause.)* She's a disturbing woman, that's why.

CHARLIE: What d'ya mean, disturbing?

GRACE: She's unsettling, Charlie. She likes to rock the boat. Like some other people I know.

CHARLIE: It's a job, Mom!

GRACE: Charlie, you flunked Latin. You have to tutor Latin every Tuesday.

CHARLIE: I'll do that, too!

GRACE: Well, the answer is No, Charlie. N.O. And that's final. *(She looks out.)* Oh look. Look at the corn. It's not as high as an elephant's eye, but I'll bet we'll be having corn on the cob before you know it.

CHARLIE: Big deal.

GRACE: Your favorite thing. Mmmm. Yummy.

CHARLIE: Goodie goodie gum-drop, rah-rah.

(She glances at him. They drive for a moment in silence. Finally.)

CHARLIE: Can I drive? Can I at least do that?

GRACE: No you may not.

CHARLIE: Why not?

GRACE: Because it's against the law, Charlie.

CHARLIE: Ted drives.

GRACE: Well he shouldn't.

CHARLIE: Well he does.

GRACE: Well that's because he's Canadian. They do things differently… *(She looks out.)* There are the Robinsons. Wave to the Robinsons! Hi, hi! *(She waves as they go by. Charlie gives them the finger out his window.)*

CHARLIE: It's just back roads, Mom.

GRACE: I don't care if it's back roads or Delaware Avenue.

CHARLIE: I've been practicing in our driveway.

GRACE: That's not the open highway.

CHARLIE: Please, Mom.

GRACE: I'm sorry.

CHARLIE: You never let me do anything.

GRACE: I don't let you kill yourself, no.

CHARLIE: You wouldn't even let me have a beer at the Potters'.

GRACE: Not at fourteen, no.

CHARLIE: You're a real wet blanket, Mom. All the time.

GRACE: Who took you and your friends to the movies, just the other night?

CHARLIE: Took us. TOOK us. You wouldn't even let us hitchhike.

GRACE: Not at night. No.

CHARLIE: And we had to see *your* movie. We had to see *Mrs. Miniver* again, for Chrissake.

GRACE: I've asked you not to swear, please.

CHARLIE: *(Softly, out the window.)* Yeah well go to hell.

(Grace slams on the "brakes." They both rock suddenly forward.)

GRACE: What did you say?

CHARLIE: Never mind.

GRACE: What did you *say?*

CHARLIE: *(Grimly.)* I said "Go to hell."

GRACE: Out of the car.

CHARLIE: Oh, Mom…

GRACE: Out. Right now. People who swear at their mothers can learn to walk the rest of the way home.

CHARLIE: I was just—

GRACE: OUT, Charlie. Right now. I mean it.

(She leans grimly across him, and opens his "door." Charlie groans, gets out of the "car," slams the door, walks a little way off. Grace starts the car forward Charlie fades upstage. She stops the car, and sits for a moment, staring ahead. Charlie watches her. She relents, calls to him, opens the door.)

GRACE: Come on.

(Charlie approaches the "car" sullenly, and gets back in, closing the "door." Grace starts the "car" forward. Finally.)

GRACE: Honestly, Charlie, I'm at the end of my rope. I miss Daddy so much, I'm trying so hard to keep things going, and the last thing I need is you being rude to my friends or swearing at me in the car.

CHARLIE: I didn't—

GRACE: You did, Charlie. And you're not much help around the house, either. You leave your breakfast dishes all over the kitchen, and you use twice as much butter as you're supposed to, and I find damp, sandy towels all over your bedroom floor. And I notice that Hitchcock chair by your bed is broken again.

CHARLIE: I'll fix it, Mom.

GRACE: You can't, Charlie. And you can't fix that sugar bowl you broke either. There are special men who do that, and they're all away in the war…Well anyway… *(She pulls up.)* Here we are. *(She turns, looks at him.)* I'm just asking you to be more helpful, Charlie.

CHARLIE: O.K., Mom. *(He starts to get out of the "car.")*

GRACE: Wait, Charlie. One more thing…Now this is awkward, but your father is not around, so it's up to me to say it…If ever you have…an accident at night, Charlie…if ever you have what is known as a nocturnal emission,…

(Charlie puts a hand in front of his face.)

GRACE: …*don't* throw the bedsheets over it and pretend that nothing's happened. Change the *sheets,* Charlie. Or tell me. And I'll change them.

(Long pause. He sits, ultimately humiliated.)

GRACE: Did you hear me, sweetheart?

CHARLIE: Oh…My…God!

GRACE: I'm sorry, darling, but I thought I should bring it up.

CHARLIE: *(Jumping out of the "car.")* That does it!

GRACE: Oh now…

CHARLIE: That really DOES it, Mom! *(He starts off.)*

GRACE: Where are you going?

CHARLIE: To get a job with the Pig Woman!

GRACE: Oh no you're not!

CHARLIE: Oh yes I am! *(He runs off.)*

GRACE: *(Calling after him.)* You come back here and unload this car!

CHARLIE: *(From offstage.)* Let Elsie do it!

GRACE: *(Calling.)* Charlie!

(Elsie, sitting up from her sunbathing downstage right, as the lights come on her again.)

ELSIE: Let Elsie do what?

GRACE: *(Opening the "trunk.")* Help with the groceries, please.

ELSIE: Why can't Charlie?

GRACE: *(Picking up a grocery bag.)* Don't argue, Elsie. Just do it, please. Just do it right now.

(She starts off. Elsie begins to poke around in the remaining bag.)

ELSIE: Did you get melon, Mother? I see cookies for Charlie, but I don't see melon for me. How am I supposed to lose weight if you don't even get any melon? *(She looks up, sees that Grace has gone, upstage left turns to audience.)* Oh boy. I'll tell you one thing this play is *not* about. It's not about *me*. It's not about how it feels to grow up during a war when all the boys your age are away. And you can't even go visit your friends from college because "this trip isn't really necessary." And it's not about how someone can miss her father terribly, and how she dreams about him at night, and how he taught her to drive a car, and gave her the confidence to do it, and now he's not around, she's scared even to try. So what does she do with her summer? She sits around, and gripes, and reads, and smokes, and argues, and EATS! And turns herself into a big, fat, slobby PIG! *(She starts off.)* That's what this play is not about, if anyone wants to know. *(She goes off, upstage left.)*

(Lights might change to give a greener and leafier effect.)

CHARLIE: *(From off left.)* Hello? *(No answer. He calls louder.)* Anybody here? *(Charlie comes on, from left.)* Hello!

(Anna Trumbull, the Pig Woman, comes on from upstage right, as if from around the corner of her cottage. She wears an old, paint-spattered smock, sneakers with holes cut in them for her corns, ankle socks falling around them, and a strange bandanna on her head. Her hair is cut in bangs, and straight all around Her skin is swarthy and sunburned. There is no way of telling her age.)

ANNA: Scram.

CHARLIE: I just want to—

ANNA: Are you one of those boys who threw crabapples at me from the old orchard?

CHARLIE: No!

ANNA: You sure?

CHARLIE: I never hit you.

ANNA: Get off my land.

CHARLIE: I just want to ask you something.

ANNA: The answer is no.

CHARLIE: Wait till I ask!

ANNA: No, I do not have any tin cans for the war effort.

CHARLIE: I'm not collecting tin cans.

ANNA: Then what?

CHARLIE: I read your notice…At Brodie's…"Man wanted. Odd jobs."

ANNA: Oh that. I put that up in March.

CHARLIE: It's still there.

ANNA: Tell them to take it down.

CHARLIE: You found a man?

ANNA: I did not. There are no men to be found. And where do you think they are? Shooting, maiming, killing each other in all four corners of the globe.

CHARLIE: My father's in the Pacific.

ANNA: I'm sure he is.

CHARLIE: So can I work for you?

ANNA: You?

CHARLIE: Me.

ANNA: What can you do?

CHARLIE: Me?

ANNA: You.

CHARLIE: I can cut your grass.

ANNA: What grass? Do you see any grass around here?

CHARLIE: No.

ANNA: Grass. The very idea galls me. The very notion. Think about grass. Have you ever thought about it?

CHARLIE: No.

ANNA: Then do. Think. Question your assumptions. Think of what grass requires. Think of the topsoil, think of the fertilizer, think of the precious water. Have you ever thought about that?

CHARLIE: No.

ANNA: Have you ever thought of the poor human souls who spend their lives planting it and rolling it and keeping it trim?

CHARLIE: My friend Ted cuts grass.

ANNA: There you are. Think of that.

CHARLIE: I will.

ANNA: And think of the history of grass. Explore its origins. Do you know where it came from?

CHARLIE: No.

ANNA: Grass came directly from the English aristocracy. They thought it up, in order to play their silly games. They bred it and fed it and put signs on it saying keep off it. Got the picture? Wherever there's grass, there's class. Will you remember that? Remember I told you?

CHARLIE: Yes.

ANNA: Good. Then the day's not lost. *(She starts off upstage right.)*

CHARLIE: I could do something else, though.

ANNA: *(Wheeling on him.)* Can you put in plumbing? Can you dig a ditch all the way out to the new sewer line? Can you put in pipes? Can you pay for them?

CHARLIE: No.

ANNA: Can you fix a pump?

CHARLIE: I fixed the fuel pump on our Ford station wagon.

ANNA: I don't care about cars.

CHARLIE: What about that old car I saw in your barn?

ANNA: It doesn't work any more.

CHARLIE: I could try and fix it.

ANNA: I don't want a car. I've learned to get along without one. *(She starts off right again.)*

CHARLIE: Then I could do something else. You could teach me.
    (She stops, turns.)

ANNA: How old are you?

CHARLIE: Sixteen. *(Pause.)* A year from next November.

ANNA: Which means what?

CHARLIE: Fourteen.

ANNA: A babe. A mere babe. Where are you from?

CHARLIE: Up the beach. Rose Hill.

ANNA: A lost boy. From the Fort. Who's wandered into Indian territory…Did you know I had Indian blood?

CHARLIE: Yes.

ANNA: My great-grandmother was a Tuscarora Indian princess.

CHARLIE: Oh.

ANNA: My father was vice-president of the Erie County Street Railway Corporation. I'll bet you didn't know that.

CHARLIE: No.

ANNA: Did you know that my cottage was once a pigsty?

CHARLIE: No.

ANNA: Oh yes. That's why they call me the Pig Woman. Do you think it suits me?

CHARLIE: Um...

ANNA: Don't answer that. I like the name. It sets me off. It makes me different. Does that frighten you?

CHARLIE: No.

(Pause.)

ANNA: When could you work?

CHARLIE: Any time. *(Pause.)* Except Wednesday and Saturday afternoons.

ANNA: Why not then?

CHARLIE: That's when they have the sailing races.

ANNA: Good-bye.

CHARLIE: I have to. I signed up.

ANNA: I refuse to accommodate myself to the leisure class.

CHARLIE: I'll work every morning for you.

ANNA: Every morning?

CHARLIE: Except Tuesdays.

ANNA: Scram. Vamoose.

CHARLIE: I have to tutor on Tuesdays.

ANNA: Bye-bye.

CHARLIE: I flunked Latin! I have to tutor!

ANNA: Back to Rose Hill! Back to the stockade, white man! *(She goes off right.)*

CHARLIE: *(Calling after her.)* O.K. I'll work it *out.* I'll quit the sailing, if I can have the job.

(Pause; she comes back on.)

ANNA: I can see you're willing to make a momentous sacrifice...All right. I'll hire you.

CHARLIE: Thanks.

ANNA: I'll give you twenty-five cents an hour.

CHARLIE: Huh?

ANNA: Twenty-five.

CHARLIE: That's all?

ANNA: That's enough for a beginner.

CHARLIE: My friend Ted gets fifty.

ANNA: For what?

CHARLIE: Cutting grass.

ANNA: You see what grass does to the economy?

CHARLIE: I got twenty-five cents two *years* ago just for walking the Watsons' dog.

ANNA: I know that dog. That dog isn't worth a dime.

CHARLIE: Well I just can't work for twenty-five cents an hour. I just can't.

ANNA: Well I just can't afford to pay you anything more. Sorry.

CHARLIE: Which means I got to go back to Rose Hill and tell everybody and his uncle I couldn't get a job, and take a lot of crap from my mother and sister, and listen to Ted sling the bull all summer, and feel like a baby in front of Bonny! Darn it! Darn it all! Damn it! Goddammit to hell! *(He turns and starts off left.)*

ANNA: Stop!

(He does.)

ANNA: Come here!

(He does.)

ANNA: Let me see your hands.

CHARLIE: *(Stopping.)* My hands?

ANNA: Let me see them.

(Charlie wipes his hands on his pants, then holds them up. Anna crosses, takes them, looks them over.)

ANNA: You have very expressive hands.

CHARLIE: I do?

ANNA: You also have strong feelings.

CHARLIE: I sure do.

ANNA: *(Dropping his hands.)* Because of your hands, and your feelings, I have decided to give you more than twenty-five cents an hour.

CHARLIE: Hey, thanks.

ANNA: I've decided to give you art lessons.

CHARLIE: Art lessons?

ANNA: I will root out your talent, wherever it lies. I will teach you to express your feelings with your hands.

CHARLIE: Every day?

ANNA: Every afternoon. And what you will get from me will be worth far more than money. Now make up your mind. Work here on these terms, or run back to Rose Hill and tell them you turned down a chance to build your body and stretch your soul with Anna Trumbull, the Pig Woman.

CHARLIE: *(Finally.)* I'll do it.

(She sits, indicates that he is to sit beside her.)

ANNA: Good. You will arrive every morning at eight o'clock. I'll probably be asleep. Walk right in and give me a good shake. I sleep soundly because I have such delicious dreams. My lover, old Doctor Holloway, used to wake me with a kiss. No need for you to do that. Just hand me a cup of strong, hot coffee, and then we will proceed to labor in the vineyards together.

CHARLIE: O.K.

ANNA: We will work primarily out of doors, in the soil, in the sun. At noon, we will swim off the rocks in my cove. Bring your bathing suit or not, as you see fit. I don't wear one myself. I find them inhibiting. Do you?

CHARLIE: Um…

ANNA: Never mind. It's not important. After our swim we will have lunch. I will provide it. It will consist of homemade bread, unprocessed cheese, and fruit in season. And one glass of good red wine. Do you have any trouble with wine?

CHARLIE: No.

ANNA: I do. Because of my Indian blood, I have a weakness for alcohol. I hope you'll keep an eye on me in that department.

CHARLIE: O.K.

ANNA: Good. And while we eat, we will sit in the shade and talk. I will tell you about town. I grew up there, and think of it with all the passion of an exile. Would you like to hear me rail against your homeland?

CHARLIE: Sure.

ANNA: Then you've come to the right place…But in the afternoon, we will get serious. We will create things together. We will seek patterns, we will make shapes, we will fabricate visions of a better world. Is that all clear?

CHARLIE: Yes, Miss Trumbull.

ANNA: Call me Anna, since we are to be colleagues in life and art.

(They get up.)

CHARLIE: O.K., Anna.

ANNA: And what do I call you?

CHARLIE: Charlie. Charlie Higgins.

ANNA: Higgins. I knew the Higgins family. Stuffy bunch, all the way down the line. Loved money, hated horses, never knew what to do about women.

CHARLIE: That's me.

ANNA: One of them married a girl named Grace Anderson.

CHARLIE: That's my mom.

ANNA: No!

CHARLIE: Sure. She's my mother.

ANNA: *(Bursting into laughter.)* Oh boy. Ohboyohboyohboyohboy. That's a pip. That's a lulu. The chickens come home to roost. Does she know you're here?

CHARLIE: Sort of.

ANNA: "Sort of." I'll bet "sort of." *(She laughs again.)* Well we'll see you tomorrow, Charlie. *If* we see you tomorrow. *(She goes off right, laughing, shaking her head.)*

(Charlie stands looking after her, then goes off slowly in the opposite direction, as Bonny comes out from upstage right, carrying a towel, calling off-stage as she enters.)

BONNY: All right! It's an hour after lunch! Everybody can go in the water! *(Bonny spreads the towel, as if she were on a beach. She speaks quietly to the audience.)* Sometimes I think this play is secretly about me. That's what I secretly think. Because, for me, this is a crucial summer. All sorts of important things are beginning to happen. My father's letting me skipper the boat occasionally. And my mother says I can smoke, as long as it's in front of her. And I've got a paid baby-sitting job three times a week. *(She calls out.)* It's not cold, Susie. Just go in slowly. Bit by bit. And it'll feel fine. *(To audience.)* And tonight, one of the most crucial things of all might happen. Tonight we might be riding this roller coaster. It's called The Cyclone, and on a calm night you can hear it roar, even though the amusement park is over five miles away! Oh it's the scariest thing! It's built right out over the lake, all rickety and shaky, and they say when you climb to the top, you can see all the way to town. And when you start down, it's so basically terrifying that *women* have thrown their *babies* over the *side!* It costs five tickets per person per ride, and there's a big sign right at the gate saying you have to be at least sixteen before you can ride it. But Ted knows the Canadian boys who take tickets, and right now he's seeing if they can sneak us on. *(Calls out.)* Nobody goes out beyond the sandbar, please! Stay in the shallow water where I can see you!

(Ted comes on eagerly, from upstage left.)

TED: Everything's copasetic.

BONNY: They'll let us on.

TED: No problem.

BONNY: Oh I'm shaking like a leaf. Did you tell Charlie?

TED: How could I tell Charlie? He's over at the Pig Woman's again.

BONNY: We'll have to wait and see if he can come too.

TED: Why Charlie?

BONNY: Because last summer we all promised to ride it together.

TED: They won't let him on. He's too young.

BONNY: He's my age.

TED: That's different. I told them you were my girl.

BONNY: Your *girl?*

TED: So they'd let you through.

BONNY: You mean you didn't mention Charlie?

TED: I said I was bringing my girl.

BONNY: Oh. *(She calls out.)* Stay together, everybody! Everybody stay close together!

(Pause.)

TED: So what do you say?

BONNY: How would we get there?

TED: How do you think? By car.

BONNY: With you driving? Or your father?

TED: I got my license, remember?

BONNY: I can't, then.

TED: How come?

BONNY: My mother doesn't want me to go out alone at night in cars with older boys. She was even mad I took you sailing with me.

TED: That wasn't a car. And it wasn't at night.

BONNY: Well I don't know. She thinks you're too old for me.

TED: She didn't think that last summer.

BONNY: Well maybe you weren't last summer. *(Calling out.)* Yes I saw, Susie! I saw you do that somersault! That was very good, Susie.

TED: Don't tell her then.

BONNY: Don't *tell* her?

TED: Just meet me out by the main road.

BONNY: Without Charlie?

TED: Look, Charlie's going his way, why can't we go ours? Come on. I'll fix it so we ride in the front row. And I'll take you to the Frozen Custard place afterwards. And introduce you to my whole gang from high school.

BONNY: Gosh...

TED: *(Touching her arm.)* Sure. It'll be like a date. A real date.

BONNY: You're distracting me, Ted. I'm supposed to be watching these… *(She looks out at the lake.)* …kids. *(She jumps to her feet.)* Uh-oh.

TED: What?

BONNY: How many heads do you see out there?

TED: *(Counting quickly.)* One…two…three…four…

BONNY: There's supposed to be five!

TED: *(Pointing.)* And five, over there!

BONNY: Thank God! *(Calling out angrily.)* Susie, when you decide to swim underwater, would you *tell* people, please?

TED: Close call, huh?

BONNY: That wouldn't have happened if I had used the buddy system.

TED: I hate the buddy system.

BONNY: Well at least it's safe. *(Clapping her hands.)* Everyone out of the water, please. I'm instigating a new rule! *(She starts off upstage right.)*

TED: What about our date?

BONNY: Tell you what: I'll ask my father.

TED: He'll say no.

BONNY: He might not. He lets me do more than my mother. *(She goes off upstage right.)* New rule, everybody! New rule! We're going to have the buddy system! *(She goes off.)*

TED: *(Calling after her.)* Your father will say no! *(To audience.)* Sure he'll say no. Lookit, someday somebody ought to write a play about a Canadian kid who hangs around Americans while his dad takes care of their summer homes. Here's the story: First, he's friends with those kids, trading comics with them, playing tennis, horsing around on the raft. Everything's hunky-dory. Then he starts growing hair on his nuts, and what do you know? The plot thickens. Suddenly when he shows up at the tennis courts, he gets the fish-eye from Mrs. Putnam for even sitting down and watching, for Christ sake. And soon he feels creepy even going down to the beach, like now it's out of bounds, or something. And then suppose he wants to take out an American girl. My God, suddenly it's like he wants to French kiss her, and bang her, and carry her off to Saskatchewan, all on the first date! I dunno. All I know is somebody ought to write about it some time.

(Elsie comes on from left and begins to organize the chairs center, and stools left and right, for supper. Grace comes on from right, and helps. No actual table is necessary.)

ELSIE: Where've you been?

GRACE: Oh, just having a quick drink with poor Mr. McAlister.

ELSIE: Did you ask him what to do about Charlie?

GRACE: I did not. Charlie is our problem, and we can deal with it by ourselves.

ELSIE: Where is he now, by the way?

GRACE: Out by the hose. Washing his hands. Which were covered with purple paint.

ELSIE: Purple?

GRACE: Don't ask *me* what she has him doing.

ELSIE: I hope you let him have it, Mother. Tonight I hope you read him the riot act. He's been late for dinner ever since he started that stupid job.

GRACE: Sssshhh.

ELSIE: And he's missed two turns to set the table.

GRACE: He'll make it up.

ELSIE: And he ruins the meal, Mother. With all those obnoxious ideas she gives him.

GRACE: Sshh. We have ideas, too. We'll just have to counteract them.

(They sit down, Grace in the chair, center, Elsie on the stool, right.)

ELSIE: Well I hope tonight you make him do the dishes, at least. Including the pots and pans. Otherwise it isn't fair.

GRACE: Ssshh. *(She hears him coming.)* We're just going to have to hold the line, Elsie. As the Marines did on Iwo Jima. Now are we allies in this, or not?

ELSIE: We're allies, Mother.

GRACE: Thank you, dear.

(They shake hands. Charlie enters from upstage right.)

GRACE: Good evening, Charlie.

CHARLIE: *(Very jauntily.)* Hi.

GRACE: Sit down, dear.

CHARLIE: O.K. *(He sits on stool, left.)*

GRACE: Pour Charlie some milk, please, Elsie.

(Elsie 'pours milk" with grim reluctance.)

CHARLIE: Thanks.

GRACE: *(Serving "food.")* Now, Charlie, am I giving you too much cauliflower? Speak now, or forever hold your peace.

(She hands him a "plate"; little pantomiming of eating is necessary.)

CHARLIE: What's this other stuff?

GRACE: Chicken croquettes, dear.

(Charlie makes a loud barfing sound.)

GRACE: Now that's enough, please.

CHARLIE: You know what they look like, don't you?

GRACE: We're not interested, Charlie.

ELSIE: We're not interested.

CHARLIE: Dog turds left on the beach.

ELSIE: Make him leave the table, Mother.

GRACE: I'll handle this, Elsie. *(Smiling, to Charlie.)* Somebody's feeling his oats a little these days. Am I right? Somebody is full of beans these days.

CHARLIE: Maybe.

GRACE: Otherwise you would not have made such an unattractive remark about the food. Which we are lucky to have. Which millions of refugees throughout Europe would give their eye*teeth* for.

CHARLIE: Send it to 'em.

ELSIE: Brat.

CHARLIE: *(To Elsie.)* Wrap it up, and put it in a Bundle for Britain.

ELSIE: Will you shut *up?*

GRACE: Now stop it, both of you. *(Pause.)* I take it you enjoy your new job, Charlie.

CHARLIE: Uh huh.

GRACE: You must, because it seems to occupy so much of your time.

CHARLIE: Uh huh.

GRACE: For example, I hear you missed your Latin lesson last Tuesday.

CHARLIE: Oh yeah.

GRACE: Missed it completely. Without even telephoning Mrs. Blackburn to cancel it.

CHARLIE: Sorry.

GRACE: Even after you promised Daddy you'd study it all summer long.

CHARLIE: I said I was sorry.

GRACE: Even though you might have to stay behind a grade if you don't pass it in the fall.

CHARLIE: I'm studying it on my own.

ELSIE: You haven't cracked a book.

CHARLIE: Well you know why, don't you?

ELSIE: No, why?

CHARLIE: Latin is the language of the leisure class.

GRACE: What?

CHARLIE: It's true. We all study Latin just because the poor people don't have time to.

ELSIE: Oh my God.

GRACE: That is a silly argument, Charlie, and I think I know where it came from.

CHARLIE: Well it's true, anyway.

GRACE: It is not true. Latin is…

(*Charlie and Elsie look at her expectantly.*)

GRACE: Latin is the basic building block of western civilization. And I don't think we need to discuss it any further.

ELSIE: Thank God.

GRACE: What is she paying you, by the way?

CHARLIE: I prefer not to say.

GRACE: I'll pay you more.

CHARLIE: To do what?

GRACE: Paint the garage.

CHARLIE: No thanks.

GRACE: I'll pay you twice what she pays you.

CHARLIE: No thanks, Mom.

GRACE: I'll just have to get someone else, then.

CHARLIE: O.K.

GRACE: I'll just have to get your friend Ted Moffatt to come over and paint our garage. For a dollar an hour.

ELSIE: *I'll* do it for that. I'll paint it.

GRACE: Stay *out* of this, Elsie. Please. (*Pause.*) What do you think of her, Charlie?

CHARLIE: Who? Elsie? She's a drip.

GRACE: I'm talking about Miss Trumbull, Charlie.

CHARLIE: Oh, you mean Anna.

GRACE: Yes. All right. Anna. What do you think?

CHARLIE: I like her.

GRACE: You do?

CHARLIE: We get along fine.

GRACE: Does she know who you are, Charlie?

CHARLIE: Who I *am?*

GRACE: Your name? Does she know the name?

CHARLIE: Oh sure.

GRACE: Did it ring a bell?

CHARLIE: What?

GRACE: When you told her your name, what did she say?

CHARLIE: She said she knew you.

ELSIE: Who knew who?

CHARLIE: Anna knew Mom.

ELSIE: What?

GRACE: Oh heavens. Years ago. For a short time. I took an art class from her.

ELSIE: You never told me that.

CHARLIE: I didn't know you were an artist, Mom.

GRACE: I'm not. Oh I thought I was. I did a few little things with water colors. Flowers and things. But that's not the point, anyway. The point is, Charlie, that when Daddy went to war, you promised to help.

CHARLIE: I will, Mom.

GRACE: Well I don't see you doing it. I don't see you lifting a finger around here since you started that job.

CHARLIE: I'll do it, Mom. I swear. *(He gets up, starts to take his "plate" off left.)*

GRACE: You haven't even cut the grass.

CHARLIE: *(Wheeling on her.)* I don't believe in grass.

ELSIE: Oh my God!

CHARLIE: Have you ever questioned your assumptions about grass?

ELSIE: Have you ever questioned your assumptions about setting the table?

GRACE: Now stop it!

CHARLIE: We should plow that lawn up! We should use it for growing vegetables! We should fertilize it with our own wastes!

ELSIE: See, Mother, how repulsive he is!

GRACE: Charlie, that's enough! Now all I know is you can't do all the things you have to do for me, and still work for Anna Trumbull!

CHARLIE: You mean, quit?

GRACE: That's what I mean.

CHARLIE: But I like her.

GRACE: Charlie, I am asking you, as a special favor, if not for me, then for your father, to give up that job. Will you, Charlie? For your father? Who's away at war?

(Charlie looks at her, then goes off left, carrying his "plate." Grace asks Elsie.)

GRACE: What does that mean?

ELSIE: Don't ask me. I only live here.

GRACE: Oh dear.

ELSIE: Some Iwo Jima, Mother.

GRACE: The battle's not over yet, Elsie.

(Charlie comes back in and sits down.)

CHARLIE: What's for dessert?

GRACE: I'll tell you when I hear your answer, Charlie.

CHARLIE: The answer is no.

GRACE: I am asking you, please.

CHARLIE: No!

GRACE: All right, Charlie, then from here on in, unless you want real trouble, I expect your room to be immaculate, and the chores done thoroughly, and a new chapter of Latin learned every single day! And if Miss Trumbull complains about your time, you tell her that your first responsibility is to your family.

CHARLIE: She says my first responsibility is to myself!

GRACE: Well she's wrong.

CHARLIE: She says the family is a dying social unit!

GRACE: She is just plain wrong!

CHARLIE: She says family pressure causes half the misery in the world, and you ought to know it more than anyone!

GRACE: Well you tell her…You tell her from me… *(Pause.)* Oh honestly— *(She throws down her "napkin," turns, and strides off, upstage left.)* *(Pause.)*

ELSIE: Now you've done it. I hope she sits down and writes Daddy a long letter. All about you!

CHARLIE: Oh gee.

ELSIE: She made the dessert especially for you, too. Cookie pudding. With whipped cream.

CHARLIE: Oh God, what'll I do?

ELSIE: First you better do those dishes, Charlie.

CHARLIE: O.K.

ELSIE: Including the pots and pans.

CHARLIE: O.K., O.K.

ELSIE: And then you better go up and knock on her door and apologize. The way Daddy used to do.

CHARLIE: O.K.

ELSIE: And you better have your Latin book right in your hand.

CHARLIE: Good idea.

ELSIE: And you better say you're quitting the Pig Woman!

CHARLIE: Never!

ELSIE: Then God help us all!

(She goes off, as the lights change to Anna's mottled world. She comes on from upstage right, carrying an old galvanized tub.)

ANNA: *(Calling to Charlie.)* Look what I got from the lake.

CHARLIE: *(Leaving the table, moving the chair.)* I fixed your chair, Anna!

ANNA: Good! All the more reason to look here. *(She places the tub on something, and regards it reverently.)* What do you think this is?

CHARLIE: *(Looking in.)* Mud.

ANNA: Mud? It's not mud at all. Clay! Good, thick, red Lake Erie clay! Which I dredged up from under a rock, like an Indian maiden, diving for pearls. *(She sits, downstage right.)*

CHARLIE: Oh.

ANNA: Is that all you can say? Just "Oh."

CHARLIE: *(Lying down, stretching.)* I'm kind of tired today, Anna. I had to do extra chores for my mother.

ANNA: That's exactly why I brought you this. Touch it. Feel it.

(Charlie sits up, begins to dip his fingers into the tub, very gingerly at first.)

ANNA: Go on. Dig in. Get your hands dirty. Squeeze it. Knead it. Make it ooze.

(He tries.)

ANNA: How does it feel?

CHARLIE: Good.

ANNA: Of course it does. It's the muck of life. It's the primal sludge. Work it around for a while. Perhaps we'll discover you're a sculptor.

CHARLIE: You don't think I'm a painter?

ANNA: I've decided you're not.

CHARLIE: I told you I wasn't.

ANNA: Well you tried. I appreciate that. But last night, I reviewed your entire *oeuvre* since you arrived, and I've decided I don't like it. There was only one drawing which had energy and vitality. And that had to do with airplanes.

CHARLIE: That was a Grumman Wildcat attacking a Japanese Zero over the Coral Sea.

ANNA: Whatever. I put it aside, with the rest. I did not come into this world to encourage young people to portray death and destruction. Try sculpture instead.

CHARLIE: How do you know I'm a sculptor?

ANNA: I know you're something. The problem is simply bringing it out.

CHARLIE: Maybe I'm a mechanic. I wish you'd let me fix your car.

ANNA: Cars come and go. Planes rise and fall. I want you to do something more permanent.... Now get at that clay.

CHARLIE: I can't decide what to make.

ANNA: Make a man. Make yourself.

CHARLIE: I don't feel much like a man.

ANNA: Good God, what are you saying?

CHARLIE: I dunno. I flunked Latin, I don't have my driver's license, Bonny treats me like her little brother. Sometimes I think I'll never be a man.

ANNA: Good heavens. Being a man or a woman isn't any of those things. It's simply realizing your potential.

CHARLIE: You think I've got some?

ANNA: I think everyone does. Even Hitler. But most people never find the right way to work it out. And then there's trouble.

CHARLIE: Have you found a way of working out yours?

ANNA: Of course.

CHARLIE: Then how come I never see you making anything?

ANNA: I'm making something right now.

CHARLIE: Huh?

ANNA: Work that clay, please.

(Charlie works the clay, Anna basks in the sun.)

CHARLIE: Anna?

ANNA: Mmm?

CHARLIE: If I hadn't shown up, would you have looked for another kid?

ANNA: They have to come to me.

CHARLIE: Do lots of people come to you?

ANNA: No. Not many. Some. Your mother did. But she didn't stay.

CHARLIE: Why not?

ANNA: I'm too dangerous.

CHARLIE: Yeah, dangerous. That's a good one, dangerous.

ANNA: I am, Charlie. Because I'm a great teacher. And all great teachers are dangerous. Such as Socrates. Or Christ. Or me.

CHARLIE: Don't be conceited, Anna.

ANNA: Yes well, ask your mother how dangerous I am.

CHARLIE: Oh hell, she thinks even comic books are dangerous.

ANNA: Yes well, keep working.

CHARLIE: *(As he works.)* Maybe next summer, some other kid will come around with more potential.

ANNA: I won't be here next summer.

CHARLIE: Sure you will.

ANNA: Oh no. I've put my ear to the ground, and I hear the cavalry coming.

CHARLIE: What cavalry?

ANNA: Never mind, but they'll be here, Charlie. So you're my last best hope. Now let's see what you've done.

CHARLIE: Not much, actually.

ANNA: It lacks commitment...We'll have to liberate your spirit. We'll tune up on my tomatoes.

CHARLIE: Your tomahtoes? Again?

ANNA: My to*may*toes, please. They're a vulgar fruit. Use the vulgar pronunciation.

CHARLIE: We've already talked about your tomaytoes.

ANNA: Then let's see how much you remember.

CHARLIE: Your seeds go way, way back.

ANNA: Yes.

CHARLIE: They came from your great-grandmother who was an Indian princess...

ANNA: Yes...

CHARLIE: And she got them from her lover, who was a French trapper.

ANNA: Yes. Who rowed them across the Niagara gorge...

CHARLIE: And so they've come down to you...

ANNA: Generation by generation...

CHARLIE: *(With more enthusiasm.)* And they'll last beyond you, too.

ANNA: Exactly. Because they're perennials. See? All the little buds are beginning. Soon we'll have flowers, and then fruit. Most people do what at this point?

CHARLIE: They pinch them and stake them and prune them.

ANNA: But not me...

CHARLIE: You let them grow any way they want...

ANNA: And all, all will bear fruit, as long as they get plenty of water, plenty of sun and plenty of...

BOTH: Good, honest shit!

ANNA: *(She bends down.)* Here. I'll pinch off a shoot. *(She brings it to him.)* Smell that. Inhale it deep into your lungs...Now close your eyes, and keep working...

(He does.)

ANNA: That's the smell of old France, and Canada, and the Niagara Frontier...At the end of the summer, I plan to give you some of my seeds. Some day, some other summer, you will have the pleasure of picking a ripe tomato from one of my plants. First, you will simply weigh it in the palm of your hand. Then you will admire its shape and color. Suddenly you will close your eyes and mash it into your mouth. You'll let the juice spill out, and the meat roll around on your tongue, and then you'll swallow—meat, juice, seeds, and all. And then you'll open your eyes, open them wide, and give out a great, loud war-whoop of praise to life, and the noble tomato, and to me, Anna Trumbull, the Pig Woman, who introduced you to it. *(She crosses to him.)* And now let's see what you've done. *(She takes up his work, looks at it.)* Hmmm.

CHARLIE: It keeps collapsing.

ANNA: Mmmm.

CHARLIE: Maybe I'm not a sculptor either.

ANNA: Of course you are. I'll tell you what you've made. What you've made is a spectacular ashtray, that's what you've made. If I smoked, I'd use it continuously. In fact, it's so good I'm thinking of taking up smoking.

CHARLIE: You're just trying to make me feel better.

ANNA: Well what's wrong with that? Go wash off in the lake while I fix lunch, and then we'll try again.

(They start off right.)

CHARLIE: After lunch, can't I work on your car? Maybe *that's* my potential.

ANNA: Nonsense. After lunch we'll try working with wood.

CHARLIE: Oh Anna…

ANNA: And if wood doesn't work, we'll try something else. We'll keep plugging, you and I, on into the night.

CHARLIE: I'm going out with my friends tonight.

ANNA: *(As they exit, right.)* Well then we'll seize the day. And if you work hard, I will tell you the story of my cucumbers. There is an amusing anecdote connecting them to the sexual member of my lover, old Doctor Holloway. I think you're man enough to hear it.

(They exit, right, Charlie carrying the tub. Ted comes on from upstage left singing "Pistol Packin' Mama." He gets into his "car," adjusts the "mirror," combs his hair, and then waits impatiently. Bonny backs on nervously from upstage left.)

TED: *(Rolling down the "window" leaning out.)* Come on.

BONNY: He's not here yet.

TED: Who? Don't tell me you asked Charlie!

BONNY: He said he'd meet me in the driveway right after supper.

TED: You and your buddy system…You'd think a guy could ask a girl for a date without her bringing along another guy.

BONNY: Charlie's not just another guy.

TED: Do you think you could at least wait for him in the car? Or would your dad think you were necking with a Canuck?

BONNY: I can wait in the car, Ted.

(Ted gets out, crosses around the front and opens the door for her. She gets in uneasily. She sneaks a peek in the "mirror" while he crosses back.)

TED: *(Getting into the "car.")* Did you tell your folks you were going to the Cyclone?

BONNY: I decided not to. I told them we were all going to see *Dumbo*.

TED: "All." I love that "all."

BONNY: They're at least letting me drive in your car, Ted. That's something, at least.

TED: Yeah well, look. Here comes your buddy.

(Charlie comes on from upstage left.)

CHARLIE: Sorry.

TED: Where were you?

CHARLIE: I fell asleep.

TED: Asleep? At eight in the evening?

CHARLIE: I was tired. O.K.? I've been working for two women.

(Charlie starts to get in next to Bonny. Ted reaches behind Bonny, to pull forward the "seat.")

TED: Get in back, O.K.?

CHARLIE: How come I can't sit in front?

TED: It's a floor gearshift. Get in back.

BONNY: He's just gotten his license, Charlie.

TED: I just want him in back.

BONNY: Be reasonable, Charlie.

(Charlie reluctantly gets into the back, shoving Bonny forward by the "seat." Bonny closes the "door.")

TED: And we are off. To the Cyclone! *(He starts up the "car.")*

CHARLIE: *(Leaning forward, between them.)* Don't you think you better put on your lights first, Ted?

TED: *(Quickly putting the "lights" on.)* I was planning to do that.

CHARLIE: *(Sitting back.)* Oh yeah. Sure. Right. You bet.

(They drive.)

TED: So, Charlie. How's the Pig Woman?

CHARLIE: Fine.

TED: Is it true she doesn't wear any underpants?

BONNY: Oh honestly…

CHARLIE: No.

TED: No she doesn't? Or no it's not true?

CHARLIE: She wears underwear, Ted.

BONNY: Of course she does.

TED: How do you know, Charlie? Have you looked?

CHARLIE: Knock it off, Ted. O.K.?

BONNY: Yes, Ted. Stop teasing. Really.

(They drive.)

TED: What does she pay you, Charlie?

CHARLIE: Never mind.

BONNY: My father says it's rude to talk about money.

TED: Hey look. I'm just a poor Canuck who wants to know what the rich Americans are paying their help this summer.

CHARLIE: She's not rich.

TED: That's why she only pays a quarter.

CHARLIE: There are more things in this world than money, Ted.

BONNY: Yes, Ted.

TED: Such as what?

BONNY: Look out for that car!

(Ted swerves. They all lean. Ted straightens the "wheel.")

CHARLIE: Jesus. Drive much?

TED: I saw him.

CHARLIE: Uh huh. You betchum, Ted.

TED: I want to know what the Pig Woman gives you that's more important than money, Charlie.

CHARLIE: Things you wouldn't understand, Ted.

TED: Such as what?

(Silence from Charlie.)

BONNY: Such as what, Charlie?

CHARLIE: Whose side are you on, Bonny?

BONNY: I'm just curious, Charlie. What does she give you?

CHARLIE: She...teaches me things.

TED: *Teaches* you? You mean, like a...*teacher?*

BONNY: What does she teach you, Charlie?

CHARLIE: She...I don't have to tell.

TED: You don't have to ride the Cyclone, either.

(He stops the "car." They all jerk forward.)

TED: Maybe we'll just sit here by the side of the road until we hear about those wonderful, secret, piggy things.

BONNY: Oh, Ted.

CHARLIE: Fine with me. Maybe there are more important things than riding some dumb machine in an amusement park.

BONNY: Oh, Charlie.

TED: O.K. We sit.

CHARLIE: You know what amusement parks are, don't you? Amusement parks are places where people fritter away their potential.

TED: Fritter away their what?

CHARLIE: Potential. Potential.

BONNY: What does that mean, Charlie?

CHARLIE: It means that everyone's got this potential, if they only use it right. I've got it, you've got it, Hitler's got it, even Ted's got it.

BONNY: Is that what she teaches you, Charlie?

CHARLIE: Sure. And she's trying to bring mine out.

TED: Yeah well tell her I got some potential right here in my pants.

BONNY: That's disgusting, Ted.

CHARLIE: Yes, Ted. Knock it off. There are ladies present.

TED: Want to make something out of it, Charlie.

BONNY: Oh stop!

TED: Or don't you have enough potential?

CHARLIE: I'll make something out of it, Ted.

TED: O.K., then let's get out of the car, you dumb little creep.

CHARLIE: *(Pushing against Bonny's seat.)* O.K., you crude Canadian townie hick!

TED: *(Leaping out of the "car.")* You'll be gumming your food, buster!

BONNY: Oh God!

CHARLIE: *(Holding his ground.)* I'm not scared of you!

(They square off. Bonny is out of the "car" by now, and comes between them.)

BONNY: Oh stop! Please! Ted, you're two years older!

CHARLIE: Just a year and a half.

(They face each other. Then Ted backs off.)

TED: You're lucky there's a woman around, Charlie.

CHARLIE: *(Making his knees shake, like a cartoon character.)* I'm scared, Ted. Help. Gasp. Shriek. *(He starts off left.)*

BONNY: How will you get home, Charlie?

CHARLIE: Who has to go home? I've got other places to go besides home! *(He runs off.)*

(Bonny returns to the "car." Ted tries to close the "door" for her. She slams it shut herself.)

TED: *(To Bonny, through the "window.")* Still want to go to the Cyclone?

BONNY: I don't know…

(Ted moodily gets into the "car." Elsie comes out with her book, settles downstage left in chair to read.)

TED: Or do you want to just sit out here, in the middle of nowhere?

BONNY: Maybe you'd better take me back, Ted.

TED: Knew it. Home to Daddy, eh?

(They drive. Bonny looks out the window. Ted turns on the "car radio." Music comes up: a wartime song like "Praise the Lord and Pass the

Ammunition." *Grace comes out from upstage left, carrying sweater and purse. She comes downstage to comb her hair, as if in a "mirror.")*

ELSIE: Where are you going?

GRACE: Mr. McAlister very sweetly asked me to go to the movies.

ELSIE: To *Dumbo?*

GRACE: *Dumbo?* I thought it was *Now Voyager.*

ELSIE: By the way, Mrs. Blackburn called. She says the Latin situation is beyond repair.

GRACE: Oh dear. Where is he?

ELSIE: Out with the gang.

GRACE: At least it's with them.

TED: *(In "car.")* Maybe I should get someone else to ride the Cyclone.

BONNY: Maybe you should.

ELSIE: *(To Grace.)* You should write Daddy about him.

GRACE: I don't want to worry him.

ELSIE: But he's a *man.* He could help.

GRACE: Maybe…

ELSIE: If you don't write him, I will, Mother.

GRACE: Now this is *my* problem, Elsie, and I'll thank you to stay out of it. *(She gives her a quick kiss.)* …I'll write him tomorrow. I promise. *(She goes upstage left to stand and wait, back to audience, as if on a porch. Elsie reads* War and Peace. *Music continues underneath. Anna and Charlie enter from upstage right, as if in moonlight.)*

ANNA: When does she want you home? What's the rule?

CHARLIE: Eleven.

ANNA: All right. Then we have a choice. We can sit out here and study the stars, or we can go inside, and read selections from the poetry of William Butler Yeats. Maybe you're an astronomer. Or a poet. Which will it be?

CHARLIE: Let me think…

ANNA: Now remember. It's a choice, and at your age, all choices are important. They tell you who you are. So which is it?

CHARLIE: Um…

(He stands thinking, Anna looking at lake. The Lights focus down on Charlie's face. The music continues.)

End of Act I

ACT II

Before Curtain: Music: another old Bing Crosby recording, such as "Accentuate the Positive." Charlie comes on hurriedly.

CHARLIE: This is still a play about me, when I was fourteen—

(Anna crosses upstage, from left to right carrying a bushel basket.)

ANNA: Come on, help me pick the peas, and then I'll show you how to put them up.

CHARLIE: *(Following her.)* I have to leave early today, Anna.

ANNA: Early? Why?

CHARLIE: We're going to a party.

ANNA: *(As they cross.)* What party? Tell me about this party.

CHARLIE: Well, you see, my mother thinks it would be good for me if...

(They are off as Grace comes on from upstage left, hurriedly, in a bathrobe.)

GRACE: *(Calling toward off left.)* Charlie! I'm in your bathroom! And I found Daddy's old razor! Now full speed ahead!

(Elsie comes on from upstage left, also in a bathrobe.)

ELSIE: Mother, I don't have anything to wear.

GRACE: Why not your little blue Lanz?

ELSIE: It makes me look fat, Mother!

GRACE: Now is that the dress's fault? Or is that somebody else's?

ELSIE: Oh, Mothurrr... *(She goes off.)*

(Grace speaks to audience.)

GRACE: *(To audience.)* Here's what's happening. We're all going to a party. The Ralph Wheelers are giving a big shindig for their daughter, Sylvia. It will be out at Prospect Point, and they plan to have music, and dancing, and the works, just like before the war. I'm thrilled. I'm absolutely delighted. It will get Charlie away from that woman, and Elsie away from her book, and me away from *myself*, at least for a while...

(Elsie comes back on from upstage left.)

ELSIE: Are you sure Charlie's invited, Mother?

GRACE: Absolutely. I called up and asked.

ELSIE: You mean, you wangled an invitation?

GRACE: I had to, Elsie.

ELSIE: But he'll be *out* of it, Mother. They all go away to school.

GRACE: That's the point, Elsie. I am thinking of the fall.

ELSIE: Oh. Right. I forgot... *(Ominously.)* The fall. *(She hurries off upstage left.)*

GRACE: *(To audience.)* Which needs explaining. Guess what arrived from the Pacific last week. A great stack of letters. For all of us! Oh he's fine! He's alive, and well, and frantic to come home, though he thinks we've got a while before the Japanese surrender. *(Takes airmail letter out of the pocket of her robe.)* But this is the crucial one. This he wrote in response to my S.O.S. about Charlie. Listen: *(She opens it, reads.)* "…Sounds to me as if the boy should go right off to boarding school. Sounds as if he's lost his bearings. I was sent to Saint Luke's when I was fifteen, and it shaped me right up. Send him away." *(She folds the letter.)* So guess who's been on the long distance telephone. I called Saint Luke's, and I called George Graham in Philadelphia, who's on the board of trustees, and I called Sam Satterfield in Greenwich who gives them scads of money—I alerted the whole network. And what with one thing and another, the school's going to take him. Latin or no Latin, in September. Off he goes, if we can just hold on till then! *(Calls off.)* Charlie!

(Charlie comes out from upstage left, in boxer shorts and socks.)

CHARLIE: Do I have to go to the party?

GRACE: Of course you do. Now here's the razor. Have you any idea how to use it?

CHARLIE: I used to watch Dad.

GRACE: Then let's see if you can end up looking halfway presentable for the Wheelers.

CHARLIE: *(Mixing "lather" in front of "mirror.")* Who's Saliva Wheeler anyway?

GRACE: Her name is Sylvia! And she's very attractive, and if you don't dance with her at least once, I'm going to personally throttle you. *(Grace goes off upstage left.)*

(Charlie begins to "shave" meticulously, facing front, as if in a mirror. Anna comes on downstage right with her bushel basket, settles down to shelling "peas.")

CHARLIE: I have to go, Anna.

ANNA: Good. Go, then. You'll learn something. I used to go myself. Years ago, when my family had money. Oh sure. I was on the list. I went. I came out. I wore white. I carried flowers. Yellow roses and Baby's breath. I danced. I was the belle of the ball. Can you imagine? Me? Anna Trumbull, the Pig Woman, dancing till dawn?…I didn't enjoy it, though. I saw too much. I saw into the kitchen and under the rug. I gave it up. But you go. Look them over. Then you'll know what you're up against.

CHARLIE: *(Into "mirror.")* I won't know anybody. I don't even know the Wheelers.

ANNA: *(Shelling peas.)* I do. Ralph Wheeler's father was on the way up while mine was on the way down. We'd nod to each other on Delaware Avenue, like freighters passing on the lake. Of course, their money is absolutely corrupt. Behind every great fortune is a great crime. Theirs was killing horses. When the automobile came in, old Walt Wheeler, who ran a livery stable down on Richmond Avenue, simply bought up every horse he could get his hands on. Dirt cheap. And then he systematically took them out behind the barn and cut their throats.

CHARLIE: *("Nicking" his neck.)* Ouch!

ANNA: He sold the hides to the shoe people, the hooves to the glue people, the hair to the mattress people, and the meat, at outrageous prices, to the poor immigrants who were coming in to break their backs for Lackawanna Steel. And with his profits, he built his place out here. So when you get there, just remember: the whole shebang is built on the bones of dead horses!

(Grace comes into the "bathroom" from upstage left. She carries a seersucker jacket, clean khakis, a striped tie, a blue Oxford-cloth button-down shirt for Charlie and a pair of loafers.)

GRACE: I got out your suit. And here's a tie. And I ironed your shirt for you. And polished these. *(She lays them out on the glider.)* You can always tell a gentleman by his linen and his leather. *(She goes off left.)*

CHARLIE: *(Into "mirror.")* A lot of snooty boarding school kids will be there.

ANNA: *(Shelling "peas.")* Good. Now they've decided to ship you off, you should meet your fellow prisoners. The boarding school crowd. I knew them, too. I remember the Watson boy. He was the one who ran away from Hotchkiss. He was happy at Deerfield, though. Once he was hit on the head by a hockey puck, he fell right into line…

(Elsie comes on from left, now dressed for the party. She comes downstage left, as if she were now in Grace's bedroom, standing in front of a full-length mirror.)

ELSIE: *(Calling off.)* Mother, I'm borrowing your lipstick, please. *(She puts on lipstick in the "mirror.")*

(Charlie, center, has finished shaving, and is putting on his clothes.)

CHARLIE: And a lot of superficial girls…

ANNA: And then there was the Patterson girl. She was seduced by her riding master at finishing school. They never taught her how to cross her legs. *(Grace comes on from left, crosses downstage left into her "bedroom," now dressed for the party. She and Elsie straighten their seams, and put on make-up in front of the "mirror." Charlie continues to dress.)*

ELSIE: Do I have too much lipstick on, Mother?

GRACE: It never hurts to have less, dear.

ELSIE: I won't have anyone to dance with.

GRACE: You'd be surprised. All the boys are beginning to come home.

ELSIE: But I won't know any of them.

GRACE: All the better. You might find yourself dancing with Prince Andrei Bolkonski.

ELSIE: *(Looking at her.)* When did you read *War and Peace,* Mother?

GRACE: Oh heavens…before I was married I read a lot…Now powder your nose, and get your hair out of your eyes. *(Calling toward Charlie.)* Charlie, come into my room, please. I want to see how you've done.

CHARLIE: *(Dressed by now.)* So I gotta go, Anna.

ANNA: Sure. Fine. Go. While you're there, say hello to Bill McMartin. He built a chemical factory right on the lake. Whenever I see a dead fish, I think of Bill.

(Charlie crosses downstage left into Grace's area.)

GRACE: Well look at you! Charlie, I think tonight I'm going to break down and let you have a glass of beer. After all, you're almost fifteen.

ANNA: You'll have to drink, of course. It makes them easier to tolerate. That's how I got hooked on the old firewater.

GRACE: *(To Charlie.)* Now come here, and let's see if we all pass inspection. *(She stands between Charlie and Elsie, as if they were all in front of a full-length mirror. She puts her arms around her children.)* There. Oh, I wish someone were here to take our picture

ELSIE: And send it to Daddy.

GRACE: Yes. I happen to think we look very snappy. Except for your tie, Charlie.

CHARLIE: What's wrong with my tie?

GRACE: It's all over the place, my friend. Here. Let me fuss with it. *(She undoes Charlie's tie, starts tying it again.)*

CHARLIE: Ouch.

GRACE: Hold still.

CHARLIE: *(As Grace struggles with his tie.)* PLEASE, Mom.

GRACE: Just hold still.

ANNA: *(Gathering up her bushel basket.)* Yes, well, go on. Go to the party. Wear their uniform, drink their liquor, learn their dance steps. Maybe you'll like it. Maybe that's your potential, after all.

(She goes off right as Charlie suddenly pulls away from Grace.)

CHARLIE: Lay *off*, Mom! You're *strangling* me!

GRACE: I'm just trying to get it straight.

CHARLIE: *(Ripping off the tie, throwing it down.)* I'm not wearing this tie!

GRACE: Pick that up.

CHARLIE: Make me.

    (Pause.)

ELSIE: Uh oh.

GRACE: That is your father's necktie.

CHARLIE: I don't care.

    (Pause.)

GRACE: We are late for the party.

CHARLIE: I don't want to go.

ELSIE: Oh Lord.

    (Pause.)

GRACE: Come on, then, Elsie. We'll go without him.

CHARLIE: I don't give a shit.

GRACE: *(Wheeling on him.)* I ought to wash your mouth out with soap!

CHARLIE: I don't give a flying fuck.

ELSIE: Oh my God!

    (Grace hauls off and lets him have it, slapping him across the face, hard. Long pause.)

CHARLIE: *(Grimly.)* O.K., Mom! This is IT! *(He rips off his jacket, throws it down on the ground.)* No more parties for me! *(Rips off his shirt.)* Never again! I never want to see those people! Ever! *(Rips off his pants.)* I don't want to talk to them... *(Throws off a shoe.)* I don't want to be with them... *(Throws off the other shoe, and his socks.)* I don't want to dance on the bones of dead horses! *(He is now in his undershorts.)*

GRACE: What are you talking about?

CHARLIE: I don't want to go away to school, either! I don't want to go to *any* school, ever again! I want to stay out here, all year round! With Anna! I want to live in her barn, and eat her tomatoes, and realize my potential any time I want! And you know what I want to do now? I want to go down to the lake and dive under the water and get clean, really clean, CLEAN. *(He runs off right. From offstage, his underpants fly back onstage.)* *(Long pause.)*

GRACE: *(Quietly, to Elsie.)* Go see what he does, please.

    (Elsie exits quickly. Grace goes around the stage, quickly picking up Charlie's

scattered clothes. She sits down, gathering them all in her lap. She notices her husband's tie and smooths it out as best she can. Elsie comes back in.)

GRACE: Well? What?

ELSIE: He ran right down the steps and into the water.

GRACE: I'm sure.

ELSIE: Stark naked. While it's still light out. And Mrs. Wilson was strolling on the beach! With her sister-in-law! Who's Catholic!

GRACE: I'm sure.

ELSIE: And I'll bet when he comes out, he heads straight for the Pig Woman, Mother. I'll bet he does.

GRACE: I imagine.

ELSIE: So what'll we do, Mother? What'll we do now?

GRACE: Do? I'll tell you what we'll do. We'll go to the party, that's what we'll do. And we'll have a perfectly spectacular time. *(She stands up.)* We'll drink too much, and eat too much, and kiss every man in sight! And when we're good and loaded, we might just sneak up on old Mrs. Stockwell, and push her into the pool! And if people ask us about Charlie, we'll say, "Who's he? We don't know any Charlie. All we know is that the night is young, and we are beautiful, and we're raring to go!" And then tomorrow morning, bright and early—no, not bright and early, but at a convenient hour—I'll tell you what else I'm going to do! I'm going to make a visit! The Shadow here is going to pay one hell of a call on the Pig Woman! Meanwhile, let's move it, sister! Let's shake a leg! We are going to live it up, if it kills us! *(Grace strides out upstage left.)*
(Elsie stands, amazed, and then trots after her, as the light changes to early evening. Anna comes out from upstage right, carrying a greasy kerosene lamp, a dusty bottle of wine, and two old cups. She puts down the lantern, pours herself some wine, and sits contemplatively. Charlie comes on from right.)

ANNA: I thought you were going to catch us our breakfast.

CHARLIE: It's getting too dark to fish.

ANNA: Nonsense. Try again.

CHARLIE: *(Hesitating.)* Why hasn't she come yet?

ANNA: She will.

CHARLIE: Maybe she won't. Maybe she's so mad at me, she's just given up.

ANNA: Oh no. She'll be here. After all, this is the perfect time for a powwow: The witching hour…the children's hour…lately what's known in town as the cocktail hour. This is when she'll come. First let her get the casserole in the oven. And wash the lettuce. And comb her hair. Then she'll be on her way.

CHARLIE: You sure know my mom.

ANNA: I know her very well. She'll park her car down by the barn. She'll sit for a moment, organizing her thoughts. Then she'll get out, and start up the path. She'll come to the fork by the old elm. Will she take the short cut? No, she will not. Little Red Riding Hood will take the long way around. She'll pass the outhouse, circle the rhubarb, notice our light, take a deep breath, and call...

GRACE: *(From off left.)* ANNA!

CHARLIE: Golly, Anna. You're amazing.

ANNA: *(To Charlie.)* You see? Now *fish!* You promised.
(Charlie goes off downstage right to fish.)

GRACE: *(Off left, closer.)* Anna?

ANNA: *(Calling offstage.)* Out here.
(Grace comes on briskly. They look at each other. Grace holds out her hand. Anna holds up her hand, in mock Indian fashion.)

ANNA: How.
(A moment. Then Grace laughs.)

GRACE: Oh, Anna.
(They shake hands.)

ANNA: Long time, no see.

GRACE: I know it.

ANNA: Twenty years.

GRACE: Oh, not *twenty*...

ANNA: Twenty. Almost exactly.

GRACE: Mercy. Has it been that long? Well I mean, we've *seen* each other, haven't we? Occasionally. We've seen each other...

ANNA: You had talent twenty years ago.

GRACE: Don't be silly.

ANNA: You had potential.

GRACE: Oh please...
(Pause.)

ANNA: Well. You're looking for the boy.

GRACE: Yes, actually.

ANNA: He's down fishing off the rocks.

GRACE: How nice. *(Pause.)* I assume he spent last night here.

ANNA: In the barn.

GRACE: He didn't even have a toothbrush.

ANNA: He didn't need one.

GRACE: Well, I imagine he needs one now. And is ready for his own bed.

ANNA: No.

GRACE: No?

ANNA: No. *(Pause.)* Want a drink?

GRACE: Oh heavens no.

ANNA: Have a taste of the local wine.

GRACE: Local? Do the Canadians make wine?

ANNA: I do.

GRACE: Anna, you were always so resourceful…

ANNA: The house wine, then? *(She pours a cup.)*

GRACE: Why that sounds very nice, actually.

ANNA: Here you are. *(Hands her a cup and pours another for herself.)*

GRACE: *(Sipping.)* Mmmm.

ANNA: You like it?

GRACE: Oh yes.

ANNA: You don't. But we'll pretend you do.

GRACE: Anna…

ANNA: *(Producing a strange, ratty, multicolored patch of knitting from her pocket.)* Look at this.

GRACE: *(Taking it.)* What is it?

ANNA: We've been working with wool.

GRACE: Oh.

ANNA: What do you think?

GRACE: Looks a little…tangled, Anna.

ANNA: That's the point.

GRACE: The point?

ANNA: That's what he's trying to say.

GRACE: Look, Anna, don't you think if he had any real talent, we would have noticed it?

ANNA: No.

GRACE: Then don't you think someone at school, someone at camp might have pointed it out?

ANNA: No.

GRACE: But he's never shown the slightest interest!

ANNA: Until now.

GRACE: All right, then. Fine, Anna. Thank you. Thank you for taking him under your wing. He's had a good experience. I appreciate it. Thank you.

ANNA: You're welcome.

GRACE: But he's not the world's next Michelangelo, Anna, and he has to continue his education, and I'd appreciate it very much if you'd tell him that.

ANNA: Tell him yourself.

GRACE: I have, Anna. Of course. And I will again. But I'm afraid at this point he listens more to you.

ANNA: He won't listen to me if I tell him that.

(Grace puts down her cup.)

GRACE: All right now, Anna, let's be frank.

ANNA: You don't like my wine.

GRACE: No I don't, Anna. And I don't like what you're doing either. And I want to know why.

ANNA: I'm a teacher, remember. He came. I'm teaching him.

GRACE: Teaching him what, for God's sake?

ANNA: What I taught you, once upon a time.

GRACE: I was a poor student, Anna.

ANNA: You were the best. You could have done anything. And you settled for a Still Life.

GRACE: Oh Anna, stop. Please.

ANNA: I never stop. It's against my religion.

(Pause.)

GRACE: I'd like to make a deal with you, Anna.

ANNA: I don't make deals.

GRACE: You might make this one. Suppose you let him go by the middle of August.

ANNA: Suppose I don't.

GRACE: Suppose I give you a check if you do.

ANNA: A check?

GRACE: For all you've done. For Charlie.

ANNA: A check.

GRACE: *(Starting to open her purse.)* I brought along a check, Anna.

ANNA: *(Bursting into laughter.)* A check! Ohboyohboyohboy! It seems to me I've heard that song before.

GRACE: I'm serious, Anna.

ANNA: *(Laughing.)* Oh I know you are!

GRACE: I'm trying to find a solution here.

ANNA: Seems to me I remember another check twenty years ago.

GRACE: I don't know what you mean.

ANNA: I remember your own father showing up with a check.

GRACE: I didn't know that.

ANNA: Oh yes. Seems I was a bad influence on you, and he wanted to buy me off. And I told him just what I told you: I never stop.

GRACE: I swear I didn't know that, Anna.

ANNA: Oh yes. And when I refused the check, he said he'd see to it that I stopped. And he did! But not before his daughter landed on my doorstep in the middle of the night.

GRACE: I knew we'd get to this...

ANNA: You ran straight to me a week before your wedding!

GRACE: I had a slight case of cold feet...

ANNA: You wanted to change your life!

GRACE: I was a confused young girl!

ANNA: You were a courageous young woman! Before your parents yanked you out of my studio, postponed the wedding, and dragged you kicking and screaming across half the continent of Europe!

GRACE: Well I'm glad they did! I'm happily married now!

ANNA: You are, eh?

GRACE: Yes I am, Anna! And I've got two wonderful children to prove it!

ANNA: Prove it? How? By shipping them off to prison? By taking your son's natural energies and stifling them, just as your parents stifled your own?

GRACE: Oh, Anna, what are we talking about? What could I do? What could I paint? A few pale peonies in a pot. And what can Charlie do? That thing, that rag you've got? And what can *you* do, Anna, really, when the chips are down? What have you ever made? When have you ever been shown? When have you ever received even the smallest signal from the outside world? Oh come on. You're a captivating teacher, and you excite the young, but this is amateur night around here, and you know it. You and Charlie have been playing in the mud, and now it's time for everyone to clean up and go home.

ANNA: Home, is it? Some home! Seems to me that while your husband has been laying down his life for that home, and while your children were fast asleep in that home, you've been sneaking down the beach to the gold star home of Bob McAlister.

(Pause.)

GRACE: That's vicious and vindictive and cruel!

ANNA: Yes, well, look who else has been playing in the mud.

GRACE: Who told you?

ANNA: I'm the Pig Woman, remember. I'm good at rooting around.

(Pause.)

GRACE: Does Charlie know?

ANNA: No.

GRACE: Will you tell him?

ANNA: No.

GRACE: Thank you. *(Sits on glider.)* It's over anyway. It was a small thing at a bad time, and I regret it more than you know.

ANNA: All I know is that you were a woman of pride and promise, and you chose a shadow of a life when you left me!

GRACE: Oh, Anna! Please! No more! No more! *(Pause.)* It's been such a lonely summer.

ANNA: Welcome to the club.

GRACE: Did my father really stop you from teaching?

ANNA: Oh not directly. He simply told all the other fathers how dangerous I was. Somehow, my students stopped showing up.

GRACE: I'm sorry.

ANNA: And for some reason, I heard nothing more from you.

GRACE: I got married, Anna. I had babies…

ANNA: Oh well. Doc Holloway set me up out here. One thing about men: they put their wagons in a circle, but there's always one who's willing to sneak out after dark. *(Pointedly.)* As you also seem to have discovered, recently.

(Pause.)

GRACE: Oh, Anna, I'm hanging on by my fingernails.

ANNA: *(Handing her her cup of wine.)* Try this. It helps.

GRACE: *(Sipping her wine.)* It's not bad, after all.

ANNA: See what you've been missing. *(She sits down beside her.)*

GRACE: I've missed *you,* Anna. I admit it. Over the years. Many times, when things have gotten me down, I've wanted to come over. Just to see you.

ANNA: I've been here.

GRACE: Lately I've been wondering what I'd be like if I'd taken the other road.

ANNA: Now's the time to find out.

GRACE: Oh God, it's a little late for that.

ANNA: Not for him.

GRACE: You mean Charlie.

ANNA: That's who I mean.

GRACE: *(Gets up, crosses downstage right.)* You see, Anna, what you do?…I'd almost forgotten Charlie.

ANNA: I haven't…Let him stay.

GRACE: For how long?

ANNA: As long as he wants.

    (Pause.)

GRACE: He could decide to stay all winter.

ANNA: He could.

GRACE: Knowing Charlie…Knowing you…

ANNA: He could.

GRACE: Away from town. Away from school.

ANNA: Why not?

GRACE: He'd fall behind, Anna!

ANNA: Behind what? *(No answer.)* Hmm? Behind what?

GRACE: I want him home, Anna.

ANNA: The old story, eh?

GRACE: I want him home.

    (Anna gets up.)

ANNA: That's it, then.

GRACE: Yes.

ANNA: I'm beginning to hear drums. In Indian territory.

GRACE: I think I'd like to see him now.

ANNA: You know what he looks like.

GRACE: I'd like to talk to my own son, please.

ANNA: You've talked to him all his life.

GRACE: *(Calling out.)* Charlie!

ANNA: He's too far away.

GRACE: Then I'll get him. *(She starts off right.)*

ANNA: See if he'll come.

GRACE: *(Stopping, turning.)* I could call the police, Anna.

ANNA: Much good they'd do.

GRACE: They'd bring him home.

ANNA: And he'd run away.

    (Pause.)

GRACE: All right then, Anna. Let him choose. But let it be a fair choice. I'll have to trust you on that. And I'll have to trust myself. Trust all we've done in bringing him up. I don't think I've lived a shadow of a life, Anna. I love my family, and I've worked hard, and I'm proud of what I've done. And if I had to choose again, I'd choose this. And I think Charlie will, too! Blood is thicker than water, after all. Or mud.

ANNA: We'll see.

GRACE: Yes. Well I'll trust that it is.

ANNA: I'll trust him.

GRACE: *(Looking at her watch.)* Mercy. Look at the time. It's getting late.

ANNA: Yes.

GRACE: I've got a casserole in the oven.

ANNA: I'm sure.

GRACE: I imagine he'd like some. It's his favorite thing.

ANNA: He's already eaten.

GRACE: That never seemed to make much difference.

ANNA: Let him fish.

GRACE: Let him choose, Anna. That's the deal. Tell him we're having Shepherd's Pie.

ANNA: Why don't you just trot out your left breast, and bribe him with that? *(Pause.)*

GRACE: *(Grimly.)* Good night, Anna. *(She turns and goes off left.)*
(Anna takes a long slug of wine. Charlie comes on with his fishing rod, hurriedly.)

CHARLIE: Was that her car?

ANNA: Yes.

CHARLIE: Did she go?

ANNA: Yes.

CHARLIE: Already?

ANNA: Yes.

CHARLIE: Was she sore at me?

ANNA: No.

CHARLIE: Does she want me back?

ANNA: Yes.

CHARLIE: Do you think I should…touch base?

ANNA: Touch base?

CHARLIE: See her. Say hello. Do you think I should?

ANNA: It's up to you.
(Pause.)

CHARLIE: Maybe I better. *(He starts off toward where Grace has gone.)*

ANNA: Charlie…
(He stops. This is tough for her.)

ANNA: I've decided to let you work on my car.

CHARLIE: Hey! When?

ANNA: Any time you want.

CHARLIE: Now?

ANNA: Here. Take the light.
(Charlie takes the lantern and runs off right. Anna takes her wine bottle and

cups, and goes off behind him. Bonny comes on from upstage left. She speaks to the audience.)

BONNY: You know where this is? This is the place out on the back road where Charlie and Ted and I used to sell lemonade in the old days. I got a secret note from Charlie, asking me to meet him here, so here I am. *(Looks around.)* I shouldn't even be here. My parents would kill me if they knew. They think he's bad news from the word go. My mother thinks he's worse than Ted, even. So I had to lie to them. I told them I was going over to Janice's to listen to the "Hit Parade." Oh God, I'm lying more and more! Is this what it means to become a woman? And why is it we women are always drawn to such dangerous men? I feel like Juliet, in Shakespeare's play of the same name. Who says this whole thing isn't secretly about me? *(She shivers.)* What a scary place this is, at night. Right around here is where Margie Matthews met that skunk. And here's where the Harveys' dachshund named Pickle was run over by the milkman. If I had any sense, I'd go over to Janice's after all. Anything, but stand around and wait for a crazy boy who's run away from his own home! But I can't let him down. Maybe the Pig Woman isn't feeding him properly. Or maybe she's keeping him in sexual bondage. Whatever that means. I've got to stay. It's my duty as a friend and neighbor.

(From offstage, a flash of headlights, and the sound of an old car horn. A-hoo-ga.)

BONNY: Oh help! What's that? Maybe it's some of those fresh Canadian boys out in the car, drinking Molson's Ale!

(She starts to hide. Charlie comes on from upstage left.)

CHARLIE: Hey. It's me. *(He looks all slicked up for a date.)*

BONNY: Charlie!

CHARLIE: *(Dangling a set of car keys.)* And look what comes with me.

BONNY: A car?

CHARLIE: A 1932 Reo. It's Anna's.

BONNY: Did you steal it?

CHARLIE: Hell no. I got it started. So she's letting me drive it.

BONNY: Without a license?

CHARLIE: Licenses are simply the way the bureaucrats keep themselves in power.

BONNY: Do you like living with her, Charlie?

CHARLIE: Oh sure.

BONNY: Is she…your mistress?

CHARLIE: Naw. I sleep in the barn.

BONNY: Don't you ever see your mother?

CHARLIE: Oh sure. I stop by. Now and then. To pick up my laundry.

BONNY: What does she say?

CHARLIE: Oh she begs me to come home. A couple of times she even cried a little.

BONNY: It's hard to imagine your mother crying.

CHARLIE: Well she did. Yesterday, in fact. So I had to hang around for a while. And then Anna got all itchy when I was late. That's when she said I could drive the car.

BONNY: Oh, Charlie, you've got two grown women fighting over you, tooth and nail!

CHARLIE: I know it…Come on. I'll take you for a spin.

BONNY: I'm not supposed to even go near you, Charlie.

CHARLIE: Come on. We'll ride the Cyclone.

BONNY: The Cyclone?

CHARLIE: Why not? We'll stop by for Ted, and make him sit in the rumble seat.

BONNY: Ted's already been on the Cyclone.

CHARLIE: No kidding? When?

BONNY: Last week. He took that girl with the big chest who serves double-dips at Brodie's.

CHARLIE: That horny bastard. O.K. We go by ourselves.

BONNY: But how will we get on? We're not sixteen.

CHARLIE: That's easy. When they ask, I'll just wave these car keys under their nose.

BONNY: But will that work?

CHARLIE: Sure. Listen, Bonny, one thing I've learned around here this summer. One thing I've learned. You're sixteen, if you feel sixteen. And if you feel sixteen, you act sixteen. And when you act sixteen, people treat you like sixteen. That's what I've learned.

BONNY: How true.

CHARLIE: So come on. Let's make our move.

BONNY: My father would kill me if he knew I was riding in a car with a boy.

CHARLIE: You're not. You're riding with a man. Now come on! Let's go !

(*He goes off left. She follows. The stage goes dark. Immediately, there is the sound of a telephone ringing, stridently. It is picked up in the middle of a ring. A small light comes up, as Elsie comes on from left in her pajamas, rubbing her eyes.*)

ELSIE: (*Calling toward right.*) Mother?…Who is it, Mother? Is it about…

Daddy? *(To audience.)* Oh I know it is. This is the way it happens. Everyone's sound asleep, and then suddenly the telephone rings, and— *(Grace comes on from right in her bathrobe, dazed.)*

GRACE: That was about Charlie.

ELSIE: Charlie?

GRACE: He's had an auto accident. Bonny was with him. Nobody's dead, thank God.

ELSIE: How could he possibly…?

GRACE: He was driving Anna's car, and ran right smack into a stone wall.

ELSIE: Oh Lord.

GRACE: The police said they're lucky they weren't killed. *(She leans on the back of the chair.)* Oh I give up, Elsie. I've had it. I have no idea what to do.

ELSIE: Do? Well. The first thing we do is go see him, Mother. Where is he?

GRACE: I think they said Fort Erie.

ELSIE: Fort Erie hospital? Is he there?

GRACE: I don't even know where it is.

ELSIE: Then we find it, Mother. We get dressed, and drive to Fort Erie, and ask.

GRACE: I couldn't drive. Not in a million years.

ELSIE: Mother. Come *on!* Pull yourself together! Get dressed, and while you're doing that, I'll call Doctor Burke, and ask him where the hospital is, and he can *meet* us there, and I'll even *drive,* Mother.

GRACE: *(Looking at her.)* You will?

ELSIE: Yes I will. Now go on, Mother! Hurry! Make tracks!

GRACE: Oh, thank you, Elsie.

(She hurries off right. Elsie turns to the audience.)

ELSIE: Good God! Maybe this play *is* about me, after all.

(She hurries out left, as the lights come up, bright, as if on the sunroom of a hospital. Ted comes on from right dressed for a visit. He carries a package, crudely wrapped in brown paper. Charlie comes on from left, wearing a neckbrace.)

TED: Well, well.

CHARLIE: *(Gloomily.)* Hi, Ted.

TED: *(Looking around.)* Nice sunroom they have here. Nice and sunny.

CHARLIE: Yeah well.

TED: *(Handing him the package.)* I brought you some reading material.

CHARLIE: *(Taking it.)* Thanks.

TED: Open it.

(Charlie sits and opens it diffidently. It is a stack of old comic books.)

TED: My permanent collection. Everything's there: the double issue of Hawkman, Mandrake meets the Phantom, everything.

CHARLIE: Thanks.

TED: That thing on your neck, you look like Prince Valiant, in armor.

CHARLIE: I'm supposed to be glad it's not broken.

TED: I just saw Bonny.

CHARLIE: Yeah?

TED: She's going home today.

CHARLIE: The nurse told me.

TED: Her old man was there, helping with her stuff.

CHARLIE: Oh God.

TED: She looks fine. They say she'll have just a tiny scar on her cheek. Like a permanent dimple.

CHARLIE: Is she sore at me?

TED: Naw.

CHARLIE: I'll bet she's sore.

TED: Naw. She said she wished she could have visited with you.

CHARLIE: I didn't feel like it. O.K.?

TED: O.K.

    (Pause.)

CHARLIE: Her old man's sore at me, isn't he?

TED: Naw.

CHARLIE: I'll bet he's gunning for me.

TED: Naw. He's gunning for the Pig Woman. He said it was her fault for giving you the car, and he's going to sue the pants off her.

CHARLIE: Oh jeez…

TED: I said she didn't wear any pants…Was I right?

CHARLIE: I wrecked her car, you know. They're selling it for junk.

TED: Next time remember to hit the brakes.

CHARLIE: I did, goddammit! They broke. Even the police said that.

TED: O.K., O.K. *(Pause.)* Want to read comics?

CHARLIE: Maybe later.

TED: There's a new one, where they bring in a Batgirl.

CHARLIE: I'll get 'em back to you, Ted.

TED: No, keep 'em. I got to give 'em up. We're moving.

CHARLIE: Moving? How come?

TED: My dad took a job in Toronto. He says after the war, Toronto is going up and Buffalo is going down.

CHARLIE: Bullshit.

TED: That's what he says. He says Canada's going to be a great nation, and we're getting in on the ground floor.

CHARLIE: Ho hum. Snore snore. Wake me when you're finished, O.K.?

TED: Yeah well I'm going to technical school and learn about electronics.

CHARLIE: Next summer tell me all about it.

TED: I won't be around next summer, Charlie. That's what I'm telling you.

(Pause.)

CHARLIE: Oh.

TED: So when you read those comics, think of me, O.K.?

CHARLIE: O.K. I will, Ted.

(Pause. Bonny comes on from right.)

BONNY: Hi, Charlie.

(Charlie looks away from her, sheepishly.)

TED: He's really sick. He doesn't even feel like reading comics.

BONNY: I told my father I wouldn't leave until I could see you, Charlie. I put my foot down.

(Charlie can't answer.)

TED: Don't you think he looks like Prince Valiant? Or maybe its Chester the Turtle?

BONNY: Ted, there's a cafeteria down below, where you can get cokes. Why don't you get us cokes? I'll pay you back, I swear.

TED: *(Looking from one to the other, saluting.)* Roger, Wilco, over and out. *(He goes off right.)*

BONNY: Oh, Charlie! *(She sits down next to him.)*

CHARLIE: I could of killed you.

BONNY: Oh don't be silly. As the doctor said, we were young. We bounced.

CHARLIE: I'll never drive a car again.

BONNY: Now, now…

CHARLIE: Never! I'll never drive, I'll never go out with girls, I'll never fall in love, I'll never get married…

BONNY: Oh gee…

CHARLIE: I'm a goner. I'm a chump. I'm just a dumb juvenile jerk. I'm a creep. I'm a weird, twerpy, stupid, fairy, pipsqueak slob of a son of BITCH!

BONNY: Charlie, stop!

(She kisses him impulsively. Almost at the same time, a loud church bell starts to ring energetically somewhere. They look at each other.)

BONNY: What was that?

CHARLIE: I dunno.

(He kisses her. More bells, buzzers, alarms, horns ring out, louder and louder. Ted rushes in.)

TED: Hey! Guess what? The Japs have just surrendered! They gave UP! The war's over! Come on! There's a big party down in the cafeteria! *(He runs off.)*

(Charlie and Bonny follow, as the sound of horns, bells, gongs, whistles, everything comes up louder and louder, and Grace comes out from left, now wearing a sweater. She speaks to the audience.)

GRACE: Well, it's the day after Labor Day, and time for everyone to move in. Already, there's a north wind whipping across the tennis courts, and the lake looks gray and shivery, and we've been using two blankets at night. It's time to get back to town.

(Elsie comes out from left.)

GRACE: Did you turn off the water?

ELSIE: Charlie's doing it.

GRACE: Then I'd better check. *(She goes in left.)*

ELSIE: *(To audience as she stacks the stool on the chair.)* We've got a million things to do in town, anyway. On Tuesday, Mother takes the train to San Francisco to meet Daddy, and on Thursday, it's my responsibility to get Charlie on the Pullman for Saint Luke's School. And Holyoke starts the following week. So we've all got to buy clothes, and sew on name-tapes, and pack trunks, and somewhere in all the confusion, I've got to write a ten-page paper on *War and Peace*.

(She piles the furniture to one side. Grace comes out from left.)

GRACE: Did you hide the liquor?

ELSIE: Oh no.

GRACE: Then do it, please.

(Elsie goes in left. Grace speaks to the audience.)

GRACE: As far as Anna is concerned, nobody is suing anybody, thank God. Oh, there was a lot of talk, but nothing came of it. Seems she was already in dutch with the provincial government. Hadn't paid her taxes, hadn't put in plumbing. And of course the car wasn't registered. So the accident brought everything to a head. Bonny's father made a few telephone calls to Toronto, and they lowered the boom, that's all. The poor thing couldn't pay the huge fines, so the solution was, she sells her property and gets out.

(Elsie comes out from left, carrying an old tarpaulin.)

ELSIE: I think this is it, Mother.

(She and Grace cover the porch furniture.)

GRACE: All right. Tell Charlie to check the locks on all the doors, and put the rat poison out.

ELSIE: O.K. *(She goes back in left.)*

GRACE: *(Coming downstage speaks to the audience.)* I did what I could for her. Really. I went to see her. She wouldn't even answer the door. I left her a note, telling her how sorry I was. I even enclosed a check. For the car. But I never heard a word. Nothing. Though I notice the check was cashed almost immediately. I *did* hear, through the grapevine, that there's some cousin in Niagara Falls who's willing to take her in. Thank God for that…But you know something: I almost hate to see her go.

(Elsie comes out again from left, carrying her War and Peace.*)*

ELSIE: All set, Mother.

GRACE: *(Calling off.)* Come on, Charlie! We're waiting!

(Elsie sits in the "car," Grace speaks to the audience.)

GRACE: I do. I don't know whether this play has been about me or not, but I know I feel sad. Oh, I suppose she shouldn't be living around here any more. Confusing the minds of the young. I know all that. But still: it's the end of something, isn't it? And that's always sad. Or do people just feel this way in the fall?

(Charlie comes out, still in his neckbrace, now wearing a sweater.)

GRACE: Did you leave a key under the mat, dear, so Mrs. Marek can get in to clean in the spring?

CHARLIE: Uh huh.

GRACE: Well then, let's go.

ELSIE: I'll drive, Mother.

GRACE: Good for you.

ELSIE: And I cleared a place in back for Charlie.

CHARLIE: Why can't I sit in front?

GRACE: Please, dear. It's easier for Elsie.

(They get into the "car"; Charlie climbs into the back, Elsie starts the "car" jerkily.)

ELSIE: Good-bye, house.

GRACE: Yes. You've given us quite a summer.

ELSIE: Just think. Next summer Daddy will be out here.

GRACE: I know…We'll all have to toe the mark, won't we?

ELSIE: *(As they "drive.")* Next year, I hear they're redoing the tennis court.

GRACE: Yes. We'll be playing on a hard surface.

ELSIE: And they're building a ramp. For motor boats.

GRACE: Yes…

CHARLIE: Turn here…

ELSIE: Oh no!

GRACE: Charlie…

CHARLIE: Turn HERE!

GRACE: Charlie, she won't see anyone. She's been very difficult.

CHARLIE: Stop the car.

ELSIE: We're behind schedule.

CHARLIE: STOP THE CAR, or I'm jumping OUT!

GRACE: Stop the car, Elsie.

ELSIE: All right, Mother.

(They stop. Charlie gets out of the "car," crosses around to downstage left.)

GRACE: Don't be too long, dear. Please.

ELSIE: *(Grabbing her book.)* Might as well start *War and Peace* all over again.

GRACE: *(Anxiously watching Charlie.)* Let's hope he's not *that* long.

(Charlie calls out from downstage left.)

CHARLIE: Anna? *(No answer.)* Anna! *(No answer.)* Come on, Anna! It's just me.
*(Anna comes out from right. She wears an old raincoat and a hat. She looks
strangely suburbanized.)*

CHARLIE: Hey, Anna. Look at you!

ANNA: Yes. Look at me. All gussied up for town. Just like one of the summer
ladies.

CHARLIE: I came to apologize, Anna.

ANNA: For what? Oh you mean, for ruining my life.

CHARLIE: The brakes broke, Anna.

ANNA: So they say.

CHARLIE: Oh Anna, I'm sorry.

ANNA: Yes well, let's bury the hatchet, shall we?…What's that they put you
in? A halter? A straightjacket?

CHARLIE: Just a neckbrace. They're taking it off next week.

ANNA: Don't be too sure.

CHARLIE: Where will you be, Anna? I'll write you a letter.

ANNA: Didn't they tell you? I'm returning to my roots. I'll be living in the
Tuscarora Trailer Park. Near the old Reservation.

CHARLIE: I'll come see you, Anna. Christmas vacation. I swear.

ANNA: Nonsense. The war is over. The men are coming home. Think what
they'll be bringing us: New cars. Television. Jet travel. When you've got
a choice between all that, and me, which will you take?

CHARLIE: You, Anna. Any day.

ANNA: Oh sure. You bet.

ELSIE: *(Calling out, impatiently.)* Come on, Charlie!

GRACE: *(Restraining her.)* Don't, Elsie. Give him time.

ELSIE: But what's he doing?

GRACE: Saying good-bye…

ANNA: *(To Charlie.)* Well, the world seems to be calling you.

CHARLIE: *(Crossing to Anna.)* What about my stuff?

ANNA: Your stuff?

CHARLIE: The stuff I made.

ANNA: You want it? I was going to consign it to the rubbish heap of history.

CHARLIE: I want it.

ANNA: Wait, then. *(She goes off right.)*

ELSIE: *(In "car.")* What if he decides to stay with her again?

GRACE: He won't.

(Anna comes out immediately from right carrying an old cardboard box.)

ANNA: Here you are. Fragments of a lost age. *(She hands him the box.)* Your *oeuvre*. Your complete works.

CHARLIE: *(Taking out an inept clay object.)* I never found my potential, did I?

ANNA: That's all right. I seem to have lost mine.

CHARLIE: *(Rummaging in the box.)* What about my tomahtoe seeds?

ANNA: *(Automatically.)* Tomaytoe seeds.

CHARLIE: You promised me some in June.

ANNA: They're in there.

(Charlie finds them in the box.)

CHARLIE: What about you? Aren't you keeping some?

ANNA: Where would I plant them?

CHARLIE: I don't know, Anna. Anywhere. Come on. Keep plugging. And so will I.

ANNA: Oh hell. Maybe I'll drop a few over the bones of my great-grandmother, and see what comes up.

CHARLIE: That's the ticket. *(He shakes some seeds into her hand.)*

ANNA: Well. They're picking me up any minute.

CHARLIE: *(Attempting to shake hands.)* Good-bye, Anna. Thank you for a wonderful summer.

ANNA: What is this? A coming-out party?

(She gestures for him to bend down. He bends stiffly over the box. She takes his head in her hands, and kisses him on the forehead.)

ANNA: There. Now scram. I want to look at the lake.

(She moves downstage right. He watches her, then moves away, carrying the box and the seeds.)

ELSIE: *(Seeing him, from the "car.")* At last...hurry, please. I have a dentist appointment in forty-five minutes.

(Charlie arrives at the "car.")

GRACE: *(Indicating the box.)* What did she give you?

CHARLIE: Personal stuff. *(He starts to slide into the front seat.)*

ELSIE: Mother, ask him to sit in back, please.

GRACE: *(Sliding over, making room.)* That's all right, Elsie. We're all in this thing together.

(Charlie slides in, sits, holding the box in his lap. They drive. Charlie reaches over and turns on the radio. Music comes up loud: a song from 1945 such as "It's Been a Long, Long Time." Elsie reaches over and turns it off.)

ELSIE: Can't we have some adult conversation?

CHARLIE: *(Turning it on again.)* It's a democracy, isn't it? It's a free country.

GRACE: *(Turning it down.)* Let's at least not have it quite so loud...

(The music continues under more softly.)

CHARLIE: *(In "car"; to audience.)* So I tried photography in boarding school. And took up writing in college. And finally, last summer, I wrote this play.

ELSIE: *(Looking out.)* Oh look. There's the Peace Bridge.

GRACE: And the city beyond.

(They look. Anna stands, isolated in her own light, looking out at the lake. The music comes up as the lights fade on all.)

The End